Hispanic/Latino Ministry—Past, Present, Future

A New Beginning

Special Anniversary Edition

UNITED STATES CONFERENCE OF CATHOLIC BISHOPS
WASHINGTON, DC

Excerpts from Pope John Paul II, *Puebla*, copyright © 1979, Libreria Editrice Vaticana (LEV), Vatican City; excerpts from Pope John Paul II, Homily, January 25, 1979 © 1979, LEV; excerpts from Pope Paul VI, *Gravissimum Educationis* © 1965, LEV. Used with permission. All rights reserved.

Scripture texts used in this work are taken from the *New American Bible*, copyright © 1991, 1986, and 1970 by the Confraternity of Christian Doctrine, Washington, DC 20017 and are used by permission of the copyright owner. All rights reserved.

Los textos de la Sagrada Escritura utilizados en esta obra han sido tomados de los *Leccionarios I, II y III*, propiedad de la Comisión Episcopal de Pastoral Litúrgica de la Conferencia Episcopal Mexicana, copyright © 1987, quinta edición de septiembre de 2004. Utilizados con permiso. Todos los derechos reservados.

Excerpts from Vatican Council II: *The Conciliar and Post Conciliar Documents* edited by Austin Flannery, OP, copyright © 1975, Costello Publishing Company, Inc., Northport, NY, are used with permission of the publisher, all rights reserved. No part of these excerpts may be reproduced, stored in a retrieval system, or transmitted in any form or by any means—electronic, mechanical, photocopying, recording, or otherwise—without express written permission of Costello Publishing Company.

Illustrations: pp. 1, 25, 33, 38, 39, 44, 59, 73, 89, 129, 139, 141, 143-149, 178, 197 copyright © 2012, Carmen Soto Fernandez.

ISBN 978-1-60137-314-4

First printing, August 2012

Primera impresión, agosto de 2012

Copyright © 2012, United States Conference of Catholic Bishops, Washington, DC. All rights reserved. No part of this work may be reproduced or transmitted in any form or by any means, electronic or mechanical, including photocopying, recording, or by any information storage and retrieval system, without permission in writing from the copyright holder.

Copyright © 2012, United States Conference of Catholic Bishops, Washington, DC. Se reservan todos los derechos. Ninguna porción de este trabajo puede reproducirse o ser transmitida en forma o medio alguno, ya sea electrónico o mecánico, incluyendo fotocopias, grabaciones, o por cualquier sistema de recuperación y almacenaje de información, sin el permiso por escrito del propietario de los derechos.

Contents

Foreword vii

Encuentro and Mission: A Renewed Pastoral
Framework for Hispanic Ministry (2002). 1

Many Faces in God's House: A Catholic
Vision for the Third Millennium (1999, excerpts). 25

The Hispanic Presence in the New Evangelization in the United States (1996) 33

National Pastoral Plan for Hispanic Ministry (1987) 59

The Hispanic Presence: Challenge and Commitment (1983) 73

Study on Best Practices for Diocesan Ministry Among Hipanics/Latinos (2006) 89

Appendix I: The Bishops Speak with the Virgin: A Pastoral Letter
of the Hispanic Bishops of the United States (1981) 103

Appendix II: Letter of the Hispanic/Latino Bishops to Immigrants (2011) 113

Índice

Presentación 119

**Encuentro y Misión: Un Marco Pastoral Renovado
para el Ministerio Hispano (2002)** 121

**Muchos Rostros en la Casa de Dios: Una Visión
Católica para el Tercer Milenio (1999, extractos)** 129

La Presencia Hispana en la Nueva Evangelización en los Estados Unidos (1996) 139

Plan Pastoral Nacional para el Ministerio Hispano (1987) 165

La Presencia Hispana: Esperanza y Compromiso (1983) 179

**Estudio sobre las Mejores Prácticas de
Ministerios Diocesanos entre Hispanos/Latinos (2006)** 197

**Apéndice I: Los Obispos Hablan con la Virgen:
Carta Pastoral de los Obispos Hispanos de los Estados Unidos (1981)** 211

Apéndice II: Carta de los Obispos Hispanos/Latinos a los Inmigrantes (2011) 221

Foreword

The year 2012 marks a new beginning in Hispanic/Latino ministry: a coming of age in which Catholic leaders of Hispanic/Latino descent take to heart the call to provide leadership to the entire Church in the United States.

This new beginning is highlighted by a number of significant anniversaries that have made Hispanic/Latino ministry an integral part of the history of the Church and its evangelizing mission over the past forty years.

One of these anniversaries is the celebration of the first National Encuentro for Hispanic Ministry in 1972. This groundbreaking event was the spark that launched ministry among Hispanics/Latinos forty years ago and shaped it as a ministry of accompaniment, one in which the ministers enter the life of Hispanics/Latinos, walking with them and listening to their concerns, so that in turn the ministers can share the Good News of the Living Christ with their companions and lead them to recognize the Lord in the liturgical life of the community and to share in its mission.

Ministry modeled as accompaniment has inspired all subsequent *encuentros*, events, and documents on Hispanic/Latino ministry, including the *National Pastoral Plan for Hispanic Ministry* in 1987 and *Encuentro and Mission: A Renewed Pastoral Framework for Hispanic Ministry* in 2002.

As we celebrate the twenty-fifth and tenth anniversaries, respectively, of these documents in 2012, we are grateful that a new beginning in Hispanic/Latino ministry is based on a solid foundation that has produced much fruit.

At this moment of graced anniversaries and new beginnings, we, the bishops of the United States, offer this special edition of United States Conference of Catholic Bishops (USCCB) documents on Hispanic/Latino ministry to accompany an entire new generation of Catholics being formed for ministry today. The documents have an emphasis on the New Evangelization called forth by Popes John Paul II and Benedict XVI.

This publication provides an opportunity to reflect on the past of Hispanic/Latino ministry with gratitude for all that has been accomplished over the years. It also provides an opportunity to carry out our present ministries with renewed enthusiasm and to look at future ministerial opportunities with a greater sense of hope.

The documents in this publication speak to this sense of urgency and to the call for a New Evangelization:

Encuentro and Mission: A Renewed Pastoral Framework for Hispanic Ministry (2002) calls all ministers to be bridge builders between cultures and to develop new ministry models to bring the Good News of Christ to second-generation Hispanic/Latino young people.

Many Faces in God's House: A Catholic Vision for the Third Millennium (1999) emphasizes our common Catholic identity and the call to a transforming hospitality that enables us to be one Body of Christ and yet come from diverse cultures and ethnicities.

The Hispanic Presence in the New Evangelization in the United States (1996) highlights the unique contribution Hispanic/Latino Catholics can make to the dialogue between faith and culture that is at the heart of the New Evangelization.

National Pastoral Plan for Hispanic Ministry (1987) calls for a way of being a church that is evangelizing, communitarian, and missionary, and makes Hispanic/Latino ministry integral to the life and mission of the Church.

The Hispanic Presence: Challenge and Commitment (1983) calls Hispanics a blessing from God and affirms their Catholic culture, including a profound faith in God, a strong sense of family, an authentic Marian devotion, and a sense of hospitality and fiesta in gratitude for God's gift of life.

Study on Best Practices for Diocesan Ministry Among Hispanics/Latinos (2006) provides examples of successful diocesan ministry based on key elements such as ministerial vision, structure, ongoing development, resources, and collaboration.

The publication also includes two letters written by Hispanic/Latino bishops:

The Bishops Speak with the Virgin (1981) presents a conversation between the bishops and Our Lady of Guadalupe as they echo Our Lady's promise to take care of, protect, and accompany Hispanic/Latino Catholics in their journey in the United States.

In their *Letter of the Hispanic/Latino Bishops to Immigrants* (2011), the bishops express to undocumented immigrants their commitment to walk with them in solidarity and to offer their unconditional pastoral care and welcome as they face persecution, deportation, and discrimination. The letter also extends a call for reconciliation.

All these documents have proven helpful in articulating the Church's response to the Hispanic/Latino presence. They have also articulated the contributions of Hispanic/Latino Catholics as active members of the Church.

We celebrate the gifts and the fruits of this mutual response as a blessing from God. For as we are missionary to the new immigrants in our own parishes, schools, and other Catholic institutions, new immigrants are also missionary to us, bringing with them God's unique presence through their steadfast faith and their unwavering search for God and God's promises in their lives.

Today, millions of Hispanic/Latino Catholics feel at home in more than five thousand parishes. Lay ecclesial movements also gather millions through retreats, conferences, and thousands of small communities. And practically every year, new bishops, priests, religious men and women, and lay ecclesial ministers of Hispanic/Latino descent are added to the ministry of our increasingly culturally diverse church.

However, never before has it been so urgent for all ministers to serve Hispanics/Latinos in parishes, schools, and other Catholic institutions. Nor has it been as important for Hispanic/Latino ministers to reach out to Catholics from different cultural backgrounds and ethnicities in the spirit of the New Evangelization.

Catholic Hispanic/Latino leaders are keenly aware that their leadership is of the utmost importance for the present and future of the whole Church in our country. And so they commit themselves to a new beginning in Hispanic/Latino ministry, in the spirit of the New Evangelization and in the trusting hands of Mary, Mother of God and Mother of the Church.

Our prayerful hope is that this document will be a source of inspiration, guidance, and accompaniment for Hispanic/Latino leaders and for all Catholic leaders as we continue to bring the Good News of Christ to every human situation in the United States and beyond.

Your brother in Christ,

Most Reverend Gerald Barnes
Bishop of San Bernardino
Chairman, Subcommittee on Hispanic Affairs

Encuentro and Mission
*A Renewed Pastoral Framework
for Hispanic Ministry*

The document *Encuentro and Mission: A Renewed Pastoral Framework for Hispanic Ministry* was developed by the Committee on Hispanic Affairs of the United States Conference of Catholic Bishops (USCCB). It was approved by the full body of U.S. Catholic bishops at its November 2002 General Meeting and has been authorized for publication by the undersigned.

Msgr. William P. Fay
General Secretary
USCCN

Preface

1. We, the bishops of the United States, have heard the voices of Hispanic leaders—both laity and clergy. We especially affirm those pastoral efforts of Hispanic ministry that promote the general objective and the specific dimensions of the 1987 *National Pastoral Plan for Hispanic Ministry* ("National Pastoral Plan" or "Pastoral Plan"). This pastoral statement, *Encuentro and Mission: A Renewed Pastoral Framework for Hispanic Ministry*, is addressed to all Catholics, but particularly to pastoral leaders involved in ministry among Hispanics. This pastoral statement provides basic pastoral principles, priorities, and suggested actions to develop efforts in Hispanic ministry while strengthening the unity of the Church in the United States. To ensure continuity in ministry among Hispanics, *Encuentro and Mission* serves as an addendum to the National Pastoral Plan and is meant to be a renewed pastoral framework to assist dioceses, parishes, and Catholic organizations and institutions in their response to the Hispanic presence. As such, *Encuentro and Mission* is a pastoral framework to help further develop ministry among Hispanics.

2. The titles chosen for sections of this pastoral statement are inspired by Pope John Paul II's pastoral letter *Novo Millennio Ineunte*, in which the Holy Father echoes Jesus' invitation to the apostles to "put out into the deep" for a catch—"*Duc in altum.*" These words ring out for us today, inviting us to remember the past of Hispanic ministry with gratitude, to live the present challenges and opportunities with enthusiasm, and to look forward to the future of Hispanic ministry with confidence. These words have also been echoed by those in Hispanic ministry leadership as they read the signs of the times, seize the opportunity for action, and expand the vision of Hispanic ministry in order to respond to the Hispanic presence in a culturally diverse context.

3. The basic pastoral principles and priorities and the suggested actions included in this pastoral statement are framed for Hispanic ministry. However, they can also serve as a tool for all communities and ministries seeking to respond to the challenges and opportunities presented to the Church in the United States by the diversity of cultures in our faith communities.

Introduction

4. **In February 2001,** the U.S. Catholic bishops' Committee on Hispanic Affairs convened a national symposium with the leadership of Hispanic ministry in Colorado Springs, Colorado. The purpose of the symposium was to assess and develop Hispanic ministry efforts further while strengthening the unity of the Body of Christ in our increasingly culturally diverse communities. Keenly aware of the pastoral nuances and challenges facing the Church, the bishops' committee asked the leadership to review existing pastoral priorities based on the values and principles of the 1987 *National Pastoral Plan for Hispanic Ministry*,[1] Encuentro 2000: Many Faces in God's House,[2] the pastoral challenges of *Ecclesia in America*,[3] the New Evangelization,[4] and recent demographic data on the Hispanic presence in the United States.

5. The National Symposium to Refocus Hispanic Ministry included the participation of sixty representatives from national and regional Catholic Hispanic organizations and representatives from the USCCB's Department of Migration and Refugee Services; the Catholic Campaign for Human Development; the Secretariat for Family, Laity, Women, and Youth; and the Secretariat for Evangelization.

6. This pastoral statement, *Encuentro and Mission*, is our response to the voices of the leadership of Hispanic ministry about the Hispanic presence at the beginning of the new millennium. Hispanic Catholics are a blessing from God and a prophetic presence that has transformed many dioceses and parishes into more welcoming, vibrant, and evangelizing faith communities. We bishops see Hispanic ministry as an integral part of the life and mission of the Church.

GROWTH OF HISPANIC MINISTRY

7. Hispanic ministry has experienced tremendous growth in the United States since the mid-1980s. This growth has taken place during the experience of three national Encuentros, the development of the Pastoral Plan, an increase in the number of Hispanic Catholic organizations, and a growing pastoral effort in dioceses and parishes to welcome and serve Hispanic Catholics. Our response to the Hispanic[5] presence, coupled with the prophetic voices and actions of Hispanic Catholics throughout the country, has brought Hispanic ministry to a crossroads at the beginning of a new century. Today, Hispanic ministry faces two central questions. First, what model of leadership will Hispanic Catholics offer as they continue to become a strong presence within the Catholic Church in the United States? And second, how will this model strengthen the unity of the Body of Christ in increasingly culturally diverse communities?

A RESPONSE TO CULTURALLY DIVERSE COMMUNITIES

8. As a response to the challenges of serving culturally diverse communities, and especially the Hispanic community, we convened a national intercultural gathering during the Jubilee Year. The Committee on Hispanic Affairs and Hispanic Catholics served as the hosts and lead agents of Encuentro 2000: Many Faces in God's House, which took place in Los Angeles, California, in July 2000. Encuentro

2000 marked the first time that the Church in the United States gathered to recognize, affirm, and celebrate the cultural and racial diversity of its members. With the participation of more than five thousand leaders representing the many faces of the Church—from 150 dioceses and 157 different ethnic groups and nationalities[6]—Encuentro 2000 inspired and challenged Catholics in the United States to embrace a Catholic vision for the third millennium in which all are welcomed to the Father's table.

A NEW PHASE FOR HISPANIC MINISTRY

9. We are aware that the implementation of the values and principles of Encuentro 2000 is a long-term process, one of building unity and solidarity among all Catholics. The Hispanic presence reminds the Church that people of different nationalities bring with them beautiful and useful gifts that are usually embraced by the broader community. We are called to "welcome the stranger among us"[7] and to build more welcoming, evangelizing, and missionary faith communities.

10. For Hispanic ministry, a new phase should include further development in three fundamental areas: (1) ministry structures and network, (2) relationship building and collaboration, and (3) active participation. Structures and ministry networks that have effectively served the ministry should be strengthened, such as diocesan and regional offices and pastoral institutes. Hispanic ministry should build closer relationships and collaboration with ethnic, racial, and ministerial groups and organizations. In addition, ministry efforts should foster the active participation of Hispanic Catholics in the social mission of the Church.

Remembering *the* Past *with* Gratitude

HISTORICAL MEMORY OF HISPANIC MINISTRY

11. **Hispanic ministry leaders** have generated a *memoria histórica* (historical memory) and a unique identity since the first establishment of a national office for Hispanic ministry in 1945. Some aspects of this identity are expressed in the themes of the Encuentros: *Pueblo de Dios en Marcha/People of God on the Journey*, *Voces Proféticas/Prophetic Voices*, *Muchos Rostros en la Casa de Dios/Many Faces in God's House*. We have recorded the unique history of Hispanic Catholics in the United States in our publications of the proceedings of the I, II, and III National Encuentros, as well as in many other publications.[8]

12. Because Hispanics are a blessing to the entire Church in the United States, and because Hispanic ministry is integral to its mission, appreciating and embracing the contributions this community has made are important. Hispanic Catholics have developed a vision of ministry inspired by the social and ecclesiological context of the Second Vatican Council in the United States and in Latin America. This vision is articulated in the Pastoral Plan as a model of Church that seeks to strengthen communion and participation with a strong emphasis on evangelization, social justice, and the integral education of the faithful. All leaders in the Church are called to bring Hispanics and all other Catholics to a deeper love of Jesus Christ, of the Catholic faith, and of Mary, the mother of God. In addition, the Pastoral Plan calls for the assessment of needs, the establishment of priorities, and the development of strategies to respond to needs and aspirations of Hispanics in the United States. The vision of the National Pastoral Plan and its continued implementation has helped to promote a ministry that goes beyond Hispanics. This understanding is articulated in the Encuentro 2000 parish guide *Many Faces in God's House*,[9] with its Catholic vision for the new millennium. *Many Faces in God's House* seeks to strengthen the unity of the Body of Christ while honoring and celebrating the cultural diversity of the Church.

13. Over the years, Hispanic ministry leaders have identified values and principles that have guided the development of Hispanic ministry and its historical memory. Several of these values and principles are discussed here.

1. Common Faith, Culture, and Language

14. Hispanics have emerged from the blending of different races and cultures, which has resulted in a new people. Even though Hispanics find their ancestors in many different countries, most share a common faith and language, as well as a culture rooted in the Catholic faith. These elements, which give a common identity to Latin American and Caribbean people, are even more important for Hispanics in the United States as they struggle to define their own identity in a culturally diverse context and under pressure to assimilate. The commitment of Hispanics to become active participants and to offer their unique contributions in the life of the Church and society—versus *being assimilated*—has been a key value and principle for Hispanics in ministry.

2. A Culture Born Catholic

15. Since the first Spanish missionaries brought the Catholic faith to the new continent, many of the gospel values and

church traditions became inculturated into the cultures of the Latin American people. These values include a profound faith in God, a strong sense of solidarity, an authentic Marian devotion, and a rich popular religiosity. Hispanics have a profound respect for the human person and value relationships over tasks or possessions. Personal relationships are at the heart of a spirituality of *encuentro* and the need to develop strong family, community, and parish ties. Hispanics understand culture as an integral part of the human person that should be respected and honored.[10]

3. A Profound Ecclesial Vocation

16. Hispanics have a profound ecclesial vocation that leads them to work hard at belonging to the Church in a more meaningful way. This has been the case in the process of the National Encuentros, Convocation '95, and other important events that we have convened and that have been affirmed by the Holy See. This ecclesial vocation has raised the level of awareness of the Hispanic presence—the presence of a population that will continue to have an impact on the life of the Church for years to come. The desire to promote collaboration with ministries of other ethnic communities has strengthened the ecclesial identity of Hispanic Catholics. Most importantly, this desire has defined Hispanic ministry as integral to the mission of the Church and as key to its future.

4. A Prophetic Model of Church

17. Hispanic ministry leaders, with the full approval of the U.S. bishops, have articulated a model of Church that is deeply rooted in the reality of Hispanic peoples. As such, this model of Church seeks to respond to the needs and aspirations of the poor, the undocumented, the migrant workers, the incarcerated, and the most vulnerable, particularly women and children. This prophetic model calls for a strong commitment to social justice, for advocacy and action in favor of new immigrant families and young people, and for the empowerment of Hispanics and all Catholics to enter into the full life of the Church and society.

5. Leadership Understood as Discipleship

18. Since the I National Encuentro (1972), Hispanic Catholics have understood leadership as discipleship, and pastoral ministry as *seguimiento* (accompaniment). This model of leadership in ministry, which is based on Jesus' call to follow him, has two dimensions. The first is the encounter with Christ, which leads to conversion and to a personal relationship with the Lord. This relationship with Christ generates a *mística* and a spirituality that permeate every aspect of the faithful's life-journey as members of the Church. The second element of *seguimiento* is the commitment to follow Jesus by continuing his mission to be leaven for the reign of God in the world.

6. A *Pastoral de Conjunto* (Communion in Mission)

19. The principle of *pastoral de conjunto* (communion in mission) has been key to incorporating Hispanic ministry in dioceses and parishes.[11]

20. *Pastoral de conjunto* has led to the promotion of diocesan offices for Hispanic ministry and the increase in the number of parishes serving Hispanics. To date, over 75 percent of the dioceses have an office for Hispanic ministry, and almost four thousand parishes provide pastoral services to Hispanics in the Spanish language.[12] In addition, *pastoral de conjunto* has helped to encourage development and growth in the number of Hispanic Catholic organizations and apostolic movements. The principle of *pastoral de conjunto* can serve the broader Church by modeling and promoting collaborative ministry as an effective vehicle for carrying out the mission of the Church. Regional offices for Hispanic ministry and national Catholic organizations and apostolic movements have been effective promoters of this principle as they work with the local church.

7. A Process of Consultation

21. Since the I National Encuentro (1972), Hispanics have used a methodology of pastoral discernment that focuses on the needs and aspirations of the faithful, judges that reality in light of the Scriptures and Tradition, and moves into transforming action. This methodology, known as SEE—JUDGE—ACT—CELEBRATE—EVALUATE, has generated critical thinking and a strong commitment on the part of the leadership to the mission of the Church. This methodology has also led to strategies and pastoral actions that are relevant, timely, and effective. The components of celebration and evaluation have been very helpful in renewing and redirecting the efforts of Hispanic ministry over the years. This methodology has been applied in the context of a consultation process that promotes participation and works under the assumption that *how* we do things is as important as *what* we do.

Living *the* Present *with* Enthusiasm

THE PASTORAL VISION OF THE NATIONAL PASTORAL PLAN

22. The 1987 *National Pastoral Plan for Hispanic Ministry* has been a beacon for dioceses and parishes serving Hispanic Catholics in the United States. The Pastoral Plan offers an evangelizing ecclesial model and pastoral principles that have strengthened the ministry since its approval in 1987. The vision that the Pastoral Plan offers, as articulated in its general objective,[13] resulted from the consultative and pastoral theological reflection processes of the national Encuentros of 1972, 1977, and 1985.

23. The vision, values, and pastoral priorities established in the Pastoral Plan are still relevant today. However, the "signs of the times" call for refocusing our efforts in ministry. One sign is the ever-growing Hispanic presence in the United States. Another is the unprecedented leadership role that Hispanic Catholics will play in building the future of the Church. A third sign is the Church's concern with the growing number of Hispanics who are joining other Christian denominations or religious traditions. A critical fourth sign is the emergence of new leadership in need of training and formation on the values and principles of the National Pastoral Plan and of Encuentro 2000.

24. *Encuentro and Mission* revisits our pastoral dimensions that have been developed and implemented since 1987. In this renewed framework, we offer new perspectives and challenge pastoral leaders to appreciate the efforts of the past while responding to the ministry efforts of a new generation of lay and ordained leaders.

RESPONSE TO THE CALL FOR A NEW EVANGELIZATION

25. Pope John Paul II, in emphasizing the urgent need for humanity to listen to Jesus Christ's message of hope, has called for a New Evangelization. This renewed commitment to evangelization was already present in each of the priorities of the II Encuentro (1977), and it was included as one of the four specific dimensions in the Pastoral Plan (the other three being *pastoral de conjunto*, missionary option, and formation).

26. Evangelization is the fundamental mission of the Church. It is also an ongoing process of encountering Christ, a process that Hispanic Catholics have taken to heart in their pastoral planning. This process generates a *mística* (mystical theology) and a spirituality that lead to conversion, communion, and solidarity, touching every dimension of Christian life and transforming every human situation. As we have said in our national plan for evangelization, *Go and Make Disciples*, "The fruit of evangelization is changed lives and a changed world—holiness and justice, spirituality and peace."[14]

27. In order to reach out more effectively to inactive Hispanic Catholics and the unchurched, we recommend that the New Evangelization, with its emphasis on spirituality and *mística*, be integral to all the specific dimensions of the Pastoral Plan. That is, the New Evangelization must now become an integral part of *pastoral de conjunto*, missionary option, and formation. This is of particular importance as Hispanics continue to be lured away to fundamentalist groups.

28. A new fourth pastoral dimension for Hispanic ministry is that of **liturgy and prayer life**, a dimension of Christian life that was witnessed in the first Christian communities (Acts 2:42-47). Liturgy and prayer life were included in the National Pastoral Plan under spirituality and *mística*, but with this renewed framework they become a distinct dimension that is also infused with the New Evangelization.

A Call to Build and Nurture Community

29. Just as the New Evangelization, with its emphasis on encountering the living Jesus Christ, suffuses each specific dimension for Hispanic ministry, so does the building of the reign of God, with its emphasis on communion and solidarity. Every action taken in the life of the faith community should nurture and strengthen the fraternal bonds between all its members. Whether through a formation program, an advocacy strategy, a liturgical celebration, or a whole pastoral plan, fraternal human relationships and a truly Christian experience of community should be strengthened within each cultural group and across all cultures.

SPECIFIC DIMENSIONS FOR A COMPREHENSIVE HISPANIC MINISTRY

1. The New Evangelization and Formation
"They devoted themselves to the teachings of the apostles. . . ." (Acts 2:42)

30. An evangelizing catechesis and a solid formation are more necessary today than ever. Such formation is about the acquisition of wisdom, understood as truth in love:

> Wisdom is communicated, transmitted, shared. It requires an interpersonal relationship with those who possess it. That is why wisdom is related to the experience of community, of a common culture, of being a people. The wisdom at the heart of the formation for which the Pastoral Plan calls is the wisdom of the Church.[15]

31. This formation also includes the acquisition of communication skills, organizational and leadership skills, and a greater sense of responsibility to and desire to participate in the life of the Church and society. The Pastoral Plan describes this dimension as the transition "from good will to skills." It calls for leadership development and catechetical formation within a cultural context and for theological-pastoral reflections on the grassroots level. It also calls for seminars and study sessions with pastoral specialists in the areas of liturgy, catechesis, theology, and evangelization. Research is recommended in the social, economic, cultural, religious, and psychological aspects of family, popular religiosity, and issues involving youth, women, and the poor and marginalized.

2. The New Evangelization and Missionary Option
"Awe came upon everyone, and many wonders and signs were done through the apostles." (Acts 2:43)

32. This dimension of the Pastoral Plan calls people to move from being merely recipients of the Good News to being committed witnesses of it to those who need to experience its life-giving power. We reaffirm the emphasis of the 1987 Pastoral Plan on reaching out to those who have not encountered the living Jesus Christ in their lives. "The story of the Samaritan woman also shows the need to evangelize by reaching out to the poor, the 'outsiders,' and those who are victims of discrimination and injustice."[16] The mission of the Church to those who suffer—particularly young people, women, and families—requires both works of mercy and a committed struggle against all forms of injustice. The Pastoral Plan calls for the promotion of opportunities for the poor and the marginalized to participate in political, social, economic, and religious processes. It also calls for a pastoral and social response to the needs of families suffering from many difficulties, including abuses, divorce and separation, abortion, domestic violence, alcoholism and drug abuse, isolation, legal residence issues and rights, and the lack of educational opportunities. The plan calls for coordination and collaboration. It recommends using regional and diocesan *encuentros* as a vehicle for helping leaders become aware of the broader community's needs for community building, pastoral planning, and solidarity in action among all the baptized.

3. The New Evangelization and *Pastoral de Conjunto* (Communion in Mission)
"All who believed were together and had all things in common. . . ." (Acts 2:44)

33. *"Pastoral de conjunto"* refers to the reality of the Church as communion. At its most fundamental level, this communion is the expression of God's desire that all may be one. "Since that communion is a communion of love . . . every

single member is 'responsible' for the well-being of others. This promotion for the well-being of all, this concern and care for their 'holiness,' is the basis of *pastoral de conjunto*."[17] In his apostolic letter *Novo Millennio Ineunte*, Pope John Paul II says that we must "make the Church *the home and the school of communion*" (no. 43). The Pastoral Plan describes communion in mission as movement "from fragmentation to coordination." It calls for collaborative efforts and the distribution of resources among ministries and groups. To develop a *pastoral de conjunto* requires the close collaboration in ministry among all ethnic and cultural groups. This dimension calls all to recognize each other's unique vocation while living out their common responsibility for the Church.[18]

4. The New Evangelization and Liturgy and Prayer Life

"Every day they devoted themselves to meeting together in the temple area and to breaking bread in their homes. They ate their meals with exultation and sincerity of heart, praising God. . . ." (Acts 2:46)

34. The liturgy and prayer life of the Church are privileged opportunities for the faithful to experience a true spirit of community—hence the importance of achieving full participation in the celebration of the sacraments by all those who form the assembly. So that the liturgy may be the summit and source of Christian life, the celebration of the sacraments, particularly the Eucharist, must foster a feeling of being "at home." All are invited to share ways of prayer that reflect their different cultural values and traditions and welcome their talents. The Pastoral Plan seeks to promote liturgical celebrations that are inculturated in the reality of the community that celebrates them, while bringing the many faces of God's house into a greater communion. This pastoral dimension is strongly implied but not directly included as such in the 1987 Pastoral Plan.

PASTORAL RESPONSES AND PRINCIPLES IN HISPANIC MINISTRY

35. Hispanic ministry has empowered millions of Hispanic Catholics to become active participants in the life of the Church and society. This success has been made possible due to a consultative process by which challenges have been identified and priorities established.

36. Ministry in the twenty-first century requires a commitment to welcome and foster the cultural identity of the many faces of the Church while building a profoundly Catholic and culturally diverse identity through an ongoing process of inculturation. The following basic pastoral responses are based on principles that have proven very useful in developing Hispanic ministry over the last thirty years of a national pastoral effort. We bishops are confident that they will continue to help the Church respond to the Hispanic presence.

1. Articulate a Clear Vision of Ministry Based on Unity in Diversity

37. As full members of the Body of Christ, Hispanic Catholics have an understanding of their role in the mission of the Church that serves to empower the ministerial leadership to be aware of the Church's culturally diverse dimension and to work toward building the one Body of Christ while honoring cultural differences. This principle of unity and diversity involves a commitment that affirms and fosters cultural identity for all groups while promoting the transformation of cultures by gospel values.

38. Unity in diversity stems from the spiritual discipline of inclusion rooted in the Gospel. Inclusion calls all Christians to open themselves up in such a way that they risk being changed by whoever is the stranger, the foreigner, in our lives.[19] Through inclusion, the newcomer tries to participate fully in U.S. life by loving it and learning the language and the laws; but the native culture is also maintained, along with the native tongue and values. This process of gospel inclusion adds to the U.S. culture the specific richness of other cultures while guiding all Catholics beyond a shared tolerance of one another towards greater acceptance and respect.

2. Foster a Spirituality of Communion in Mission

39. The fostering of a spirituality of *pastoral de conjunto* (communion in mission) needs to be a strong value and principle for pastoral planning and action for all Catholics. This model of ministry helps to increase the level of inclusion and of mutual collaboration among all Catholics in dioceses, parishes, and national organizations. *Pastoral de conjunto* helps to build more vibrant faith communities by making them more welcoming, evangelizing, missionary, and committed to solidarity with the disenfranchised. Forming leaders who are motivated to serve within a culturally diverse Church is an essential component for a fruitful *pastoral de conjunto*.

3. Promote Small Ecclesial Communities and Apostolic Movements

40. The Pastoral Plan recommends many projects and programs to respond to the Hispanic presence in the Church, such as small ecclesial communities and apostolic movements that are parish-based. These are effective for promoting evangelization, leadership formation, and vocations to priestly and consecrated life.

41. Among Hispanics, small ecclesial communities have been and continue to be a valuable expression of the evangelization efforts of the Church. "These small ecclesial communities promote experiences of faith and conversion as well as concern for each person and an evangelization process of prayer, reflection, action, and celebration."[20] They are a prophetic challenge for the renewal of our Church and the humanization of our society and can serve to stem the loss of Hispanic Catholics to other faith traditions.

42. In *Encuentro and Mission*, we bishops affirm these small communities, along with vibrant apostolic movements, as an effective response that brings families together within cultural and faith contexts that affirm and support family life, the language and culture of the community, and parish involvement. In 1995, in *Communion and Mission*, the Committee on Hispanic Affairs said,

> When solidly rooted in Scripture, church tradition, and Hispanic religiosity, small church communities constitute a new moment in the Church's self-understanding, epitomizing the celebration and proclamation of the Church. These gatherings of the People of God are integrally linked to the parish, and through it, to the diocesan and universal Church.[21]

43. The Pastoral Plan calls for trained mobile teams to go into the community to visit families and to invite them to become closer to the life of the Church, especially those families who feel distant and marginalized. The development of small church communities and apostolic movements as a pastoral response is only one example of the richness and the dynamic character of the *National Pastoral Plan for Hispanic Ministry*.

4. Plan With the People, Not For the People

44. It is of paramount importance that we continue the participatory and consultative process that has been the trademark of the national Encuentros. The process has traditionally been based on grassroots consultation, convened by us and conducted in collaboration with clergy, religious, and lay people. In the Encuentro process, pastoral planning and ministry are conducted with the people, not for the people. Today there exists a strong need to utilize such a process, for it is an effective tool for responding to the pastoral challenges found in parishes throughout the country. We bishops call for a renewed commitment to promote the vision and process of the Pastoral Plan and to implement its prophetic general objective and specific pastoral dimensions.

5. Promote and Support Vocations to the Priesthood, Diaconate, and Consecrated Life

45. The promotion of vocations to the priesthood, diaconate, and consecrated life must be integral to the efforts of Hispanic ministry. As the number of parishes providing pastoral services to Hispanic Catholics continues to grow, the availability of ordained ministers to provide for the sacramental and spiritual life of the parish is imperative. The growth in the number of ordained and consecrated ministers, particularly within the Hispanic community, is dependent on a proactive effort involving the diocesan offices for vocations, religious communities, the parish community, and Catholic families. However, we must state clearly and loudly that efforts in the area of vocations must include a clearly understood sensitivity to cultures being served, to the culture of those men preparing for the priesthood or the diaconate, and to the culture of women and men entering or living a consecrated life.

6. Form Lay Leaders as Bridge-Builders for Today's Culturally Diverse Church

46. Today's culturally diverse Church needs leaders who are deeply rooted in a personal relationship with Christ. Some essential qualities include an openness to embracing people from different cultures, a flexibility for working and journeying with them, and an understanding of the broader Church. Also required is a commitment to serve all Catholics. Leaders need to be excellent listeners and have great sensitivity to and interest in people's lives, needs, aspirations, and ideas. They need to believe in and be models of service, with a profound commitment to solidarity with the most vulnerable. In short,

leaders need to be *gente-puente* (bridge-builders)—pioneers in opening doors to self and to others.

7. Develop Relevant Stewardship Models

47. Hispanic Catholics have always responded with great generosity to the efforts of the Church to reach out to other Hispanics. Millions of Hispanics share their time and talents week after week in thousands of faith communities throughout the country. This contribution takes the form of countless hours of dedicated volunteer service in catechesis, liturgy and prayer, community services, and many other ministries. Even though many Hispanics find themselves affected by poverty, they also share their treasure through creative and culturally relevant fund raisers, in-kind professional services, and individual contributions. However, a significant number of Hispanic Catholics do not yet respond to the needs of the Church and its mission in proportion to what they possess.

48. Stewardship among Hispanics does not happen in a vacuum. In our pastoral letter on stewardship, we said, "How to affirm racial, cultural, and ethnic minorities, how to overcome poverty and oppression . . . remain vexing questions, as well as opportunities."[22] Experiences in Hispanic ministry have shown that stewardship is the result of a process of discipleship that moves through the stages of inviting, welcoming, building relationships, building a sense of belonging, sharing decision making, taking ownership, and finally arriving at stewardship. As Hispanics become better established in U.S. society, they will share more of their time, talent, and treasure with the faith communities that journey with them on the path from newcomers to stewards.

8. Strengthen Diocesan, Parish, and Regional Structures

49. The Church must ensure that dioceses and parishes are equipped with appropriate resources to serve the ever-growing Hispanic population. In addition, there exists a need to affirm and strengthen regional structures and pastoral institutes that assist dioceses in their pastoral efforts and in the formation and leadership development of Hispanic lay leaders. At the national level, greater collaboration with national organizations is also necessary to ensure a stronger tie and a closer relationship with the bishops' Committee for Hispanic Affairs and the Secretariat for Hispanic Affairs and with other offices of the United States Conference of Catholic Bishops.

9. Commit to Social Justice

50. A commitment to social justice is one of the pillars of Hispanic ministry. This commitment should involve ongoing formation on Catholic social teaching and collaboration on advocacy and public policy issues. Issues of immigration, education, human rights, border concerns, voter registration, and dialogue with labor union leaders are all issues relevant to the Hispanic community. Lay leaders should be formed and trained to participate in these arenas, for they have an impact on not only their community but also the entire Church. The renewed sense of solidarity called for in *Ecclesia in America* can serve to strengthen the civic responsibility of Hispanics and all Catholics in all aspects of human life.

10. Promote Intercultural Dialogue and Collaboration

51. The general objective of the *National Pastoral Plan for Hispanic Ministry* calls for a Church incarnated in the reality of Hispanic Catholics while being open to the diversity of cultures. The values and principles of Encuentro 2000 stem from this affirmation and take it one step further—that is, to recognize that the face of the Church is changing and that all are called to foster a vision that welcomes the many faces of the Church to the table where decisions are made. Relentlessly promoting intercultural dialogue and a better understanding of the universality of the Church can accomplish these ends.

11. Give the Church a Voice in Spanish

52. According to population figures in the *2000 World Almanac*, the Hispanic population in the United States is the fifth largest in the world, after Mexico, Spain, Argentina, and Colombia. This population has led to an extensive use of the Spanish language by corporations and the media in the United States. In the Church, care should be taken that pastoral letters and statements, as well as other church documents and resources, are sent to parishes in Spanish. Catholic newspapers, as well as radio and television programs hosted by the Church, should include news stories in Spanish and features on Hispanic Catholic life.

Looking Forward *to* the Future *with* Confidence

53. As a responsibility of the entire Church, the Hispanic presence calls for the strongest pastoral response from every diocese and parish where Hispanic Catholics live. This most important ministry also calls for an equally strong pastoral response on the part of all Catholic institutions and organizations, particularly those involved in education, social services, and advocacy.

54. The following suggested actions are based on recommendations generated by the more than sixty representatives from national and regional organizations who participated in the National Symposium to Refocus Hispanic Ministry for the New Century, which took place in spring 2001. The recommendations were reviewed by our Committee on Hispanic Affairs and are organized under the four specific dimensions of this pastoral statement, *Encuentro and Mission*:

a. The New Evangelization and formation
b. The New Evangelization and missionary option
c. The New Evangelization and *pastoral de conjunto*
d. The New Evangelization and liturgy and prayer life

THE NEW EVANGELIZATION AND FORMATION

55. (1) Commit to the academic and professional development of Hispanics.

a. Develop and support programs designed to help Hispanic lay people attain degrees for church ministry. This includes identifying financial resources for ministers' professional development in collaboration with colleges, universities, and other programs committed to the higher education of Hispanic Catholics in ministry.

b. Support the hiring of a diocesan coordinator and of DREs able to train and support Hispanic catechists and the people they serve in catechetical programs and new evangelizing efforts in the parishes. These programs and efforts should emphasize education in the faith, especially through Catholic education during all school years.

c. Include Hispanics and other ethnic communities in the planning and implementation of catechetical, evangelization, and ministry development programs, celebrations, and other diocesan and parish activities. Active participation in certification programs and ongoing education are of particular importance.

55. (2) Foster an integral leadership formation model.

a. Strengthen and develop formation programs for ordained, religious, and lay ecclesial ministers that include the particularity of each group. Offices for Hispanic ministry should collaborate with schools, colleges, and universities, as well as with seminaries. Formation of all ministers is an extended process in which Hispanics are ministers of the entire Church, not only of Hispanics.

b. Include the perspective of women and young people in formation programs by using a methodology of social analysis that focuses on their reality, experiences, and contributions.

c. Incorporate Hispanic ministry, culture, and language into programs in offices of evangelization, religious education, and formation, as well as in seminaries. Seminarians must learn Spanish and become familiar with Hispanic culture. Also, provide clergy and religious with opportunities to learn Spanish and to gain an understanding of the customs, cultures, and histories of Latin America. This is no longer an option—it is a need.

55. (3) Establish solid and accessible faith formation programs.

a. Develop—in collaboration between offices for Hispanic ministry, departments of evangelization and religious education, and other departments—catechetical, pastoral, and theological formation programs designed for Hispanics.

b. Form ministers able to serve in a culturally diverse context. The formation of all ministers, including Hispanic deacons, should affirm cultural and ministerial identity. Leadership skills, social analysis, community organizing, and pastoral planning should also be included. A Spanish-track program, one of equal quality with the English track, is encouraged.

c. Develop guidelines for culturally diverse formation programs that include the vision, values, and principles of the Pastoral Plan for Hispanic ministry, of the renewed pastoral framework given in *Encuentro and Mission*, and of other documents.[23]

55. (4) Make the formation of young Hispanics, especially young adult Hispanics, an urgent priority.

a. Support young Hispanics on their educational attainment efforts, catechetical formation, and human and leadership development. Promoting the involvement of Hispanics in school boards, education commissions, and parent organizations can be a key component of this effort.

b. Parish leaders must collaborate with public school officials, teachers, and especially parents to help improve the educational attainment level of Hispanic young people, the majority of whom attend public schools. Dioceses and parishes should take steps to help increase Catholic school accessibility and attendance by Hispanic children, possibly through scholarships and other incentives.

c. Encourage religious congregations to renew their historic commitment to Catholic education in communities that are poor and immigrant, especially in the Hispanic community.

d. Promote the inclusion of different ethnic and cultural perspectives in the curricula of elementary, middle, and high schools. Involvement of Hispanic professionals as mentors and the hiring of more Hispanic teachers can be particularly effective in this effort.

THE NEW EVANGELIZATION AND MISSIONARY OPTION

56. (1) Renew the Church's commitment to reach out to inactive Catholics.

a. Develop strategies to strengthen Hispanic families in their personal relationships with Jesus Christ by implementing the strategies and actions outlined in *Go and Make Disciples*. Small ecclesial communities, apostolic movements, and specific programs on the New Evangelization are effective in reaching out to inactive Catholics and the unchurched.

b. Encourage and engage Hispanic professionals in active participation in the life of the Church. This should be done through a personal invitation to celebrate, dialogue about, and discern the leadership role of Hispanics in the Church.

c. Open doors for ecumenical and interfaith dialogue and collaboration with Hispanics from other Christian traditions. Special attention should be given to families whose members belong to different faith traditions.

56. (2) Develop ministry models that serve young people, women, and families.

a. Develop youth and young adult ministry models that effectively reach both U.S.-born and newly arrived Hispanics who live in culturally diverse parishes and dioceses. A collaborative effort between the offices for Hispanic ministry and youth ministry is key to carrying out this action.

b. Involve Hispanic young people and families in the plans and programs of diocesan offices for youth and family ministry. Involvement is measured by the level of participation of Hispanics and other ethnic communities in the planning and implementation of youth and family diocesan celebrations, gatherings, and parish activities.

c. Promote the leadership and spiritual development of women and their inclusion in key positions of ministry with an equal-pay policy. This may also include developing a process to invite and consult with Hispanic lay women who exercise a natural leadership in the Church and who need assistance and support for their development.

d. Promote the family as domestic church, and develop programs for family catechesis, spiritual direction, and human development. Special attention should be given to Hispanic families affected by divorce, single parenting, domestic violence, and isolation of the elderly and people with disabilities.

56. (3) Promote active participation in civic life and advocacy efforts.

a. Strengthen the commitment and promote the active participation of Hispanic Catholics in the areas of social justice—including pro-life concerns—civic responsibility, and working for the common good in their parishes and communities. The diocesan office for Hispanic ministry, in collaboration with the state Catholic conference, should promote legislation that supports educational opportunities for young people at risk and programs to reach new immigrants.

b. Intensify advocacy efforts on behalf of new immigrants, poor families, disadvantaged young people, and those suffering from discrimination and abuse by working more closely with advocacy groups and the state Catholic conferences. Special attention should be given to undocumented immigrants affected by family separation, fear of deportation, discrimination, and violence.

c. Involve Hispanics and other professionals in the life of the Church, and create opportunities for them to contribute their talent, time, and treasure. This effort requires identifying Hispanic professionals and creating opportunities for dialogue and collaboration. In addition, it should affirm the contribution of Hispanic women to Church and society and further promote their formation, leadership development, and placement in decision-making positions.

56. (4) Intensify social ministry.

a. Strengthen the safety net for all people, especially women and children suffering from domestic violence, sexual abuse, abortion, chemical dependency, gang activity, and alcoholism. This effort should include consideration of working with local authorities and organizations to establish centers with interpreters for family services that provide counseling and support to Hispanic families, women, and young people.

b. Develop ministries with the incarcerated and their families, including programs that mentor those recently released from jail and reentering society.

c. Promote dialogue with Hispanics from other Christian denominations, and encourage collaboration on common issues that affect the lives of Hispanic families.

THE NEW EVANGELIZATION AND *PASTORAL DE CONJUNTO* (COMMUNION IN MISSION)

57. (1) Develop a common vision and mission for Hispanic ministry.

a. Promote the understanding that Hispanic Catholics are full members of the Body of Christ and are a blessing to the entire Church, and that Hispanic ministry is integral to its mission. This understanding empowers the ministerial leadership to provide regular opportunities for the faithful to come together to have a personal encounter with the living Jesus Christ. All Catholics should be given the opportunity to commit and contribute to the mission of Christ while honoring cultural differences.

b. Engage diocesan and parish leadership in a pastoral planning process based on the vision and mission articulated in the Pastoral Plan. This process is most effective when convened by the bishop and supported by the pastors and diocesan and parish leaders.

c. Establish formal channels of communication between the bishop and the diocesan director for Hispanic ministry, and create opportunities for ongoing dialogue with pastors and other parish leaders.

57. (2) Strengthen the structures for Hispanic ministry.

a. Establish, in each diocese, an office for Hispanic ministry to coordinate pastoral efforts based on the Pastoral Plan and this renewed framework, *Encuentro and Mission*. The office should serve as a resource to parishes and other ministries. Parishes with a Hispanic population within their boundaries should find ways to serve Hispanic Catholics.

b. Strengthen Hispanic ministry structures such as diocesan, parish, and regional ministry offices and centers for pastoral formation. This effort should include adequate resources and support for implementation of programs and projects.

c. Promote and support small ecclesial communities and apostolic movements, especially those serving young people, women, and families, with New Evangelization efforts.

57. (3) Develop a strategy for *pastoral de conjunto*.

a. Establish channels of communication between the different departments, offices, and agencies within diocesan and parish structures. This is particularly important during the planning process since the work of the office for Hispanic ministry often includes multiple ministry areas, such as youth, family, religious education, catechesis, liturgy, and advocacy.

b. Build relationships with leadership in all ministries to achieve a common vision and pastoral planning process. Such relationships should lead to common projects and programs that build the unity of the Church and gather Catholics from different ethnic and cultural groups.

c. Create a place for Hispanics and other ethnic and cultural communities at the table where decisions are made. This involves decisions that affect the Church as a whole, not only a particular community or ministry. The bishop's cabinet, diocesan and parish councils, financial committees, Catholic universities and theological institutes, commissions, and advisory groups are some examples where broader participation is needed.

57. (4) Foster the development of Hispanic ministry leaders.

a. Develop Hispanic leaders able to minister in the context of a culturally diverse and pluralistic society while strengthening their Hispanic cultural and ministerial identity. This requires that the Church honor, embrace, and bridge the cultural, racial, and linguistic differences.

b. Promote the involvement of Hispanic church professionals as leaders and experts in different ministries and disciplines, not only in Hispanic ministry issues. This is particularly important in planning diocesan events such as catechetical conferences, youth conventions, ministerial days, and formation programs.

c. In collaboration with the office for social concerns and the state Catholic conferences, offices for Hispanic ministry should educate Hispanic Catholics about public policy issues and processes as well as basic community organizing skills. The diocesan office for Hispanic ministry should promote political legislative action on issues affecting Hispanics and other Catholics, such as immigration, human rights, and education.

THE NEW EVANGELIZATION AND LITURGY AND PRAYER LIFE

58. (1) Increase participation in the liturgical life of the Church.

a. Multiply the number of parishes equipped to celebrate the liturgy in Spanish, particularly the celebration of the Sunday Eucharist. This effort should include the formation of committees for the liturgy in Spanish that closely collaborate with the pastor and parish staff.

b. Deepen the experience of welcoming and communion in the liturgy in dioceses and parishes. Foster liturgical and religious expressions including the careful selection of music, the creation of environment and art, and a sensitivity to the precise use of languages. This involves making ritual books and other liturgical resources readily available in Spanish.

c. Affirm and support Hispanic Catholics seeking the sacraments, particularly when their situation requires special attention. Provide timely information and preparation classes in Spanish to the faithful about the requirements for receiving the sacraments. A welcoming attitude and personal attention are essential.

58. (2) Make God's saving grace more visible in the lives of the faithful.

a. Identify important cultural events and moments in the life of the local community for which liturgical celebrations would be most relevant.

b. Develop or continue emphasis on evangelization and the use of Catholic devotions in liturgical formation programs for all Catholic ministers, particularly Hispanics.

c. Provide Eucharistic liturgies or prayer services in times of difficulty and during civic events that affect the life of Catholics, particularly Hispanics.

58. (3) Intensify the formation of liturgical ministers.

a. Develop and provide—through collaboration between the diocesan offices for worship and for Hispanic ministry—training to ordained and other liturgical ministers in Spanish, particularly in the areas of preaching and selection of liturgical music.

b. Provide opportunities for formation and immersion experiences that serve to foster better understanding of popular religiosity among different Hispanic Catholic communities and their inclusion in liturgical celebrations and traditional fiestas.

c. Place greater emphasis on the Rite of Christian Initiation for Adults among Hispanics in order to respond to the growing number of Protestant-raised Hispanics seeking admission into the Catholic Church.

58. (4) Create opportunities for all the faithful to celebrate together (popular piety).

a. Provide opportunities that promote a spiritual understanding of the liturgy as a culturally diverse celebration of the faith community that is a common and dynamic spiritual encounter, a *mística*, with God in the search for unity in our diversity.

b. Develop guidelines and models for culturally diverse liturgies. This should involve the participation of Hispanics and members of other ethnic groups in the planning and implementation stages of liturgical celebrations. The use of cultural gestures and symbols during these celebrations is strongly recommended, as well as the promotion of different forms of personal, familial, and small community prayer in everyday life.

c. Encourage diocesan and parish leaders to ensure that diocesan liturgies are inclusive of the cultures and languages present in the diocese. The liturgies of the Encuentro 2000 national event offer an excellent model for culturally diverse liturgies.

d. Incorporate popular faith expressions—such as devotion to the Blessed Virgin Mary and the saints—into liturgical celebrations. Use the preparation and organization times before country patron saints' celebrations and other popular religiosity practices as opportunities to evangelize and to provide ongoing spiritual formation and leadership development.

Pastoral Application

59. **Ministry among Hispanics** requires an openness to pastoral and social realities that challenge the Church to respond with new ardor, methods, and expressions in ministry. For this reason, collaboration and communion in mission are critical for an effective ministry. It is not possible for one ministry, or one minister, to do everything that is required. Guidelines for ministering among Hispanics may be helpful in responding to pastoral and social needs, but they must come from the local church. While each parish is different, common elements can be effective in an implementation process.

MISSION

60. Hispanic ministry is the Church's response to the Hispanic presence. This ministry must be seen as an integral part of the life and mission of the Church in this country. We must be relentless in seeking ways to promote and facilitate the full incorporation of Hispanic Catholics into the life of the Church and its mission. It entails a collaborative effort with the entire community and honors their history, their faith traditions, and the contributions Hispanic Catholics have made in service to the Church and society.

VISION

61. The *National Pastoral Plan for Hispanic Ministry* provides a general objective and four pastoral dimensions that guide the ministry and serve as the basis for pastoral planning for parishes, dioceses, and Catholic organizations. The general objective calls the faithful to live and promote the unity of the Body of Christ and its mission through faith communities and Catholic organizations. This call is defined through the following pastoral priorities.[24]

a. Welcome all the baptized and build community.

b. Reach out to the baptized who may not be involved in the life of the Church and those who do not know Christ.

c. Affirm and promote the cultural identity of Hispanics and of all the faithful.

d. Celebrate and express the faith in a spirit of communion and participation.

e. Promote and be an example of justice through a spirit of solidarity with the most vulnerable.

f. Invite and provide formation to Hispanic leaders through an evangelizing catechesis that prepares them to teach and serve the Hispanic and other Catholic communities.

g. Build faith communities in which all cultures are constantly transformed by gospel values in order to be leaven for the reign of God in society.

62. Perhaps the best summary for this pastoral statement lies in words that are often attributed to Oscar Arnulfo Romero, Archbishop of San Salvador, who was assassinated on March

24, 1980, while celebrating Mass. These words, which are widely used in pastoral circles in the United States, are a profound prophetic message that should serve all in ministry:

> It helps now and then, to step back and take the long view. The kingdom is not only beyond our efforts, it is even beyond our vision.
>
> We accomplish in our lifetime only a tiny fraction of the magnificent enterprise that is God's work. Nothing we do is complete, which is another way of saying that the kingdom always lies beyond us.
>
> No statement says all that could be said. No prayer fully expresses our faith. No confession brings perfection, no pastoral visit brings wholeness. No program accomplishes the Church's mission. No set of goals and objectives includes everything.
>
> This is what we are about: We plant seeds that one day will grow. We water seeds already planted, knowing that they hold future promise. We lay foundations that will need further development. We provide yeast that produces effects far beyond our capacity.
>
> We cannot do everything, and there is a sense of liberation in realizing that. This enables us to do something, and to do it very well. It may be incomplete, but it is a beginning, a step along the way, an opportunity for the Lord's grace to enter and do the rest.
>
> We may never see the end results, but that is the difference between the master builder and the worker. We are workers, not master builders; ministers, not messiahs. We are prophets of a future not our own.

Appendix: Challenges Faced *in* Hispanic Ministry

63. **Challenges were identified** by the leadership participating in the 2001 National Symposium to Refocus Hispanic Ministry as being common realities affecting the development of Hispanic ministry in all regions of the country.[25]

1. PROSELYTISM OF HISPANIC CATHOLICS

64. While data are generally lacking about the number of Hispanics who have left the Church, current data suggest that a significant number of Hispanics join other Christian denominations and religious traditions every year. This challenge includes a growing number of Hispanic families who are experiencing diversification of commitments to other religious traditions besides Catholicism. Today, Hispanics have family members who belong to fundamentalist groups or who have espoused mainline traditions. Another perspective on this particular concern notes that studies have not yet been conducted on what "leaving the Church" really means. Because of their mobility, Hispanics find themselves in new environments that are totally different from what they know, love, and understand. New arrivals have to adapt to a new language, to different institutions, and to new support systems. The structure of the parish and the style of worship are usually very different from what they experienced in their native country. Adapting and determining where one belongs takes time. In many parishes throughout the country, Hispanics find familiarity and a welcoming atmosphere. However, that is not always possible where Hispanic clergy and personnel are not available. A transforming hospitality, then, becomes extremely important in welcoming the stranger among us, which includes providing opportunities for Catholic formation and spiritual nourishment.

65. The Committee on Hispanic Affairs's 1999 report *Hispanic Ministry at the Turn of the New Millennium* identified several factors that make Hispanics feel unwelcomed in the Catholic Church. These make them more open to experiencing and choosing other faith traditions. Among these factors are excessive administrative tasks and rules in Catholic parishes, which often override a spontaneous, personal, and warm reception. For example, some Hispanics complain about having to fill out complicated forms and produce evidence of being registered, such as showing contribution envelopes, before they can receive the sacraments. In contrast, evangelical churches conduct home visits, provide powerful preaching that skillfully links Scripture with everyday life, and foster a notion of Church as extended family that provides Hispanics with a sense of belonging to God's family.

66. Another factor that can affect the sense of belonging in the Catholic Church is the lack of priests, religious, and lay pastoral ministers to serve the many needs of the Hispanic community. The formation and recognition of a potential leader in the Hispanic community can also be difficult, due to a lack of formal education.

2. THE GROWTH OF THE HISPANIC POPULATION AND THE IMPACT OF FEWER PRIESTS

67. Priestly vocations among Hispanics are on the rise. Thirteen percent of all U.S. seminarians are Hispanic.[26] This growth is overshadowed, however, by the ever-growing number of Hispanic Catholics, estimated to be

at least 25 million—constituting nearly 40 percent of all Catholics in the United States. According to the committee's findings in *Hispanic Ministry at the Turn of the New Millennium*, there is one Hispanic priest for 9,925 Hispanic Catholics in the United States. In contrast, there is one Catholic priest for every 1,230 Catholics in the general Catholic population.[27] Even though nearly four thousand parishes are already serving Hispanics, the demand for services in Spanish continues to outpace the response from the Church.[28] There is an urgent need to increase the number of parishes that provide for the sacramental, catechetical, spiritual, and social needs of the community. This increase should include more ordained, religious, and lay pastoral ministers serving Hispanic Catholics.[29]

3. NEED FOR MORE CONTINUITY IN MINISTRY

68. Participants in the National Symposium to Refocus Hispanic Ministry identified the need to intensify efforts for leadership development, as well as the need for continual training of new leadership in dioceses, parishes, and Catholic organizations in order to give continuity to Hispanic ministry.[30] Ministry does not draw its strength from specific programs alone. Rather, it favors an ongoing process of community building and leadership formation nurtured by a common vision. This underscores the importance of hiring Hispanic ministers who are familiar with the collective history of Hispanic ministry and who are committed to its vision as outlined in the Pastoral Plan and Encuentro 2000. The presence of lay ecclesial ministers as parish staff and of Hispanics serving on parish councils is particularly critical when faith communities face the unavoidable challenge of changing pastors and parochial vicars.

4. A MULTICULTURAL MODEL THAT PROMOTES A ONE-SIZE-FITS-ALL APPROACH TO MINISTRY

69. Participants in the symposium spoke with concern about a "multicultural" model that consolidates minorities under one office, which is headed by a coordinator. In the experience of the participants, this model often dilutes the identity and vision of Hispanic ministry and those of other ethnic ministries.[31] It can reduce effectiveness in dioceses, parishes, and Catholic organizations and institutions. The leadership in Hispanic ministry is particularly concerned about the reduction of resources and the limited access to the bishop that can follow the establishment of multicultural offices. Also expressed was concern about the exclusion of Hispanic ministry staff from the decision-making process, particularly in the areas of budgets, plans, and programs specific to Hispanic ministry and its impact in other ministerial areas and in the mission of the Church as a whole. We bishops are mindful of the cultural diversity of the Church and of the need for effective ministry models. However, the size and long-standing presence of the Hispanic population call for an assertive response by the Church to the challenge of ministering among Hispanic Catholics.

5. NEED FOR DIVERSITY OF MINISTRY MODELS SERVING YOUTH AND YOUNG ADULTS

70. Presentations during the symposium highlighted the need to develop alternative models for ministry with Hispanic young people. Census 2000 shows that out of 35.3 million Hispanics living in the United States, approximately 12.5 million are younger than eighteen years of age.[32] The majority of young people in this age group do not participate in Catholic youth programs or attend Catholic schools. The traditional model of parish youth ministry does not, for the most part, reach Hispanic young people because of economic, linguistic, cultural, age, and educational differences.[33] At the same time, there is resistance to accepting, affirming, and supporting emerging models that attempt to fill the void by reaching out to Hispanic young people, particularly new immigrants. Generally speaking, the majority of parish youth ministry programs serve a population that is mostly European white, mainstream, middle-class, and English-speaking. Many live in the suburbs, are more likely to attend Catholic high school, and are college-bound; the parents of many are registered in the parish. On the other hand, Hispanic youth groups serve youth and young adults from working- and middle-class families who live in the inner city. They tend to have a low educational attainment level, to have limited access to Catholic schools, and to not be college-bound. They conduct their meetings in Spanish or bilingually, and they foster cultural identity as an integral part of membership in a Hispanic youth group. U.S.-born Hispanic teenagers are the largest segment of Hispanic young people—and the least served. This group does not naturally gravitate to either of these models. It is of vital importance to develop ministerial models that respond to the specific needs and aspirations of U.S.-born Hispanic youth.

6. NEED FOR MORE CONSISTENT MINISTRY MODELS

71. Research commissioned by the Committee on Hispanic Affairs shows that diocesan offices for Hispanic ministry are not consistent in their structure or do not have equitable access to resources.[34] The offices are often housed under different departments or pastoral services. Participants at the symposium expressed concern that Hispanic ministry is often perceived as a specialized ministry separate from the mission of the diocese or the parish. Such ambiguity makes it difficult to adequately fund a comprehensive Hispanic ministry effort and impedes its relation to other ministries.[35]

7. PASTORAL PLANNING IN ISOLATION

72. A survey of bishops and diocesan directors for Hispanic ministry showed that even though the Pastoral Plan has existed since 1987, few ministers outside Hispanic ministry know about the plan, or they rarely conduct pastoral planning in collaboration with Hispanic ministry. The leadership in Hispanic ministry is concerned that such lack of awareness fosters the perception that Hispanics are the exclusive responsibility of the office for Hispanic ministry.[36] Inconsistent pastoral planning in Hispanic ministry, isolation, and a tendency to view Hispanic ministry as a parallel structure has limited collaboration with other ministries and Catholic groups in the past.[37]

8. COMPLEXITY OF HISPANIC POPULATION

73. In most regions of the country, Hispanic ministry has focused its energy on serving new immigrant Hispanics facing language barriers, poverty, low educational attainment, isolation, discrimination, and limited catechetical formation. This focus has led, at times, to tensions between new immigrants and U.S.-born Hispanics. The recent influx of new immigrants from Mexico and Central America into areas traditionally populated by Puerto Ricans, Cubans, or Mexican Americans is presenting new challenges to Hispanic ministry in dioceses throughout the country. Adding to this complexity are other ethnic groups with comparatively small migrations, such as Latinos of African descent who have long suffered racial prejudice, as well as indigenous peoples from rural regions of Mexico and other countries who may possess a low level of Spanish literacy. Training in language—particularly in speaking the language of the heart in dialogue with men and women—culture, and social structures are a necessity for foreign-born priests and other pastoral ministers.[38]

9. LIMITED ACCESS TO LEADERSHIP POSITIONS

74. Participants at the symposium shared that church leadership is often reluctant to establish relationships and develop closer collaboration with and across cultures and ministries. In general, Hispanic theologians, educators, and ecclesial ministers are considered knowledgeable only in Hispanic ministry and are kept from positions of leadership such as chancellor, department director, school principal, pastor, and seminary rector. Some reluctance on the part of Hispanic leaders also prevents their applying for positions or addressing groups not connected with Hispanic ministry.[39]

10. LIMITED RESOURCES AND LOW EDUCATIONAL ATTAINMENT

75. Participants at the symposium identified the lack of adequate economic resources and training programs that respond to the leadership needs of the community; in addition, programs that provide intercultural communication skills are urgently needed. Hispanics, particularly young people, have a low educational attainment compared with other groups and may suffer from poor self-esteem. This situation leads Hispanics to settle for certificates instead of degrees.[40] We bishops are encouraged to know that nearly 25 percent of all students enrolled in lay formation programs in the United States are Hispanic.[41] However, the Church is challenged by seeing that the number of Hispanics enrolled in degree programs is quite low, particularly in theology and related fields. The limitation of resources dedicated to the education of Latinos has a direct impact on the number of Hispanics who have the necessary credentials to hold leadership-level positions.

Notes

1. U.S. Catholic Bishops, *National Pastoral Plan for Hispanic Ministry* (1987), in U.S. Catholic Bishops, *Hispanic Ministry: Three Major Documents* (Washington, D.C.: United States Conference of Catholic Bishops, 1995). Also referred to herein as "National Pastoral Plan" or "Pastoral Plan."

2. The National Celebration of Jubilee 2000, Encuentro 2000: Many Faces in God's House, in Los Angeles, Calif., July 6-9, 2000, was hosted by Hispanic Catholics and focused on hospitality and strengthening the unity of the Church in a cultural context.

3. John Paul II, post-synodal apostolic exhortation *Ecclesia in America* (Washington, D.C.: United States Conference of Catholic Bishops, 1999).

4. John Paul II, Address to the Assembly of CELAM (March 9, 1983), III: AAS 75 (1983), 778.

5. The term "Hispanic" was used during the 1970 Census and was adopted by the church leadership of the time to help define a people with a common identity, vision, and mission. It has been integral to the *memoria histórica* of Hispanic ministry since 1970 and continues to be integral to the pastoral efforts of the entire Church today. In recent years, the term "Latino" has become widely used by church and community leaders, particularly in urban areas. It is a self-identifying term that has emerged from the community and is embraced by the Church. Even though this population is labeled "Hispanic," however, it is essential for understanding and for effective working relationships to recognize that the people come from different countries and come with special identities. The binding forces are the faith tradition, language, and values.

6. U.S. Catholic Bishops, Secretariat for Hispanic Affairs, Message from the Director, *En Marcha* (Summer 2000): 2.

7. See U.S. Catholic Bishops, *Welcoming the Stranger Among Us: Unity in Diversity* (Washington, D.C.: United States Conference of Catholic Bishops, 2000).

8. Our other publications reflecting the history of U.S. Hispanic Catholics include the following: *The Bishops Speak with the Virgin*; *The Hispanic Presence: Challenge and Commitment*; the *National Pastoral Plan for Hispanic Ministry*; *Communion and Mission: A Guide for Bishops and Pastoral Leaders on Small Church Communities*; *The Hispanic Presence in the New Evangelization in the United States*; *Reconciled Through Christ: On Reconciliation and Greater Collaboration Between Hispanic American Catholics and African American Catholics*; and *Encuentro 2000: Many Faces in God's House*. The documents of the Latin American Episcopal Council (CELAM) produced after its gatherings in Medellín, Puebla, and Santo Domingo are also an important part of the *memoria histórica* of Hispanic ministry, as is the wealth of publications produced by various ministries related to the ecclesial experience, theology, and pastoral practices within the Church.

9. U.S. Catholic Bishops, Committee on Hispanic Affairs, *Many Faces in God's House: Parish Guide* (Washington, D.C.: United States Conference of Catholic Bishops, 1999).

10. See U.S. Catholic Bishops, *The Hispanic Presence: Challenge and Commitment* (1983), in *Hispanic Ministry: Three Major Documents*, 5-7.

11. The term "*pastoral de conjunto*" has been used since the 1987 Pastoral Plan to refer to the idea of communion in mission. *Leaven for the Kingdom of God*, no. 3.2, explains further: "Since that communion [of God] is a communion of love, every member . . . finds his or her identity in a relation of love with the others. . . . This promotion of the well-being of all, this concern and care for their 'holiness,' is the basis of the *pastoral de conjunto*. When we speak of the *pastoral de conjunto*, therefore, . . . we are speaking of the very nature of the Church's mission" (U.S. Catholic Bishops, Committee on Hispanic Affairs, *Leaven for the Kingdom of God* [Washington, D.C.: United States Conference of Catholic Bishops, 1990]).

12. U.S. Catholic Bishops, Committee on Hispanic Affairs, *Hispanic Ministry at the Turn of the New Millennium* (Washington, D.C.: United States Conference of Catholic Bishops, 1999), 17, 41.

13. It is a model of Church that is evangelizing, communal, and missionary. This model is to be a ministry that is incarnated, or rooted, in the reality of the Hispanic people and is open to the diversity of cultures. This model of Church must promote justice by its example and be committed to developing leadership through integral education. Such an educational process touches on the different dimensions of the human person: spiritual life, intellectual development, affective maturity, and the acquisition of human virtues. All these elements combined are essential for the Church to be leaven for the reign of God in society.

14. U.S. Catholic Bishops, *Go and Make Disciples: A National Plan and Strategy for Catholic Evangelization in the United States* (Washington, D.C.: United States Conference of Catholic Bishops, 1996), 3.

15. *Leaven for the Kingdom of God*, no. 6.3.

16. *Leaven for the Kingdom of God*, no. 5.1.

17. *Leaven for the Kingdom of God*, no. 3.2.

18. See *Leaven for the Kingdom of God*, no. 3.4.

19. See Eric H. F. Law, *Inclusion: Making Room for Grace* (St. Louis, Mo.: Chalice Press, 2000), 42-43.

20. *National Pastoral Plan for Hispanic Ministry*, no. 38. See also nos. 38-40.

21 U.S. Catholic Bishops, Committee on Hispanic Affairs, *Communion and Mission: A Guide for Bishops and Pastoral Leaders on Small Church Communities* (Washington, D.C.: United States Conference of Catholic Bishops, 1995), 1.

22 U.S. Catholic Bishops, *Stewardship: A Disciple's Response* (Washington, D.C.: United States Conference of Catholic Bishops, 1992), 3.

23 Documents such as *Encuentro 2000: Many Faces in God's House*, *Go and Make Disciples*, *Welcoming the Stranger Among Us: Unity in Diversity*, and *Brothers and Sisters to Us* are especially recommended.

24 Cf. Bishop Arthur N. Tafoya, opening remarks, National Symposium to Refocus Hispanic Ministry, in U.S. Catholic Bishops, Committee on Hispanic Affairs, *Proceedings of the National Symposium to Refocus Hispanic Ministry* (Washington, D.C.: United States Conference of Catholic Bishops, 2002): "All leaders and ministers in the Church are called to accept responsibility and share talents and resources to respond to the many pastoral challenges the Church faces every day. But unless this is done in the name of the Holy Trinity—the Father, the Son, and the Holy Spirit—and with the intention of building the kingdom of God, what is done in ministry will not last. All ministries have one fundamental responsibility: to be leaven for the kingdom of God."

25 See *Proceedings of the National Symposium to Refocus Hispanic Ministry*.

26 U.S. Catholic Bishops, Committee on Priestly Life and Ministry et al., *The Study of the Impact of Fewer Priests on the Pastoral Ministry* (Washington, D.C.: United States Conference of Catholic Bishops, 2000), 31. While 13 percent is a promising number, it must be pointed out that most of these are foreign-born.

27 *Hispanic Ministry at the Turn of the New Millennium*, 5.

28 *Hispanic Ministry at the Turn of the New Millennium*, 40.

29 *Hispanic Ministry at the Turn of the New Millennium*, 5.

30 *Proceedings of the National Symposium*, 39.

31 *Proceedings of the National Symposium*, 38.

32 U.S. Census Bureau, *NP-D1-A Projections of the Population by Age, Sex, Race, and Hispanic Origin for the United States, 1999-2100 Middle Series*, Internal Release Date: November 2, 2000.

33 *Proceedings of the National Symposium*, 38, 52-53.

34 *Hispanic Ministry at the Turn of the New Millennium*, 16.

35 *Proceedings of the National Symposium*, 37.

36 *Hispanic Ministry at the Turn of the New Millennium*, 17.

37 *Proceedings of the National Symposium*, 37.

38 *Proceedings of the National Symposium*, 38.

39 *Proceedings of the National Symposium*, 38.

40 *Proceedings of the National Symposium*, 38.

41 U.S. Catholic Bishops, Subcommittee on Lay Ministry, *Lay Ecclesial Ministry: The State of the Questions* (Washington, D.C.: United States Conference of Catholic Bishops, 1999), 54.

Many Faces in God's House

A Catholic Vision for the Third Millennium

In November 1997, the National Conference of Catholic Bishops approved a request from the bishops' Committee on Hispanic Affairs that the U.S. bishops convoke a fourth national Encuentro in the jubilee year 2000. *Encuentro 2000* builds on the previous three Encuentros and also takes into consideration the pastoral challenges and demographic realities we face today. In November 1998, the bishops' Committee on Hispanic Affairs, under the chairmanship of Most Rev. Gerald R. Barnes, Bishop of San Bernardino, approved the bilingual publication of *Encuentro 2000*, **Many Faces in God's House: A Catholic Vision for the Third Millennium** as a parish guide to help implement the *Encuentro 2000* process at the local level, and it is authorized for publication by the undersigned.

Monsignor Dennis M. Schnurr
General Secretary
NCCB/USCC

VISION STATEMENT

The greatest homage which all the Churches can give to Christ on the threshold of the third millennium will be to manifest the Redeemer's all-powerful presence through the fruits of faith, hope and charity present in the men and women of many different tongues and races who have followed Christ. (Tertio Millennio Adveniente, no. 37)

Now is the appropriate time for us to proclaim that we are one Church of many faces, which represent the many peoples of God. *Encuentro 2000* is an opportunity for the Church in the United States to gather to engage in profound conversations about life and faith: to worship together, to learn from each other, to forgive one another and be reconciled, to acknowledge our unique histories, and to discover ways in which we as Catholic communities can be one Church yet come from diverse cultures and ethnicities. *Encuentro 2000* is a process by which we can rediscover and gain greater appreciation of the universality of the Catholic Church and renew our commitment to our common identity and mission. As members of one family of God, we are called to encounter the living Jesus Christ by authentically receiving and reflecting his gracious hospitality in and through one another, as the way to conversion, communion, and solidarity.

An Invitation to Participate in Encuentro 2000

Sensing the movement of the Spirit at the threshold of the year 2000, the bishops of the United States invite the Church, in all its cultural and ethnic diversity, to come together to cherish the histories of all our peoples and discover Christ in each others' stories, so that in solidarity we may cross into the new millennium.

Encuentro 2000 provides the Church with an opportunity to proclaim anew to the world that profound faith in Jesus Christ is the key, the focal point, and the goal of all human history (cf. *Gaudium et Spes*, no. 10). Following the initiative of the Committee on Hispanic Affairs and treasuring the experience of Hispanic Catholics both in their history and in the prior processes of the Encuentro, the bishops of the United States convoke *Encuentro 2000*.

THEOLOGICAL REFLECTION: MANY FACES IN GOD'S HOUSE

I will give, in my house
 and within my walls, a monument and a name
Better than sons and daughters;
 an eternal, imperishable name will I give them. . . .
Them I will bring to my holy mountain
 and make joyful in my house of prayer;
Their holocausts and sacrifices
 will be acceptable on my altar,
For my house shall be called
 a house of prayer for all peoples.
Thus says the Lord God,
 who gathers the dispersed of Israel:
Others will I gather to him
 besides those already gathered. (Is 56:5, 7-8)

Our Human Diversity

Each of us is made in the image and likeness of God. Each of us is a gift from God to the world, and each of us is unique. I am the color, the race, and the ethnicity that I am, and yet, I am more. I am American: African American, Asian American, Hispanic American, European American, Native American, Arabic American, and I am a blend of some, and yet, I am more. My roots can be found in Africa, Asia, South and Central America, the Caribbean, Europe, North America, the Middle East, and yet, I am more. I live in the inner city, and I live in a small town; I live in the suburbs, and I live in a gated community; and yet, I am more.

Our Lifestyles

I am mother and father, sister and daughter, son and brother, friend and colleague, and yet, I am more. I am a construction worker and a nurse, I am a doctor and a factory worker, I work at home and I travel great distances, and yet, I am more. I am constantly moving from city to city, and I have lived in this place for generations. I am a parent whose children are my life and joy, and I am a single mother struggling to raise three children, and yet, I am more. I am a newly ordained priest struggling to serve a multicultural parish, and I am a religious, enriched by the experience of working with others. I am fifteen years old and give thanks for the Church I have always known, and I am sixty years old, now lost and desperately looking for a place in the Church I used to know, and yet, I am more. I am a divorced father who sees my children every other weekend, and I am a mother who has chosen to be a stay-home mom. I am blessed with good health, and I struggle with ill health, and yet, I am more. I am a single adult, and I am a newlywed. I am surrounded by wonderful friends, and I am lonely, seeking a good friend, and yet, I am more.

Our Lives in the Faith Community

I live my faith daily in the workplace, and my work is caring for the poor in my community. I am a lawyer who advocates for the oppressed, and I am a trades person building homes for the homeless. I visit the sick, comfort the lonely, and mourn with those who grieve. I am a farm worker who provides food for the table, and I am a Eucharistic minister who brings nourishment to the sick. I am a catechist teaching youth about our faith, and I am a sponsor for adult catechumens. I belong to an interfaith group, and I am a member of a church-based community. I am a proud father, present at my daughter's Confirmation, and I am a mother worried about my son's initiation into a new religious group. I am a charismatic renewed by the animating power of the Spirit, and I am a contemplative resting in the quiet of a great mystery. I am Catholic in faith, but was raised in a country where Christians are a very small minority. My culture is often seen as belonging to a different faith tradition, but my culture is an integral part of my Catholic faith. I am elderly, preserving traditions of the Church, and I am young, full of energy, discovering new dimensions to these traditions. I am a member of a parish, and yet I do not feel at home.

I am who I am because of God's love for me. It is God who seeks me. It is God who loved me first. It is God who makes a room for me in his house.

Sharing the Vision of Encuentro 2000

"I am" describes some of the many faces of the Church in the United States. "I am" also names the One within the faces. As such, it offers a vision of the many places, cultures, situations, and contexts that describe a truly graced multicultural reality, and offers a new meaning to multiculturalism in the United States today. *Encuentro 2000* concerns these two visions—the one Lord and the many faces. *Encuentro 2000* realizes that life in the United States finds each of us in different relationships with one another and with the Body of Christ which is the Church. The bewildering variety of relationships may be seen as obstacles to being family, community, society, and ultimately, Church. Yet *Encuentro 2000* sees Jesus opening a door leading beyond each of these obstacles, inviting us in and repeating the words from Isaiah:

Them I will bring to my holy mountain
    and make joyful in my house of prayer;
Their holocausts and sacrifices
    will be acceptable on my altar,
For my house shall be called
a house of prayer for all peoples. (56:7)

Jesus opening a door and inviting us in describes a gracious and transforming hospitality. It is gracious in that Jesus becomes present to us in the midst of this variety of peoples and relationships that were once thought to be closed doors but now have come open. This hospitality is transforming in that Jesus asks us to cross the threshold of that open door into a new house, a house of prayer for all peoples. We are to follow our Lord in becoming gracious hosts, as we acknowledge and embrace our cultural, ethnic, and linguistic diversity and God's unique presence in each other's lives, histories, and cultures. This gracious and transforming hospitality also describes a truly Christian understanding of multiculturalism—a multiculturalism that focuses less on a gathering place for many peoples and more on a gracious hospitality that has made a welcoming space for each face among us.

Encuentro 2000, then, sees the Church of the third millennium like Jesus who washed the feet of the disciples, as host of the house for all peoples. We are asked to become the welcoming Lord, gracious hosts to a world filled with dissonant and meaningless conversations. We are asked to start a new conversation in this house of prayer. Such hospitality transforms differences of culture, language, race, gender, class, and circumstance into an invitation to speak from the deepest longings of our hearts. Such hospitality recognizes the invitation of the Host who knows us better than we know ourselves, so that we, in turn, become hosts to one another. As such, this grace-filled hospitality transforms any obstacles to faithfulness into opportunities to speak from the depths of our hearts. In this house of welcoming, even those who find themselves wandering tired and afraid in this world can hear the words of Isaiah:

Thus says the Lord God,
    who gathers the dispersed of Israel:
Others will I gather to him
    besides those already gathered. (56:8)

PARISH SESSION: BRIDGING THE GAP BETWEEN FAITH AND LIFE

This is how all will know that you are my disciples, if you have love for one another. (Jn 13:35)

Welcome and Prayer
(15 minutes)

Welcome the participants and ask them to briefly introduce themselves. Start the session with a simple prayer and a bilingual song, such as Cesareo Gabarain's "Id y Enseñad/Go and Teach" (*Flor y Canto*, #336, Oregon Catholic Press).

Objective: To renew our commitment to create a culture inspired by gospel values, by living out our faith in all areas of life.

Sharing Our Experiences
(40 minutes)

What does faith have to do with daily life and culture? Should there be a relationship between Sunday Mass and Monday morning; between what I believe in faith and what I live every day? People who live their faith in everyday life make a difference in our community and inspire others to do the same. Inspiring people are found in every community of faith. In many cases they are simple folk like the grandmother of the family, a youth of the parish, a neighborhood couple, or a teacher in the local school. Inspirational individuals do not always stand out by being the most popular or the ones who speak best. What is common to all of them is their commitment to live according to gospel values day-in and day-out, especially in adverse circumstances. Their life witness is the best example of discipleship. It is an enthusiastic invitation for others to live the good news of Jesus in every human situation (*Go and Make Disciples*, p. 2). On the other hand, many baptized men and women live their Christian faith without energy, while others have separated themselves from the Church (*Redemptoris Missio*, no. 33). Conversion is incomplete if we are not aware of the demands of Christian life and if we do not strive to live them (*Ecclesia in America*, no. 27). The New Evangelization calls us to an ongoing process of conversion. It aims to bridge the gap between our faith and our daily duties in family, work, and social life.

Discussion questions:

- Who in your community inspires others to live the gospel values in everyday life?
- Give examples of how you live the Gospel.
- What makes it difficult for you to live your faith in everyday life?

Reflecting on Our Faith Tradition
(40 minutes)

Jesus Christ is not an idea, but a concrete, historic individual: the Son of God who became the son of Mary in a given time, place, and culture so as to redeem us (*The Hispanic Presence in the New Evangelization in the United States*, p. 20). Jesus lived faithfully the gospel values in his own particular culture. He also had to challenge expectations and attitudes contrary to those values. The Gospel is full of examples in which Jesus transformed these enslaving situations by inculturating them with the values of the kingdom of God. With the healing on the Sabbath day, Jesus teaches that the Sabbath is for the good of the individual, not the individual for the Sabbath. In mixing with sinners and publicans and having social contacts with non-Jews, Jesus teaches that God's love and his plan of salvation reach across cultural and geographic boundaries toward everyone. With his miracles, Jesus witnesses to God's will, and this implies, above all, bringing forgiveness, reconciliation, healing, and liberation to everyone. With his teachings and deeds, Jesus brings faith, life, and culture together by affirming what is genuine and good in the culture, and challenging what is false, mistaken, and undesirable.

Evangelization consists precisely in continuing this good work: in transforming, in the name of Jesus Christ and with the power of the Holy Spirit, every belief, attitude, and behavior in our culture, so as to affirm the life and dignity of each person, in accord with the values and promises of the kingdom of God. This process of inculturation of the Gospel calls us to promote a new expression of the Gospel in accordance with evangelized culture, looking to a language of the faith that is the common patrimony of the faithful and thus a fundamental element of communion (*General Directory for Catechesis*, no. 203).

Discussion questions:

- By which activities or actions does your community of faith give witness to Jesus' message of love, hope, and faith?
- What attitudes, beliefs, and behaviors present in your community and culture need to be challenged and transformed by the Good News of Jesus Christ?

Putting Our Faith into Action
(40 minutes)

Pope John Paul II warns that we live amidst a cultural crisis of unsuspected proportions, in which fundamental gospel and human values tend to disappear and give way to attitudes, deeds, and situations that separate us from God and from one another (CELAM 1992, no. 230). Putting things before persons, getting rich at the expense of the weakest, fomenting racial contempt, and educating without moral values are some examples of the cultural crisis. John Paul II calls for a New Evangelization that will renew the commitment of the Church, and of each believer, to bridge the gap between faith and life. For a faith that does not build a culture based on gospel values is a sterile faith (*The Hispanic Presence in the New Evangelization in the United States*, p. 16). To better respond to this challenge, the New Evangelization calls for a "new apostolic zeal" capable of generating "new enthusiasm" in the proclamation of the Gospel with "new methods" that effectively use imagination, creativity, and the technical and scientific resources available to share the good news.

Action steps:

- Identify actions that can bring about a New Evangelization in the five areas listed below. (One such action is to go on a one-day pilgrimage to a cathedral or a local shrine to pray for new understanding in living our faith in the world.)
  — In the lifestyle of the faith community (*koinonia*)
  — In the celebration of the liturgy and prayer (*liturgia*)
  — In the teaching of the faith and the values of the Gospel (*didache*)
  — In the service of others and the work for charity and justice (*diaconia*)
  — In the proclamation that Jesus Christ is the Way, the Truth, and the Life, yesterday, today, and forever (*kerygma*)
- Develop a plan to implement actions.

Gathering Our Experiences
(15 minutes)

- What facilitated participation in the session, and what made it difficult?
- To what extent was there greater knowledge of each other and mutual acceptance achieved?
- Was a deeper knowledge of our faith achieved, and was a commitment made to implement the identified course of action?

Celebrating Our Faith as a Community
(25 minutes)

- Opening hymn/song
- Invocation or invitation to prayer
- Scriptural reading
- Prayer of thanksgiving or petition
- The Lord's Prayer
- Final prayer and sign of peace
- Closing hymn

REFERENCES

Bishops of the Diocese of Galveston-Houston. Pastoral Letter on Cultural and Ethnic Diversity, *Many Members, One Body* (Galveston-Houston, Texas: Diocese of Galveston-Houston, 1994).

Catechism of the Catholic Church (Washington, D.C.: United States Catholic Conference, 1994).

Catholic Campaign for Human Development, United States Catholic Conference. Faith and Human Development Series (available in English and Spanish): *A Justice Prayer Book, Novena for Justice and Peace, A Scriptural Rosary for Justice and Peace, Scripture Guide, Way of the Cross* (Washington, D.C.: United States Catholic Conference, 1998).

CELAM. *Puebla: La Evangelización en el Presente y Futuro de America Latina* (México D.F.: Librería de Clavería, 1979).

CELAM. *Santo Domingo: Nueva Evangelización, Promoción Humana, Cultura Cristiana* (Santafé de Bogotá, Colombia: Ediciones Paulinas, FSP-SAL, 1992).

Committee on Migration, National Conference of Catholic Bishops. *One Family Under God* (Washington, D.C.: United States Catholic Conference, 1995).

Congregation for the Clergy. *General Directory for Catechesis* (Washington, D.C.: United States Catholic Conference, 1998).

Flannery, Austin, OP, ed. *Vatican Council II* (Northport, N.Y.: Costello Publishing Company, 1996).

John Paul II. *The Church in America (Ecclesia in America)* (Washington, D.C.: United States Catholic Conference, 1999).

John Paul II. *On the Coming of the Third Millennium (Tertio Millennio Adveniente)* (Washington, D.C.: United States Catholic Conference, 1994).

John Paul II. *On the Permanent Validity of the Church's Missionary Mandate (Redemptoris Missio)* (Washington, D.C.: United States Catholic Conference, 1991).

John Paul II. *On Social Concern (Sollicitudo Rei Socialis)* (Washington, D.C.: United States Catholic Conference, 1987).

John Paul II. *The Vocation and Mission of the Lay Faithful in the Church and in the World (Christifideles Laici)* (Washington, D.C.: United States Catholic Conference, 1988).

National Conference of Catholic Bishops. *Book of Readings on Reconciliation* (Washington, D.C.: United States Catholic Conference, 1999). Available only in English.

National Conference of Catholic Bishops. *Called and Gifted for the Third Millennium* (Washington, D.C.: United States Catholic Conference, 1995).

National Conference of Catholic Bishops. *Go and Make Disciples* (Washington, D.C.: United States Catholic Conference, 1997).

National Conference of Catholic Bishops. *Hispanic Ministry: Three Major Documents* (Washington, D.C.: United States Catholic Conference, 1995). Includes the National Pastoral Plan for Hispanic Ministry.

National Conference of Catholic Bishops. *The Hispanic Presence in the New Evangelization in the United States* (Washington, D.C.: United States Catholic Conference, 1996).

National Conference of Catholic Bishops. *Reconciled Through Christ* (Washington, D.C.: United States Catholic Conference, 1997).

Subcommittee on the Third Millennium, National Conference of Catholic Bishops/ United States Catholic Conference. *Open Wide the Doors to Christ: A Framework for Action to Implement Tertio Millennio Adveniente* (Washington, D.C.: United States Catholic Conference, 1997).

United States Catholic Conference. *A Catholic Framework for Economic Life* (Washington, D.C.: United States Catholic Conference, 1997).

United States Catholic Conference. *Communities of Salt and Light: Parish Resource Manual* (Washington, D.C.: United States Catholic Conference, 1994).

The Hispanic Presence in the New Evangelization in the United States

I n June 1995, the Bishops' Committee on Hispanic Affairs led the commemoration of the fiftieth anniversary of the establishment of a national office for Hispanic ministry. At their national gathering, "Convocation '95: The Hispanic Presence in the New Evangelization in the United States," held in San Antonio, Texas, the bishops hosted five hundred pastoral leaders who participated in a series of workshops dealing with Christian faith and identity. A commitment to the New Evangelization evolved at the conclusion of each workshop. A summary of these workshop statements became the "Statement of Commitment" presented at the closing of the convocation. The statement called for the bishops of the United States to share their views on the contribution of Hispanics to the Church. This statement, *The Hispanic Presence in the New Evangelization in the United States*, is a response to the pastoral leaders from the bishops of the United States on the Hispanic presence and the relationship between faith and culture. In November 1995, the National Conference of Catholic Bishops approved the bilingual publication of *The Hispanic Presence in the New Evangelization in the United States*, and it is authorized for publication by the undersigned.

Monsignor Dennis M. Schnurr
General Secretary
NCCB/USCC

Foreword

To commemorate the fiftieth anniversary of the establishment of a national office for ministry to Hispanics by the Catholic bishops of the United States, the Committee on Hispanic Affairs requested the National Conference of Catholic Bishops to issue a pastoral statement on one aspect of the New Evangelization, namely, the relationship between faith and culture. The pastoral statement, *The Hispanic Presence in the New Evangelization,* reflects the pastoral ministry experience among Hispanic Catholics as a model for the New Evangelization. The pastoral statement reaffirms the evangelization efforts of the last fifty years among Hispanic Catholics and also looks to the future and the challenges of the New Evangelization as we approach the celebration of the great jubilee of the year 2000 and the Hispanic presence in the Catholic Church in the beginning of the new millennium.

From June 23 to 25, 1995, Hispanic Catholic pastoral leaders from all parts of the United States gathered in San Antonio, Texas, to celebrate the fiftieth anniversary of the establishment of a national office for ministry to Hispanics. The event, called "Convocation '95" had as its theme "The Hispanic Presence in the New Evangelization in the United States." In addition to two general sessions dedicated to evangelization, mission, culture, and service, Convocation '95 included twenty-two workshops. There were eight morning workshops dedicated to doctrinal, theological, and spiritual issues: prayer and sacraments, life in the Spirit, the new *Catechism of the Catholic Church,* living as Church, vocations, evangelization of culture, popular religiosity, and Bible and Church. The afternoon workshops, fourteen in all, were devoted to specific areas of pastoral concerns—family, school, health, abortion and euthanasia, youth, social justice, interracial and ethnic relations, immigration issues, pastoral services to migrants, discipleship, the National Pastoral Plan for Hispanic Ministry, women issues, political responsibility, and ecclesial structures for Hispanic ministry. At the end of Convocation '95, the participants issued a "Statement of Commitment" to the New Evangelization in our country, asking the bishops to share with the entire Church their own view of the contribution of Hispanics to it. This pastoral statement is a response to the pastoral leaders' request.

The Hispanic Presence in the New Evangelization in the United States is addressed to the entire Church in our country. The Statement of Commitment says: "We will look for ways to share with the entire Church in the United States the progress brought about in Hispanic Ministry." This is essential to the unity of the Church in our country since all of us are called to its mission of evangelization, worship, and service.

Two documents issued by the National Conference of Catholic Bishops provide the basis to the Hispanic pastoral leaders' response to the call for a New Evangelization: *Go and Make Disciples,* published February 12, 1993, and the *National Pastoral Plan for Hispanic Ministry,* published January 18, 1988. All pastoral agents dedicated to the New Evangelization should become familiar with both documents since they are meant to guide all of us in this task. In this response to the Statement of Commitment of Convocation '95, the bishops limit their observations to only one aspect of the New Evangelization, namely, the *relationship between faith and culture.* Other essential aspects of evangelization are discussed in the two prior documents.

To assist in better understanding the Hispanic presence in the United States, three appendices have been included at the end of *The Hispanic Presence in the New Evangelization in the United States*. Appendix A is the message sent by our Holy Father, John Paul II, to the participants of Convocation '95. Appendix B includes a copy of the "Statement of Commitment" approved by the pastoral leaders at Convocation '95, which is quoted in this statement. Appendix C is a brief historical overview of Hispanic ministry in the United States from 1945 to 1995.

+ Roberto O. González, Chairman
Bishops' Committee on Hispanic Affairs
National Conference of Catholic Bishops

THE HISPANIC PRESENCE IN THE NEW EVANGELIZATION IN THE UNITED STATES

"At this moment of grace we recognize the Hispanic[1] community among us as a blessing from God." With this declaration we began our pastoral letter on the Hispanic presence in our Church twelve years ago.[2] Today, at the dawn of a third millennium of Christian history, we wish to reaffirm and expand on this conviction. We affirm that the Hispanic presence in our Church constitutes a providential gift from the Lord in our commitment to that New Evangelization to which we are called at this moment of history.

We see the present moment as a time of great opportunity. True, this century has seen some of the greatest offenses ever against human dignity. This has been the century of global wars, genocides, and totalitarian regimes. All yearn for a new beginning, a new hope, a new confidence that the thirst for liberty is not a vain illusion and that the search for the truth that sets us free is not an empty dream. This yearning provides us with the opportunity to proclaim Jesus Christ as the only answer to the questions that torment the human heart. Led by our Holy Father, Pope John Paul II, the Church responds to this challenge by the joyful proposal of the Gospel of life as the basis for a culture truly responsive to all human needs, spiritual and material. The Gospel of life proclaims that human rights have their origin in the Creator's wisdom, that liberty is inseparable from the truths of which we are not the authors, and that a peace founded on authentic solidarity between men and women of different racial and ethnic origins can be secure.

Many around the world still see the United States as the land of hope for liberty and justice. Yet our country has not been spared from the advances made by the "culture of death" described by the Holy Father, in which the weak are abandoned to the manipulations of the powerful. Still, when we look at the future we are not afraid. We know Jesus Christ, who has conquered sin and death, is the Lord of the Church guiding her at every moment, providing her with the wisdom to interpret the signs of the times and the spiritual resources to respond to the challenges of the moment.

We consider the Hispanic presence in our country a great resource given to us by the Lord himself for our struggle against the culture of death. In our pastoral letter of twelve years ago, we referred to the Hispanic presence as *prophetic*. We called upon our Hispanic brothers and sisters to share with us the prophetic witness of an identity forged by the Catholic faith. This summer, more than five hundred Catholic leaders in Hispanic ministry who gathered in San Antonio exer-

> *In our pastoral letter of twelve years ago, we referred to the Hispanic presence as prophetic. We called upon our Hispanic brothers and sisters to share with us the prophetic witness of an identity forged by the Catholic faith.*

cised their prophetic role. Clergy, religious, and laity from 110 dioceses of our country came together from June 23 to June 25 to celebrate the fiftieth anniversary of the establishment by our Conference of a national office for Hispanic ministry. At the end of their gathering, called Convocation '95, they issued a "Statement of Commitment"[3] to the New Evangelization in our country. Our statement today is our enthusiastic response to this statement of commitment.

We address this statement, however, not only to the participants of Convocation '95. We write to the entire Church in our country, calling all to the blessing offered to us by our Hispanic brothers and sisters' commitment to the New Evangelization. There is but one Catholic Church in the United States, as it is everywhere around the world. Evangelization is always the task of the entire Church. Our Church has been truly blessed by the presence of a great variety of cultures, races, and ethnic backgrounds, all contributing to the richness of our ecclesial life. The commitment of our Hispanic Catholics is a gift to all of us, and by welcoming it, we commit ourselves to work together for the spread of the Gospel.

In this statement we do not intend to discuss all the aspects of the New Evangelization. This discussion can be found in our 1993 statement *Go and Make Disciples*. Neither do we intend this statement to contain a discussion of the ministry to Hispanics, its history, its characteristics, and its goals. We reaffirm what we said in our pastoral letter on the Hispanic presence and urge all to implement the *National Pastoral Plan for Hispanic Ministry*, published on January 18, 1988. This pastoral plan is the fruit of the *encuentro* process, which engaged Hispanics from all regions and walks of life in formulating goals and objectives.

Instead, in this statement we wish to respond to what happened in Convocation '95. We see this statement as a dialogue with those who offered their "Statement of Commitment" to the New Evangelization. The New Evangelization must be based on a dialogue engaging all segments of our Catholic community, seeking the contribution of their experiences of faith, and learning from the witness of all. The participants at Convocation '95 recognized this when they wrote: "We will look for ways to share with the entire Church in the United States the progress brought about in Hispanic ministry."[4] It is in this spirit of dialogue that we offer now our thoughts on what we believe can be the most important contribution of our Hispanic Catholics to the New Evangelization, namely, the experience of how faith in Christ generates a culture that protects, sustains, and promotes human dignity. It is in this area, the area of the relation between faith and culture, where the contribution of our Hispanic faithful can be truly prophetic and providential.

In his message to the participants in Convocation '95, our Holy Father Pope John Paul II recognized the importance of the Hispanic contribution in the area of faith and culture. His Holiness expressed the wish that "by drawing on its rich history and experience, the Hispanic community can offer a unique contribution to the dialogue between faith and culture in American society today, and thus open new paths for the spread of the Gospel in the Third

> *The New Evangelization must be based on a dialogue engaging all segments of our Catholic community, seeking the contribution of their experiences of faith, and learning from the witness of all.*

Millennium."[5] *We believe this to be the most important contribution of Hispanic Catholics to the New Evangelization in the United States.* Therefore, we welcome the commitment by the participants in Convocation '95 to "share with our Catholic brothers and sisters in the United States what a faith incarnate in culture is."[6]

FAITH AND CULTURE

The relationship between faith and culture is at the heart of the New Evangelization. The word *culture* comes from the Latin verb *colere*, which means to cultivate the ground. Eventually, the expression *cultura animi*, the culture of souls, came to designate the personal formative process of the individual. When the process of personal formation is understood in intellectual terms, a "cultured person" is someone who simply knows a lot. However, personal formation is a process with intellectual, affective, ethical, and practical components. It touches on everything that is characteristically human. Culture is what shapes the human being as specifically human. The Second Vatican Council sees culture as the cultivation of "natural goods and values"[7] through which we reach full human maturity[8] by means of the dominion over the world which develops the resources of creation. Culture thus designates the perfection of the human person, the construction of a just social order, and the service of others.[9] The document of Puebla defines culture as "the specific way in which human beings belonging to a given people cultivate their relationship with nature, with each other, and with God in order to arrive at 'an authentic and full humanity.'"[10] As such, culture designates the style of life that characterizes different peoples. Thus it is appropriate to speak of a plurality of cultures.

The New Evangelization is aimed in a special way at those to whom the Gospel has already been proclaimed but for whom it has not become a lived experience of reality in all its dimensions. The Gospel enlightens us as to what is true and false, right and wrong, desirable and undesirable. It informs and transforms our experience of nature, of the passage of time, of work and rest, of other people, of the purpose of life and the meaning of death. *These are the experiences that characterize a culture.* The Gospel, therefore, touches the foundation of all cultures. Although addressed to each person, the invitation to follow Jesus Christ has a necessary cultural dimension. Without it the Gospel becomes an abstract system of ideas and values that can be manipulated to excuse individual and social sin. The New Evangelization is intended to bridge the gap between faith and culture by showing that *a faith that does not generate culture is a sterile faith.*

The common and absolutely essential point of departure of all authentic human cultures is the *recognition of human personhood as valuable for its own sake*, as the Second Vatican Council affirms.[11] That is, the human person may never be reduced to an "instrument" to achieve a purpose, no matter how good the purpose may be. The human person, each single human person regardless of circumstances, must be recognized and respected as such unconditionally. All authentic human cultures depend on this fact. *To say that the Gospel has a necessary cultural dimension is to say that it will promote the recognition, the affirmation, and the development of all human persons as such*. The Gospel thus compels the quest for freedom, personal growth, care for the weak and needy, and liberation from alienating economic, political, and religious structures of individual and social life.

PREFERENTIAL OPTION FOR THE POOR

On March 9, 1983, when Pope John Paul II said to the bishops of Latin America and the Caribbean that the present moment required an evangelization new in ardor, expression, and methods, he was building precisely on this process of renewal carried out by the Church in Latin America after the Second Vatican Council.[12] Central to this process is the recognition that a successful evangelization occurs only when faith shapes culture. That is, evangelization is inseparable from the affirmation and defense of the dignity of all human persons. However, because the Gospel touches the foundations of cultures, this truth about human dignity is meant to become incarnate in the culture. It is meant to affect those *social structures* through which the human person exercises dominion over the goods of nature and the distribution of the fruits of their development. These structures must be at the service of the human person, recognized and affirmed as valuable for his or her own sake. In order to judge whether this is or is not the case, it is necessary to embrace the experience of those who have no other claim to respect than their own identity as persons, *joining them in their quest for justice*. This experience becomes a criterion for interpretation of the demands of the Gospel in particular social situations.[13] In Latin America this solidarity was given a name: the "preferential option for the poor."

The Statement of Commitment issued by Convocation '95 reminds us of this criterion when it recognizes that a sign of a culture formed by the Gospel is the existence of a *preferential option for the poor* in society. Hence the commitment to "give witness to how the preferential option for the poor, an essential aspect of the Catholic faith, becomes a cultural reality."[14] *We welcome this commitment and recognize it as the contribution to the Church in our country of the last decades of ecclesial reflection and practice in the Church in Latin America.*

The Statement of Commitment correctly understands this term as "the affirmation of the dignity of the human person as created by God with no other purpose than the good of its own existence."[15] Thus the participants express a commitment to "struggle against all attempts to instrumentalize the human person, valuing only its possible contribution to the material progress of society."[16]

THE CENTRALITY OF CHRIST

In order to understand the deepest reason for the link between the preferential option for the poor and the impact of faith on culture, we must remember that communion with Jesus Christ

> *The New Evangelization is intended to bridge the gap between faith and culture by showing that a faith that does not generate culture is a sterile faith.*

involves a stand with respect to life in this world in all its dimensions. Through faith and the sacraments, we enter into the relationship between Jesus Christ and the Father. We acquire a vision of reality and an experience of nature, others, and God consistent with this relationship made possible by the gift of the Spirit of God. This vision and this experience define an outlook or *stand* with respect to reality that is oriented towards the consummation of God's plan for creation at the end of time. Thus we begin to live now, on this earth, the life of the kingdom of God which will be fully manifested at the end of time. It is this outlook or stand that is expressed culturally through social structures, especially those pertaining to work and leisure. The Statement of Commitment issued by Convocation '95 expresses it this way: "We shall seek ways to show that our efforts on behalf of social justice are the result of our faith in Jesus Christ, the Lord, the center of history and the universe. In the truth about Jesus Christ, true God and true Man, we discover what the human person is in all its dimensions: individual, social, material, and spiritual."[17]

The Gospel is not a system of concepts to be taught by a teacher to a pupil and adapted to different circumstances. The Gospel is the proclamation of the Person of Jesus Christ, of his mission, teachings, and promises. Jesus Christ is not an idea, but a concrete, specific, historical individual: the Son of God who became the Son of Mary. This individual, and he alone, is the Savior. There is no liberation of any kind without him. He became the "Poor One" in whom we experience solidarity with the poor. He is the Redeemer, the Second Person of the Holy Trinity in whom all were predestined to reach their fulfillment as human persons by faith and the sacramental incorporation into his saving death and resurrection. Without this proclamation of Jesus Christ and his worship through faith and the sacraments there is no true evangelization.[18]

Therefore, we wish to emphasize the importance of the commitment of the participants of Convocation '95 to the renewal of our "liturgical, sacramental, and catechetical life,"[19] to the promotion of vocations to the sacramental ministries of priesthood and diaconate, as well as to lay and religious vocations. We especially welcome the commitment to an adequate doctrinal and pastoral formation process based on Sacred Scripture and the new *Catechism of the Catholic Church*, as well as its insistence on the need for prayer and the popular expression of our religious beliefs.

WITNESS TO HOPE

The liturgical, sacramental, and catechetical life of the Church aims at introducing us into a personal relationship with Jesus Christ. Through this union with him, we experience the power of God's love, which is stronger than the power of sin and death. We experience the redemption of our personal and collective history by a love greater than all the evil in the world. This love conveys to us an experience of the horror of sin precisely as it awakens us to the reality of redemption and true freedom. Thus it gives rise to a hope which "will not leave us disappointed."[20] Evangelization is the proclamation of this hope rooted in Jesus Christ and committing us to the struggle against the power of sin in our lives. It is this hope, and not a utopian dream, that sustains our struggle for liberation and justice in the world, our preferential option for the poor.

The Church is the people of God formed by the Holy Spirit into the body of Christ. The Church is the place of *communio* or interpersonal communion of faith and love with the Lord and among believers. The life of the

> *Evangelization is the proclamation of this hope rooted in Jesus Christ and committing us to the struggle against the power of sin in our lives. It is this hope, and not a utopian dream, that sustains our struggle for liberation and justice in the world, our preferential option for the poor.*

Church is the proclamation, beginning, and anticipation of the kingdom of God. The Church evangelizes when its members proclaim the word of God, catechize, worship in the liturgy, serve the need of others, and give witness to their faith by the lives they lead. *The impact of faith on cultures, such as the preferential option for the poor, must be understood as the consequence of this way of life.*

THE CULTURE OF DEATH

In our country, the modern technological, functional mentality creates a world of replaceable individuals incapable of authentic solidarity. In its place, society is grouped by artificial arrangements created by powerful interests. The common ground is an increasingly dull, sterile, consumer conformism—visible especially among so many of our young people—created by artificial needs promoted by the media to support powerful economic interests. Pope John Paul II has called this a "culture of death." In the Holy Father's words, "this culture is actively fostered by powerful cultural, economic, and political currents which encourage an idea of society excessively concerned with efficiency. . . . A life which would require greater acceptance, love, and care is considered useless, or held to be an intolerable burden, and is therefore rejected in one way or another. . . ."[21] In such a culture, "society becomes a mass of individuals placed side by side, but without any mutual bonds."[22] The New Evangelization, therefore, requires the Church to provide refuge and sustenance for ongoing growth to those rescued from the loneliness of modern life. It requires the promotion of a culture of life based on the Gospel of life.

THE CULTURE OF LIFE

Hence the importance for the New Evangelization in our country of the commitment by the participants in Convocation '95 to "defend the value of each human life from the first moment of conception to natural death."[23] The struggle against abortion and euthanasia is an integral part of the New Evangelization, as well as the struggle against capital punishment, contraception, drugs, and the arms trade. Our defense of life requires "solidarity with all who defend the victims of the culture of death in our country, overcoming all racial or ethnic hostility, seeking to be an authentic leaven of unity, and struggling against racism and discrimination which denies access to the necessary resources to escape the poverty in which a large part of our Hispanic population is still immersed."[24]

Specifically, the Statement of Commitment calls for the recognition of the "right to a dignified work, a just salary, decent housing, an education that respects our cultural origins, and the access to health care programs worthy of the value of each human being, regardless of age."[25] Convocation '95 also identified as particularly urgent the defense of the family, the promotion of the dignity of women, and the care of the elderly and the terminally ill. Of particular importance to our Hispanic brothers and sisters is the need to reject immigration policies destructive of families, seeking instead immigration policies free from all racist motivations and selfish fears. In the same spirit, we have frequently denounced the unjust treatment of migrant agricultural workers.

> *Of particular importance to our Hispanic brothers and sisters is the need to reject immigration policies destructive of families, seeking instead immigration policies free from all racist motivations and selfish fears.*

To say all of this is not to reduce evangelization and the mission of the Church to the improvement of life in this world.[26] *Evangelii Nuntiandi* insists on the profound link between the invitation to faith in Christ and the promotion of social justice. The link between them is part of the very mystery of faith being proclaimed through evangelization. It is rooted in the relation between creation and redemption.[27] In *Redemptoris Missio*, John Paul II confirms this teaching and expands it in terms of the *prophetic mission* of the Church at the service of the poor.[28] The Holy Father talks of the Church's solidarity with the poor as a sign of redemption. The Church, he says, is the Church of the poor.[29] The Holy Father refers specifically to the example of the Church in Latin America, where the preferential option for the poor has been recognized as an integral part of the Church's mission. Indeed, this is one of the great insights central to the Latin American ecclesial experience, as articulated in the great declarations of Medellin and Puebla and reaffirmed in Santo Domingo. We welcome the importance given to it by our Hispanic Catholics in the Statement of Commitment of Convocation '95. We see this as an example of how Hispanic Catholics are a "logical bridge between the Church in the United States and the Church in Latin America,"[30] as the Statement of Commitment declares.

THE BLESSING OF THE HISPANIC PRESENCE

With the Holy Father, we recognize the Hispanic presence in our Church as a blessing, a privileged opportunity to work for a culture that reflects the truth about the human person revealed in the truth about Jesus Christ. As Pope John Paul II wrote to Convocation '95, "From the dawn of evangelization in the New World, the name of Jesus Christ and the liberating power of the Gospel have taken root among the Spanish-speaking peoples of the Americas. The preaching and evangelical witness of the first missionaries bore fruit in lives of holiness and in the growth of a new culture marked by deep faith and authentic Christian values. Today this living heritage continues to be a source of enrichment for the Church in the United States as it faces the challenge of proclaiming the Good News of our salvation and of building up the Body of Christ in the context of an ethnically diverse society."[31]

In our pastoral letter *The Hispanic Presence, Challenge and Commitment*, published in 1983, and in the *National Pastoral Plan for Hispanic Ministry* of 1987, we have already highlighted the Hispanic contribution to the life of the Church in the United States. The fact is that *the future of the Church in the United States will be greatly affected by what happens to Hispanic Catholics*, who constitute a large percentage of its members. The contribution of Hispanic Catholics in the United States to the New Evangelization and the future of our Church will depend on the Church's presence in the Hispanic community.

> *The participants ask the Church that its programs of education and religious formation in schools, universities, institutes, and seminaries reflect the true significance of the Hispanic presence.*

When we speak of the Hispanic presence, it is important to realize we are speaking about a complex, varied, and dynamic reality. The Statement of Commitment of Convocation '95 correctly underlines "the importance of a Hispanic presence in the communications media, in order to present an adequate image of the reality of our communities, their real needs, and their contributions to the life of the Church and society."[32] The participants ask the Church that its programs of education and religious formation in schools, universities, institutes, and seminaries reflect the true significance of the Hispanic presence.

In a way, a new Hispanic-American identity is still in the process of being forged in the United States as people from different Latin American cultures come together, discover what they have in common, and interrelate with the dominant North American culture. This new Hispanic-American identity will take its place next to all the other expressions of the Hispanic identity, all having a common origin.

The majority of Hispanic people were born here, and their ancestors have been in our country for a long time, some including many generations. Convocation '95 provided the participants with the opportunity to reflect on the origins of the Hispanic presence in our land long before the settlement of the first thirteen English colonies. Today the vast majority of Hispanics are engaged in a struggle similar to that of all previous American immigrant groups, namely, care for the family, work, health, and education. Their needs are obviously different from the needs of those recently arrived. Different responses to different needs are required. In this regard, we agree with the need to "search for ways in which Hispanics who have achieved success in society will contribute with their talents so that [their] experience of faith and culture will assist the Church in the evangelization of the professional world."[33]

The experience of living in the United States is bringing the people of Latin American descent to recognize what they have in common. As the Statement of Commitment says: Hispanics are "the fruit of an inculturation of the Catholic faith which constitutes the basis of our Hispanic identity."[34] This inculturation of the faith has generated similar attitudes about personal and social life that unite Hispanics despite their differences.

Traditional Hispanic cultures preserve many experiences of self, nature, others, and God, which characterize this inculturation of the faith. We have in mind similar attitudes such as openness of spirit; a welcoming disposition to what is unexpected, new, and unplanned; simplicity; a recognition that a need for companionship and support is not a weakness, but a necessary part of personal growth; creative fidelity and determination to honor promises given; a sense of honor and respect for self and others; patience and willingness to follow the rhythms of nature; a sense of walking together toward a common destiny; a truly creative imagination capable of rising above immediate appearances in order to reach the inner core of reality; a love for home, land, and an extended view of family; a trust in divine providence; and an awareness that what is proper and right is more worthy of sacrifice than immediate satisfaction, that persons are more important than things, personal relations more fulfilling than material success, and serenity more valuable than life in the fast lane. All of this is combined with a joyful resignation born of the awareness that life is greater than any temporary frustration. These similar attitudes, characteristic of an Hispanic *ethos*, are the fruit of the inculturation of the Catholic faith through the tremendous encounter with Iberian, Native American, and African spiritualities at the origin of the history of Hispanics. *The Hispanic ethos is historically inseparable from the Catholic faith. Indeed, sometimes fear and opposition to the Hispanic presence is motivated more by anti-Catholicism than by anything else.*

Of course Hispanics are not the only people who possess these qualities! These are truly attributes of all who are authentically human. Moreover, as with all that is human, these attitudes can also be corrupted by sin and can hide the reality of prejudice and selfishness. Still, with the Holy Father we are convinced that the presence in our Church of such large numbers of Hispanics can be understood spiritually as a *providential opportunity* for all of us to rediscover

> *In order to participate in the current debate and assist our country to be faithful to the truths and values upon which it claims to be founded, it is necessary for us as Catholics to appreciate the relationship between faith and culture.*

qualities necessary for our service to society in the name of the liberating Gospel of Jesus Christ. These qualities are not merely folkloric stereotypes. Behind them lies a definite, courageous stand originating in the Catholic faith and sustained throughout the vicissitudes of what is often a very harsh and difficult life.

PROPHETIC PRESENCE
─────────────────

In our pastoral letter on the Hispanic presence and in the *National Pastoral Plan for Hispanic Ministry*, we referred to the Hispanic presence as *prophetic*. This prophetic presence is due above all to those aspects of the Hispanic ethos arising from its Catholic origins. As prophetic, we believe that the Hispanic presence provides the Church in our country an opportunity to recall its mission to preserve and foster a Catholic identity in the midst of an often hostile culture.

For most of its history, the Catholic Church in the United States sought to convince American society of the patriotism of the Catholic people and their adherence to the fundamental and "self-evident truths" mentioned in our Declaration of Independence. Although anti-Catholicism still remains in our country, much of this effort achieved some success, especially after the Second Vatican Council's Declaration on Religious Liberty. At the present time, however, the influence of secularism has led to a debate about the proper interpretation of the American founding principles. Some of the interpretations being proposed—and even adopted in judicial decisions—are absolutely incompatible with our faith. In order to participate in the current debate and assist our country to be faithful to the truths and values upon which it claims to be founded, it is necessary for us as Catholics to appreciate the relationship between faith and culture. The Hispanic presence is prophetic because it is the bearer of traditions flowing from an authentic inculturation of the Catholic faith.[35] Our efforts to help Hispanics preserve and grow in their faith will put us in a position to better understand those currents of thought and practice in our society that undermine the faith of all Catholics.

The Church in the United States began as a Church of poor immigrants who struggled against discrimination in order to obtain their share of the American dream. Yet many times anti-Catholicism excluded them from participation in society. Ironically, in the name of freedom, freedom was denied; in the name of tolerance, tolerance was denied and doors were closed. *We believe this is again increasingly the case,* going even beyond Catholicism to all expressions of biblical faith different from the secularist ethos seeking cultural dominance in our society.

In the past, the Catholic Church created a space within American society where the Catholic people could be nourished and supported in the faith while being cared for in their needs. This was accompanied by a relentless effort to show that Catholics were as fully committed to freedom, pluralism, and democracy as anyone else in the country. As a result of this effort, most of our Catholic immigrants were assimilated into the American mainstream. This was possible because of the commitment of the American people to the rights of the human person based on the unsurpassable dignity of each human being created by God. Of course there were differences of opinion concerning those rights and their ultimate origin and meaning, but a common discourse about this was possible, based on the biblical Jewish and Christian experiences of life and on the great tradition about a natural law grasped by all human beings, regardless of their different beliefs concerning religion.

In the present cultural crisis, this common discourse is not always possible. The crucial and key concepts upon which this discussion was based are the same—concepts such as rights, persons, justice, liberty, and happiness—but the experiences to which these concepts point can no longer be assumed to be the same for all. Of course we must continue the dialogue upon which our future as one nation depends, pursued serenely and with respect for all, but we must always try to understand the experiences at the roots of the concepts being debated. Most important of all, we must *retrieve the cultural dimension of the experiences at the root of Catholic life.* This is a crucial part of the New Evangelization, and the large Hispanic presence in our midst constitutes for us a providential resource for this task. That is why we have stated that *the most important contribution of Hispanic Catholics to the New Evangelization in our country lies in the area of faith and culture.*

PROPHETIC WARNING

The Hispanic presence is also a prophetic warning to the Church in the United States. For if Hispanic Catholics are not welcomed warmly and offered a home where they can experience our Church as their Church, the resulting loss of their Catholic identity will be a serious blow to the Church in our country. We will have missed an opportunity to be truly Catholic while the culture of death, prevalent in our society, seeks to impose its way on us all.

As the call for a New Evangelization in Latin America demonstrates, we cannot take for granted the Catholic faith of Hispanic Catholics. Hispanics do not consider themselves a chosen people protected in any special way from infidelity to the Gospel. Nor do they present themselves as living exemplars of faith. To pretend to do so is an intolerable and dangerous romanticism. A disposition to the faith is not itself faith; a strong religiosity is not identical to the ecclesial-sacramental life in Christ; appreciation of the values of personalism, family, and community are not enough for a moral life in Christ. The devastation of Hispanic families by drugs, alcohol, and licentiousness is well documented. So is the plight of so many Hispanic women who are victims of deeply ingrained *machista* attitudes, as the women attending Convocation '95 strongly reminded us. Although racism, poverty, immigrant bashing, and prejudiced discrimination are still a fact of life for many Hispanics, these vices are present also in the Hispanic communities. The commitment to struggle against these ills by embracing a preferential option for the poor is a commitment by Hispanics to other Hispanics as well.

Yet through it all, there remains a precious gift in our midst brought to us by our Hispanic brothers and sisters: a sense of the sacred, a particular and deep sensitivity to the beauty of creation festively celebrated, a sense of pride in *la hispanidad*, a capacity for profound emotions of devotion to others, a great delicacy in human contacts, and a thirst for the transcendent and divine expressed in powerful Catholic symbols. We believe with the participants of Convocation '95 that the importance of this "cultural Catholicism" should not be underestimated. It is truly a blessing, and it is upon these experiences of a faith becoming culture that the New Evangelization in our country must be based.

THE STAR OF EVANGELIZATION

In this task we commend ourselves once again to the Queen of the Americas, Our Lady of Guadalupe, as we seek to respond to the call to a New Evangelization. It was in the womb of Mary that the Word became flesh. This mystery of the incarnation is the basis for our belief in the mystery of faith becoming culture. Mary's *Magnificat* is the canticle of our preferential option of love for the poor. She is the woman, pursued by the dragon, in whose companionship the people of God, her children, are protected from the culture of death. It is Mary who prevents us from detaching our Lord from the flesh and turning him into an abstract, remote figure. Through her, the Lord becomes a concrete, tangible presence redeeming all aspects of our life, our companion and the goal of our pilgrimage to the definitive manifestation of the kingdom of God. As we welcome the commitment of our brothers and sisters in Convocation '95, we commend them and ourselves to her, Santa Maria, the Star of all Evangelization.

NOTES

1. For this document, "Hispanic" is synonymous with Latin American, Latino, Mexican-American, Spanish-American, and Chicano; it includes all Spanish-speaking persons in the United States.

2. *The Hispanic Presence: Challenge and Commitment.* Washington, D.C.: United States Cathoic Conference, 1984.

3. Statement of Commitment, Convocation '95, June 25, 1995. Hereafter designated as "SOC."

4. SOC, 9.

5. Letter of May 8, 1995, from Archbishop G. B. Re to Bishop Roberto González, chairman, NCCB Committee on Hispanic Affairs, Prot. No. 370.479 (included as Appendix A to this statement).

6. SOC, 3.

7. *Gaudium et Spes* (GS), no. 53.

8. GS, no. 57.

9. Cf. GS, nos. 55 and 57.

10. *La Evangelización en el Presente y en el Futuro de América Latina.* Puebla: CELAM, 1979, no. 386.

11. Cf. GS, no. 24.

12. Cf. AAS 75 (1983), pp. 771-779.

13. Congregation for the Doctrine of the Faith. *Instruction on Certain Aspects of Liberation Theology*, VIII, nos. 1-9.

14. SOC, 4.

15. Ibid.

16. Ibid.

17. Ibid., 8.

18. Cf. Pope Paul VI, *Evangelii Nuntiandi*, no. 22; AAS 68 (1976).

19. SOC, 8.

20. Cf. Romans 5:5.

21. Cf. Pope John Paul II, *Evangelium Vitae,* no. 12.

22. Cf. ibid., no. 20.

23. SOC, 5.

24. Ibid.

25. Ibid.

26. Congregation for the Doctrine of the Faith. *Instruction on Certain Aspects of Liberation Theology*, VI, no. 3.

27. Cf. *Evangelii Nuntiandi*, no. 31

28. Pope John Paul II, *Redemptoris Missio*, no. 43.

29. Ibid., no. 60

30. SOC, 10.

31. Cf. Appendix A, Letter to Bishop Roberto González.

32. SOC, 6.

33. Ibid.

34. Ibid., 3.

35. *Hispanic Ministry: Three Major Documents.* Washington, D.C.: United States Catholic Conference, 1995.

Appendices

A. Message from the Holy Father

May 8, 1995

Dear Bishop González,

The Holy Father was pleased to be informed that on June 23-25, 1995 the Committee on Hispanic Affairs of the National Conference of Catholic Bishops will sponsor *Convocation '95*, a program of prayer and reflection devoted to the theme: "The Hispanic Presence in the New Evangelization in the United States." He asks you kindly to convey to all assembled in San Antonio his prayerful good wishes for this significant pastoral initiative.

His Holiness joins the delegates to the Convocation in thanking Almighty God for the abundant blessings bestowed on the Church in the United States through the deep faith and Christian witness of generations of Hispanic Catholics. From the dawn of evangelization in the New World, the name of Jesus Christ and the liberating power of the Gospel have taken root among the Spanish-speaking peoples of the Americas. The preaching and evangelical witness of the first missionaries bore fruit in lives of holiness and in the growth of a new culture marked by deep faith and authentic Christian values. Today this living heritage continues to be a source of enrichment for the Church in the United States as it faces the challenge of proclaiming the Good News of our salvation and of building up the Body of Christ in the context of an ethnically diverse society.

It is the Holy Father's fervent hope that the San Antonio Convocation, by commemorating the fiftieth anniversary of the first nationwide effort to coordinate the Hispanic Apostolate in the United States, will foster a deeper and more conscious commitment by Hispanic Catholics to bearing effective witness to their faith, to strengthening the growth of the Church in love, and to serving Christ in the least of their brothers and sisters. By drawing on its rich history and experience, the Hispanic community can offer a unique contribution to the dialogue between faith and culture in American society today, and thus open new paths for the spread of the Gospel in the Third Millennium. Recognizing the importance of the younger generation for the future of the Church in the United States, His Holiness encourages the delegates to the Conference to consider the urgent need for an effective catechesis and to promote structures enabling young people to respond generously to the Lord's invitation to serve him in the Priesthood and Religious Life.

In the end, the success of the new evangelization will be measured by the response of all the baptized to Christ's call to sincere conversion, lively faith and holiness of life. To the delegates and all assembled at the Convocation the Holy Father repeats the challenging words he addressed to the Hispanic Community during his Pastoral Visit to San Antonio in 1987: "Today, it is your turn, in fidelity to the Gospel of Jesus Christ, to build your lives on the rock of your Christian faith. It is your turn to be evangelizers of each other and of all those whose faith is weak or who have not yet given themselves to the Lord. May you be no less zealous in evangelization and in Christian service than your forebears!" (*Address at Our Lady of Guadalupe Plaza*, September 13, 1987).

With these sentiments, His Holiness commends all taking part in Convocation '95 to the loving intercession of Mary Immaculate, Patroness of the Church in the United States, and he cordially imparts his Apostolic Blessing as a pledge of joy and strength in Jesus Christ our Savior.

With personal good wishes, I remain,

Sincerely yours in Christ,

+ G. B. Re
Substitute

B. Convocation '95 Statement of Commitment

(English Translation)

1. We praise God, who has been good to us, for the opportunity to meet in San Antonio to commemorate the fiftieth anniversary of the establishment of what is now the NCCB Committee on Hispanic Affairs. We have celebrated the achievements in Hispanic ministry during half a century. Profoundly conscious of the Communion in Christ Jesus uniting us as the one Catholic Church in pilgrimage proclaiming the kingdom of God, we commit ourselves to the task of a New Evangelization in the United States of America. We offer our bishops this "Statement of Commitment," eager to hear their insights about the Hispanic contribution to the New Evangelization.

2. Convocation '95 has been an evangelizing experience for the Hispanic-Catholic community, which has already begun to generate new ardor, create new expressions, and explore new methods to make present the kingdom of God in our society.

3. Although we celebrate fifty years of an organized Hispanic ministry at a national level, our reunion in San Antonio gives us the opportunity to reaffirm the origins of our Catholic identity. We are the fruit of an inculturation of the Catholic faith which constitutes the basis of our Hispanic identity. Celebrating the variety of manifestations of this common identity in our different places of origin, we commit ourselves to share with our Catholic brothers and sisters in the United States what a faith incarnate in culture is. In this way, together, we will be able to struggle against the culture of death denounced by our Holy Father Pope John Paul II, giving witness to the Gospel of life.

4. We commit ourselves to give witness to how the preferential option for the poor, an essential aspect of the Catholic faith, becomes a cultural reality. By this option we understand the affirmation of the dignity of the human person as created by God with no other purpose than the good of its own existence. We will struggle against all attempts to instrumentalize the human person, valuing only its possible contribution to the material progress of society.

5. Guided by this option, we will defend the value of each human life from the first moment of conception to natural death. We will search for ways to affirm our solidarity with all who defend the victims of the culture of death in our country—overcoming all racial or ethnic hostility; seeking to be an authentic leaven of unity; and struggling against racism and discrimination. Such discrimination denies access to the necessary resources to escape the poverty in which a large part of our Hispanic population is still immersed. We shall insist on the recognition throughout our society of the right to a dignified work, a just salary, decent housing, an education that respects our cultural origins, and the access to health care programs worthy of the values of each human being, regardless of age. In discussing health problems, we paid particular attention to the devastation brought about by AIDS, committing ourselves to be witnesses of the love of God for all the sick. The pollution of water and the environment also threatens the health of many of our communities, and we shall continue our efforts to stop the destruction of nature whose goods are meant for all human beings.

6. We will search for ways in which Hispanics who have achieved success in society will contribute with their talents so that our experience of faith and culture will assist the Church in the evangelization of the professional world. We underline the importance of a Hispanic presence in the communications media, in order to present an adequate image of the reality of our communities, their real

needs, and their contributions to the life of the Church and society. We reaffirm our commitment to solidarity with migrant agricultural workers, refugees, the victims of police abuse, and the undocumented. We shall develop goals and strategies within our ministry to struggle against the discrimination suffered by immigrants, working with political institutions and government agencies in order to inform and educate them about matters that affect new arrivals. We remind everyone that those who, for whatever reason, are in prison do not lose their dignity as persons, and we will strive so that pastoral care is attentive to the particular needs of the Hispanic population in jail.

7. We want our Hispanic communities to be at the vanguard of the efforts to defend the dignity of the family as the fundamental cell of society and of the Church. We commit ourselves to work for the recognition of the dignity of the vocation of parenthood, and we shall struggle for the recognition of the rights of women and their invaluable contributions to all aspects of ecclesial and social life. The Hispanic women in our convocation have called our attention to the problems of women in our country, and we commit ourselves to struggle against domestic violence, the violation and mistreatment of women, the abandonment of single mothers, the exclusion of poor women, and the lack of adequate resources for an integral formation and education. Concerning the family, we underline the importance of respecting the dignity of the elderly, from which we have received the faith that sustains and animates us.

8. We shall seek ways to show that our efforts on behalf of social justice are the result of our faith in Jesus Christ, the Lord, the center of history and the universe. In the truth about Jesus Christ, true God and true man, we discover what the human person is in all its dimensions: individual, social, material, and spiritual. We commit ourselves to the proclamation and witness of what it means to be the People of God that follows Jesus towards the full manifestation of his victory over sin and death. Therefore, promoting an authentic team ministry (*pastoral de conjunto*), we will do everything possible so that our liturgical, sacramental, and catechetical ministry gives witness to the truth concerning the Church founded by Christ, being faithful to the vision of the *National Pastoral Plan for Hispanic Ministry* of a Church that is authentically "communitarian, evangelizing and missionary, incarnate in the reality of the Hispanic people and open to the diversity of cultures, a promoter and example of justice, that develops leadership through integral education . . . that is leaven for the kingdom of God in society."

9. We shall promote information on the *National Pastoral Plan* and its implementation where it has not yet occurred. We shall continue to look for expressions of ecclesial life and structural changes which, in communion with the Holy Father and the bishops, will help us give clear witness to the truth about the Church, such as the small ecclesial communities, movements of ecclesial renewal, and Catholic Hispanic organizations. In this area, it is necessary to strengthen the parishes as centers of the life of the Church in the different regions. We support all efforts to strengthen Catholic schools, searching for ways in which Catholic education will be more accessible to Hispanics. We also underline the importance of a vocations ministry that will eagerly look for Hispanics called to ministry in the Church as priests, deacons, and members of religious communities. We recognize the need for Hispanic families to give greater attention to vocations, to ecclesial ministry, recognizing the great blessing this is for them. There is an urgent need for programs for the adequate religious formation of our communities and their lay leaders, with special emphasis on a profound knowl-

edge of the Scriptures as the word of God, the doctrine of the Church in accordance with the new *Catechism of the Catholic Church*, and the incomparable power of prayer. We call upon schools and other educational institutions to respond to the needs of the Hispanic people and upon seminaries so that they adequately prepare all future priests to understand the reality and the promise of the Hispanic presence in the Church. We affirm the importance of a popular religiosity faithful to the Gospel as one of the most important ways through which faith becomes culture. In our Con-vocation '95, we discussed widely the importance of pastoral programs for the young, open to their points of view and soliciting their contribution to the life of the Church. We will look for ways to share with the entire Church in the United States the progress brought about in Hispanic ministry.

10. Concluding our Convocation '95, we affirm our commitment to look for ways to continue the process of dialogue between our communities and our bishops, such as the process of the *Encuentros*, as well as this Convocation. We do not wish to wait ten years before another similar occasion. We urge, therefore, that plans be formulated to achieve the full cooperation of our Hispanic peoples in the preparation for the celebrations of the third millennium of Christianity. As part of this concern, we shall do all within our reach to help in the preparation and participation of our bishops in the upcoming Synod of the entire American Hemisphere. We are the logical bridge between the Church in the United States and the Church in Latin America.

11. We return to our homes and places of ecclesial commitment entrusting ourselves to our Mother, Mary, Queen of the Americas, *La Morenita*, our Lady of Guadalupe, constant companion of our people in their struggle for liberty, peace, and respect for our dignity.

C. Historical Context of Hispanic Ministry in the Catholic Church in the United States

The Gospel was introduced to this continent and to this hemisphere over 500 years ago. As such, ministry to the Spanish-speaking and to native peoples has been an ongoing process and an integral part of our Church's history in the Americas. In more recent times, ministry to the Spanish-speaking was established by dioceses to respond to the pastoral and social concerns of their particular Spanish-speaking communities.[1] In some dioceses, ministry offices were established at the turn of the century. In many western and southwestern dioceses, Spanish-speaking councils were established in the 1940s and 1950s.

The first bishops' committee for the Spanish-speaking was established in 1945 under the leadership of Archbishop Robert E. Lucey, of San Antonio, by the National Catholic Welfare Conference. The primary focus of the Committee was the plight of migrant workers in the southwest. Its office was located in San Antonio.[2]

At the time the bishops' committee was established, the Spanish-speaking community was largely settled in the states bordering Mexico. Other parts of the country were also seeing a significant Hispanic presence: the midwest, the northeast, and Florida also had a significant Spanish-speaking population.

In general, the population was relatively small and largely poor. Most workers received low wages, lived in substandard housing, lacked medical care, had little education or educational opportunity, and received little support or assistance. Regretfully, not even the institutional Church was present to assist. Many workers had come to the United States as *braceros* in the federally sponsored Bracero Program, which was established as a contracted labor force to support the agricultural industry during and after World War II. Needless to say, the plight of the farm workers intensified during this period.

Many social and pastoral needs in different parts of the country moved Hispanics to form new secular and ecclesial associations. These associations were important and were used by the Spanish-speaking community as vehicles for a more pro-active participation in public policy issues and in meeting the many social service needs facing their families and communities. The Church responded by continuing to provide social services and later by establishing and funding diocesan and regional offices and pastoral institutes to better coordinate Hispanic pastoral ministry efforts.[3]

Within this affirming and supportive climate, the Church established an office for ministry to the Spanish-speaking community that went beyond regional concerns. In 1968, with the reorganization of the National Catholic Welfare Conference, the National Office of the Bishops' Committee for the Spanish-Speaking became the Division for the Spanish-Speaking under the Social Action Department of the newly organized National Conference of Catholic Bishops.[4]

In 1971, the office was moved to Washington, D.C. The task of the national director was to move beyond social and material concerns to the pastoral; to increase the size of the staff to carry out the challenging work ahead; to collaborate with national organizations; and to invite them to become partners in the task at hand. The challenge of the Secretariat for Hispanic Affairs was to assist the Church in its response to the pastoral and social needs of a growing number of Hispanic Catholics. Its mission was to serve as an advocate for pastoral needs and for public policy issues that were impacting the life of the Spanish-speaking community. In June 1972, these concepts became the priorities and the basis for the *Primer Encuentro Nacional Hispano de Pastoral*. According to Pope Paul VI, the first *Encuentro* "aroused so much enthusiasm and so many expectations."[5]

The conclusions of the *Primer Encuentro* called for "greater participation of the Spanish speaking in leadership and decision-making roles at all levels within the American Church."[6] Further, it called for the establishment of regional and pastoral centers, to be established and coordinated nationally, for the purpose of research and reflection and the development of programs of Christian leadership formation at all levels of the Church. Finally, the conclusions of the participants state that "being convinced of the unity of the American Church" and of the values of their heritage, they were "impelled by the Spirit to share responsibility for the growth of the kingdom" among the Spanish speaking and the peoples of the United States.[7]

During the period following the *Primer Encuentro*, the number of Hispanic bishops increased, and Hispanic bishops collaborated with non-Hispanic bishops, Hispanic and pro-Hispanic priests and religious were renewed, apostolic movements were revitalized, and small Christian communities increased.

On January 1, 1975, the Division for the Spanish-speaking was elevated to the Secretariat for the Spanish-Speaking. Within its first year of existence, the bishops' committee called for a second national *encuentro* to develop a more concrete pastoral orientation. The following year, the national secretariat took advantage of the International Eucharistic Congress, which was taking place in Philadelphia, to convene a meeting of national ministry leaders to consult and determine Hispanic priorities, particularly those of the grassroots Hispanic community. "Three priorities surfaced: unity in pluralism, integral education, and social change (especially in fomenting greater respect for Hispanos). Each priority gave special attention to leaders and youth."[8]

The participants at the national gathering set summer 1977 as the date for the *II Encuentro*. A national coordinating committee was established, consisting of the secretariat staff and the regional directors. Also included were the heads of the national Catholic Hispanic organizations. In January 1977, the Ad Hoc Committee of Bishops for the Spanish-Speaking supported and endorsed the *encuentro*.

In various planning meetings leading up to the II *Encuentro*, the national coordinating committee quickly discovered that the "principal strength of the process was found in the diocesan Church."[9] The number of diocesan offices for the Spanish-speaking had grown from thirty in 1972 to over one hundred in 1977.

The diocesan directors were included in the planning process and were invited to the National Meeting of Diocesan Directors of the Hispanic Apostolate. Eighty-two diocesan directors participated. The motto chosen was *Pueblo de Dios en Marcha* and the official hymn chosen was *Un Pueblo que Camina*. The theme was evangelization, and the participants chose five additional topics for discussion: *ministries, human rights, integral education, political responsibility, and unity in pluralism*. More than one hundred thousand people from all parts of the country participated in the process.[10] "The *Segundo Encuentro* recommendations express(ed) the desire of grassroots Hispanics for a more responsive, multicultural, spiritually alive, united and creative Church."[11]

In 1968 the Midwest Regional Office and the Mexican American Cultural Center had been established to assist in the formation, training, and development of diocesan staffs and pastoral leaders. In 1974, the Northeast Catholic Pastoral Center for Hispanics was established in New York. The period following the *II Encuentro* of 1977 saw the opening of five new regional offices for Hispanic ministry: the Southeast in 1978, the Far West in 1979, the Northwest in 1981, and the organization of diocesan directors in the North Central states in 1982 and in the Mountain states in 1984. These offices and regional structures were a great support to the Hispanic apostolate and continue to be an integral part of Hispanic ministry today.

In addition, during the *II Encuentro*, a National Youth Task Force was created which became the *Comité Nacional Hispano de Pastoral Juvenil*. Today this organization does not exist, though there have been attempts to reestablish it. In 1987, the NCCB reorganized and placed youth under the youth desk of the Secretariat for Laity and Family Life. In place of the *Comité*, regional and diocesan offices took on the responsibility of coordinating Hispanic youth ministry.

The successful collaboration with national Hispanic Catholic organizations during the *II Encuentro* proved to be a valuable exercise for pastoral ministry. The expertise and knowledge of the national leaders were great assets to the Ad Hoc Committee and to the Secretariat for Hispanic Affairs in formulating pastoral strategies. All the participants benefited from the national coordination. They saw a need to keep in contact and to continue to collaborate for the purpose of implementing national Hispanic pastoral priorities.

As a result of the need to continue meeting, a National Advisory Committee (NAC) was created by the National Conference of Catholic Bishops in 1978 to assist the Secretariat for Hispanic Affairs. Its members included the directors and coordinators of the regional offices and organizations, presidents of the pastoral institutes, the presidents of the apostolic movements, and the heads of Hispanic Catholic organizations, such as PADRES, HERMANAS, Hispanic Youth, and the National Farmworker Ministry. After the ad hoc committee of bishops was changed to a standing committee in 1987, the NAC was dissolved in 1990 to adapt to the structure of a NCCB/USCC permanent committee.

The Bishops Speak with the Virgin: A Pastoral Letter of the Hispanic Bishops of the U.S. was published in 1982. It was a message of the Hispanic community's pilgrimage with joy, courage, and hope; the historical reality; and the community as artisans of a new humanity. In 1983, the bishops issued a pastoral letter on Hispanic ministry titled *The Hispanic Presence: Challenge and Commitment*. In the document, the bishops of the United States made a call to

Hispanic ministry, affirmed the achievements in Hispanic ministry, listed urgent pastoral implications, and made a statement of commitment. Most importantly, in their letter, the bishops called for a third national *encuentro* and called for the conclusions to be reviewed as a basis for a national pastoral plan for Hispanic ministry.

The bishops asked "Hispanic peoples to raise their prophetic voices once again, as they did in 1972 and 1977, in a *III Encuentro Nacional Hispano de Pastoral*, so that together we can face our responsibilities well. We call for the launching of an *Encuentro* process, from *comunidades eclesiales de base* and parishes, to dioceses and regions, and to the national level, culminating in a gathering of representatives in Washington, D.C., in August 1985."[12] Further, they stated that they recognized "that integral pastoral planning must avoid merely superficial adaptations of existing ministries."[13]

The *III Encuentro* is the fruit of the efforts of many committed men and women who, for many years, dedicated their time and energy in a process of evangelization. The *III Encuentro* consisted of ten steps that required consultation and participation of the people at the diocesan, regional, or national levels: (1) formation of diocesan promoter teams (EPDs) and mobile teams; (2) evaluation of *II Encuentro*; (3) promotion of *III Encuentro* through communication; (4) local consultation through personal contact; (5) local reflection about consultation and selection of priorities for the national level; (6) national meeting of diocesan directors and delegates of the EPDs and selection of a theme; (7) study and reflection at the local level about the national theme; (8) second diocesan meeting to synthesize the local reflection on the theme; (9) regional *encuentro* on diocesan conclusions for use at the national *encuentro*; and, (10) the *III Encuentro Nacional Hispano de Pastoral*.[14]

The Ad Hoc Committee of Bishops for Hispanic Affairs proposed four objectives for the *III Encuentro*: (a) evangelization, (b) formation of leaders, (c) development of grassroots efforts, and (d) emphasis on the diocesan and regional dimensions of the process. A fifth objective came from the bishops' pastoral letter, *A National Pastoral Plan*.[15] The regional offices, the pastoral institutes, the National Advisory Committee, and representatives from the diocesan promotional teams helped design the process, which preserved the model of communion and participation.

The theme selected was *Pueblo Hispano: Voz Profética*, which came from the bishops' pastoral letter *The Hispanic Presence: Challenge and Commitment*. Practical "Prophetic Pastoral Guidelines" were approved and became the "direction and principal options of Hispanic pastoral ministry."[16]

Prophetic Voices was published in 1986 as the document on the historical context, the process, the commitments, the follow-up, the pastoral reflection, and the conclusions of the *III Encuentro Nacional Hispano de Pastoral*.

The Prophetic Pastoral Guidelines in this document were designed to be the fundamental direction for pastoral action. They included family as the core of pastoral ministry, a preferential option for and in solidarity with the poor, a preferential option for Hispanic youth, and resolve to follow *pastoral de conjunto* and to follow the pastoral approach of an evangelizing and missionary Church. The "guidelines" also promote Hispanic leadership and a "line of integral education that is sensitive to cultural identity, promotes and exemplifies justice, and values and promotes women in equality, dignity and their role in the Church, the family, and society."[17]

The National Pastoral Plan for Hispanic Ministry promotes a model of Church that is communitarian and participatory. The general objective prophetically and poetically states the vision of Church that Hispanic and non-Hispanic Catholic leaders and pastoral agents have developed and have participated in for many decades. Though there are many new leaders and Church professionals who have not been involved in the Hispanic pastoral process over the last 20 to 25 years, the vision is still very relevant and it is one of the best Hispanic ministry has developed. To a large degree, Hispanic ministry has been affirmed and supported by the Church during this process, though not always to the degree expected. However, the purpose of the process has always been to develop responsible pastoral agents of the Good News and to participate in the process of building the reign of God, regardless of age, culture, economic status, or gender.

"To live and promote . . . by means of a *Pastoral de Conjunto*, a model of Church that is: communitarian, evangelizing, and missionary, incarnate in the reality of the Hispanic people and open to the diversity of cultures, a promoter of justice . . . that develops leadership through integral education . . . that is leaven for the kingdom of God in society"[18] is the challenge all Christians must face. Through the four specific dimensions of the pastoral plan: *pastoral de conjunto, evangelization, missionary option, and formation*, and with the programs and projects delineated, the Hispanic ministry implementation strategy is in place for the Church. Since 1987, when the pastoral plan was approved by the NCCB, Hispanic ministry has had a mandate to implement the model of Church that so many participated in experiencing.

In affirmation and support of parish, diocesan, and regional efforts to minister with and among Hispanic Catholics, the NCCB's Bishops' Committee on Hispanic Affairs and nine other NCCB/USCC committees co-sponsored Convocation '95 in San Antonio, Texas, on June 23-25, 1995. The event, hosted at Incarnate Word College, marked the Catholic bishops' intent to commemorate, to celebrate, to build communion in ministry, and to re-commit to Hispanic ministry on the fiftieth anniversary of the establishment of a national office for ministry to Hispanics.

Five hundred Hispanic ministry directors and delegates, representing 110 dioceses and the eight Hispanic ministry regions, joined 35 bishops, 98 priests, 17 permanent deacons, 55 women religious, and more than 300 lay men and women, including 115 couples, at the national gathering. The bishops facilitated twenty-three different workshops dealing with themes related to Christian identity and Christian action. From the statements of commitment that were developed at the conclusion of each of the twenty-three workshops, the Convocation '95 participants gave input to the development of a "Statement of Commitment" to ministry with Hispanics that was used by the National Conference of Catholic Bishops in developing their pastoral statement on Hispanic Catholics in the United States titled *The Hispanic Presence in the New Evangelization in the United States*.

At the closing ceremony of Convocation '95, the bishops' committee awarded the first national *Archbishop Patrick F. Flores Medal* to nine individuals and one couple for their contribution and service to the Church and Hispanic ministry. These recipients, and thousands more like them, continue to make evangelization of Hispanic Catholics possible. As the year 2000 draws near, Hispanic/Latino Catholics are a major pastoral priority in the Catholic Church in the United States.[19]

At the beginning of 1996, and as the Church approaches the new millennium, the implementation of the National Pastoral Plan is integral to the work of the NCCB Secretariat for Hispanic Affairs, the five regional offices and three regional associations, and the over 140 diocesan directors and coordinators for Hispanic ministry in the United States. Other NCCB/USCC departments and secretariats, as well as most national and regional ecclesial associations and organizations working in Hispanic ministry, utilize the Pastoral Plan as their guideline and measure in developing their particular ministry. The Bishops' Committee on Hispanic Affairs and the Secretariat for Hispanic Affairs maintain a close working relationship with these ministry offices and organizations and with the various dioceses developing a ministry with Hispanics. Many dioceses have developed or are in the process of developing local pastoral plans and strategies for evangelization, formation, and catechesis among Hispanic Catholics.

NOTES

1. National Conference of Catholic Bishops. *Hispanic Ministry: Three Major Documents* (TMD); bilingual edition. Washington, D.C.: United States Catholic Conference, 1995, 68.

2. TMD, 8.

3. National Conference of Catholic Bishops. *Strangers and Aliens No Longer: Part One.* Washington, D.C.: United States Catholic Conference, 1993, 89-105.

4. Stephen A. Privett, SJ. *The U.S. Catholic Church and Its Hispanic Members: The Pastoral Vision of Archbishop Robert E. Lucey.* San Antonio: Trinity University Press, 1988, 65-67.

5. Paul VI. Salutation message in the *Proceedings of the II Encuentro Nacional Hispano de Pastoral (SE)*. Washington, D.C.: National Conference of Catholic Bishops/United States Catholic Conference, 1978, p. 49.

6. United States Catholic Conference. *Conclusiones Primer Encuentro Nacional Hispano de Pastoral (PE)*. Washington, D.C.: Division for the Spanish Speaking, 1972, 1.

7. PE, 2.

8. SE, 64.

9. Ibid., 64.

10. Ibid., 65.

11. S. Galerón, R. M. Icaza, R. Urrabazo, eds. *Prophetic Vision: Pastoral Reflections on the National Pastoral Plan for Hispanic Ministry.* Kansas City, Mo.: Sheed and Ward and the Mexican American Cultural Center, 1992, 192.

12. TMD, 18, no. 18.

13. Ibid., 18, no. 19.

14. Ibid., 30.

15. Ibid., 31.

16. Ibid.

17. Ibid., 33.

18. Ibid., 71.

19. National Conference of Catholic Bishops, *Mission Statement: Goals and Objectives 1997-99.* Washington, D.C.: United States Catholic Conference, 1995, Objective 6.6.

National Pastoral Plan for Hispanic Ministry

PREFACE

This pastoral plan is addressed to the entire Church in the United States. It focuses on the pastoral needs of the Hispanic Catholics, but it challenges all Catholics as members of the Body of Christ.

We urge that the plan be studied carefully and taken seriously. The result of years of work involving thousands of people who participated in the III Encuentro, it is a strategic elaboration based on the conclusions of that Encuentro.

We, the bishops of the United States, adopt the objectives of this plan and endorse the specific means of reaching them, as provided herein. We encourage dioceses and parishes to incorporate this plan with due regards for local adaptation. We do so with a sense of urgency and in response to the enormous challenge associated with the ever-growing presence of the Hispanic people in the United States. Not only do we accept this presence in our midst as our pastoral responsibility, conscious of the mission entrusted to us by Christ, but we do so with joy and gratitude. For, as we stated in the pastoral letter of 1983, "At this moment of grace we recognize the Hispanic community among us as a blessing from God."

We present this plan in a spirit of faith—faith in God, that he will provide the strength and the resources to carry out his divine plan on earth; faith in all the People of God, that all will collaborate in the awesome task before us; faith in Hispanic Catholics, that they will join hands with the rest of the Church to build up the entire Body of Christ. We dedicate this plan to the honor and glory of God and, in this Marian Year, invoke the intercession of the Blessed Virgin Mary under the title of Our Lady of Guadalupe.

I. INTRODUCTION

This *National Pastoral Plan* is a result of the commitment expressed in our pastoral letter on Hispanic ministry, *The Hispanic Presence: Challenge and Commitment.*

We look forward to reviewing the conclusions of the III Encuentro as a basis for drafting a National Pastoral Plan for Hispanic Ministry to be considered in our general meeting at the earliest possible date after the Encuentro.

This plan is a pastoral response to the reality and needs of the Hispanic people in their efforts to achieve integration and participation in the life of our Church and in the building of the Kingdom of God.

Integration is not to be confused with assimilation. Through the policy of assimilation, new immigrants are forced to give up their language, culture, values, and traditions and adopt a form of life and worship foreign to them in order to be accepted as parish members. This attitude alienates new Catholic immigrants from the Church and makes them vulnerable to sects and other denominations.

By integration we mean that our Hispanic people are to be welcomed to our church institutions at all levels. They are to be served in their language when possible, and their cultural values and religious traditions are to be respected. Beyond that, we must work toward mutual enrichment through interaction among all our cultures. Our physical facilities are to be made accessible to the Hispanic community. Hispanic participation in the institutions, programs, and activities of the Church is to be constantly encouraged and appreciated. This plan attempts to organize and direct how best to accomplish this integration.

The plan has its origins in our pastoral letter, and it is based on the working document of the III Encuentro and the Encuentro conclusions. It takes seriously the content of these documents and seeks to implement them.

It takes into account the sociocultural reality of our Hispanic people and suggests a style of pastoral ministry and model of Church in harmony with their faith and culture. For this reason it requires an explicit affirmation of the concept of cultural pluralism in our Church within a fundamental unity or doctrine as expressed so many times by the Church's Magisterium.

This plan employs the methodology of a *Pastoral de Conjunto* where all the elements of pastoral ministry, all the structures, and all of the activities of pastoral agents—both Hispanic and non-Hispanic—are coordinated with a common objective in view. To integrate this plan into the planning process of church organization, departments, and agencies at all levels (national, regional, diocesan, and parish) will require local adaptation so that all elements of pastoral ministry are operating in unison.

The plan's general objective is a synthesis of the prophetic pastoral guidelines approved at the III Encuentro. It provides the vision and orientation for all pastoral activity.

This document is also a response to the proselytism of the sects. Its effectiveness requires the renewal of our parish structures, active participation by pastors and administrators, and a renewed missionary attitude at all levels of our Church.

Pastoral planning is the effective organization of the total process of the life of the Church in fulfilling her mission of being a leaven of the Kingdom of God in this world. Pastoral planning includes the following elements:

- Analysis of the reality wherein the Church must carry out her mission
- Reflection of this reality in light of the Gospel and the teachings of the Church
- Commitment to action resulting from this reflection
- Pastoral theological reflection on this process
- Development of a pastoral plan
- Implementation
- Ongoing evaluation of what is being done
- And the celebration of the accomplishment of this life experience, always within the context of prayer and its relationship to life

Pastoral de Conjunto is a co-responsible, collaborative ministry involving coordination among pastoral agents of all of the elements of pastoral life and the structures of the same in view of a common goal: the Kingdom of God.

This pastoral plan is a technical instrument which organizes, facilitates, and coordinates activities of the Church in the fulfillment of her evangelizing mission. It is at the service of the *Pastoral de Conjunto*. It is not only a methodology but also an expression of the essence and mission for the Church, which is communion.

Pastoral Planning Process
III Encuentro
Reality
Ecclesial Community
Mistica
Spirituality
Celebraton
Mission
1. Analysis of Reality
2. Discernment
3. Decision
    Encuentro
    Conclusions
4. Theological Reflection
5. Plan
6. Implementation
7. Evaluation

II. FRAMEWORK OF HISPANIC REALITY

A. History

The Hispanic presence in the Americas began immediately with Christopher Columbus' first voyage of discovery in 1492, and the first Christian evangelization began in 1493 with the Spanish settlements on Hispaniola. The event was more encounter than discovery, because Europeans rapidly intermingled with Native Americans of high and sophisticated cultures, thus launching a new age and a new people—a true *mestizaje*.

In search of land and labor, Spaniards soon encountered the region that would one day become the United States. In 1513 Ponce de Leon probed the coasts of La Florida; then Pánfilo de Narvaez attempted the settlement of Florida in 1527, while Nuño de Guzman at the same time pressed overland north of Mexico. Survivors of Narvaez's failed expedition brought word of many tribes and great wealth. Fray Marcos de Niza responded in 1539 by preceding the great expedition of Francisco Vasquez de Coronado into the flanks of the Rockies. A year later Fray Juan Padilla gave his life as a martyr on the Kansas plains. Padre Luis Cáncer, a Dominican missionary, poured out his life in Florida in 1549. Despite the setbacks in conversion, Pedro Menéndez de Avilés forged ahead by founding the city of San Agustín in 1565. Jesuit missionaries moved into Chesapeake Bay, only to vanish long before Roanoke. A map of 1529 illustrated by the Royal Spanish cartographer, Diego Ribera, shows that missionaries and explorers arrived as far north as present day Maryland, New York, and New England, and gave Spanish names to the rivers and mountains they saw. Far to the west, adventurers probed into New Mexico, where missionaries lost their lives in futile attempts at evangelization; not until Juan de Oñate arrived in 1598 with scores of the new settlers did stability finally come. Generations before the Pilgrims tenuously built their colonies, Spanish missionaries struggled to bring the Americas into the fold of Christ.

In the seventeenth century Franciscan missionaries raised elegant churches in the Pueblo towns of New Mexico; Jesuits along the western slopes of New Spain wove scattered Indian *rancherías* into efficient social systems that raised the standard of living in arid America. But the primacy of evangelization as a cornerstone of Spanish royal policy was swept away by political ambitions in the eighteenth century; the missions fell victim to secularism. First, the Jesuits were exiled and the order suppressed; Franciscans and Dominicans tried valiantly to stem the tide of absolutism, but their numbers dwindled rapidly, and the Church's service to the poor crumbled.

Independence swept Mexico, and the northern provinces of New Spain, now the states of a new republic, fell to the invading armies of the United States. Under the provisions of the Treaty of Guadalupe Hidalgo in 1848, the old mission territories were annexed to the burgeoning United States. Spanish Florida and Louisiana, for a while French, were stars in the blue field of conquest; and from the Mississippi to the Pacific shores the frontiers of *mestizaje* were put under Anglo law and custom.

The nineteenth century was characterized by decades of neglect and adjustment. Hispanic and Native American populations were ill-served and overlooked. The people of the mainland continued to move north as they had for more than a millennium; only now they encountered a new tide of empire which was inundating old familiar places and families.

Political and social conditions in the twentieth century have only enhanced the northern migration. New avenues of immigration opened from the island nations; Puerto Ricans, Cubans, and Dominicans poured into the Eastern seaboard. Mexicans continued to trek north to find work and opportunities. And the worsening conditions of Central and South America have added thousands to the stream of immigrants who speak a language once dominant in North America and now scorned by all too many who remain ignorant of the deep cultural power it exercises throughout the world.

The United States of America is not all America. We speak of the Americas to describe a hemisphere of many cultures and three dominant languages—two from the Iberian Peninsula and one from a North Atlantic island. Since the Church is the guardian of the mission of Jesus Christ, it must forever accommodate the changing populations and shifting cultures of mankind. To the extent the Church is impregnated with cultural norms, to the extent it divides and separates, to the extent it replaces cultural norms with the primacy of love, it unites the many into the Body of Christ without dissolving difference or destroying identity.

B. Culture

The historical reality of the Southwest, the proximity of countries of origin, and continuing immigration all contribute to the maintenance of Hispanic culture and language within the United States. This cultural presence expresses itself in a variety of ways: from the immigrant who experiences "cultural shock" to the Hispanic whose roots in the United States go back several generations and who struggles with questions of identity while often being made to feel an alien in his own country.

Despite these differences, certain cultural similarities identify Hispanics as a people. Culture primarily expresses how people live and perceive the world, one another, and God. Culture is the set of values by which a people judge, accept, and live what is considered important within the community.

Some values that make up the Hispanic culture are a "profound respect for the dignity of each person . . . deep and reverential love for family life . . . a marvelous sense of community . . . a loving appreciation for God's gift of life . . . and an authentic and consistent devotion to Mary . . ." (*The Hispanic Presence: Challenge and Commitment* [USCCB: Washington, DC, 1983], no. 3).

Culture for Hispanic Catholics has become a way of living out and transmitting their faith. Many local practices of popular religiosity have become widely accepted cultural expressions. Yet the Hispanic culture, like any other, must continue to be evangelized.

C. Social Reality

The median age among Hispanic people is 25. This plus the continuous flow of immigrants ensures a constant increase in population.

Lack of education and professional training contribute to high unemployment. Neither public nor private education has responded to the urgent needs of this young population. Only eight percent of Hispanics graduate at the college level.

Families face a variety of problems. Twenty-five percent of the families live below the poverty level, and twenty-eight percent are single-parent families.

Frequent mobility, poor education, a limited economic life, and racial prejudice are some of the factors that result in low participation in political activities.

As a whole, Hispanics are a religious people. Eighty-three percent consider religion important. There is an interest in knowing more about the Bible and a strong presence of popular religious practices.

Despite this, eighty-eight percent are not active in their parishes. On the other hand, the Jehovah's Witnesses, Pentecostal groups, and other sects are increasing within the Hispanic community. According to recent studies, the poor, men, and second-generation Hispanics are those who least participate in the life of the Church.

D. Assessment

The Catholic heritage and cultural identity of Hispanics are threatened by the prevailing secular values of the American society. They have marginal participation in the Church and in the society: they suffer the consequences of poverty and marginalization.

This same person, due to its great sense of religion, family, and community, is a prophetic presence in the face of the materialism and individualism of society. Since the majority of Hispanics are Catholic, their presence can be a source of renewal within the Catholic Church in North America. Because of its youth and growth, this community will continue to be a significant presence in the future.

The current pastoral process offers some exciting possibilities on both social and religious levels: more active participation in the Church, a critique of society from the perspective of the poor, and a commitment to social justice.

As the year 1992 approaches, celebrating the five-hundredth anniversary of the evangelization of the Americas, it is more important than ever that Hispanics in the United States rediscover their identity as well as their Catholicity, be re-evangelized by the Word of God, and forge a much needed unity among all Hispanics who have come from the entire spectrum of the Spanish-speaking world.

III. DOCTRINAL FRAMEWORK

The mission of the Church is the continuation of Jesus' work: to announce the Kingdom of God and the means for entering it. It is the proclamation of what is to come and also anticipation of that plenitude here and now in the process of history. The Kingdom which Jesus proclaims and initiates is so important that, in relation to it, all else is relative.

The Church, as community, carries out the work of Jesus by entering into the cultural, religious, and social reality of the people, becoming incarnate in and with the people; "in virtue of her mission and nature she is bound to no particular form of human culture, nor to any political, economic, or social system." Therefore, she is able to preach the need for conversion of everyone, to affirm the dignity of the human person, and to seek ways to eradicate personal sin, oppressive structures, and forms of injustice.

The Church in its prophetic voice denounces sin and announces hope and in this way continues the historic and tangible presence of Jesus. Since Jesus proclaimed Good News to the poor and liberty to captives, the Church continues to make an option for the poor and the marginalized.

The Church likewise identifies with the risen Christ, who reveals himself as the new creation, as the proclamation and realization of a new values of solidarity among all: through his simplicity; in peace; through the proclamation of his Kingdom which implies a new social order; through a new style of Church as leaven; and above all, through his gift to us of his Spirit.

This Spirit unites the members of the community of Jesus intimately one with another, all in Christ with God. Our solidarity comes from this indwelling Spirit of Christ The Spirit impels the community to accomplish in life a prophetic commitment to justice and love and helps it to live, within an experience of missionary faith, its union with the Father.

This responsibility falls on the whole Church—the People of God: the Pope and bishops, priests, religious, and laity, who with a sense of co-responsibility must accomplish Jesus' work. All this is expressed in a singular way in the Eucharist. It is here that Jesus offers himself as victim for the salvation of all and challenges the entire People of God to live out the commitment of love and service.

IV. SPIRITUALITY

The spirituality or *mystic* of the Hispanic people springs from their faith and relationship with God.

Spirituality is understood to be the way of life of a people, a movement by the Spirit of God, and the grounding of one's identity as a Christian in every circumstance of life. It is the struggle to live the totality of one's personal and communitarian life in keeping with the Gospel; spirituality is the orientation and perspective of all the dimensions of a person's life in the following of Jesus and in continuous dialogue with the Father.

The pastoral plan is a gospel reflection of the spirituality of the Hispanic people. It is a manifestation and response of faith.

When we look at this spirituality, we find that one of the most important aspects of its content is a sense of the presence of God, which serves as a stimulus for living out one's daily commitments. In this sense the transcendent God is nevertheless present in human affairs and human lives. Indeed, one might go so far as to speak of God as a member of the family, with whom one converses and to whom one has recourse, not only in moments of fervent prayer but also in one's daily living. Thus, God never fails us. He is Emmanuel, God-with-Us.

The Hispanic people find God in the arms of the Virgin Mary. That is why Mary, the Mother of God, as goodness, compassion, protection, inspiration, and example . . . is at the heart of the Hispanic spirituality.

The saints, our brothers and sisters who have already fulfilled their lives in the following of Jesus, are examples and instruments of the revelation of God's goodness through their intercession and help. All this makes Hispanic spirituality a home of living relationships, a family, and a community. It will find expression and consequence more in ordinary life than in theory.

Hispanic spirituality has as one of its sources the "seeds of the Word" in the pre-Hispanic cultures, which considered their relationships with the gods and nature to be an integral part of life. In some cases, the missionaries adopted these customs and attitudes: they enriched and illuminated them so as to incarnate the Divine Word of Sacred Scripture and the Christian faith to make them come alive in religious art and drama. All this has taken shape in popular devotions which preserve and nourish the peoples' spirituality. At the same time, Christian principles have been expressed in attitudes and daily behavior which reveal divine values in the experience of the Hispanic people. This spirituality has been kept alive in the home and has become a profound tradition within the family.

The spirituality of the Hispanic people, a living reality through its journey, finds expression in numerous ways. At times it takes the form of prayer, novenas, songs and sacred gestures. It is found in personal relationships and hospitality. At other times it surfaces as endurance, patience, strength, and hope in the midst of suffering and difficulties. Their spirituality can also inspire a struggle for freedom, justice, and peace. Frequently it is expressed as commitments and forgiveness as well as in celebration, dance, sacred images, and symbols. Small altars in the home, statues, and candles are sacramental of God's presence. The *pastorelas, posadas, nacimientos, via crucis,* pilgrimages; processions; and the blessings offered by mothers, fathers and grandparents are all expressions of this fait and profound spirituality.

At various times through the centuries, these devotions have gone astray or have been impoverished due to the lack of a clear and enriching catechesis. This pastoral plan with its evangelizing, community-building, and formative emphasis can be a source of evangelization for these popular devotions and an encouragement for enriching liturgical celebrations with cultural expressions of faith. It seeks to free the Spirit who is alive in the gatherings of our people.

The III Encuentro process was yet one more step in the development and growth of their spirituality. Many participants appeared to have moved from a personal and family spirituality to one that is communitarian and ecclesial. They moved from a sense of individual and family injustice, to recognition of general injustice to all people. This growth was sensed also in their awareness and experience of being church, in their familiarity with ecclesial documents, in their active participation in liturgies and prayers.

For people who celebrate life and death with great intensity and meaning, the Eucharistic liturgy has a special place. The liturgy and sacraments offer to a people imbued with a profound religious sense the elements of community, the assurance of grace, the embodiment of the Paschal Mystery, in the dying and rising of the Lord in his people. This is especially true of what happens in the celebration of the Eucharist—the source of our unity. Numerous possibilities are found for artistic elements that enrich the sacramental celebrations with originality and joyfulness. These sacramental moments capture the spirituality and *mística*, which overflow from the living of their Christian vocation and their Hispanic identity.

In the gathering around a simple, common table, Jesus told his disciples to "do this in memory of me." It was to this gathering that Jesus revealed his mission, his life, his innermost prayer to his friends and then asked them to do the same in his memory. He mandated them to do all that he had done, had lived for, in their lives. This consistent stopping to share a common meal has nourished the Hispanic people throughout history. As Jesus' disciples, they reserve a place for him at the table.

Since spirituality penetrates the totality of life, it is likewise made manifest in a multitude of expressions. At this particular moment of their journey, Hispanic Catholics are revealing their spirituality through the nine prophetic pastoral guidelines of the III Encuentro, which have been summarized in *the General Objective and Specific Dimensions* of this plan. The pastoral plan is thus not only a series of goals and objective but also a contribution to the development, growth, and fruition of the people's life of faith as discerned in the Spirit of God and incarnated in our time.

Through the process of the III Encuentro, many Hispanic Catholics have sought to live in dialogue with their God who inspires and motivates, with Mary who accompanies Jesus 'disciples. The pastoral plan takes its source out of the gathering and sharing of the Hispanic people. It is an expression of his presence in us. The pastoral plan provides a way for this people of God to express their life with the Spirit, a life deeply rooted in the Gospel.

V. GENERAL OBJECTIVE

---✚---

TO LIVE AND PROMOTE . . .
by means of a *Pastoral de Conjunto*
A MODEL OF CHURCH that is:
communitarian, evangelizing, and missionary,
incarnate in the reality of the Hispanic people and
open to the diversity of cultures,
a promoter and example of justice . . .
that develops leadership through integral education . . .
THAT IS LEAVEN FOR THE KINGDOM OF GOD IN SOCIETY.

SITUATION FRAMEWORK OF THE HISPANIC COMMUNITY	DOCTRINAL FRAMEWORK
HISTORY CULTURE SOCIAL REALITY	LIFE AND MISSION OF JESUS AND THE CHURCH

ASSESSMENT

GENERAL OBJECTIVE

To live and promote by means of a *Pastoral de Conjunto* a model of church that is: communitarian, evangelizing, and missionary; incarnate in the reality of the Hispanic people and open to the diversity of cultures; a promoter and example of justice; active in developing leadership through integral education; leaven for the Kingdom of God in society.

SPECIFIC DIMENSIONS
PASTORAL DE CONJUNTO
EVANGELIZATION
MISSIONARY OPTION
FORMATION

PASTORAL DE CONJUNTO:
From Fragmentation to Coordination

To develop a *Pastoral de Conjunto*, which through pastoral agents and structures manifests communion in integration, coordination, in-servicing, and communication of the Church's pastoral action, in keeping with the general objective of this plan.

EVANGELIZATION:
From a Place to a Home

To recognize, develop, accompany, and support small ecclesial communities and other church groups (e.g. *Cursillos de Cristiandad, Movimiento Familiar Cristiano*, RENEW, Charismatic Movement, prayer groups, etc.), which in union with the bishop are effective instruments of evangelization for the Hispanic people. These small ecclesial communities and other groups within the parish framework promote experiences of faith and conversation, outreach and evangelization, interpersonal relations and fraternal love, and prophetic questioning and actions for justice. They are a prophetic challenge for the renewal of our Church and humanization of our society.

MISSIONARY OPTION:
From Pews to Shoes

To promote faith and effective participation in Church and societal structures on the part of these priority groups (the poor, women, families, and youth) so that they may be agents of their own destiny (self-determination) and capable of progressive and becoming organized.

FORMATION
From Good Will to Skills

To provide leadership formation adapted to the Hispanic culture in the United States that will help people to live and promote a style of Church that will be leaven of the Kingdom of God in society.

EVALAUTION
CELEBRATION-SPIRITUALITY-MISTICA

The Hispanic Presence: Challenge and Commitment

I. A Call to Hispanic Ministry

1. At this moment of grace we recognize the Hispanic community among us as a blessing from God. We call upon all persons of good faith to share our vision of the special gifts which Hispanics bring to the Body of Christ, his pilgrim Church on earth (1 Cor 12:12-13).

   Invoking the guidance of the Blessed Virgin Mary, we desire especially to share our reflections on the Hispanic presence in the United States with the Catholic laity, religious, deacons, and priests of our country. We ask Catholics, as members of the Body of Christ, to give our words serious attention in performing the tasks assigned to them. This Hispanic presence challenges us all to be more *catholic*, more open to the diversity of religious expression.

2. Although many pastoral challenges face the Church as a result of this presence, we are pleased to hear Hispanic Catholics voicing their desire for more opportunities to share their historical, cultural, and religious gifts with the Church they see as their home and heritage. Let us hear their voices; let us make all feel equally at home in the Church (PHB, I. b & III. c); let us be a Church which is in truth universal, a Church with open arms, welcoming different gifts and expressions of our "one Lord, one faith, one baptism, one God and Father of all" (Eph 4:5-6).

3. Hispanics exemplify and cherish values central to the service of Church and society. Among these are:

   (a) Profound respect for the dignity of each *person*, reflecting the example of Christ in the Gospels;

   (b) Deep and reverential love for *family life*, where the entire extended family discovers its roots, its identity, and its strength;

   (c) A marvelous sense of *community* that celebrates life through "fiesta;"

   (d) Loving appreciation for God's gift of *life*, and an understanding of time which allows one to savor that gift;

   (e) Authentic and consistent *devotion to Mary*, the Mother of God.

4. We are *all* called to appreciate our own histories, and to reflect upon the ethnic, racial, and cultural origins which make us a nation of immigrants. Historically, the Church in the United States has been an "immigrant Church" whose outstanding record of care for countless European immigrants remains un-matched. Today that same tradition must inspire in the Church's approach to recent Hispanic immigrants and migrants a similar authority, compassion, and decisiveness.

   Although the number of Hispanics is increasing in our country, it would be misleading to place too much emphasis on numerical growth only. Focusing primarily on the numbers could very easily lead us to see Hispanics simply as a large pastoral problem, while overlooking the even more important fact that they present a unique pastoral opportunity.

   The pastoral needs of Hispanic Catholics are indeed great; although their faith is deep and strong, it is being challenged and eroded by steady social pressures to assimilate. Yet the history, culture, and spirituality animating their lively faith deserve to be known, shared, and reinforced by us all. Their past and present contributions to the faith life of the Church deserve appreciation and recognition.

   Let us work closely together in creating pastoral visions and strategies which, drawing upon a memorable past, are made anew by the creative hands of the present.

5. The Church has a vast body of teaching on culture and its intimate link with faith. "In his self-revelation to his people culminating in the fullness of manifestation in his incarnate Son, God spoke according to the culture proper to each age. Similarly the Church has existed through the centuries in varying circumstances and has utilized the resources of different cultures in its preaching to spread and explain the message of Christ, to examine and understand it more deeply, and to express it more perfectly in the liturgy and in various aspects of the life of the faithful" (*GS*, 58).

   As with many nationalities with a strong Catholic tradition, religion, and culture, faith and life are inseparable for Hispanics. Hispanic Catholicism is an outstanding example of how the Gospel can permeate a culture to its very roots (*EN*, 20). But it also reminds us that no culture is without defects and sins. Hispanic culture, like any other, must be challenged by the Gospel.

Respect for culture is rooted in the dignity of people made in God's image. The Church shows its esteem for this dignity by working to ensure that pluralism, not assimilation and uniformity, is the guiding principle in the life of communities in both the ecclesial and secular societies. All of us in the Church should broaden the embrace with which we greet our Hispanic brothers and sisters and deepen our commitment to them.

Hispanic Reality

6. No other European culture has been in this country longer than the Hispanic. Spaniards and their descendants were already in the Southeast and Southwest by the late sixteenth century. In other regions of our country a steady influx of Hispanic immigrants has increased their visibility in more recent times. Plainly, the Hispanic population will loom larger in the future of both the wider society and the Church in the United States.

Only 30 years ago the U.S. census estimated there were 6 million Hispanics in the country. The 1980 census counted almost 15 million—a figure which does not include the population on the island of Puerto Rico, many undocumented workers, recent Cuban refugees, those who have fled spiraling violence in Central and South America, nor countless other Hispanics missed in the census. A number of experts estimate a total U.S. Hispanic population of at least 20 million.[1]

The United States today ranks fifth among the world's Spanish-speaking countries; only Mexico, Spain, Argentina, and Colombia have more Hispanics.[2]

Hispanic Catholics are extremely diverse. They come from 19 different Latin American republics, Puerto Rico, and Spain. The largest group, comprising 60 percent, is Mexican-American. They are followed by Puerto Ricans, 17 percent, and Cubans, 8 percent. The Dominican Republic, Peru, Ecuador, Chile, and increasingly Central America, especially El Salvador, as well as other Latin American countries, are amply represented.

Hispanics vary in their racial origins, color, history, achievements, expressions of faith, and degree of disadvantage. But they share many elements of culture, including a deeply rooted Catholicism, values such as commitment to the extended family, and a common language, Spanish, spoken with different accents.

They are found in every state of the Union and nearly every diocese. Although many, especially in the Southwest, live in rural areas, over 85 percent are found in large urban centers like New York, Chicago, Miami, Los Angeles, San Antonio, and San Francisco. In places like Hartford, Washington, D.C., and Atlanta, a growing number of advertisements in Spanish and English, as well as large Hispanic barrios,[3] are evidence of their increasing presence.

It is significant that Hispanics are the youngest population in our country. Their median age, 23.2, is lower than that of any other group; 54 percent are age 25 or younger.

Socioeconomic Conditions

7. In general, most Hispanics in our country live near or below the poverty level. While limited improvements in their social and economic status have occurred in the last generation, the Hispanic community as a whole has yet to share equitably in this country's wealth—wealth they have helped produce. Despite rising expectations, Hispanic participation in the political process is limited by economic and social underdevelopment. Thus Hispanics are severely underrepresented at decision-making levels in Church and society.

The annual median income for non-Hispanic families is $5,000 higher than the median for Hispanic families; 22.1 percent of Hispanics live below the poverty level, compared with 15 percent of the general population.[4]

Historically, unemployment has been higher among Hispanics than other nationalities. The Puerto Ricans are the hardest hit, with unemployment rates generally a third higher than for other Hispanics.[5] In times of crisis, such as in the economic downturn of the early 1980s, Hispanics are among the last hired and the first fired.

Well over half the employed Hispanics work at non-professional, non-managerial jobs, chiefly in agricultural labor and urban service occupations. In both occupational areas, the courageous struggle of workers to obtain adequate means of negotiation for just compensation has yet to succeed.

Lack of education is an important factor keeping Hispanics poor. While more Hispanics now finish high school and college than did ten years ago, only 40 percent graduate from high school, compared with 66 percent of the general population. Hispanics are underrepresented even within the Catholic school system, where they account for only 9 percent of the student population.

Educational opportunities are often below standard in areas of high Hispanic concentration. Early frustration in school leads many young Hispanics to drop out without the skills they need, while many of those who stay find themselves in an educational system which is not always supportive. Often Hispanic students are caught in a cultural cross fire—living their Hispanic culture at home, while feeling pressured at school and at work to assimilate and forsake their heritage.

Impersonal data tell us that Hispanics are numerous, rapidly increasing, of varied national origins, found everywhere in the United States, socioeconomically disadvantaged, and in need of greater access to education and the decision-making processes. But there is a human reality behind the dry, sometimes discouraging data. We see in the faces of Hispanics a profound serenity, a steadfast hope, and a vibrant joy; in many we recognize an evangelical sense of the blessing and prophetic nature of poverty.

II. Achievements in Hispanic Ministry in the United States

8. In responding to the pastoral needs of Hispanics, we are building on work begun many years ago. We recognize with gratitude what was done by farsighted men and women, Hispanic and non-Hispanic, who, pioneers in this apostolate, helped maintain and develop the faith of hundreds of thousands. They deserve credit for their courageous efforts.

9. In many respects the survival of faith among Hispanics seems little less than a miracle. Even at times when the institutional Church could not be present to them, their faith remained, for their family-oriented tradition of faith provided a momentum and dynamism accounting for faith's preservation. But let us not depend only on that tradition today; every generation of every culture stands in need of being evangelized (*EN*, 54).

One of the glories of Hispanic women, lay and religious, has been their role in nurturing the faith and keeping it alive in their families and communities. Traditionally, they have been the basic leaders of prayer, catechists, and often excellent models of Christian discipleship.

The increasing number of lay leaders and permanent deacons (20 percent of the U.S. total) is a sign that lay leadership from the grass roots has been fostered and called to service in the Church.

Also noteworthy are the various apostolic *movimientos* (movements) which have helped ensure the survival of the faith for many Hispanic Catholics. For example, *Cursillos de Cristiandad, Encuentros Conyugales, Encuentros de Promoción Juvenil, Movimiento Familiar Cristiano, Comunidades Eclesiales de Base*, and the Charismatic Renewal, as well as others, have been instrumental in bringing out the apostolic potential in many Hispanic individuals, married couples, and communities. A number of associations, such as PADRES and HERMANAS, have provided support networks to priests and women in the Hispanic movement.

Religious congregations of men and women are among those who have responded generously to the challenge. That a substantial percentage of Hispanic priests are religious is a sign of their expenditure of resources, personnel, and energy. In a special way religious congregations of women have contributed to meeting the spiritual and material needs of migrant farm workers, the inner-city poor, refugees from Latin America, and the undocumented. North American missionaries returning from Latin America have likewise brought with them a strong attraction and dedication to Hispanics.

As far back as the 1940s, the bishops showed genuine concern for Hispanic Catholics by establishing, at the prompting of Archbishop Robert E. Lucey of San Antonio, a committee for the Spanish-speaking to work with Hispanics of the Southwest. In 1912 Philadelphia began its Spanish apostolate. New York and Boston established diocesan offices for the Spanish speaking in the 1950s. Early efforts to minister to Hispanics were made in other areas as well.

Later, persistent efforts by bishops who recognized the need for a Hispanic presence at the national Church leadership level culminated in 1970 with the establishment of the USCC Division for the Spanish-speaking as part of the USCC Department of Social Development. In 1974 the division became the NCCB/USCC Secretariat for Hispanic Affairs.

Under the leadership of the bishops, and with the support of the NCCB/USCC Secretariat for Hispanic Affairs, Hispanic Catholics have been responsible for two national pastoral *Encuentros*. In 1972 and 1977 these gatherings of lay men and women dedicated to their own local communities concluded with prophetic calls to the Church-at-large. Also, as a result of the *II Encuentro Nacional Hispano de Pastoral* in 1977, ministry with Hispanic youth was encouraged at the regional, diocesan, and parish levels through the National Youth Task Force, now renamed *Comité Nacional Hispano de Pastoral Juvenil* (National Hispanic Committee for Youth Ministry).[6]

The appointment of Hispanic bishops and archbishops since 1970 has greatly enhanced this apostolate. We rejoice with all the Hispanic Catholics who see in these new bishops a visible and clear sign that the Holy See is recognizing their presence and the contribution they are capable of making to the life of the Church in the United States. Recent apostolic delegates have voiced their concern for ethnic and minority groups in the Church in this country and have urged the leadership of the Church to address their needs.

The past decade has also seen the emergence of regional offices, pastoral institutes, diocesan commissions and offices, and *centros pastorales* (pastoral centers), all of which have become effective pastoral instruments working with Hispanics.

III. Urgent Pastoral Implications

10. We urge all U.S. Catholics to explore creative possibilities for responding innovatively, flexibly, and immediately to the Hispanic presence. Hispanics and non-Hispanics should work together, teach and learn from one another, and together evangelize in the fullest and broadest sense. Non-Hispanic clergy, especially religious, priests, and bishops who have been at the forefront of the Hispanic apostolates, are needed more than ever today to serve with the Hispanic people.

The Church's Mission and the Hispanic Presence

11. From an ecclesial perspective, evangelization, which is the Church's central mission and purpose, consists not just in isolated calls to individual conversion but in an invitation to join the People of God (*EN*, 15). This is reflected in the Hispanic experience of evangelization, which includes an important communitarian element expressed in an integral or "holistic" vision of faith and pastoral activity carried out in community (*II ENHP*, I.4.c).

This experience is summed up in the concept of the *pastoral de conjunto*, a pastoral focus and approach to action arising from shared reflection among the agents of evangelization (Puebla, 650, 122, and 1307).

Implicit in a *pastoral de conjunto* is the recognition that both the sense of the faithful and hierarchical teaching are essential elements in the articulation of the faith. This pastoral approach also recognizes that the Church's essential mission is best exercised in a spirit of concord and in group apostolate (*AA*, 18).

An effective Hispanic apostolate includes the application of this experience, which can benefit the Church in *all* its efforts to fulfill its mission. Essential to this is an integral vision, forged in community, which encompasses the totality of human challenges and opportunities as religious concerns.

Creative Possibilities

12. We therefore invite all our priests, deacons, and religious and lay leaders to consider the following creative opportunities.

a. Liturgy

Universal in form, our Church "respects and fosters the spiritual adornments and gifts of the various races and peoples" in its liturgical life (*SC*, 37). As applied to the Hispanic presence, this requires making provision for Spanish and bilingual worship according to the traditions and customs of the people being served. We are thus challenged to greater study of Hispanic prayer forms. It is encouraging in this regard that Hispanic Catholic artists and musicians are already contributing to the liturgy in our country.

The presence of Hispanic liturgists on parish and diocesan commissions is essential. Every effort should be made to bring this about.

As their homes have been true "domestic churches" for many Hispanic Catholics, so the home has traditionally been for them the center of faith and worship. The celebration of traditional feasts and special occasions in the home should therefore be valued and encouraged.

The choice of liturgical art, gestures, and music, combined with the spirit of hospitality, can refashion our churches and altars into spiritual homes and create in our communities an inviting environment of family fiesta.

b. Renewal of Preaching

The recasting and proclamation of the Word in powerful, new, liberating images are unavoidable challenges for Hispanic ministry. As the apostle Paul asked, "How can they believe unless they have heard of him? And how can they hear unless there is someone to preach?" (Rom 10:14).

Those who preach should always bear in mind that the ability to hear is linked to the hearer's language, culture, and real-life situation. In proclaiming the gospel message, they should strive to make these characteristics and realities their own, so that their words will transmit the Gospel's truly liberating content.

Thirsting for God's Word, Hispanics want clear and simple preaching on its message and its application to their lives. They respond to effective preaching, and they often express a keen desire for better, more powerful preaching which expresses the gospel message in terms they can understand.

We strongly recommend that priests engaged in ministry with Hispanics, such as parish priests and chaplains, enroll in Spanish courses so that they can readily speak with and listen to Hispanics. Similarly, we urge Hispanic permanent deacons to develop their preaching skills. We ask that these men be called on more often to exercise the ministry of the Word. The continuing education of permanent deacons and periodic evaluation of their ministry are necessary in this regard.

c. Catechesis

Like initial evangelization, catechesis must start where the hearer of the Gospel is (*EN*, 44). In the case of Hispanics, this suggests not merely the use of Spanish but also an active dialogue with their culture and their needs (*NCD*, 229). Since religious education is a lifelong process for the individual (*NCD*, 32), parishes should provide an atmosphere for catechesis which in every respect encourages the ongoing formation of adults, as well as children. Such efforts will match the effectiveness of grade-level programs for children among the English-speaking and explore new methods in adult catechesis.

It is essential, too, that dioceses sponsor catechist formation courses in Spanish for Hispanics. They should be assured of having appropriate, effective materials and programs in Spanish (*NCD*, 194, 195). Catechists should take advantage of every "teachable moment" to present the Church's doctrine to Hispanic Catholics. Hispanic family celebrations[7] like baptisms, *quinceaños*, weddings, anniversaries, *fiestas patrias*, *novenarios*, *velorios*, and funerals often provide excellent teachable moments which are also moments of grace enabling the catechist to build upon the people's traditions and use them as living examples of Gospel truths (Puebla, 59 and *CT*, 53).

Throughout our country there is a deep yearning and hunger, "not a famine for bread, or a thirst for water, but for hearing the word of the Lord" (Amos 8:11). We urge continuing efforts to begin bible study groups in Hispanic communities, and to call forth Hispanic leaders to guide and direct such programs.

d. Vocation and Formation of Lay Ministers

Adequate training must have a high priority in Hispanic ministry. In planning such training, the goals of enhancing pluralism and catholicity will suggest the means. Formation should aim to incorporate the knowledge and practical experience necessary to minister effectively, while also fostering a serious commitment of service.

Although Hispanics lack sufficient clergy trained to minister with them, there are among them many lay people who are well disposed to respond to the call to be apostles (*AA*, 3).

From this we conclude that fostering vocations and training for lay ministries will help provide the much needed laborers in the vineyard.

One model in this direction is the *escuela de ministerios*,[8] which helps train lay leaders, calls youths to greater participation in the Church, and is likely to serve as a place of election for priestly and religious vocations.

e. Vocations to Priestly, Religious Ministries

The scarcity of Hispanic priests, religious sisters, brothers, and permanent deacons is one of the most serious problems facing the Church in the United States. There are historical reasons, among them neglect, for the unfortunate lack of Hispanic vocations. In the past, too, a major reason for the failure of many Hispanic young people to persevere in pursuing vocations has been the presence in seminaries and convents of cultural expressions, traditions, language, family relationships, and religious experiences which conflicted with their own. Today, however, we are pleased to note that these conflicts are fewer and the situation is vastly improved. In recent years many, if not most, seminaries and convents have made significant strides in meeting the needs of Hispanics. We congratulate these institutions and encourage them to continue improving their programs for Hispanic ministry.

We also encourage seminaries to provide courses in Spanish, Hispanic culture and religiosity, and Hispanic pastoral ministry for seminarians, priests, religious, permanent deacons, and all pastoral ministers.

In light of the present situation, we commit ourselves to fostering Hispanic vocations. Bishops, priests, religious, and laity now must aggressively encourage Hispanic youth to consider the priestly or religious vocation. We call upon Hispanic parents to present the life and work of a priest or religious as a highly desirable vocation for their children, and to take rightful pride in having a son or daughter serve the Church in this way. Without their strong support, the Church will not have the number of Hispanic priests and religious needed to serve their communities.

This requires encouraging a more positive image of priests and religious than presently exists in many Hispanic families. The Church's presence in Hispanic communities must be one which makes it possible for people to experience the reality of its love and care. Priests and religious have a serious responsibility to give Hispanic youth a positive, joyful experience of the Church and to invite them to consider the priesthood or religious life as they make decisions about their future. Diocesan vocation offices are urged to make special efforts to reach Hispanic youth with the invitation to follow Jesus in a priestly or religious vocation.

Above all, the Church in the United States must pray to the Lord of the harvest to send the Hispanic vocations that are sorely needed. We urge special, unceasing prayer in Hispanic parishes for this purpose, and we call upon parents to pray that one or more of their children will be given the grace of a vocation to the priesthood or religious life.

f. Catholic Education

Catholic educators in the United States have a long record of excellence and dedication to the instruction and formation of millions of the Catholic faithful. Now they must turn their skills to responding to the educational needs of Hispanics. Education is an inalienable right; and in nurturing the intellect, Catholic schools and institutes of learning must also foster the values and culture of their pupils (*GE*, 178).

We therefore urge Catholic schools and other Catholic educational institutions to offer additional opportunities, including scholarships and financial aid, to Hispanics who cannot now afford to attend them.

We also recommend adaptations which respond adequately to the Hispanic presence in our schools. Curricula should provide opportunities for bilingual education; teachers should be familiar with the Spanish language and should respect and understand Hispanic culture and religious expression. At the same time, care must be taken to ensure that bilingual education does not impede or unduly delay entrance into the political, socioeconomic, and religious mainstream because of inability to communicate well in the prevalent language.

It is important not only to affirm to Hispanic youths the inherent value of their heritage, but also to offer instruction in Hispanic history and culture. Society often tells them that their parents' culture, so deeply steeped in Catholicism, is valueless and irrelevant. The Church can teach them otherwise.

The Church must also become an advocate for the many young Hispanics who attend public schools, doing all it can to ensure that provision is made for their needs. Particular attention should be given to those who have dropped out of school, whether Catholic or public, and who need remedial education or assistance in developing technical skills.

g. Communications

Ours is an era in which "the medium is the message." The Church has recognized this fact by supporting the modernization of the means of communications at its disposal. For the most part, however, the Church press and electronic media lag in the area of Hispanic ministry. While a few worthy publications in Spanish have been begun in the past decade, the Catholic press largely ignores coverage of Hispanic news. Similarly, the Church lacks a solid body of television and radio programming that addresses the needs of the Hispanic community, although some fine first efforts have been launched through the Catholic Communication Campaign and the Catholic Telecommunications Network of America.

This suggests the need for greater efforts toward planned and systematic programming and regular coverage of issues relevant to the Hispanic community. Training and hiring of talented Hispanics in communications and journalism are required to produce fresh and lively material. Materials and programming imported from Latin America may also help in the short term to bridge our communications gap.

h. Effective Ecumenism

The Lord Jesus prayed for the unity of his followers (Jn 17:21), yet the division of the churches is a major obstacle to evangelization. This is underlined in the United States by instances of active proselytizing among Hispanics carried on in an anti-ecumenical manner by Protestant sects. A variety of fundamentalist groups divide Hispanics and their families with their preaching, which reflects an anti-Catholic spirit hardly emanating from the Gospel of Jesus Christ (PHB, II. c).

Our response as Catholics is not to attack or disparage brothers and sisters of other Christian traditions, but to live the Gospel more authentically in order to present the Catholic Church as the fullness of Christianity and thus nourish the faith of our Hispanic peoples. Other Christian churches have been part of the history of salvation. Prayer, dialogue, and partnership in efforts of common concern remain high on the Catholic agenda. In the Hispanic context, however, the Catholic Church and its tradition has played the major historical role of inculturation of the Gospel; the Church is committed to continuing this mission.

i. Hispanic Youth

Desiring to be the light of the world and salt of the earth, many Hispanic young people dedicate their energies and talents to the mission of the Church. Their values are deeply Christian. Whatever their circumstances, they feel themselves members of a spiritual family led by their Mother Mary. This is evident in their art, poetry, and other forms of expression. Yet pressures on Hispanic youth to adapt and live by self-seeking values have led many away from the Church.

Like youths of other backgrounds, Hispanic young people have a spirit of generosity toward the disadvantaged. In their case, however, this is often more than sensitivity toward the poor; it is of solidarity with people who have as little as they or less. If they are not to fall prey to dreams of success at any price in order to escape poverty, they need to see their talents and potential valued by the Church.

In responding to their needs, the wise pastoral minister will note the marvelous potential of their abundant energies and their ability to speak the language of youth. Committed Hispanic youths grasp with the immediacy of their own experience how to share their Christian vision with their peers through means such as modern and traditional Hispanic music and art.

Hispanic youths and young adults with leadership qualities must be offered opportunities for religious education, biblical studies, catechesis, and special training, so that their vocations to serve the Church will flourish. Such programs should take into account the fact that these youths will develop best in familiar, warm environments.

j. Family

The tradition of commitment to family is one of the distinguishing marks of Hispanic culture. Although there are variations among Mexican-Americans, Puerto Ricans, Cubans, and other Hispanics, there are shared family values and cultural attributes among all Hispanics.[9]

Whether *nuclear* or *extended*, the family unit has been the privileged place where Christian principles have been nurtured and expressed and evangelization and the development of spirituality have occurred. The Hispanic family often exemplifies Pope John Paul II's description of family prayer: "Joys and sorrows, hopes and disappointments, births and birthday celebrations, wedding anniversaries of parents, departures, separations and homecomings, important and far-reaching decisions, and the death of those who are dear, etc.—all of these mark God's loving intervention in the family history. They should be seen as suitable moments for thanksgiving, for petition, for trusting abandonment of the family into the hands of the common Father in heaven" (*FC*, 59).

In our pastoral planning, however, we must not take for granted the continued strength and unity of the Catholic Hispanic family. Hispanic nuclear families are already experiencing the same social pressures faced by other groups. The unity of the Hispanic family is threatened in particular by the uprooting caused by mobility, especially from a rural to an urban life style and from Latin American countries to our own; by poverty, which a high proportion of Hispanic families endure; and by pressures engendered by the process of assimilation, which often leads to generation gaps within the family and identity crises in young people.

There is an urgent need for pastoral ministries that will prepare our people well for married life, for parenthood, and for family counseling and religious education. We make a special plea for measures to assist Hispanic families which are "hurting," as well as the divorced, the separated, single parents, and victims of parental or spousal abuse.

Because of their unique family ties, we invite Hispanic families, along with those from other cultural groups with strong family traditions, to contribute to the gradual unfolding of the richness of Christ's truth. "In conformity with her constant tradition, the Church receives from the various cultures everything that is able to express better the unsearchable riches of Christ. Only with the help of all the cultures will it be possible for these riches to be manifested ever more clearly and for the Church to progress toward a daily, more complete and profound awareness of the truth which has already been given her in its entirety by the Lord" (*FC*, 10).

k. *Migrant Farm Workers*

As noted, Hispanics are highly mobile and are found in both urban and rural settings. As a result, they tend to escape the attention and care of the urban Church. This underlines the need for adaptations in pastoral care, particularly in the case of migrant workers.

There are three major migrant streams in the United States. In the East, farm workers migrate from Mexico, South America, and Florida north to New York and New England working on sugar cane, cotton, tobacco, apple, and grape crops. In the Central Plains, migrants go north from Texas to the Great Lakes to harvest fruits, vegetables, and grains. There is also a substantial number of Puerto Rican seasonal laborers, most of them young and single, who work mainly in the Northeast. In the West, migrants move northward through California, Nevada, and Idaho up to the Northwest; some even go as far as Alaska in search of seasonal jobs. Migration usually begins in the spring and ends in late fall, when the migrants return to their southern home bases.[10]

Abuses of farm workers are notorious, yet they continue to go unrelieved. Conditions are worsening in many regions. Men and women are demoralized to the point where the riches of Hispanic culture, strong family ties, and the profound faith life are sometimes lost. We denounce the treatment of migrants as commodities, cheap labor, rather than persons. We urge others to do the same. Economic conditions often require children to be part of the labor force. Along with the other problems associated with mobility, their education suffers. In the same vein, we find deplorable the abuse of the rights of undocumented workers. All this makes it imperative for the Church to support the right of migrant farm workers to organize for the purpose of collective bargaining.

Experience in the Hispanic apostolate suggests the need for mobile missionary teams and various forms of itinerant ministries. Dioceses and parishes in the path of migrant streams also have a responsibility to support this work and coordinate the efforts of sending and receiving dioceses.

Undoubtedly, too, Hispanic migrants themselves, whose agricultural understanding of life so closely resembles that of Jesus the Galilean,[11] have much to contribute to meeting the challenge.

l. Social Justice and Social Action

The integral evangelization described earlier as the central focus of the pastoral strategy we envisage will be incomplete without an active component of social doctrine and action. As we said in our pastoral letter on war and peace, "at the center of all Catholic social teaching, are the transcendence of God and the dignity of the human person. The human person is the clearest reflection of God's presence in the world" (*CP*, I). This thought must be applied specifically to the reality of the Hispanic presence and the ministry which responds to it.

In the past 20 years Catholic teaching has become increasingly specific about the meaning of social justice. From Pope John XXIII's encyclical *Pacem In Terris* to Pope John Paul II's *Laborem Exercens*, we have seen social teaching define as human rights such things as good governance, nutrition, health, housing, employment, and education. In the United States we have applied these teachings to the problems of our time and nation.

Now we call attention to those social concerns which most directly affect the Hispanic community, among them voting rights, discrimination, immigration rights, the status of farm workers, bilingualism, and pluralism. These are social justice issues of paramount importance to ministry with Hispanics and to the entire Church.

As it engages in social teaching, the Church embraces the quest for justice as an eminently religious task. Persons engaged in this endeavor must be involved with, informed by, and increasingly led by those who know from experience the paradoxical blessings of poverty, prejudice, and unfairness (Mt 5:3). Accordingly, we urge Hispanics to increase their role in social action, and non-Hispanics increasingly to seek out Hispanics in a true partnership.

m. Prejudice and Racism

Within our memory, Hispanics in this country have experienced cruel prejudice. So extensive has it been in some areas that they have been denied basic human and civil rights. Even today, Hispanics, blacks, the recent Southeast Asian refugees, and Native Americans continue to suffer from such dehumanizing treatment, treatment which makes us aware that the sin of racism lingers in our society. Despite great strides in eliminating racial prejudice, both in our country and in our Church, there remains an urgent need for continued purification and reconciliation. It is particularly disheartening to know that some Catholics hold strong prejudices against Hispanics and others and deny them the respect and love due their God-given human dignity.

This is evident even in some parish communities where one finds a reluctance among some non-Hispanics to serve with Hispanics or to socialize with them at parochial events. We appeal to those with this unchristian attitude to examine their behavior in the light of Jesus' commandment of love and to accept their Hispanic brothers and sisters as full partners in the work and life of their parishes. Our words in our pastoral letter on racism deserve repeating: "Racism is not merely one sin among many; it is a radical evil dividing the human family and denying the new creation of a redeemed world. To struggle against it demands an equally radical transformation in our own minds and hearts, as well as the structure of our society" (*BSU*, p. 10).

We urge those who employ Hispanics to provide them with safe and decent working conditions and to pay them salaries that enable them to provide adequately for their families. The inhuman condition of pervasive poverty forced on many Hispanics is at the root of many social problems in their lives. Decent working conditions and adequate salaries are required by justice and basic fairness.

n. Ties with Latin America

Hispanics in our midst are an as yet untapped resource as a cultural bridge between North and South in the Americas. The wellspring of Hispanic culture and faith is historically and geographically located in Latin America. For this reason, a dynamic response to the Hispanic presence in the United States will necessarily entail an ever greater understanding of and linkage with Latin American society and Church.

Latin America, the home of 350 million Catholics, continues to experience grave socioeconomic injustice and, in many nations, a severe deprivation of the most basic human rights. These conditions are oppressive and dehumanizing; they foster violence, poverty, hatred, and deep divisions in the social fabric; they are fundamentally at variance with Gospel values.[12] And yet our fellow Catholics in Latin America, especially the poor, are often vibrant witnesses to the liberating quality of the Gospel, as they strive to build a "civilization of Love" (Puebla, 9).

We shall continue to support and assist the Church in Latin America. We also look forward to a continuing exchange of missionaries, since the cooperation we envision is not one-sided. For our part, we shall continue to send those most prepared to evangelize in Latin America, including our Hispanic personnel, as they grow in numbers. With careful regard to circumstances in the areas from which they come, we welcome Latin American and other priests and religious who come to serve Hispanics in the United States. We recommend that upon arrival they receive special language and cultural preparation for pastoral activity. The Church in the United States has much to learn from the Latin American pastoral experience; it is fortunate to have in the Hispanic presence a precious human link to that experience.

o. Popular Catholicism

Hispanic spirituality is an example of how deeply Christianity can permeate the roots of a culture. In the course of almost 500 years in the Americas, Hispanic people have learned to express their faith in prayer forms and traditions that were begun and encouraged by missionaries and passed from one generation to the next.

Paul VI recognized the value inherent in popular Catholicism. While warning against the possible excesses of popular religiosity, he nonetheless enumerated values that often accompany these prayer forms. If well-oriented, he pointed out, popular piety manifests a thirst for God, makes people generous, and imbues them with a spirit of sacrifice. It can lead to an acute awareness of God's attributes, such as his fatherhood, his providence, and his loving and constant presence (*EN*, 48).

Hispanic spirituality places strong emphasis on the humanity of Jesus, especially when he appears weak and suffering, as in the crib and in his passion and death. This spirituality relates well to all that is symbolic in Catholicism: to ritual, statues and images, holy places, and gestures. It is also a strongly devotional spirituality. The Blessed Virgin Mary, especially under the titles of Our Lady of Guadalupe (Mexico), Our Lady of Providence (Puerto Rico), and Our Lady of Charity (Cuba), occupies a privileged place in Hispanic popular piety.

A closer dialogue is needed between popular and official practice, lest the former lose the guidance of the Gospel and the latter lose the active participation of the unsophisticated and the poorest among the faithful (Medellin, 3). An ecclesial life vibrant with a profound sense of the transcendent, such as is found in Hispanic popular Catholicism, can also be a remarkable witness to the more secularized members of our society.

p. Comunidades Eclesiales de Base

Hispanics in the Americas have made few contributions to the Church more significant than the *comunidades eclesiales de base* (Basic Ecclesial Communities). The small community has appeared on the scene as a ray of hope in dealing with dehumanizing situations that can destroy people and weaken faith. A revitalized sense of fellowship fills the Church in Latin America, Africa, Europe, and Asia with pastoral joy and hope. The Synod of Bishops in 1974 witnessed an outpouring of such hope from Latin American pastors, who saw in *comunidades eclesiales de base* a source of renewal in the Church. Since these communities are of proven benefit to the Church (*EN*, 58), we highly encourage their development.

The *comunidad eclesial de base* is neither a discussion or study group, nor a parish. It is "the first and fundamental ecclesiastical nucleus, which on its own level must make itself responsible for the richness and expansion of the faith, as well as of the worship of which it is an expression" (*JPP*, 10). It should be an expression of a Church that liberates from personal and structural sin; it should be a small community with personal relationships; it should form part of a process of integral evangelization; and it should be in communion with other levels of the Church. The role of the parish, in particular, is to facilitate, coordinate, and multiply the *comunidades eclesiales de base* within its boundaries and territories. The parish should be a community of communities. The ideal *comunidad eclesial de base* is a living community of Christians whose active involvement in every aspect of life is nourished by profound commitment to the Gospel.

q. Other Possibilities

We urge U.S. Catholics to use their best creative talents to go boldly beyond these first steps, which are merely prerequisites for effective action.

One opportunity for creative action arises from the presence of Hispanics in the U.S. military. We encourage the Military Vicariate to explore new means of integral evangelization, with particular attention to this Hispanic presence.

Similarly, as those in prison ministry know, incarcerated Hispanics are in dire need of attention. There is a need for pastoral ministers to assist in this area.

Among Hispanics there are also handicapped persons whose special needs are compounded by many of the problems we have described. According to estimates nearly 2 million Hispanic Catholics have one or more disabling conditions, including blindness, deafness, mental retardation, learning disabilities, and orthopedic impairments. There is a serious need for programs of ministry that encourage participation by disabled Hispanic Catholics.

This is only a partial list. As throughout this document, our intent here has been to encourage further reflection, dialogue, and action, not limit them.

IV. Statement of Commitment

13. While conscious of the many ethnic and racial groups who call legitimately upon our services and resources, and grateful for the present significant, if limited, outreach to the Hispanic people of the United States, we commit ourselves and our pastoral associates to respond to the call to Hispanic ministry. Awareness of the good works of the past and present must not make us slow to read the signs of the times. Our preparations today will make it easier to carry out tomorrow's task.

    We recognize the realities of the U.S. Hispanic presence, the past efforts of those involved in the Hispanic apostolate, and the urgent need to launch new and creative efforts. To inaugurate this new era in the Church, considerable adjustments will be required on the part of Hispanics and non-Hispanics alike. Yet we are hopeful that commitment to minister with Hispanics will lead to a reaffirmation of catholicity and a revitalization of all efforts to fulfill the Church's essential mission.

Commitment to Catholicity

14. The universal character of the Church involves both pluralism and unity. Humanity, in its cultures and peoples, is so various that it could only have been crafted by the hand of God. The Church recognizes this in saying that "each individual part contributes through its special gifts" (*LG*, 13). Yet the Church transcends all limits of time and race; humanity as a whole is called to become a People of God in peace and unity.

    The Gospel teaching that no one is a stranger in the Church is timeless. As the Apostle Paul says, "there does not exist among you Jew or Greek, slave or freeman, male or female. All are one in Christ Jesus" (Gal 3:28).

    Our commitment to Hispanic ministry therefore leads us, as teachers, to invite *all* Catholics to adopt a more welcoming attitude toward others. Hispanics, whose presence in this land is antedated only by that of Native Americans, are called to welcome their brothers and sisters, the descendants of other European immigrants. Similarly, the latter are called to embrace Hispanic newcomers from Latin America. Where all are freed from attitudes of cultural or ethnic dominance, the gifts of all will enrich the Church and give witness to the Gospel of Jesus Christ.

Commitment to Respond to Temporal Needs

15. Evangelization is a spiritual work that also extends to all that is human and seeks to bring it to fulfillment. Pope John Paul II reminded us of this when he said, "The Church will never abandon man, nor his temporal needs, as she leads humanity to salvation" (*ABUS*).

    Our Hispanic faithful proclaimed this same reality in their II Encuentro; there they make a commitment to integral evangelization, "with the testimony of a life of service to one's neighbor for the transformation of the world" (*II ENHP*, Evangelization, 1).

    We in our turn pledge to raise our voices and go on raising them as leaders in defense of the human dignity of Hispanics. We remind our pastoral associates that their work includes the effort to gain for Hispanics participation in the benefits of our society. We call all U.S. Catholics to work not just *for* Hispanics but *with* them, in order to secure their empowerment in our democracy and the political participation that is their right and duty. In this way we deepen our preferential option for the poor which, according to Jesus' example and the Church's tradition, must always be a hallmark of our apostolate (Puebla, 1134).

Call to Recognize the Hispanic Reality

16. In committing ourselves to work *with* Hispanics and not simply *for* them, we accept the responsibility for acknowledging, respecting, and valuing their presence as a gift. This presence represents more than just potential; it now performs a valuable service for our Church and our society, although this service is often overlooked; it is a prophetic presence, one to be encouraged and needed.

Commitment of Resources

17. Also part of our commitment, as shepherds and stewards of the common resources of the Church, is the pledge to harness these resources for Hispanic ministry. We make this explicit when we keep in mind and take steps to make visible the spirit of the early Christian community (Acts 2:44).

More than an expression of sentiment, this declaration of commitment includes the recognition that we must secure the financial and material resources necessary to reach our goals.

We see the need to continue to support, on a more permanent basis, the existing national, regional, and diocesan entities of the Hispanic apostolate. Given the obvious limitations of resources, it is also necessary to supervise and evaluate current efforts more thoroughly, so as to encourage the best use of personnel, monies, and physical plants. In addition, it is imperative to call to the attention of the appropriate administrators the need to seek more qualified Hispanics to serve their communities. More Hispanics are also needed in the offices of the National Conference of Catholic Bishops and the United States Catholic Conference, in our regional and diocesan offices, our schools, our hospitals, and in the many other agencies of the Church.

What now exists is not sufficient to meet all the needs and challenges. Serious efforts to assess these needs more carefully and earmark resources for Hispanic ministry must take place at every level. The Church in the United States is fortunate in having at its disposal a variety of institutions and ministries whose energies can and should be applied to the task. Schools, parishes, pastoral institutes, communication media, and a variety of specialized ministries must all be encouraged to make this commitment their own.

In the face of very real financial constraints we pledge to explore new possibilities for funding. We are aware of creative budgeting formulas that encourage all ministries and agencies to respond to the Church's priorities; we shall study these as we strive to respond to this clear pastoral need.

Convocation for the III Encuentro

18. We ask our Hispanic peoples to raise their prophetic voices to us once again, as they did in 1972 and 1977, in a *III Encuentro Nacional Hispano de Pastoral*, so that together we can face our responsibilities well. We call for the launching of an Encuentro process, from *comunidades eclesiales de base* and parishes, to dioceses and regions, and to the national level, culminating in a gathering of representatives in Washington, D.C., in August 1985.

Toward a Pastoral Plan

19. Beyond the Encuentro process, in which we shall take part, we recognize that integral pastoral planning must avoid merely superficial adaptations of existing ministries. We look forward to reviewing the conclusions of the III Encuentro as a basis for drafting a National Pastoral Plan for Hispanic Ministry to be considered in our general meeting at the earliest possible date after the Encuentro.

Study on Best Practices for Diocesan Ministry Among Hispanics/Latinos

The document *Study on Best Practices for Diocesan Ministry Among Hispanics/Latinos* was developed as a resource by the Bishops' Committee on Hispanic Affairs of the United States Conference of Catholic Bishops (USCCB). It was reviewed by the committee chairman, Bishop Plácido Rodríguez, CMF, and has been authorized for publication by the undersigned.

Msgr. David J. Malloy, STD
General Secretary, USCCB

Acknowledgments

We express our gratitude to the bishops of the participating arch/dioceses and their staff for their openness and generosity during the consultation process. We thank the National Catholic Association of Diocesan Directors for Hispanic Ministry (NCADDHM) and the National Association of Regional Directors and Coordinators for Hispanic Ministry for their leadership and collaboration. In particular, we thank Mr. Rudy Vargas IV and Ms. Elisa Montalvo for their invaluable input and guidance throughout the project. We also thank the team of interviewers who shared in the task of visiting the participating arch/dioceses and writing the reports: Sr. Angela Erevia; Sr. Leticia Salazar; Ms. Mar Muñóz-Visoso; Rev. Thomas Florek SJ; Mr. Miguel León, PhD; Mr. Alfonso Barros; Mr. Ronaldo Cruz; and Mr. Alejandro Aguilera-Titus.

Background

Representatives from the National Catholic Association of Diocesan Directors for Hispanic Ministry (NCADDHM) and the National Association of Regional Directors and Coordinators for Hispanic Ministry addressed the Bishops' Committee on Hispanic Affairs during its November 2004 meeting on concerns related to the closing of diocesan offices for Hispanic ministry or their placement under multicultural ministry offices. The concerns raised by the Hispanic ministry network pointed to the fact that while the Hispanic presence continues to grow and demands a more robust ministerial response, diocesan personnel and/or resources for Hispanic ministry are diminishing in a number of arch/dioceses. The Committee was asked to consider conducting a survey to assist the bishops in discerning the best models for diocesan Hispanic ministry at this time of restructuring. In response, the Committee directed staff to develop a strategy to identify best practices for diocesan Hispanic ministry structures and functions. This response was in keeping with the need for strong diocesan structures for Hispanic ministry called for by the United States Conference of Catholic Bishops (USCCB) in *Encuentro and Mission: A Renewed Pastoral Framework for Hispanic Ministry*.

Purpose

To provide the bishops with models of best practices in diocesan Hispanic ministry that would serve to assist in (1) assessing the level of development of Hispanic ministry in their own dioceses and identifying next steps, (2) applying pastoral criteria to ensure a more systematic, collaborative, and structurally sound approach to diocesan Hispanic ministry, and (3) developing or updating a pastoral plan for Hispanic ministry in the context of a culturally diverse Church.

Methodology

A questionnaire based on ten indicators was developed, and twenty arch/dioceses considered to be highly effective in Hispanic ministry were identified in collaboration with the leadership from the NCADDHM and the National Association of Regional Directors and Coordinators for Hispanic Ministry. A team of interviewers conducted onsite visits in the twenty selected arch/dioceses. The indicators that were selected evolved from the field experience of staff and the input provided by the regional and diocesan directors for Hispanic ministry.

Indicators

1. Vision
2. Mission
3. Pastoral planning
4. Structure
5. Sustained growth
6. Leadership development and formation
7. Decision-making process
8. Collaboration
9. Resources
10. Evaluation

Arch/Dioceses Identified for Benchmarking as "Best Practices" Arch/Dioceses

The selected arch/dioceses were chosen upon the recommendation of the two national organizations mentioned above. The criteria used for the selection took into consideration geographical location, size, Hispanic population and percentage in the arch/dioceses, rural or urban environment, and the stage of development of Hispanic ministry. At least two arch/dioceses were selected within each of the eight Hispanic ministry regions in order to maximize geographical representation. Therefore, the selected arch/dioceses do not necessarily represent the absolute top 20 best practices for diocesan Hispanic ministry in the country.

Arch/Dioceses	Region
Grand Rapids, Chicago	Midwest
Raleigh, Richmond, Charlotte	Southeast
Washington, D.C.; Wilmington	Northeast
Denver, Salt Lake City	Mountain States
Orange, Monterey, San Bernardino, Stockton	Far West
Yakima, Portland	Northwest
Omaha, St. Paul-Minneapolis	North Central States
Galveston-Houston, Fort Worth, El Paso	Southwest

Summary of Responses

1. Vision

Building Hispanic ministry on the foundation set by the United States Conference of Catholic Bishops in the 1987 *National Pastoral Plan for Hispanic Ministry* (NPPHM) is a historic and key element to successful ministry among Hispanic Catholics. The understanding that Hispanics are the responsibility of the entire Church and not just of some parishes and willing priests has taken hold in all participating arch/dioceses. This clear understanding of ministry has changed the response of arch/diocesan and parish staff from asking whether they need to respond to the Hispanic presence to asking how to do it effectively. All twenty arch/dioceses identified as best practices have an understanding of Hispanic ministry based on the NPPHM and other documents of the United States Conference of Catholic Bishops, particularly *Encuentro and Mission: A Renewed Pastoral Framework for Hispanic Ministry*. Inservices on this document have been conducted in all twenty arch/dioceses. In sixteen of them, the inservices included participants from the various arch/diocesan offices and Catholic organizations and institutions. With the exception of those arch/dioceses that are relatively new in developing Hispanic ministry, the vision for Hispanic ministry has been incorporated into the work of various arch/diocesan offices and Catholic organizations and institutions. This incorporation is evidenced by the presence of professional staff responsible for developing ministry among Hispanics within those offices and organizations, particularly in arch/dioceses with sustained growth and long-standing efforts.

2. Mission

All twenty participating arch/dioceses show a robust and ongoing response to the Hispanic presence. The number of Hispanic Catholics actively participating in the life and mission of the Church has grown dramatically. This is a direct result of the steady increase in the number of parishes with Hispanic ministry—particularly over the past ten years. In most cases, the growth has been remarkable, as the number of these parishes now reaches a total of 854 in the twenty arch/dioceses combined. In one archdiocese, the number of parishes serving Hispanics jumped from eight to forty-two in nine years. The percentage of priests and lay professional ministers directly ministering among Hispanic Catholics has also increased significantly, according to the respondents to the survey. As an example, in one archdiocese the number of priests directly involved in Hispanic ministry went from six to forty-two in a span of seven years. During the same time, the number of paid Hispanic lay leaders working in parishes went from four to twenty-six. Despite this growth, all participating arch/dioceses said that the increase in population outpaces the pastoral response. Thus, more parishes are projected to welcome Hispanics in the next few years. It is worth noting that all participating arch/dioceses expect their seminarians to take classes on Hispanic ministry, language, and culture. In some cases, this expectation is a requirement of the ordinary bishop. Moreover, in sixteen of the twenty arch/dioceses, the ordinary bishop speaks Spanish well. In the other four, the bishops can communicate in Spanish to some extent and do so on special occasions.

Participation of Hispanics continues to grow in the various parishes and arch/diocesan ministries such as catechesis, liturgical ministries, adult faith formation, youth and young adult ministry, migrant ministry, ministry with the incarcerated, evangelization, and social services. Within the Church, there is a proliferation of apostolic movements and evangelizing programs, such as *Cursillo de Cristiandad*, Charismatic Renewal, Small Christian Communities, RENEW, Bible study groups, Disciples in Mission, *Jóvenes para Cristo*, *Movimiento de Jornadas*, *Neocatecumenales*, and others. Ministry with Hispanics in the broader community is done through social services, cultural events, radio programs, and printed media. The number of Hispanics participating in social action activities such as lobby days, advocacy projects, voting registration drives, and other civic activities is also growing in all arch/dioceses surveyed.

3. Pastoral Planning

Pastoral plans are instrumental for sustained growth and effectiveness in Hispanic ministry. All but three arch/dioceses have developed or are in the process of developing a multi-year arch/diocesan pastoral plan for Hispanic ministry, usually a three- to five-year plan. The remaining three have one-year plans. In arch/dioceses where Hispanic ministry is relatively new, the plan is mainly the responsibility of the Office for Hispanic Ministry (OHM). In contrast, in those arch/dioceses with a long-standing history and maturity in ministry among Hispanics, the plans are a responsibility of the various arch/diocesan ministry offices, institutions, and organizations. In this case, the OHM is an active participant in the pastoral planning process of the entire arch/diocese. Moreover, a number of other ministerial offices and organizations are equipped with bilingual staff directly responsible for ministry among Hispanics. This ministerial capacity translates into a larger number of Hispanics participating in arch/diocesan events and activities (e.g., catechetical and ministry days, youth rallies and conventions, and liturgical celebrations). Joint projects in the areas of catechesis, youth and young adult ministry, and formation are also evidence of organic pastoral planning. It is worth noting that only one participating diocese mentioned having an office for planning. Also interesting is that a number of arch/dioceses do not have a pastoral plan in place for the arch/diocese as a whole. Some respondents mentioned that their arch/diocese was engaged in a synod process at the time the interview was conducted and that this process was leading to the development of a plan.

4. Structure

A well established Office for Hispanic Ministry, with a highly effective director who has direct access to the local ordinary, is a key element of best practices. Nineteen of the twenty arch/dioceses have a director for Hispanic ministry. Thirteen of the arch/dioceses have a lay person as full-time director, three have full-time religious sisters, and three have priests (two full-time and one part-time) as directors. Out of the eighteen with full-time directors, all have supportive staff and seven have associates. These OHMs also have their own budget, as opposed to arch/dioceses where Hispanic ministry is a line item within an office or department. Most directors have direct access to the ordinary bishop and are placed under the supervision of the ordinary or auxiliary bishop (four arch/dioceses), chancellor (four), moderator of the curia (three), and vicar general (two). In some cases, the OHM is under a department, most frequently the Department of Pastoral Services. Seventeen arch/dioceses have professional staff in other diocesan offices specifically hired to minister among Hispanics. In three arch/dioceses, most of the diocesan staff is bilingual—in one of these, twenty-seven out of fifty professional staff are Hispanic and hold positions as directors and associate directors. In three arch/dioceses, the OHM is the only office with staff serving Hispanics as their main responsibility. The one diocese without an OHM has bilingual directors for most of its diocesan offices and Catholic organizations and institutions. Most priests in that diocese are bilingual. Hispanics constitute the vast majority of the Catholic population in the diocese, and most parishes provide ministries in English and Spanish.

5. Sustained Growth

Four different stages have been identified in the development of Hispanic ministry at the arch/diocesan level. Each level is defined by the primary task to be accomplished as Hispanic ministry evolves:

i. **Outreach Stage**: At this level, Hispanic ministry is localized in certain areas or parishes of the diocese without diocesan coordination. Social services, advocacy, and the establishment of the Sunday Liturgy in Spanish are the primary activities and top priorities. All twenty arch/dioceses have gone through this stage. However, these priorities are ongoing in migrant ministry efforts.

ii. **Diocesan Team Stage**: Hispanic ministry is coordinated through a diocesan office that provides direct ministry services to Hispanics. During this stage the primary goal of the OHM is to advocate with parishes and assist them in welcoming Hispanics. However, Hispanic Catholics are the responsibility of the OHM more than that of the parishes themselves. It is typical to have priests and/or religious as directors during this stage, given the need for sacramental ministry. Five of the twenty arch/dioceses are in this stage of development and are moving quite successfully to the next stage.

iii. **Parish-Based Stage**: At this level, Hispanic ministry is the responsibility of the parish, and the OHM is a resource for the parishes and other arch/diocesan ministerial offices. In this stage, the top priority is to have Hispanics become the responsibility of the parishes. Rapid growth in the number of parishes with Hispanic ministry is characteristic. Also typical is the development of programs and projects to assist parishes in their Hispanic ministry efforts. A change in who serves as director of the OHM is also typical—a lay ecclesial minister or a religious sister may serve as director instead of a priest. The office begins to hire staff to serve Hispanics within different ministerial areas. Twelve arch/dioceses are in this stage of development. Nine of them have a lay person as director, two have priests, and one has a religious sister. All but one have staff serving in other diocesan offices and Catholic organizations (e.g., catechesis, adult faith formation, youth and young adults, Catholic Charities). It is important to keep in mind that the opening of Hispanic ministry offices in new parishes is ongoing and at the beginning requires a strong component of advocacy and pastoral planning as well as some direct assistance.

iv. **Diocese-Wide Stage**: The Office for Hispanic Ministry is highly influential and collaborative at this level. The other diocesan ministry offices are equipped to provide resources to parishes in their pastoral efforts with Hispanics within their own ministerial responsibility. Most parishes with a significant Hispanic presence provide a comprehensive Hispanic ministry. Two dioceses have reached this stage of development, while four are well on their way. In five of these six arch/dioceses, the director for Hispanic ministry also serves on the arch/diocesan cabinet.

6. Leadership Development and Formation

All twenty arch/dioceses participating in the survey see leadership development and formation as a high priority, particularly for Hispanic lay leaders. This level of priority is made evident by the existence of well-established diocesan formation programs in eighteen of the twenty arch/dioceses. The other two dioceses are at an early stage of development; and even though they provide formation opportunities for ministries, a more systematic program is not yet in place. Based on the input generated by the respondents to the survey, a well-established formation program has staff specifically responsible for administering the program; has a good faculty; is appreciated and used by a significant number of parishes; offers formation that is systematic, ongoing, and comprehensive; and is recognized and connected with the various diocesan ministry offices. Seven of the arch/dioceses have a full-time person directing the formation program. In these cases, the program tends to be more sophisticated, offering a variety of formation opportunities ranging from certificate programs to programs offering college credit and/or full degrees. Some of the arch/dioceses are partnering with a university to promote degree programs so they are not limited to a certification-only program.

In ten arch/dioceses, the director for Hispanic ministry is also responsible for the formation program, making that a part-time position. In five arch/dioceses the formation program is provided by a regional Hispanic pastoral institute such as the Southeast Pastoral Institute (SEPI), the Northeast Pastoral Institute, or the Midwest Center for Leadership Formation.

In eleven arch/dioceses, the formation program was established more than fifteen years ago. It is noteworthy that once a program is established, it grows very consistently. This is due in part to the great level of interest shown by Hispanic lay leaders in their own ministerial formation. This fact reflects the findings included in the United States Conference of Catholic Bishops' 1999 statement *Lay Ecclesial Ministry: The State of the Question* (page 54), which show that Hispanics constitute 23 percent of all lay people involved in arch/diocesan formation programs. Another contributing factor to the success of these programs is the relationship that exists between the programs and the parishes. Representatives of the twenty arch/dioceses spoke of the importance of having the pastors recognize the formation program as a valuable resource to develop leadership within the parish.

The existence of a well-established formation program is a strong sign of a best practice in diocesan Hispanic ministry. This indicator is further enhanced by formation efforts in different ministerial areas such as catechesis, youth and young adult ministry, marriage preparation, and migrant ministry. Fourteen of the twenty arch/dioceses surveyed conduct such programs on a regular basis, particularly in the area of catechesis. Eleven have a program on Hispanic youth and/or young adult ministry. Among the eleven, some have developed their own programs, while others use regional or national pastoral institutes such as the ones mentioned above, or the programs offered by Instituto Fe y Vida and the Mexican American Cultural Center (MACC).

In the area of Catholic education, the percentage of Hispanic students attending Catholic schools varies significantly between the surveyed arch/dioceses. The disparity can be linked to the size of the Hispanic population and its length of residency in a particular area. Surveyed arch/dioceses with a long-standing Hispanic population show that approximately 20 percent of children in Catholic schools are of Hispanic descent. This number is expected to grow as a number of arch/dioceses are becoming more deliberate about making Catholic education more accessible to Hispanics. In arch/dioceses where the Hispanic presence is relatively new, the percentage of Hispanics in Catholic schools is about 10 percent. However, two arch/dioceses with a relatively recent and/or limited Hispanic presence have a high percentage of Hispanics getting a Catholic education.

7. Decision-Making Process

The following question was asked in the survey of arch/dioceses. How do you rate the inclusion of Hispanics in the decision-making process in your diocese: high, good, or low? The surveyed arch/dioceses responded as follows: high (six), good (eleven), low (five).

The arch/dioceses with the "high" and "good" decision-making levels were the ones where the OHM is well established and its director is a member of the bishop's cabinet. Based on the responses, a well-established OHM, in arch/dioceses that have reached a diocese-wide stage of development (thus including Hispanics in different departments and ministerial offices), reported a "high" involvement of Hispanics in the decision-making process. Out of the five arch/dioceses indicating "low" participation, four are in the second stage of development (diocesan focus). One of them is well into the third stage (parish-based) but has only one full-time staff person serving Hispanics, who has the title of director for Hispanic ministry.

The following areas were identified as key decision-making processes impacting Hispanic ministry: assignments of priests to parishes, hiring of new staff, pastoral planning, diocesan events and programs, allocation of resources, and restructuring strategies. In addition, the participation of Hispanics in presbyteral councils, in liturgical commissions, as priest personnel, and in vocations boards is also pivotal. The number of Hispanics in these decision-making bodies is increasing.

The number of Hispanics sitting on arch/diocesan councils and/or commissions tends to be good. A number of arch/dioceses do not have councils in place yet. Some of the arch/dioceses are currently conducting a synod process with a significant Hispanic participation. Participation of Hispanics in the decision-making process at the parish level appears to be strong. All arch/dioceses that were surveyed reported that participation of Hispanics in parish councils is significant. Many parishes have a bilingual pastor, and a significant number have a Hispanic priest. The number of parishes with Hispanics as staff members is also on the rise in all twenty arch/dioceses surveyed.

8. Collaboration

Collaboration is both a fruit and a sign of highly effective Hispanic ministry. Just as in the area of pastoral planning, collaboration is more deliberate and better coordinated in arch/dioceses with long-standing Hispanic ministry. The six arch/dioceses that have reached, or are close to reaching, the diocese-wide stage of development report a much higher level of sharing perspectives and resources, both on behalf of Hispanic Catholics and also in relationship with the entire local church. Arch/diocesan events like catechetical days, youth conventions, leadership development initiatives, formation programs, and lobby days are commonplace in five of the twenty participating arch/dioceses. In these, the OHM is a partner with other ministerial offices under a common goal or even a common pastoral plan for Hispanic ministry that involves other ministries directly.

In arch/dioceses where Hispanic ministry has reached the parish-based stage of development, the OHM is more of a resource to other ministerial offices and Catholic institutions and organizations. This is due to the fact that the OHM is the only ministry office equipped with the personnel, expertise, and skills required for ministry among Hispanics. In these arch/dioceses, collaboration takes place mainly in the planning of diocesan events within specific ministerial areas. The depth of this collaboration can depend a great deal on the personal relationship between directors and/or the collaborative style within a specific department, such as pastoral services. Collaboration increases significantly when staff are hired to develop ministry among Hispanics in a particular department, office, or Catholic institution.

In the case of arch/dioceses at the beginning stages of Hispanic ministry, collaboration is quite limited because the OHM provides direct services to Hispanic Catholics, which leaves limited time for staff to collaborate with other offices or institutions. However, the participating arch/dioceses at this level of development expressed that more collaboration is needed and should increase as ministry evolves. Overall, the concept of *pastoral de conjunto* (communion in mission) in Hispanic ministry predisposes its leadership to collaborate. Several responses to the survey emphasized this point, well illustrated by one respondent who said, "We constantly convey to our colleagues that it is not 'us' and 'they' but 'we' as one Church."

9. Resources

All participating arch/dioceses said that the personnel and financial resources assigned to Hispanic ministry come short of what is needed. However, seventeen arch/diocesan respondents said that the commitment of their arch/diocese to Hispanic Catholics is generous but not sufficient to respond to a fast-growing Hispanic population. With two exceptions, no personnel reduction in the OHM or of Hispanics in other ministerial offices has taken place in the past few years. In three of them, there has been an increase in diocesan personnel serving Hispanics. Five reported a decrease in budget due to economic limitations that were applied across the board. Three of them reported an increase in their budget in the past few years.

While the level of arch/diocesan personnel has remained almost the same over the past few years, personnel and resources at the parish level have grown significantly in all twenty arch/dioceses. The percentage of priests involved in Hispanic ministry ranges from 25 percent up to 65 percent in arch/dioceses that have reached the third stage of development (parish-based). Even in those arch/dioceses where Hispanic ministry is young, the percentage of priests ministering among Hispanics is quite significant and growing. It is noteworthy that twelve arch/dioceses have a fund to help parishes hire Hispanic ministry coordinators and/or subsidize part of priests' salaries. Two of them give priority to hiring vicariate coordinators.

In the area of Catholic education, nine arch/dioceses said that they were making a special effort to increase the number of Hispanic students in Catholic schools. These efforts took the form of a particular fund for this purpose or a specific emphasis within a fund to support all students with limited resources. One of the arch/dioceses stands out in this area by having the highest reported percentage of Hispanic students in Catholic schools (25 percent), even though it is a relatively small diocese with a relatively small Hispanic population.

In the area of stewardship, eighteen arch/dioceses are engaging the Hispanic community through their annual stewardship program. In most of them, the OHM is a resource that provides translation of materials and identifies Spanish-speaking leaders to help promote the effort at the parish level. Some OHMs offer classes on the importance of developing a sense of belonging to the faith community and being good stewards. One diocese has two Spanish-speaking professionals in the Office for Stewardship. The responses reflect the need to do more in this area.

10. Evaluation

Evaluation is an important element in all of the arch/dioceses surveyed. Specific events such as ministry days, retreats, inservices, or workshops are always evaluated. Annual performance evaluations for the OHM are done in sixteen of the twenty arch/dioceses. Pastoral plans and formation programs are generally evaluated upon completion, but a more systematic process is needed in some arch/dioceses.

In terms of criteria used to measure growth and effectiveness in Hispanic ministry, the following aspects were the most commonly used by the participating arch/dioceses:

- Number of parishes with Hispanic ministry
- Number of Masses in Spanish, and average Sunday attendance
- Percentage of priests directly involved in ministry among Hispanics
- Number of Hispanics in diocesan and parish staff and in councils
- Number and quality of arch/diocesan programs, events, and activities for Hispanics and number of Hispanics participating in them
- Number of Hispanics participating in all arch/diocesan events
- Number of workshops offered to or requested by parishes and/or apostolic movements
- Number of people served by social services agencies
- Number of Hispanic priests, deacons, seminarians, and religious men and women ministering in the arch/diocese, and total number of bilingual priests
- Hispanic population growth and percentage of the population reached by the Church

Conclusion

After analyzing the combined responses generated by the twenty arch/dioceses participating in the survey, the following elements have been identified as decisive in making an arch/diocese a best-practice arch/diocese in diocesan Hispanic ministry.

1. Building Hispanic ministry on the foundation set by the United States Conference of Catholic Bishops in the 1987 *National Pastoral Plan for Hispanic Ministry* (NPPHM) is a historic and key element to successful ministry among Hispanic Catholics. The understanding that Hispanics are the responsibility of the entire Church and not just of some parishes and willing priests has taken hold in all participating arch/dioceses.

   Highlight: All twenty arch/dioceses identified as best practices arch/dioceses have an understanding of Hispanic ministry based on the NPPHM and other documents of the United States Conference of Catholic Bishops, particularly *Encuentro and Mission: A Renewed Pastoral Framework for Hispanic Ministry*. Inservices on this document have been conducted in all twenty archdioceses.

2. A ministry that is culturally specific consistently brings a growing number of Hispanic Catholics into a more enthusiastic participation in the life and mission of the Church in parishes, Catholic institutions, apostolic movements, diocesan events, and programs and activities. The number of parishes with Hispanic ministry reaches a total of 854 in the twenty arch/dioceses combined.

   Highlight: All twenty arch/dioceses show a robust and ongoing response to the Hispanic presence. In one archdiocese, the number of priests directly involved in Hispanic ministry went from six to forty-two in a span of seven years, and the number of paid Hispanic lay leaders working in parishes went from four to twenty-six. During that time, the archdiocese went from twelve missions serving Hispanics to thirty-nine parishes. In sixteen of the twenty arch/dioceses, the ordinary bishop speaks Spanish well. In the other four, the bishops can communicate in Spanish to some extent and do so on special occasions.

3. An ongoing pastoral planning process makes Hispanic ministry more focused, systematic, deliberate, and collaborative. Pastoral plans for Hispanic ministry require the response of the various departments, offices, and institutions to the Hispanic presence. Plans maximize the use of resources and offer the benefit of measuring progress and building on previous efforts.

   Highlight: All but three arch/dioceses have developed or are in the process of developing a multi-year arch/diocesan pastoral plan for Hispanic ministry, usually a three- to five-year plan. The remaining three have one-year plans.

4. A well-established Office for Hispanic Ministry has a competent director and/or staff in place, with direct access to the local ordinary who is bilingual to some degree. In arch/dioceses where Hispanic ministry is more developed, the OHM is placed under direct supervision of the local ordinary or a member of the curia. In other arch/dioceses, it falls under a department—most frequently pastoral services.

   Highlight: Nineteen of the twenty arch/dioceses have a director for Hispanic ministry. The one diocese without an OHM has bilingual directors for most of its diocesan offices and Catholic organizations and institutions.

5. A sustained growth initiative recognizes developmental stages for Hispanic ministry and promotes its advancement. Through the stages of outreach, diocesan focus, parish-based focus, and diocese-wide focus, the OHM goes from being primarily a direct service office to a mainly resource office, and then to a fully engaged partner office.

   Highlight: In dioceses with advanced development, the Office for Hispanic Ministry is highly influential and collaborative. The other diocesan ministry offices are equipped to provide resources to parishes in their pastoral efforts with Hispanics within their own area of ministerial responsibility.

6. A vibrant and well-established leadership development and formation process includes programs, workshops, and activities in various ministerial areas. Programs are sufficiently staffed and constantly

expanding. They move from occasional workshops to certificate programs to full degrees in ministry. Programs include courses for seminarians and priests in Hispanic culture, language, and ministry.

Highlight: Eighteen of the twenty arch/dioceses have well established diocesan formation programs in Spanish. This fact reflects the findings included in the United States Conference of Catholic Bishops' 1999 statement *Lay Ecclesial Ministry: The State of the Question* (page 54), which shows that Hispanics constitute 23 percent of all lay people involved in arch/diocesan formation programs.

7. Best practice includes shared leadership, where Hispanics and other bilingual staff are members of the cabinet and other decision-making bodies in the arch/diocesan structure, and different ministerial offices have staff directly responsible for ministry development among Hispanics. A growing number of priests, particularly pastors, are bilingual, and Hispanic membership in parish councils is increasingly representative.

Highlight: The arch/dioceses with the high (six) and good (eleven) decision-making levels are the ones where the OHM is well established and its director is a member of the bishop's cabinet.

8. A spirit of collaboration and common mission permeates the interaction of the OHM with other offices and Catholic organizations and institutions. Joint projects on specific ministerial areas are common; and arch/diocesan celebrations, programs, and events are planned and implemented with full or significant input and participation of the OHM and therefore of Hispanic Catholics.

Highlight: Collaboration increases significantly when staff are hired to develop ministry among Hispanics in a particular department, office, or Catholic institution. Overall, the concept of *pastoral de conjunto* (communion in mission) in Hispanic ministry predisposes its leadership to collaborate.

9. A well-informed leadership in Hispanic ministry is aware of the limitations in resources and knows that the arch/diocese is committed to the Hispanic presence. Staff and program budget levels for the OHM are maintained for the most part, and increases are attainable when well articulated. Program budget cuts are applied across the board. At the parish level, resources increase consistently in terms of personnel and services. The Hispanic community responds by sharing more fully their time, talent, and treasure, particularly when stewardship efforts are consistent and ongoing.

Highlight: With two exceptions, no personnel reduction in the OHM or of Hispanics in other ministerial offices has taken place in the past few years in the twenty best-practices arch/dioceses. In three of them, there has been an increase in diocesan personnel serving Hispanics. Seventeen arch/diocesan respondents said that the commitment of their arch/diocese to Hispanic Catholics is generous.

10. An evaluation process is in place to measure accomplishment of goals included in the pastoral plan and/or specific programs and activities. There is a very good picture in terms of quantitative growth. Awareness of developmental growth and articulation of future direction and priorities needs more discussion within Hispanic ministry, with other diocesan ministries, and with the broader community.

Highlight: Annual performance evaluations for the OHM are done in sixteen of the twenty arch/dioceses. Pastoral plans and formation programs are generally evaluated upon completion.

Highlights by Arch/Diocese

Charlotte

- A well-established diocesan office and regional structure within Hispanic ministry provides effective coordination and assistance to parishes ministering among Hispanics.
- Diocesan coordination of Hispanic youth and young adult ministry is in place, and migrant ministry is very effective.

- A pastoral plan for Hispanic ministry is in place, and pastoral planning is an ongoing process.

Chicago

- Well-established lay formation programs and catechetical ministries benefit thousands of Hispanics through archdiocesan formation opportunities and parish programs.
- Well-organized and vibrant Hispanic young adult ministry with paid staff coordinating its efforts is present at the archdiocesan level.
- The archdiocese has a very strong parish-based Hispanic ministry.

Denver

- A well-established archdiocesan office for Hispanic ministry includes a coordinator for Hispanic youth and young adult ministry.
- Centro San Juan Diego is an archdiocesan gathering place and multipurpose center offering an array of pastoral and social services and activities for the Hispanic community.
- The archdiocese has a very strong parish-based Hispanic ministry. The number of parishes with Hispanic ministry went from eight to forty-two in the past ten years.

El Paso

- The well-established lay ministry formation program serves more than seven hundred Hispanics every year (*Instituto Tepeyac*).
- The highly effective Diocesan Migration and Refugee Services center (DMRS) provides counseling on immigration and other legal issues. All staff are bilingual and very professional.
- Practically every priest is bilingual, and Hispanics are served in most parishes in English and Spanish.

Fort Worth

- A high percentage of diocesan directors and associate directors are Hispanic; and, every diocesan office is equipped with Hispanic ministry capabilities.
- Collaboration between diocesan offices is very high, and pastoral planning is done consistently in the various ministerial areas, including adult faith formation, catechesis, youth ministry, migrant ministry, and family life.
- The Office for Hispanic Ministry is an effective channel for the Church's involvement in civic activities, projects, and initiatives impacting Hispanics.

Galveston-Houston

- A well-established archdiocesan network has representatives from every parish with Hispanic ministry.
- Effective programs and projects among Hispanics include the areas of catechesis, youth and young adult ministry, faith formation, and leadership development.
- Collaboration with other archdiocesan offices and agencies is well coordinated through a pastoral plan for Hispanic ministry.

Grand Rapids

- A well-established diocesan office and regional structure within Hispanic ministry provides effective coordination and assistance to parishes ministering among Hispanics.
- There is a high level of collaboration with other diocesan ministry offices, particularly in the area of youth and young adult ministry.
- A comprehensive *Diocesan Pastoral Plan for Hispanic Ministry* has been in place or ten years, and the growth has been very significant.

Monterey

- A vibrant migrant ministry reaches thousands of Hispanics every year.
- The diocesan advisory committee for Hispanic ministry (*Comité Consejero Católico Hispano*) is an effective coordinating body with a clear vision for ministry.
- An ongoing pastoral planning process and continuity in diocesan leadership have resulted in well-established programs and structures benefiting Hispanic Catholics in a growing number of parishes.

Omaha

- The director of the Office for Hispanic Ministry sits on the cabinet and plays a key role in the overall pastoral planning process in the archdiocese.

- The archdiocese has a well-established Institute for Ministry Formation (*Instituto Pastoral San Juan Diego*).
- The Office for Hispanic Ministry is a highly regarded resource to the community at large on issues related to the Hispanic presence.

Orange

- Ministry among Hispanic youth and young adults has grown consistently and has a very strong diocesan and parish presence.
- Collaboration with civic institutions and organizations on issues affecting Hispanics is high.
- More than 50 percent of all parishes have a comprehensive Hispanic ministry: Liturgy, religious education, service and advocacy, evangelization, and community building programs and activities.

Portland, in Oregon

- There is very strong Hispanic ministry at the parish level, with bilingual priests in fifty-six parishes (a significant number of them have Hispanic lay people on staff).
- The archdiocese has a well-established lay ministry formation program (*Comunidades Evangelizadoras*).
- There is a special grants program to assist parishes in hiring lay people as staff to coordinate Hispanic ministry.

Raleigh

- There is very strong Hispanic ministry at the parish level (sixty-six out of seventy-eight parishes in the diocese have Hispanic ministry).
- Excellent knowledge of the Hispanic presence in the diocese and a clear vision for ministry lead to a timely and highly relevant pastoral planning process for Hispanic ministry.
- Ministry with Hispanic youth and young adults and a lay leadership formation program are ongoing and very successful.

Richmond

- The diocese has a well-established Office for Hispanic Ministry with a strong Hispanic ministry network.

- There is a high level of collaboration with other diocesan offices and agencies, including involvement of Hispanic Catholics in social justice and advocacy activities and events (e.g., lobby days).
- Ministry with Hispanic youth and young adults and a lay leadership formation program are ongoing and very successful.

Salt Lake City

- A very significant percentage of children in Catholic schools is Hispanic (24 percent) in comparison with most dioceses in the country.
- A Diocesan Commission for Hispanic Ministry appointed by the bishop is very effective in providing guidance on the pastoral planning process.
- Ongoing diocesan events and activities provide formation opportunities and resources to a growing number of parishes and apostolic movements ministering among Hispanics in a highly proselytizing environment.

San Bernardino

- Highly educated, bilingual staff head practically every diocesan ministry office and Catholic agency under a clear vision of ministry in a culturally diverse Church.
- Lay ministry formation, catechesis, and leadership programs at the certificate and degree levels are well established and attended.
- Ministry among Hispanic youth and young adults is vibrant in many parishes and diocesan programs and activities.

St. Paul-Minneapolis

- Continuity in Hispanic ministry leadership over an extended period of time has led to a strong Hispanic ministry network with a common vision.
- There is ongoing implementation and evaluation of the *Archdiocesan Pastoral Plan for Hispanic Ministry* with the participation of parish leaders.
- Solid knowledge of the Hispanic presence in the archdiocese is generated and shared in a timely fashion with other ministry offices for further collaboration.

Stockton

- A very effective and collaborative Office for Hispanic Ministry has evolved over the years, and Hispanics sit on various boards and commissions.
- The diocese has a highly developed ministry among migrants with an array of services and resources, including a handbook for migrants.
- Most parishes have a very strong Hispanic ministry including catechesis and ministry with Hispanic youth and young adults.

Washington, D.C.

- There is a comprehensive and highly collaborative *Archdiocesan Pastoral Plan for Hispanic Ministry*.
- Most archdiocesan offices and agencies are equipped with bilingual staff responsible for ministry among Hispanics.
- The archdiocese produces a weekly publication of one of the best Catholic newspapers in the country (*El Pregonero*).

Wilmington

- Continuity in leadership since the creation of the diocesan Office for Hispanic Ministry has led to a strong diocesan ministry network with common vision.
- The pastoral planning process has been consistent, systematic, and consultative over an extended period of time.
- The diocese has seen rapid growth in the number of parishes with Hispanic ministry and the development of ministry among Hispanic youth and young adults.

Yakima

- Besides the Office for Hispanic Ministry, every diocesan ministry office and agency has bilingual staff.
- More than 85 percent of the parishes have Hispanic ministry and a bilingual pastor and/or parish vicar.
- The diocesan office and structure for youth and young adult ministry among Hispanics is highly developed and well integrated with the overall pastoral ministry with young people in the diocese.

References

United States Conference of Catholic Bishops (USCCB). *Encuentro and Mission: A Renewed Pastoral Framework for Hispanic Ministry*. Washington, DC: USCCB, 2002.

USCCB, Committee on the Laity. *Lay Ecclesial Ministry: The State of the Questions*. Washington, DC: USCCB, 1999.

USCCB. *National Pastoral Plan for Hispanic Ministry* (NPPHM; 1987). In *Hispanic Ministry: Three Major Documents*. Bilingual edition. Washington, DC: USCCB, 1995.

Appendix I
The Bishops Speak with the Virgin

A Pastoral Letter of the Hispanic Bishops of the United States

"I have a living desire that there be built a temple, so that in it I can show and give forth all my love, compassion, help and defense, because I am your loving mother: to you, to all who are with you, to all the inhabitants of this land and to all who love me, call upon me and trust in me. I will hear their lamentations and will remedy all their miseries, pains and sufferings."

(Message of Our Lady, December 1531)

GREETINGS

Four hundred and fifty years after Your apparition in our lands, we, Your sons, come as the shepherds of our Hispanic people in the United States of North America. We come full of joy and hope, but we also come saddened and preoccupied with the suffering of our people.

We are the shepherds of a people on the march. Walking with our people, we come to You, Mother of God and our Mother, so that we may receive a renewed spirit. We want to be filled with enthusiasm to go out and proclaim the wonders of God that have taken place in our history, that are taking place at this time in our lives and that will take place in the future.

Although the world has often misunderstood us, You do understand and hold us in esteem. You, too, were always a pilgrim. You were always on the march. You visited Your cousin Elizabeth in the mountains (Lk 1:39-56); Your Son was born at the end of Your long trek from Nazareth to Bethlehem (Lk 2:1-7); You went on pilgrimage to the temple to present Jesus (Lk 2:21-44); You lived in exile as a threatened and pursued stranger (Mt 2:13-15); You returned to Your land after the tyrant King Herod died (Mt 2:19-23); and You again went on the march toward Jerusalem for the Feast of the Passover (Lk 2:41-52). You were present at the beginning and at the end of the ministry of the Lord; at Cana in Galilee, when the signs of the Kingdom were first made manifest (Jn 2:1-12) and at the foot of the Cross (Jn 19:25-27). And here, at the birth of the Americas, You have appeared as a sign from heaven (Apoc 12:1), new life and new light.

You went on all of Your journeys, pilgrimages and marches as a poor woman, at the service of Jesus, of the Kingdom of God, of the poor and those in need. The Spirit covered You. You put the Word of God into practice and You shared the life of Jesus with a believing people. After the death of Jesus, You hoped against all hope and You were called to the heavens as the "favored one of God" (Lk 1:28).

You were the faithful one . . .
You formed the body of Jesus and gave Him to the world . . .
You are the Mother of God and our Mother . . .
You are the Mother of all the inhabitants of these lands . . .
You are the Mother of the Americas!

I. OUR PILGRIMAGE THROUGHOUT HISTORY

Mientras recorres la vida
tu nunca solo estás
contigo por el camino
Santa María va

a. The Birth of a New People

At a unique moment in the history of this world, three radically different and totally unknown worlds met: indigenous America, Africa and Europe.

The clash carried many of the indigenous people to slavery and death, and made them strangers in their own land. The Africans were violently wrenched from their lands and transplanted to far-off countries as slaves. This initiated a shock whose reverberations are experienced even today. There also began at that time a *mestizaje*, an intertwining of blood and culture, that in effect brought about the birth of a new people.

"Do not let your heart be troubled . . . Am I not here who am your Mother?"

(Story of Guadalupe)

"My being proclaims the greatness of the Lord, my spirit finds joy in God my Savior. For he has looked upon his servant in her lowliness; all ages to come shall call me blessed."

(Lk 1:46-48)

The roots of our Latin American reality are grounded in this three-fold inheritance. It is our identity, our suffering, our greatness and our future.

Four hundred and fifty years ago, at the birth of our Latin American *mestizo* race, during the deep and sharp labor pains of our people, our Mother came to be with us.

A great sign came from the sky (Apoc 12:1), *a beautiful woman who visited our lands and spoke to us in our native tongue with gentle love, tenderness and compassion. You are that woman.*

Just as she had been chosen for her littleness and humility, so Mary chose Juan Diego, a humble Indian. From the many she could have chosen, she singled out a poor man.

The faithful child, Juan Diego, listened to his Mother, trusted in her and accepted her command. The bishop asked her for a sign, and she gave it to him *con gusto*—not only beautiful roses but she also gave him the first flower of all flowers: Her image miraculously imprinted on Juan Diego's *tilma*.

"The Lord said: 'I have witnessed the afflictions of my people . . . and have heard their cries of complaint against their slave drivers, so I know well what they are suffering. Therefore I have come down to rescue them. . . .'"

(Ex 3:7-8)

At a painful time in our history, God gave us a great gift—the portrait of His Mother who is also our Mother. Her image is the visible sign of her loving presence among us. A woman with a compassionate face and heart, but whose eyes are sad because she is conscious of the suffering of her people and hears their mourning.

Ever since then You have shared our suffering and joys, our struggles and fiestas, and all of our attempts to bring about the Reign of God. You inspire us, You stir us, and You continue to walk beside us. You are the source of our identity and of the unity of our people in the Americas.

Today we come to You, our Mother, filled with gratitude and admiration, to bring to You the portrait of Your family, to tell you of our life and to share with You the enduring dreams of the Hispanic people of the United States of North America.

"The fact is that the soil of America was prepared to receive the new Christian seeds by movements of its own spirituality."

John Paul II, Santo Domingo, January 25, 1979

---

b. Our Faith

Our ancestors had a strong sense of religiosity. Their lives were centered in their God. They were a people of spiritual values, of wisdom and humanizing customs.

The missionaries brought us the knowledge of a personal God who, through His Son, invites us to a new life. The Gospel purified and enriched the beliefs of our lands.

Because of this, our faith is personal and cultural, because the Word was made flesh on our land when His Mother arrived on the hill of Tepeyac. Little by little, the Gospel has penetrated every aspect of our life and culture. It is the alpha and omega, the center of our very being. Faith penetrates our music, art, poetry, language, customs, *fiestas*—every expression of our life.

Faithful to our tradition we hope that the Gospel continues to transform our life and our culture.

"*The Word became flesh and made its dwelling among us.*"

(Jn 1:14)

---

c. Our Mestizaje

The Hispanic people of the United States of North America is a people of *mestizaje*, an interlacing of the blood and culture of the indigenous, African and European peoples. In the present reality of our people we find a new intertwining: that of the Latin American people and those of the United States. From this second *mestizaje*, the Hispanic American people begin to emerge.

"*It is the Gospel, fleshed out in our peoples, that has brought them together to form the original and historical entity known as Latin America. And this identity is glowingly reflected in the mestizo countenance of Mary of Guadalupe, who appeared at the start of the evangelization process.*"

(Puebla, no. 446)

We are thus a new people and within our very being we combine the cultural riches of our parents. The Virgin of Guadalupe, our *Madrecita mestiza*, comes to fill with joy and blessings the painful and difficult process of our *mestizaje*.

d. Our Cultures

In the shaping of this people, many beautiful values from different cultures have been incorporated, all of which have enriched us today. Our culture is rich in imagery, art, music, dances, food, poetry, even to the point of embodying a certain sense of mischievousness.

Our language is rich in expressions that come from the Gospel. This facilitates the transmission of the Word.

"*The people's religious life is not just an object of evangelization. Insofar as it is a concrete embodiment of the Word of God, it itself is an active way in which the people continually evangelize themselves.*"

(Puebla, no. 450)

Our personal faith is expressed very beautifully: "Mi Padre Dios" [God my Father], "Nuestra Madrecita María" [Our dear Mother Mary], "Nuestro Señor y Hermano Jesucristo" [Our Lord and Brother Jesus Christ], "Mis Santitos" [My little saints]. *A true spiritual environment is fostered in our homes and many houses even become household churches. The little altar with the crucifix, Your statue,* Madrecita, *and our "little saints" hold a special place in the home. The vigil lights and blessed palms speak to us of Your Most Holy Son. Our culture is the expression of the Gospel incarnated in our people and it is a rich form of passing on the divine teachings to new generations.*

e. Our Families

It is almost impossible to explain this great gift from God. Words do not tell the whole story. For us, the meaning of family is extended and includes parents, children, grandparents, aunts and uncles, "distant" relatives, neighbors, godparents, and *compadres*, or intimate friends. The family is the first school of love, tenderness, acceptance, discipline and respect. In our homes we have come to experience the bonds of friendship, mutual support, concern for one another and the presence of God.

We have received from our families the thoughts and values that are the foundation and primary orientation of our lives.

The new Juan Diego who carried the message from heaven to the Church of the United States was also a humble messenger: our mothers and grandmothers. They taught their sons and grandsons to pray while their fathers struggled to earn their daily bread.

Their voice has echoed insistently: "Don't miss Mass," "Marry in the Church," "May God go with you." They have marked our souls with the love of God and have caused Your image of Guadalupe, full of tenderness, to blossom throughout the nation.

Madrecita, You know the miseries and faults of our families. They have not been perfect. But, even with their defects, they have been a great source of security, community and happiness. In the most difficult moments of our march through history, our people have never lost their joy of living. Throughout all of the burdens of life, we sing—even in the midst of pain.

Faith has made us a joyful people. In our *fiestas*, we celebrate the mystery of life that, in its successes and failures, joys and sadness, birth and even death, is a gift from God.

"The family is therefore the principal school of the social virtues which are necessary to every society. It is therefore above all in the Christian family, inspired by the grace and the sacrament of matrimony, that children should be taught to know and worship God and to love their neighbor, in accordance with the faith which they have received in earliest infancy in the sacrament of baptism. In it also, they will have their first experience of a well-balanced human society and of the Church."

(Gravissimum Educationis, no. 3)

---

f. People Who Fill Us with Admiration

Madrecita, *Our history is filled with men and women who have been a great inspiration for us. They have struggled and have given their lives that we might have a better life.*

We give You thanks:

- *for the Indians who suffered the pain of the conquest and who fought for the good of their people;*
- *for the Africans, victims of slavery and humiliation;*
- *for the missionaries You brought from Spain, men of apostolic vision, filled with courage, love and compassion;*
- *for our forgotten heroes, who have remained hidden in obscurity;*
- *for the saints who have blossomed in our lands like the roses of Tepeyac.*

What joy we feel, Madrecita, seeing so many who have brought beauty to our people with the gifts Your Son has given to them:

- *the artists, writers, singers and poets who dream;*
- *the educators, the learned and the technicians;*
- *the businessmen, farmers, professionals and shop owners;*
- *domestic and farm workers;*
- *migrant workers and labor unions who give strength to the voice of the worker;*
- *politicians who truly represent the people;*
- *soldiers who have fought to defend freedom.*

Madrecita, *a very special thanks for the priests and religious, our co-workers in the vineyard of the Lord, who have given themselves to our people and who have truly loved them.*

Without the wealth of their talents and the totality of their commitment, the Gospel of Your Son would not be proclaimed in all its fullness.

We give thanks to God, Madrecita, *for having called us to be the apostles of Your Son in our day. We ask You to walk with us still.*

II. OUR REALITY

Aunque te digan algunos
que nada puede cambiar
lucha por un mundo nuevo
lucha por la verdad

Much has been gained but the suffering continues. We are conscious of the oppression and exploitation of our people. We have seen bodies disfigured by hunger and saddened by the fear of the law; we have heard the cries of abandoned children, mistreated by their own parents. We sense the loneliness of the elderly, ignored by their relatives, and the depression of prisoners whose greatest crime has been the lack of money to pay someone to defend them in court. We have shared the pain and the heat of farm workers and domestic laborers, the invisible slaves of modern society. In the jails and the detention camps, there are some who have come to our country in search of work and freedom, yet who have been considered criminals. We have seen our youth with empty eyes because they have nothing to look forward to in life. We have been with the countless victims of the violence that grows daily in our neighborhoods and even in our families. We will not rest until all injustice is eliminated from our life.

"Christ has delivered us from the power of the law's curse by himself becoming a curse for us, as it is written: 'Accursed is anyone who is hanged on a tree.' This has happened so that through Christ Jesus the blessing bestowed upon Abraham might descend on the Gentiles in Christ Jesus, thereby making it possible for us to receive the promised Spirit through faith."

(Gal 3:13-14)

We have shared with our people the fear that comes from racism and discrimination. The knowledge that we might be rejected, ridiculed or insulted paralyzes us.

Just as Juan Diego accepted his challenge, we now accept ours: that of being artisans of a new people.

"For we do not have a High Priest who is unable to sympathize with our weakness, but one who was tempted in every way that we are, yet never sinned."

(Heb 4:15)

a. Our Identity

We are a people twice *mestizado*. We are in the beginning stages of our life as Hispanic Americans.

Every birth is at one and the same time joy and sadness. Our birth as a people has been the same. Constant rejection has been a part of our daily life.

Nevertheless, our parents taught us to love the United States, although the struggle has been difficult. Our people have always struggled to improve themselves. We love the peace founded on truth, justice, love and freedom [*Pacem in Terris*]. We have not taken up arms against our country but instead have defended it. We have fought to eliminate the injustices that rule our lives. The road has been long and difficult, littered with many obstacles, but we have made progress and will continue ahead with firmness and determination.

b. Our Accomplishments

Morenita, we give You thanks for the many beautiful things that have been happening to us lately.

Our people are beginning to count in society. Their voice is now being heard. Each day they are becoming more responsible for the religious and social structures that shape their life.

Your children have already celebrated pastoral conventions on a national level.

The efforts of the farm workers have brought forth their fruits. Many of our people today enjoy a better life, thanks to the heroic efforts of our leaders.

Fourteen sons of our people have been called to be successors of the Apostles.

Vocations to religious life and to the priesthood are on the rise.

Catholic movements and associations have arisen, dedicated to the social and apostolic progress of our people.

We have Pastoral Centers, dedicated to research, theological reflection, the production of materials and the formation of pastoral leaders.

The bishops have established national and regional offices to serve Your people.

We give thanks to Your Son for all that is being achieved. But we ask Him to give us the strength and courage to continue facing the gigantic problems of our day. As John Paul II said in Mexico, "We want to be the voice of those who have no voice." The poor have the right to our love and special care.

"In each nation and social group there is a growing number of men and women who are conscious that they are the craftsmen and molders of their community's culture. All over the world the sense of autonomy and responsibility increases with effects of the greatest importance for the spiritual and moral maturity of mankind. . . . We are witnessing, then, the birth of a new humanism, where man is defined before all else by his responsibility to his brothers and at the court of history."

(*Gaudium et Spes*, no. 55)

c. Challenges

There are certain challenges in our society which we must meet.

Our betterment in social life does not mean that we forget our roots—our Latin American *mestiza* tradition. The more we value our past, the more strength will we have to launch ourselves toward the building of our future.

Development of a more human life does not mean that we allow ourselves to be enslaved and destroyed by materialism, consumerism, social climbing, the desire for continuous pleasure and immediate gratification. All of this comes from the idolatry of gold. These values are the cancer of society.

The *modernization of the family* does not mean that we abandon the greatest treasure of our Hispanic culture. The family is in great danger today. Divorce is on the rise, the elderly are forgotten and even cheated, children are abandoned and young people make the street their home. The spirit of individualism is killing the spirit of community that is the core of the family.

Christian unity does not mean religious indifference. Ecumenism must not lead us to lose our identity as Catholics. Affirming ecumenism, we reject every type of active proselytizing which is anti-ecumenical and destructive to our people. The great diversity of fundamentalist groups and their anti-Catholic spirit divide our families and our peoples. Our response is not one of fighting against these groups, nor one of speaking ill of them or their intentions, but rather we will take their activities as a challenge to us Catholics to live more authentically and apostolically the life of the Gospel.

III. ARTISANS OF A NEW HUMANITY

Ahora que estamos unidos
juntos en la verdad
danos fuerza te pedimos
fuerza para triunfar

a. A Rediscovery of the Gospel

The greatest strength of our people comes from the rediscovery of the Gospel that is our truth, our way and our life. The power of God in us is this:

- His light illuminating the meaning of our life and the goal of our mission;
- His love transforming our hearts of stone into human hearts;
- His compassion moving us to action;
- His hope encouraging us to continue struggling even when, humanly speaking, there is no hope;
- His strength transforming our weaknesses and converting them into strengths for the good.

"I came that they might have life and have it to the full."

(Jn 10:10)

"I am the Way, the Truth and the Life."

(Jn 14:6)

"Love one another as I have loved you."

(Jn 15:12)

"His heart was moved with pity, and he cured their sick."

(Mt 14:15)

"Father, into your hands I commend my spirit."

(Lk 23:46)

b. A Rebirth of the Church

The word of the Gospel takes human form the more it penetrates, encompasses and ennobles our culture. It is expressed by means of images, symbols, music, art and wisdom. The Church is born out of our response to the word of Jesus. Today we are living a true rebirth of the Hispanic American *mestizo* Church.

"The Lord said to Paul: 'My grace is enough for you, for in weakness power reaches perfection.' And so I willingly boast of my weaknesses instead, that the power of Christ may rest upon me."

(2 Cor 12:9)

"The seed which is the word of God grows out of good soil watered by the divine dew, it absorbs moisture, transforms it, and makes it part of itself, so that eventually it bears much fruit. So too, indeed, just as happened in the economy of the Incarnation, the young churches, which are rooted in Christ and built on the foundations of the apostles, take over all the riches of the nations which have been given to Christ as an inheritance

(cf. Ps 2:8).

They borrow from customs, traditions, wisdom, teaching, arts and sciences of their people, everything which could be used to praise the glory of the Creator, manifest the grace of the Savior, or contribute to the right ordering of Christian life."

(Ad Gentes, no. 22)

"The Church can never be without the lay apostolate; it is something that derives from the layman's very vocation as a Christian."
"Laymen ought to take on themselves as their distinctive task the renewal of the temporal order."

(Apostolicam Actuositatem, nos. 1 & 7)

"United in a CEB and nurturing their adherence to Christ, Christians strive for a more evangelical way of life amid the people, work together to challenge the egotistical and consumeristic roots of society, and make explicit their vocation to communion with God and their fellow humans. Thus they offer a valid and worthwhile point of departure for building up a new society, 'the civilization of love.'"

(Puebla, no. 642)

c. The Life of the Church

Faith comes to us from the Church and calls us to be Church. In time and space, this life of the Church takes various forms depending on concrete needs and conditions. With great joy, we see:

- The birth of new parish life where each member places his or her talents at the service of the community. The wide participation of parishioners in the mission of the Church is the beginning of a new day and the source of great hope for the Church of the future;
- In the renewed parishes, the Church is the natural center of the life of the community. The parish forms leaders and moves the people to work together for the good of all;
- The base communities [comunidades eclesiales de base] cause the individual to experience faith and to feel like Church;
- New family movements and Bible study groups have brought new life to our communities;
- The resurgence of ministries has engendered a new ecclesial life that has incorporated many into the mission of the Church. We are all called to actively take part in the apostolate;
- Permanent deacons, men prepared and ordained for services to the people of God, have renewed the presence of the Church in many places with their dedication and apostolic zeal.

d. Popular Expressions of Faith

The missionaries knew how to understand the Indians, discovering their desires and inclinations in order to make these the basis for evangelization. They made dances expressions of faith.

Pilgrimages and processions offered occasions for teaching Christian doctrine. They created forms such as the *pastorela*, the *posadas* and the *siete palabras* to pass on the biblical message by means of dance, drama, music and art.

These expressions of a Christian people are a true gift of the Spirit and a beautiful treasure of our people. We invite pastoral leaders and catechists to rediscover these values.

"The Catholic Church rejects nothing of what is true and holy in these religions. She has a high regard for the manner of life and conduct, the precepts and doctrines of which, although differing in many ways from her own teaching, nevertheless often reflect a ray of that truth which enlightens all men. Yet she proclaims, and is in duty bounds to proclaim without fail, Christ who is the way, the truth and the life (Jn 1:6)."

(Nostra Aetate, no. 2)

---

e. Catechesis

Religious education continues to be a most important task in the Church. Through it we grow and mature in Christian commitment.

- Catechesis must take into account our Hispanic American tradition.
- Proper methods must be utilized, especially radio and television.
- The preparation and motivation of catechists merit special attention.

Catechists today, as in the time of the missionaries, must be based on the Bible and Church tradition, taking into account the concrete signs of the times, using the methods of our tradition: dramatic interpretations of the Gospel, artistic expression of the mysteries of faith and songs with catechetical content.

"If the Church does not reinterpret the religion of the Latin American people, the resultant vacuum will be occupied by sects, secularized political forms of messianism, consumptionism and its consequences of nausea and indifference, or pagan pansexualism. Once again the Church is faced with stark alternatives: what it does not assume in Christ is not redeemed, and it becomes a new idol replete with all the old malicious cunning."

(Puebla, no. 469)

---

f. Liturgy

The community celebration of faith is the manifestation of the Christian life of the people. So that these celebrations might be authentically those of the people, they ought to incorporate:

- the local language of the people in the prayers, readings and preaching;
- the art of our people in the representations of sacred images.

Some forms of celebration are beginning to emerge today that incorporate these fundamental principles of the Second Vatican Council. We applaud these efforts and we hope that this liturgical dawning may continue glowing and that soon it may come to shine in all its fullness.

"The great challenge posed by the people's piety . . . we must see to it that the liturgy and the people's piety cross-fertilize each other, giving lucid and prudent direction to the impulses of prayer and charismatic vitality that are evident today in our countries. In addition, the religion of the people, with its symbolic and expressive richness, can provide the liturgy with creative dynamism. When examined with proper discernment, this dynamism can incarnate the universal prayer of the Church in our culture in a greater and better way."

(Puebla, no. 465)

g. Theological Reflection

Theology helps to discover how to live and proclaim our faith. Every ecclesial community has the privilege and obligation of discovering the theological meaning of its life.

- We are grateful for the theological contributions of other local ecclesial communities and, in a very special way, we value the inspiration of the theological thought of Latin America.
- Our Hispanic American people are beginning to point out the theological significance of our identity in the United States.
- We invite our people to continue this process.

"It is necessary that in each of the great socio-cultural regions, as they are called, theological investigation should be encouraged and the facts and words revealed by God, contained in sacred Scripture, and explained by the Fathers and Magisterium of the Church, submitted to a new examination in the light of the tradition of the universal Church. In this way it will be more clearly understood by what means the faith can be explained in terms of the philosophy and wisdom of the people, and how their customs, concept of life and social structures can be reconciled with the standard proposed by divine revelation. Thus a way will be opened for a more profound adaptation in the whole sphere of Christian life . . . the Christian life will be adapted to the mentality and character of each culture, and local traditions together with the special qualities of each national family, illuminated by the light of the Gospel, will be taken up into a Catholic unity."

(AG, no. 22)

Each people and every generation has the privilege and the obligation to respond to Jesus' question to Peter: "And who do you say that I am?" (Mt 16:17). The particular response of other local churches enriches us, but at the same time inspires and encourages us to search for our own response. Who is this Jesus who lives and speaks in our Christian people? Together we must search, formulate and proclaim our answer to this question.

h. Vocations

The blossoming of new vocations for our people fills us with joy. However, the number is minimal in relation to the need. This apostolate must grow. Many men and women can respond to the Lord's call.

"The Church is more firmly rooted in a people when the different communities of the faithful have ministers of salvation who are drawn from their own members—bishops, priests and deacons, serving their own brothers—so that these young churches acquire a diocesan structure with their own clergy.

(Ad Gentes, no. 16)

Our Hispanic American *mestizaje* Church will reach maturity when our people have enough vocations not only for our own needs but also for the universal mission of the Church.

"To fulfill my duty to evangelize all of humanity, I myself will never tire of repeating: 'Do not be afraid. Open wide the doors for Christ. To his saving power open the boundaries of State, economic and political systems, the vast fields of culture, civilization and development.'"

(John Paul II, opening address, Puebla, January 28, 1979)

i. A More Authentic Following of Jesus

Christ is our only model and like Him we ought to be ready to commit ourselves and to be steadfast in the proclamation of truth, always filled with compassion and mercy.

Our following of Him demands us to raise our voice when life is threatened, defending and respecting everyone as persons created by God. We are obligated to fight for peace and justice.

Just as He opened up new horizons for us, so too must we raise up the farmworker, the migrant and the laborer. We must aid in the self-improvement of all in search of a better place in society.

IV. A PILGRIMAGE WITH JOY, COURAGE, AND HOPE

The imitation of Christ allows us to see others in their dignity as children of God.

> Ahora que estamos unidos
> juntos en la verdad
> danos fuerza te pedimos
> fuerza para triunfar
> ¡Ven con nosotros a caminar
> Santa María, ven!

We are heading into the 21st Century!

Conscious of all that God has achieved through us, we call on our people to assume an attitude of leadership to create a more human society. We are all the Church, and together we can triumph.

We invite our people to be strong co-workers with us in ministry. Jesus told every one of us: "Go out and proclaim the good news." Christians, by nature, are evangelizers. The lay person, if Christian, evangelizes.

We invite young men and women, especially, to place their enthusiasm, their sense of commitment and their sincerity at the service of the Gospel. May they be young apostolic bearers of the Gospel to the youth of today.

We invite our brother priests to continue living their commitment. Do not be discouraged. We always walk with Jesus. We never go alone. He gives us the strength to be enduring guardians of the faith. May we also care for our traditions and language that are the means of spreading the Gospel. May we form the lay and religious ministers that God gives us, that they may be effective co-workers with us.

We congratulate them on all the good that has been done and we invite them to be the Good Shepherd with us. May they be men of prayer, devoted sons of the *Guadalupana*.

We invite our brother and sister religious to continue giving witness to the value of the life of poverty, chastity and obedience, in a world that values riches, pleasure and power. We commend them because they have been a prophetic voice for justice and peace. We invite them, according to the particular charism of their community, to be united with the efforts of the local church in which they work so that, in conjunction with the bishops and the people of God of that diocese, they may build up the Kingdom of God.

We invite the contemplative religious to continue offering to the Church the strength of their prayers and good example.

We invite our brother deacons to join our efforts, and those of all the clergy, in the apostolate. Faithful to their vocation as deacons, may they be men of service to the people. Let them not forget that the primary field of their apostolate is their home, their community and their place of work.

We challenge seminarians to commit themselves seriously to their studies and spiritual formation. Our people need compassionate priests, with thorough knowledge of the sacred mysteries and a profound sense of the urgency of the social teachings of the Church.

NUESTRO ADIOS

O Mother of the Americas, just as You trusted Juan Diego, we beg you to trust in us, the Hispanic bishops. May You send us to places we are unaccustomed to visit; may You send us to proclaim Your mandate: that a Temple be built wherein we may feel the love and tenderness of our Mother. We want to be the artisans and the builders of this new Temple—a society in which all will be able to live as brothers and sisters. We want to build up the Kingdom of God, where peace is found because hate, jealousy, lies, dissension, and every kind of injustice will have disappeared.

Madre de Dios—*Mother of God*
Madre de la Iglesia—*Mother of the Church*
Madre de las Américas—*Mother of the Americas*
Madre de todos nosotros—*Mother of us all*
Ruega por nosotros—*Pray for us*

Most Reverend Patricio Flores
Archbishop of San Antonio

Most Reverend Roberto Sánchez
Archbishop of Santa Fe

Most Reverend Rene H. Gracida
Bishop of Pensacola-Tallahasee

Most Reverend Joseph J. Madera
Bishop of Fresno

Most Reverend Manuel Moreno
Bishop of Tucson

Most Reverend Raymond Peña
Bishop of El Paso

Most Reverend Arthur Tafoya
Bishop of Pueblo

Most Reverend Juan Arzube
Auxiliary Bishop of Los Angeles

Most Reverend Gilbert Chavez
Auxiliary Bishop of San Diego

Most Reverend Alphonse Gallegos
Auxiliary Bishop of Sacramento

Most Reverend Francisco Garmendia
Auxiliary Bishop of New York

Most Reverend Ricardo Ramirez
Auxiliary Bishop of San Antonio

Most Reverend Agustín Román
Auxiliary Bishop of Miami

Most Reverend Rene Valero
Auxiliary Bishop of Brooklyn

Appendix II
Letter of the Hispanic/Latino Bishops to Immigrants

The Hispanic/Latino Bishops of the United States greeted us early today, the Feast of Our Lady of Guadalupe, with their own very special version of the "Mañanitas," a letter to immigrants. Signed by 33 bishops, the letter was released simultaneously from Los Angeles and San Antonio, the sees of the two highest ranking Hispanic archbishops.

The full text of the letter along with the signatories is reproduced below.

ESTAS SON LAS MAÑANITAS... OF THE HISPANIC BISHOPS

Dear immigrant sisters and brothers,
May the peace and grace of Our Lord Jesus Christ be with all of you!

We the undersigned Hispanic/Latino Bishops of the United States wish to let those of you who lack proper authorization to live and work in our country know that you are not alone, or forgotten. We recognize that every human being, authorized or not, is an image of God and therefore possesses infinite value and dignity. We open our arms and hearts to you, and we receive you as members of our Catholic family. As pastors, we direct these words to you from the depths of our heart.

In a very special way we want to thank you for the Christian values you manifest to us with your lives—your sacrifice for the well-being of your families, your determination and perseverance, your joy of life, your profound faith and fidelity despite your insecurity and many difficulties. You contribute much to the welfare of our nation in the economic, cultural and spiritual arenas.

The economic crisis has had an impact on the entire U.S. community. Regretfully, some in reaction to this environment of uncertainty show disdain for immigrants and even blame them for the crisis. We will not find a solution to our problems by sowing hatred. We will find the solution by sowing a sense of solidarity among all workers and co-workers—immigrants and citizens—who live together in the United States.

In your suffering faces we see the true face of Jesus Christ. We are well aware of the great sacrifice you make for your families' well-being. Many of you perform the most difficult jobs and receive miserable salaries and no health insurance or social security. Despite your contributions to the well-being of our country, instead of receiving our thanks, you are often treated as criminals because you have violated current immigration laws.

We are also very aware of the pain suffered by those families who have experienced the deportation of one of their members. We are conscious of the frustration of youth and young adults who have grown up in this country and whose dreams are shattered because they lack legal immigration status. We also know of the anxiety of those whose application process for permanent residency is close to completion and of the anguish of those who live daily under the threat of deportation. This situation cries out to God for a worthy and humane solution.

We acknowledge that, at times, actions taken in regard to immigrants have made you feel ignored or abandoned, especially when no objection is raised to the false impressions that are promoted within our society. Through the United States Conference of Catholic Bishops we have testified before the U.S. Congress for change in our immigration laws and for legislation that respects family unity and provides an orderly and reasonable process for unauthorized persons to attain citizenship. The new law should include a program for worker visas that respects the immigrants' human rights, provides for their basic needs and ensures that they enter our country and work in a safe and orderly manner. We will also continue to advocate on behalf of global economic justice, so that our brothers and sisters can find employment opportunities in their countries of origin that offer a living wage, and allow them to live with dignity.

Immigrants are a revitalizing force for our country. The lack of a just, humane and effective reform of immigration laws negatively affects the common good of the entire United States.

It pains and saddens us that many of our Catholic brothers and sisters have not supported our petitions for changes in the immigration law that will protect your basic rights while you contribute your hard work to our country. We promise to keep working to bring about this change. We know how difficult the journey is to reach the border and to enter the United States. That is why we are committed to do all that we can to bring about a change in the immigration law, so that you can enter and remain here legally and not feel compelled to undertake a dangerous journey in order to support and provide for your families. As pastors concerned for your welfare, we ask you to consider seriously whether it is advisable to undertake the journey here until after just and humane changes occur in our immigration laws.

Nevertheless, we are not going to wait until the law changes to welcome you who are already here into our churches, for as St. Paul tells us, "You are no longer aliens or foreign visitors; you are fellow-citizens with the holy people of God and part of God's household" (Eph 2:19).

As members of the Body of Christ which is the Church, we offer you spiritual nourishment. Feel welcome to Holy Mass, the Eucharist, which nourishes us with the word and the body and blood of Jesus. We offer you catechetical programs for your children and those religious education programs that our diocesan resources allow us to put at your disposal.

We who are citizens and permanent residents of this country cannot forget that almost all of us, we or our ancestors, have come from other lands and together with immigrants from various nations and cultures, have formed a new nation. Now we ought to open our hearts and arms to the recently arrived, just as Jesus asks us to do when he says, "I was hungry and you gave me to eat; I was thirsty and you gave me to drink; I was an alien and you took me into your house" (Mt 25:35). These words of the Lord Jesus can be applied to the new immigrants among us. They were hungry in their land of origin; they were thirsty as they traveled through the deserts, and they find themselves among us as aliens. (See Daniel G. Groody, CSC, "Crossing the Line," in *The Way*, Vol. 43, No. 2, April 2004, p. 58-69). Their presence challenges us to be more courageous in denouncing the injustices they suffer. In imitation of Jesus and the great prophets we ought to denounce the forces that oppress them and announce the good news of the Kingdom with our works of charity. Let us pray and struggle to make it possible for these brothers and sisters of ours to have the same opportunities from which we have benefited.

We see Jesus the pilgrim in you migrants. The Word of God migrated from heaven to earth in order to become man and save humanity. Jesus emigrated with Mary and Joseph to Egypt, as a refugee. He migrated from Galilee to Jerusalem for the sacrifice of the cross, and finally he emigrated from death to life in the resurrection and ascension to heaven. Today, he continues to journey and accompany all migrants on pilgrimage throughout the world in search of food, work, dignity, security and opportunities for the welfare of their families.

You reveal to us the supreme reality of life: we are all migrants. Your migration gives a strong and clear message that we are migrants on the way to eternal life. Jesus accompanies all Christians on our journey toward the house of our Father, God's Kingdom in heaven (see Pope John Paul II, *Tertio Millennio Adveniente*, no. 50).

We urge you not to despair. Keep faith in Jesus the migrant who continues to walk beside you. Have faith in Our Lady of Guadalupe who constantly repeats to us the words she spoke to St. Juan Diego, "Am I, who am your mother, not here?" She never abandons us, nor does St. Joseph who protects us as he did the Holy Family during their emigration to Egypt.

As pastors we want to continue to do advocacy for all immigrants. With St. Paul we say to you: "Do not be mastered by evil; but master evil with good" (Rom 12:21).

May Almighty God, Father, Son and Holy Spirit, accompany you and bless you always.

Sincerely in Christ our Savior,
The Hispanic/Latino Bishops of the United States

Most Rev. José H. Gómez
Archbishop of Los Angeles

Most Rev. Gustavo García-Siller, MSpS
Archbishop of San Antonio

Most Rev. Gerald R. Barnes
Bishop of San Bernardino

Most Rev. Alvaro Corrada del Rio, SJ
Apostolic Administrator of Tyler
Bishop of Mayaguez, PR

Most Rev. Felipe de Jesús Estevez
Bishop of St. Augustine

Most Rev. Richard J. García
Bishop of Monterey

Most Rev. Armando X. Ochoa
Apostolic Administrator of El Paso
Bishop-designate of Fresno

Most Rev. Plácido Rodríguez, CMF
Bishop of Lubbock

Most Rev. James A. Tamayo
Bishop of Laredo

Most Rev. Raymundo J. Peña
Bishop Emeritus of Brownsville

Most Rev. Arthur Tafoya
Bishop Emeritus of Pueblo

Most Rev. Daniel E. Flores
Bishop of Brownsville

Most Rev. Fernando Isern, DD
Bishop of Pueblo

Most Rev. Ricardo Ramírez
Bishop of Las Cruces

Most Rev. Jaime Soto
Bishop of Sacramento

Most Rev. Joe S. Vásquez
Bishop of Austin

Most Rev. Carlos A. Sevilla, SJ
Bishop Emeritus of Yakima

Most Rev. Oscar Cantú, STD
Auxiliary Bishop of San Antonio

Most Rev. Arturo Cepeda
Auxiliary Bishop of Detroit

Most Rev. Manuel A. Cruz
Auxiliary Bishop of Newark

Most Rev. Rutilio del Riego
Auxiliary Bishop of San Bernardino

Most Rev. Eusebio Elizondo, MSpS
Auxiliary Bishop of Seattle

Most Rev. Francisco González, SF
Auxiliary Bishop of Washington

Most Rev. Eduardo A. Nevares
Auxiliary Bishop of Phoenix

Most Rev. Alexander Salazar
Auxiliary Bishop of Los Angeles

Most Rev. David Arias, OAR
Auxiliary Bishop Emeritus of Newark

Most Rev. Octavio Cisneros, DD
Auxiliary Bishop of Brooklyn

Most. Rev. Edgar M. da Cunha, SDV
Auxiliary Bishop of Newark

Most Rev. Cirilo B. Flores
Auxiliary Bishop of Orange

Most Rev. Josu Iriondo
Auxiliary Bishop of New York

Most Rev. Alberto Rojas
Auxiliary Bishop of Chicago

Most Rev. Luis Rafael Zarama
Auxiliary Bishop of Atlanta

Most Rev. Gabino Zavala
Auxiliary Bishop of Los Angeles

Feast of Our Lady of Guadalupe, December 12, 2011

Ministerio Hispano/Latino—Pasado, Presente, Futuro

Un Nuevo Comienzo

Edición Especial de Aniversario

Presentación

El año 2012 marca un nuevo comienzo en el ministerio hispano/latino: una mayoría de edad en la cual los líderes católicos de descendencia hispana/latina toman en serio el llamado a proveer liderazgo a toda la Iglesia en Estados Unidos.

Este nuevo comienzo se destaca por una serie de aniversarios importantes que han hecho del ministerio hispano/latino una parte integral de la historia de la Iglesia y de su misión evangelizadora, en los últimos cuarenta años.

Uno de estos aniversarios es la celebración del *Primer Encuentro Nacional del Ministerio Hispano*, en 1972. Este evento novedoso fue la chispa que puso en marcha el ministerio entre los hispano/latinos hace cuarenta años y lo definió como un ministerio de acompañamiento en el cual los ministros entran en la vida de los hispano/latinos, caminando con ellos y escuchando sus preocupaciones, para que a su vez los ministros puedan compartir la Buena Nueva de Cristo Vivo con sus compañeros, llevándolos a reconocer al Señor en la vida litúrgica de la comunidad y a participar en su misión.

Este modelo de ministerio de acompañamiento ha inspirado todos los encuentros y documentos posteriores del ministerio hispano/latino, incluyendo el "Plan Pastoral Nacional para el Ministerio Hispano" en 1987, y "Encuentro y Misión: Un Marco Pastoral Renovado para el Ministerio Hispano" en 2002.

Al celebrar en el 2012 los respectivos 25° y 10° aniversario de estos documentos, estamos agradecidos de que esta nueva etapa del ministerio hispano/latino se fundamente en una base sólida que ha producido mucho fruto.

En este momento de gracia, de aniversarios y nuevos comienzos, nosotros, los obispos de los Estados Unidos, ofrecemos esta edición especial de documentos de la Conferencia de Obispos Católicos de Estados Unidos sobre el ministerio hispano/latino, para acompañar a toda una nueva generación de católicos que se forman para el ministerio hoy. Los documentos tienen un énfasis en la Nueva Evangelización proclamada por los Papas Juan Pablo II y Benedicto XVI.

Esta publicación proporciona una oportunidad para reflexionar con gratitud sobre el pasado del ministerio hispano/latino, y todo lo que se ha logrado en los últimos años. También proporciona una oportunidad para llevar adelante nuestros ministerios presentes con renovado entusiasmo, y reconocer futuras oportunidades ministeriales con una mayor esperanza.

Los documentos contenidos en esta publicación enfatizan la llamada urgente a una nueva evangelización:

Encuentro y Misión: Un Marco Pastoral Renovado para el Ministerio Hispano (2002) hace un llamado a todos los ministros a ser *gente-puente* entre culturas, y desarrollar nuevos modelos de ministerio para llevar la Buena Nueva de Cristo a la segunda generación de jóvenes hispano/latinos.

Muchos Rostros en la Casa de Dios: Una Visión Católica para el Tercer Milenio (1999) hace énfasis en nuestra identidad católica común y el llamado a una hospitalidad transformadora que nos permita ser un solo Cuerpo de Cristo y aún viniendo de diversas culturas y etnicidades.

La Presencia Hispana en la Nueva Evangelización en los Estados Unidos (1996) pone de relieve la contribución única los católicos hispanos/latinos pueden hacer para el diálogo entre fe y cultura, que está en el corazón mismo de la Nueva Evangelización.

El *Plan Pastoral Nacional para el Ministerio Hispano* (1987) propone un modelo de Iglesia evangelizadora, comunitaria y misionera, y hace del ministerio hispano/latino parte integral de la vida y misión de la Iglesia.

La Presencia Hispana: Esperanza y Compromiso (1983) llama a los Hispanos "bendición de Dios" y afirma su cultural católica incluyendo: una profunda fe en Dios, fuerte valoración de la familia, autentica devoción Mariana y sentido de hospitalidad y fiesta en agradecimiento a Dios por el don de la vida.

Estudio sobre las Mejores Prácticas de Ministerios Diocesanos entre Hispanos/Latinos (2006) ofrece ejemplos de éxito en el ministerio diocesano, basado en elementos claves como la visión ministerial, la estructura, el desarrollo continuo, recursos y colaboración.

Esta edición especial también incluye dos cartas escritas por los obispos hispanos/latinos: *Los Obispos Hablan con la Virgen* (1981) presenta una conversación entre los obispos y Nuestra Señora de Guadalupe, haciéndose eco de la promesa de Nuestra Señora de cuidar, proteger y acompañar a los católicos hispano/latinos en su jornada de vida en Estados Unidos.

Carta de los Obispos Hispanos/Latinos a los Inmigrantes (2011). Los obispos expresan a los inmigrantes indocumentados su compromiso de caminar con ellos en la solidaridad, ofreciéndoles sus cuidados pastorales sin condiciones y haciéndolos sentir bienvenidos mientras se enfrentan a la persecución, la deportación y la discriminación. Esta carta es también un llamado a la reconciliación.

Todos estos documentos han sido útiles en la articulación de la respuesta de la Iglesia a la presencia hispano/latina. También han articulado los aportes de los católicos hispanos/latinos como miembros activos de la Iglesia.

Celebramos los dones y los frutos de esta respuesta mutua como una bendición de Dios, porque así como somos misioneros hacia los nuevos inmigrantes en nuestras propias parroquias, escuelas y otras instituciones católicas, los nuevos inmigrantes también son misioneros para nosotros, trayendo con ellos la presencia única de Dios a través de su fe inquebrantable, y su búsqueda constante de Jesucristo vivo y sus promesas.

Hoy en día, millones de católicos hispanos/latinos se sienten como en casa en más de cinco mil parroquias. Movimientos laicos eclesiales también unen a millones a través de retiros, conferencias y miles de pequeñas comunidades. Prácticamente todos los años, nuevos obispos, sacerdotes, religiosos y religiosas, y ministros eclesiales laicos de descendencia hispana/latina se suman al ministerio de nuestra Iglesia, cada vez más diversa culturalmente.

Sin embargo, nunca antes ha sido tan urgente para todos los ministerios el servir a los hispanos/latinos en parroquias, escuelas y otras instituciones católicas. También ha sido de igual importancia para los ministros hispanos/latinos el desafío de llegar a los católicos de diferentes orígenes culturales y étnicos en el espíritu de la Nueva Evangelización.

Los líderes católicos hispanos/latinos están muy conscientes de que su liderazgo es de suma importancia para el presente y futuro de toda la Iglesia en nuestro país. De ahí su compromiso con un nuevo comienzo en el ministerio hispano/latino, en el espíritu de la Nueva Evangelización y en las manos confiables de María, Madre de Dios y Madre de la Iglesia.

Nuestra oración y esperanza es que esta edición especial de documentos sobre el Ministerio Hispano/Latino sea fuente de inspiración, orientación y acompañamiento para los líderes hispanos/latinos y para todos los líderes católicos, en su visión de llevar la Buena Nueva de Cristo a toda situación humana en Estados Unidos y en el mundo.

Fraternalmente en Cristo,

Rev. Mons. Gerald Barnes
Obispo de San Bernardino
Presidente, Subcomité de Asuntos Hisponos

Encuentro y Misión

*Un Marco Pastoral Renovado
para el Ministerio Hispano*

El documento *Encuentro y Misión: Un Marco Pastoral Renovado para el Ministerio Hispano* fue elaborado por el Comité para Asuntos Hispanos de la Conferencia de Obispos Católicos de Estados Unidos (USCCB). El documento fue aprobado por el cuerpo de obispos católicos de Estados Unidos durante su Reunión General en noviembre de 2002 y ha sido autorizado para su publicación por el suscrito.

Monseñor William P. Fay
Secretario General
USCCB

Prefacio

1. Nosotros, los obispos de Estados Unidos, hemos escuchado las voces de los líderes hispanos —de los laicos y del clero. Afirmamos especialmente aquellos esfuerzos pastorales en el ministerio hispano que fomentan el objetivo general y las dimensiones específicas del Plan Pastoral Nacional para el Ministerio Hispano ("Plan Pastoral Nacional" o "Plan Pastoral") de 1987. Esta declaración pastoral, *Encuentro y misión: Un marco pastoral renovado para el ministerio Hispano*, está dirigida a todos los católicos, particularmente a los líderes pastorales involucrados en el ministerio con los hispanos. Esta declaración pastoral ofrece principios pastorales básicos, prioridades, y acciones sugeridas para continuar esfuerzos en el ministerio hispano, a la vez que fortalece la unidad de la Iglesia en Estados Unidos. Para asegurar la continuidad en el ministerio con los hispanos, *Encuentro y Misión* sirve como un adendum del Plan Pastoral Nacional y está diseñado como un marco pastoral renovado para ayudar a las diócesis, parroquias, y organizaciones e instituciones católicas en su respuesta a la presencia hispana. Por lo tanto, *Encuentro y Misión* es un marco pastoral para continuar desarrollando el ministerio hispano.

2. Los títulos seleccionados para las secciones de esta declaración pastoral están inspirados en la Carta Pastoral del Papa Juan Pablo II *Novo Millennio Ineunte*, en la cual el Santo Padre se hace eco de la invitación de Jesús a los apóstoles a "remar mar adentro" para pescar —*"Duc in altum"*. Estas palabras resuenan también hoy para nosotros y nos invitan a recordar con gratitud el pasado del ministerio hispano, a vivir con pasión los desafíos y oportunidades de hoy, y a abrirnos con confianza al futuro. Estas palabras también han encontrado eco entre los líderes del ministerio hispano que leen los signos de los tiempos, aprovechan la oportunidad para la acción, y expanden la visión del ministerio hispano a fin de responder a la presencia hispana dentro de Estados Unidos en un contexto culturalmente diverso.

3. Los principios pastorales y prioridades básicas, y las acciones sugeridas, que se incluyen en esta declaración pastoral, surgen de la realidad del ministerio hispano. Sin embargo, también pueden servir de instrumento a todas las comunidades y ministerios, que buscan, responder a los desafíos y oportunidades con que se enfrenta la Iglesia en Estados Unidos debido a la diversidad de culturas en nuestras comunidades de fe.

Introducción

4. **En febrero de 2001**, el Comité para Asuntos Hispanos convocó a los líderes del ministerio hispano a un simposio nacional en Colorado Springs, Colorado. El propósito del simposio era evaluar y desarrollar más ampliamente los esfuerzos en el ministerio hispano y, al mismo tiempo, fortalecer la unidad del Cuerpo de Cristo en nuestras comunidades siempre crecientes y culturalmente diversas. El comité de obispos, muy consciente de los matices y desafíos pastorales que enfrenta la Iglesia, solicitó a los líderes que revisaran las prioridades pastorales existentes a la luz de los valores y principios del *Plan Pastoral Nacional para el Ministerio Hispano* de 1987,[1] Encuentro 2000: Muchos Rostros en la Casa de Dios,[2] los desafíos pastorales de *Ecclesia in America*,[3] la Nueva Evangelización,[4] y los recientes datos demográficos sobre la presencia hispana en Estados Unidos.

5. El Simposio Nacional, cuyo objetivo fue reenfocar el ministerio hispano, incluyó la participación de sesenta representantes de organizaciones hispanas católicas a nivel nacional y regional, y representantes de los departamentos de Migración y Servicios a los Refugiados, la Campaña Católica para el Desarrollo Humano; el Secretariado para la Familia, los Laicos, las Mujeres y los Jóvenes; y el Secretariado para la Evangelización, de la USCCB.

6. La declaración pastoral, *Encuentro y Misión*, es nuestra respuesta a las voces del liderazgo en el ministerio hispano y a la presencia hispana al inicio del nuevo milenio. Los católicos hispanos son una bendición de Dios y una presencia profética que ha convertido a muchas diócesis y parroquias en unas comunidades de fe más acogedoras, vibrantes, y evangelizadoras. Nosotros, los obispos, consideramos al ministerio hispano como parte integral de la vida y la misión de la Iglesia.

EL CRECIMIENTO DEL MINISTERIO HISPANO

7. El ministerio hispano ha experimentado un tremendo crecimiento en Estados Unidos desde mediados de los años 80. Este crecimiento ocurrió durante la experiencia de los tres Encuentros nacionales, la elaboración del Plan Pastoral, el aumento del número de organizaciones hispanas católicas y el incremento de los esfuerzos pastorales en las diócesis y parroquias para acoger y servir a los católicos hispanos. Nuestra respuesta a la presencia hispana,[5] junto con las voces y acciones proféticas de los católicos hispanos en todo el país, han llevado al ministerio hispano a un cruce de caminos al inicio de un nuevo siglo. Hoy, el ministerio hispano enfrenta dos interrogantes principales. Primero, ¿qué modelo de liderazgo ofrecerán los católicos hispanos, quienes se están convirtiendo progresivamente en una fuerte presencia dentro de la Iglesia Católica en Estados Unidos? Segundo, ¿en qué forma fortalecerá este modelo la unidad del cuerpo de Cristo en comunidades cada vez más diversas culturalmente?

UNA RESPUESTA A LAS COMUNIDADES CULTURALMENTE DIVERSAS

8. Como respuesta a los desafíos que se encuentran al servir a comunidades culturalmente diversas y, en especial, a la comunidad hispana, convocamos a un encuentro nacional intercultural durante el Año del Jubileo. El Comité para Asuntos Hispanos y los católicos hispanos fueron los anfitriones y los líderes de este evento histórico llamado

Encuentro 2000: Muchos Rostros en la Casa de Dios, el cual se realizó en Los Angeles, California, en julio de 2000. Encuentro 2000 fue la primera vez que la Iglesia en Estados Unidos se reunía para reconocer, afirmar, y celebrar la diversidad cultural y racial de sus miembros. Con la participación de más de cinco mil líderes que representaban los muchos rostros de la Iglesia —procedentes de 150 diócesis y 157 grupos étnicos y nacionalidades diferentes[6]— Encuentro 2000 inspiró y desafió a los católicos en Estados Unidos a abrazar una visión católica para el tercer milenio, en la cual todos sean bienvenidos a la mesa del Padre.

UNA NUEVA FASE PARA EL MINISTERIO HISPANO

9. Estamos conscientes de que la implementación de los valores y principios de Encuentro 2000 es un proceso a largo plazo, un proceso para construir unidad y solidaridad entre todos los católicos. La presencia hispana recuerda a la Iglesia que las personas de distintas nacionalidades traen consigo bellos y útiles dones que, generalmente, son bien recibidos por toda la comunidad. También nos recuerda que hemos sido llamados a "acoger al forastero entre nosotros"[7] y a construir comunidades de fe más acogedoras, evangelizadoras y misioneras.

10. Para el ministerio hispano, la fase nueva deberá incluir un mayor desarrollo en tres áreas fundamentales: (1) en las estructuras y redes ministeriales; (2) en la construcción de relaciones ministeriales y colaboración; y (3) en la participación activa. Las estructuras y redes ministeriales que han servido efectivamente a la pastoral hispana, como las oficinas diocesanas y regionales, y los institutos pastorales, deberán ser fortalecidas. El ministerio hispano deberá desarrollar una relación y colaboración más estrecha con los diversos grupos y organizaciones étnicas, raciales, y ministeriales. Además, los esfuerzos ministeriales deberán fomentar la participación activa de los hispanos católicos en la misión social de la Iglesia.

Recordar con gratitud *el pasado*

MEMORIA HISTÓRICA DEL MINISTERIO HISPANO

11. **Los líderes del ministerio hispano** han generado una *memoria histórica* y una identidad singular desde 1945 cuando, por primera vez, se estableció una oficina nacional para el ministerio hispano. Algunos aspectos de esta identidad han sido expresados en los temas de los Encuentros: *Pueblo de Dios en Marcha, Voces Proféticas, Muchos Rostros en la Casa de Dios*. Los obispos hemos recogido la rica historia de los católicos hispanos en Estados Unidos en nuestras publicaciones de las conclusiones del I, II, y III Encuentros, así como en muchas otras publicaciones.[8]

12. Ya que los católicos hispanos son una bendición para toda la Iglesia en Estados Unidos y el ministerio hispano es una parte integral de su misión, es importante apreciar y recibir con agrado las contribuciones hechas por esta comunidad. Los católicos hispanos han desarrollado una visión de ministerio inspirada por el contexto social y eclesiológico del Concilio Vaticano II en Estados Unidos y en América Latina. Esta visión está articulada en el Plan Pastoral como un modelo de Iglesia que busca fortalecer la comunión y la participación, enfatizando fuertemente la evangelización, la justicia social y la educación integral de los fieles. Todos los líderes de la Iglesia están llamados a traer a los hispanos, y a todos los demás católicos, a un amor más profundo por Jesucristo, por la fe católica, y por María, la madre de Dios. Además, el Plan Pastoral pide una evaluación de las necesidades de los fieles, el establecimiento de prioridades y el desarrollo de estrategias a fin de responder a las necesidades y aspiraciones de los hispanos/latinos en Estados Unidos. La visión del Plan Pastoral Nacional y su continua implementación, han ayudado a generar una visión de ministerio que va más allá de la comunidad hispana. Esta visión universal se expresa en la Guía para Parroquias del Encuentro 2000, *Muchos Rostros en la Casa de Dios*[9] como una visión católica para el nuevo milenio. *Muchos Rostros en la Casa de Dios* busca fortalecer la unidad del cuerpo de Cristo, a la vez que honra y celebra la diversidad cultural de la Iglesia.

13. A través de los años, los líderes del ministerio hispano han identificado valores y principios que han guiado el desarrollo de sus esfuerzos pastorales y han constituido su memoria histórica. Varios de los valores y principios más fundamentales se enumeran aquí.

1. Una fe, cultura e idioma comunes

14. Los hispanos emergen de una mezcla de diferentes razas y culturas, lo que ha resultado en un pueblo nuevo. Aunque los hispanos encuentran que sus ancestros vinieron de diferentes países, la mayoría comparte una fe y un idioma común, así como una cultura enraizada en la fe católica. Estos elementos, que dan una identidad común a los pueblos de América Latina y del Caribe, son aún más importantes para los hispanos en Estados Unidos, pues son ellos quienes luchan por definir su propia identidad dentro de un contexto culturalmente diverso y bajo la presión de la asimilación. El compromiso de los hispanos a ser participantes activos en la vida de la Iglesia y la sociedad, y a ofrecer sus singulares contribuciones, a la misma, en vez de simplemente *asimilarse*, ha sido un valor y principio primordial para los hispanos en el ministerio.

2. Una cultura que nació católica

15. Desde que los primeros misioneros españoles trajeron la fe católica al nuevo continente, muchos de los valores del Evangelio y las tradiciones de la Iglesia se fueron inculturando en el pueblo nuevo de América Latina. Estos valores incluyen una profunda fe en Dios, un fuerte sentido de solidaridad, una auténtica devoción mariana, y una rica religiosidad popular. Los hispanos tienen un profundo respeto por la persona humana y le dan más valor a las relaciones que a los trabajos o posesiones. Las relaciones personales son el núcleo de una espiritualidad de *encuentro* y de la necesidad de desarrollar fuertes vínculos familiares, comunitarios, y parroquiales. Los hispanos entienden que la cultura es parte integral de la persona humana y, por tanto, ésta debe ser respetada y honrada.[10]

3. Una profunda vocación eclesial

16. Los hispanos tienen una profunda vocación eclesial que los lleva a trabajar arduamente para pertenecer a la Iglesia de una manera más significativa. Esto se ha puesto de manifiesto en el proceso de los Encuentros Nacionales, de la Convocación '95, y de otros eventos importantes que convocamos y que fueron reafirmados por la Santa Sede. Esta vocación eclesial ha elevado el nivel de concientización sobre la presencia hispana, como una población que continuará influenciando e impactando a la Iglesia en el futuro. El deseo de fomentar la colaboración con los ministerios de otras comunidades étnicas, ha fortalecido la identidad eclesial de los católicos hispanos. Más importante aún, es que este deseo define al ministerio hispano como realidad integral de la misión de la Iglesia y como factor clave para su futuro.

4. Un modelo profético de Iglesia

17. Los líderes del ministerio hispano, en comunión con los obispos de Estados Unidos, han articulado un modelo de Iglesia que está enraizado profundamente en la realidad del pueblo hispano. Como tal, este modelo busca responder a las necesidades y aspiraciones de los pobres, los indocumentados, los trabajadores migrantes, los encarcelados, y los más vulnerables, particularmente mujeres y niños. Este modelo profético llama a un firme compromiso por la justicia social, a la defensa de los intereses y la acción a favor de las nuevas familias inmigrantes y de los jóvenes, y a facultar a los hispanos y a todos los católicos a participar plenamente en la vida de la Iglesia y la sociedad.

5. Un liderazgo entendido como discipulado

18. Desde el I Encuentro Nacional (1972), los católicos hispanos entienden el liderazgo como discipulado, y el ministerio pastoral como seguimiento. Este modelo de liderazgo en el ministerio, basado en el llamado de Jesús a seguirlo a él, tiene dos dimensiones. La primera es el encuentro con Cristo, el cual lleva a la conversión y a una relación personal con el Señor. Esta relación con Cristo genera una mística y una espiritualidad que impregnan cada aspecto de la vida-jornada de los fieles como miembros de la Iglesia. El segundo elemento del seguimiento es el compromiso de seguir a Jesús para continuar su misión de ser fermento para el reino de Dios en el mundo.

6. *Una pastoral de conjunto* (comunión en misión)

19. El principio de *pastoral de conjunto* (comunión en misión) ha sido clave para incorporar el ministerio hispano en las diócesis y parroquias.[11]

20. La pastoral de conjunto ha llevado al fomento de las oficinas diocesanas para el ministerio hispano y al incremento del número de parroquias que sirven a los hispanos. A la fecha, más del 75 por ciento de las diócesis tiene una oficina para el ministerio hispano, y casi cuatro mil parroquias brindan servicios pastorales en español.[12] Además, la pastoral de conjunto ha ayudado a fomentar el desarrollo y el crecimiento en el número de organizaciones hispanas católicas y movimientos apostólicos. El principio de la pastoral de conjunto puede servir de modelo a toda la Iglesia promoviendo un ministerio colaborativo como una herramienta eficaz para cumplir con la misión de la Iglesia. Las oficinas regionales para el ministerio hispano, las organizaciones católicas y los movimientos apostólicos a nivel nacional han sido eficaces promotores de este principio al trabajar con la iglesia local.

7. Un proceso de consulta

21. Desde el I Encuentro Nacional (1972), los hispanos han utilizado una metodología de discernimiento pastoral que se enfoca en las necesidades y aspiraciones de los fieles, juzga esa realidad a la luz de las Escrituras y la Tradición, y se concretiza en acción transformadora. Esa metodología, conocida como VER—JUZGAR—ACTUAR—CELEBRAR—EVALUAR, ha generado un pensamiento crítico y un firme compromiso, de parte del liderazgo, con la misión de la Iglesia. Esta metodología también ha conducido a estrategias y a acciones pastorales que

son relevantes, oportunas y efectivas. A través de los años, los componentes de celebración y evaluación han servido de mucha ayuda en la renovación y redirección de los esfuerzos del ministerio hispano. Esta metodología ha sido aplicada en el contexto de un proceso de consulta que fomenta la participación y obra bajo la suposición de que *la manera de hacer* las cosas es tan importante como *las cosas en sí*.

Muchos Rostros en la Casa de Dios

Una Visión Católica para el Tercer Milenio

En noviembre de 1997, la National Conference of Catholic Bishops aprobó la petición del Comité de Obispos para Asuntos Hispanos de que los obispos estadounidenses convocaran un cuarto encuentro nacional en el Jubileo del Año 2000. *Encuentro 2000* parte desde los tres encuentros anteriores, y toma en consideración los desafíos pastorales y las realidades demográficas de hoy. En noviembre de 1998, el Comité de Obispos para Asuntos Hispanos aprobó la publicación bilingüe *Encuentro 2000*, **Muchos Rostros en la Casa de Dios: Una Visión Católica para el Tercer Milenio,** como una guía parroquial para facilitar la implementación del proceso del *Encuentro 2000* a nivel local y su publicación fue autorizada por el que suscribe.

Monseñor Dennis M. Schnurr
Secretario General
NCCB/USCC

DECLARACIÓN DE VISIÓN

El mayor homenaje que todas las Iglesias tributarán a Cristo en el umbral del tercer milenio, será la demostración de la omnipotente presencia del Redentor mediante frutos de fe, esperanza y caridad en hombres y mujeres de tantas lenguas y razas, que han seguido a Cristo. (Tertio Millennio Adveniente, no. 37)

Este es el momento oportuno para proclamar que somos una Iglesia de muchos rostros que representan los diversos pueblos de Dios. El *Encuentro 2000* brinda a la Iglesia en Estados Unidos la oportunidad de reunirse para dialogar profundamente sobre su vida y su fe: para rendir culto juntos, para aprender uno del otro, para perdonarnos y reconciliarnos, para honrar nuestras singulares historias y para descubrir formas en las cuales, como comunidades católicas, podemos ser una Iglesia aunque vengamos de diferentes culturas y razas. *Encuentro 2000* es un proceso por el cual redescubriremos y lograremos una mejor apreciación de la universalidad de la Iglesia Católica y de renovar nuestro compromiso con nuestra identidad y misión comunes. Como miembros de la familia de Dios, estamos llamados a encontrar a Jesucristo vivo recibiendo y reflejando auténticamente su amable hospitalidad en cada uno de nosotros y por medio de cada uno, como el camino a la conversión, la comunión, y la solidaridad.

Una Invitación para Participar en *Encuentro 2000*

Sintiendo el movimiento del Espíritu en el umbral del año 2000, los obispos de Estados Unidos invitan a la Iglesia en toda su diversidad cultural y étnica, a reunirse para celebrar las historias de todos nuestros pueblos y descubrir a Cristo en cada una de ellas, para que crucemos juntos hacia el nuevo milenio, en solidaridad. *Encuentro 2000* brinda a la Iglesia la oportunidad de proclamar nuevamente al mundo que una profunda fe en Jesucristo es la clave, el centro y el fin de toda historia humana (cf. *Gaudium et Spes*, 10).

Siguiendo la iniciativa del Comité para Asuntos Hispanos e inspirados por la experiencia del pueblo hispano, tanto en su historia como en los procesos anteriores de los encuentros, los obispos de Estados Unidos convocan *Encuentro 2000*.

REFLEXIÓN TEOLÓGICA: MUCHOS ROSTROS EN LA CASA DE DIOS

Les daré dentro de los muros de mi casa
　un monumento de piedra y un nombre que vale
más que hijos e hijas,
　una fama que nunca se acabará o se olvidará. . . .
Los llevaré a mi cerro santo
　y haré que se sientan felices en mi Casa de oración.
Serán aceptados los holocaustos y sacrificios
　que hagan sobre mi altar,
ya que mi casa será llamada
　Casa de oración para todo el mundo.
Esto dice el Señor Yavé,
　que reúne a todos los israelitas que estaban dispersos:
Agregaré todavía más gente
　a todos los que ya se habían juntado. (Is 56:5, 7-8)

Nuestra Diversidad Humana

Cada uno de nosotros está hecho a imagen y semejanza de Dios. Cada uno de nosotros es un regalo de Dios para el mundo, y cada uno es muy singular. Yo soy del color, de la raza, y de la cultura que soy, y soy algo más. Soy Americano: Africano-Americano, Asiático Americano, Hispano Americano, Europeo Americano, Nativo Americano, y tengo antepasados de más de uno y soy algo más. Mis raíces se encuentran en África, Asia, Sudamérica, Centroamérica, el Caribe, Europa, el Cercano Oriente, Norteamérica, y soy algo más. Vivo en la ciudad y en un pueblo pequeño; vivo en los suburbios y en una comunidad privada, y soy algo más.

Nuestros Estilos de Vida

Soy madre y padre, hermana e hija, hijo y hermano, amigo y colega, y soy algo más. Soy trabajador de construcción y enfermera, soy doctor y obrero, trabajo en casa y viajo grandes distancias, y soy algo más. Viajo constantemente de ciudad en ciudad y he vivido en el mismo lugar por generaciones. Soy un padre para quien los hijos son vida y alegría y soy una madre soltera que se esfuerza por educar a sus tres hijos, y soy algo más. Soy un sacerdote ordenado recientemente tratando de servir a una parroquia multicultural y soy una religiosa enriquecida por la experiencia de trabajar con los demás. Tengo quince años y doy gracias a Dios por la iglesia que me es familiar y tengo sesenta años y me siento perdida buscando desesperadamente mi lugar en la iglesia a la que estaba acostumbrada, y soy algo más. Soy un padre divorciado que veo a mis hijos cada dos semanas y soy una madre que ha escogido su familia sobre una profesión. Disfruto de muy buena salud y sufro por mis enfermedades, y soy algo más. Soy un joven soltero y estoy recién casada. Estoy rodeado de maravillosos amigos y me siento sola buscando una buena amiga, y soy algo más.

Nuestra Vida en la Comunidad de Fe

Vivo mi fe a diario en mi centro laboral y mi trabajo es velar por los pobres en mi comunidad. Soy un abogado que defiende a los oprimidos y un trabajador que construye casas para los desamparados. Visito a los enfermos, consuelo a los que están solos, sufro con quienes lloran a un ser querido. Soy un campesino que provee comida en la mesa y un ministro de la Eucaristía que lleva alimento a los enfermos. Soy un catequista que enseña a la juventud en la fe y soy madrina de catecúmenos adultos. Pertenezco a un grupo interreligioso y soy miembro de una pequeña comunidad eclesial. Soy un padre orgulloso por la confirmación de mi hija y una madre preocupada por la participación de mi hijo en un grupo religioso nuevo. Soy un carismático renovado por el poder del Espíritu y soy una contemplativa postrada ante el silencio de un gran misterio. Soy católico y crecí en un país donde los cristianos son una minoría pequeña. Mi cultura es vista como una religión, pero mi cultura es una parte integral de mi fe católica. Soy una persona mayor que conserva las tradiciones de la Iglesia y soy una joven llena de energía que descubre nuevas formas de vivir esas tradiciones. Soy un miembro de la parroquia y, sin embargo, no me siento en casa.

Soy quien soy porque Dios me ama. Es Dios quien me busca. Es Dios quien me amó primero. Es Dios quien tiene un lugar para mí en su casa.

Compartiendo la Visión del *Encuentro 2000*

"Soy" describe algunos de los muchos rostros de la Iglesia en Estados Unidos. "Soy" también nombra a Aquel que está dentro de esos rostros. Como tal, "soy" ofrece una visión de muchos lugares, culturas, situaciones y contextos que describen una realidad multicultural verdaderamente bendecida, y que hoy ofrece un nuevo significado al multiculturalismo en Estados Unidos. *Encuentro 2000* propone estas dos visiones *un Único Señor* y *los muchos rostros*. *Encuentro 2000* reconoce que la vida en Estados Unidos nos encuentra en diferentes relaciones unos con otros y con el Cuerpo de Cristo que es la Iglesia. Esta desconcertante variedad de relaciones puede ser vista como un obstáculo para ser familia, comunidad, sociedad y, finalmente, Iglesia. Sin embargo, *Encuentro 2000* ve a Jesús abriendo la puerta, llevándonos más allá de cada uno de estos obstáculos, invitándonos a pasar y repitiendo las palabras del profeta Isaías:

Los llevaré a mi cerro santo y haré que se sientan
    felices en mi Casa de oración.
Serán aceptados los holocaustos y sacrificios
    que hagan sobre mi altar,
ya que mi casa será llamada
    Casa de oración para todo el mundo. (56:7)

Jesús describe una hospitalidad amable y transformadora al abrirnos la puerta e invitarnos a pasar. Es amable porque Jesús se nos presenta en medio de esta variedad de pueblos y de relaciones que parecían puertas cerradas, y que ahora están abiertas. Esta hospitalidad es transformadora porque Jesús nos invita a cruzar el umbral de esa puerta abierta hacia una casa nueva, una casa de oración para todos los pueblos. Debemos seguir al Señor y convertirnos en amables anfitriones al reconocer y abrazar nuestra diversidad cultural, étnica, y lingüística y honrar la presencia única de Dios en nuestras vidas, historias y culturas. Esta hospitalidad amable y transformadora también describe el significado verdaderamente cristiano del multiculturalismo. Un multiculturalismo que se enfoca menos en un lugar donde se reúnen muchos pueblos y más en una hospitalidad amable que crea un espacio de bienvenida para cada uno de estos rostros.

Encuentro 2000, entonces, ve a la Iglesia del tercer milenio como Jesús que lava los pies de sus discípulos, como el anfitrión de la casa para todos los pueblos. Esa visión nos llama a convertirnos en el amable Señor, en el cordial anfitrión de un mundo lleno de conversaciones disonantes y sin sentido. Se nos pide empezar una nueva conversación en esta casa de oración. Tal sentido de hospitalidad transforma las diferencias culturales, raciales, sociales, de género, de lenguaje y las distintas circunstancias, en una invitación a hablar desde los más profundos anhelos de nuestro corazón. Tal hospitalidad reconoce la invitación del anfitrión, que nos conoce mejor que nosotros mismos, de convertirnos en anfitriones unos de otros. Como tal, esta visión de amable hospitalidad transforma cualquier obstáculo a la fidelidad en oportunidades de hablar desde lo más profundo de nuestro corazón. En esta casa de bienvenida, incluso aquellos que se encuentran sin rumbo, cansados y temerosos en este mundo, pueden escuchar las palabras de Isaías:

Esto dice el Señor Yavé,
    que reúne a todos los israelitas que estaban dispersos:
Agregaré todavía más gente a todos
    los que ya se habían juntado. (56:8)

Haciendo Realidad la Visión del *Encuentro 2000*

Encuentro 2000 nos llama hacia una nueva primavera del Cristianismo al entrar en el tercer milenio. Nos extiende una invitación abierta hacia una hospitalidad amable que nos invita a sentirnos en casa. Tal llamada a la hospitalidad acepta sin condiciones nuestros dones y contribuciones al banquete de sueños futuros que celebramos en la mesa de la cocina. Nos llama a la sala para compartir nuestro álbum de fotografías y contar nuestras historias familiares. Nos llama hacia la puerta cerrada con rabia, para ofrecer una confesión de errores y palabras de perdón que puedan llevarnos hacia la reconciliación y a sanar las heridas. Nos llama al patio para tener una nueva experiencia del jardín como un lugar de oración para todos los pueblos. Finalmente, nos llama a la mesa eucarística para compartir nuestras alegrías y dolores con Aquel que es al mismo tiempo nuestro Señor y nuestro Anfitrión, en una deslumbrante visión de comunión. El Cuerpo de Cristo reunido en la mesa del banquete es cima y fuente de la hospitalidad transformadora. Es la casa de oración en donde habitan los muchos rostros de la casa de Dios.

SESIÓN PARROQUIAL: CERRANDO LA BRECHA ENTRE LA FE Y LA VIDA

Así reconocerán todos que ustedes son mis discípulos: si se tienen amor unos a los otros. (Jn 13:35)

Bienvenida y Oración (15 minutos)

Se da la bienvenida a los participantes y se les pide que se presenten brevemente. Se inicia la sesión con una oración sencilla, incluyendo un canto bilingüe como el de Cesáreo Gabarain "Id y enseñad/Go and Teach" (*Flor y Canto*, #336, Oregon Catholic Press).

Objetivo: Renovar nuestro compromiso para crear una cultura inspirada en el Evangelio viviendo los valores de la fe en todas las áreas de la vida.

Compartiendo Nuestras Experiencias (40 minutos)

¿Qué tiene que ver la fe con la vida diaria y la cultura? ¿Acaso debe haber una relación entre la Misa del domingo y la mañana del lunes; entre lo que creemos por la fe y lo que vivimos todos los días? Las personas que viven su fe en la vida diaria son un gran ejemplo en nuestras comunidades e inspiran a otros a ser mejor. En cada comunidad de fe existen personas que nos sirven de inspiración. En muchos casos, se trata de personas sencillas como la abuela de la familia, un joven de la parroquia, un matrimonio del barrio, o una maestra de la escuela local. Las personas inspiradoras no siempre se distinguen por ser las más populares o las que mejor hablan. Lo que es común a todas ellas es su compromiso de vivir de acuerdo al Evangelio todos los días, especialmente en situaciones adversas. Su testimonio de vida es el mejor ejemplo del discipulado; es una invitación entusiasta para que los demás vivan la Buena Nueva de Jesús en toda situación humana (*Vayan y Hagan Discípulos*, p. 2). Por otro lado, muchos hombres y mujeres bautizados viven su fe cristiana sin energía, mientras que otros se han alejado de la Iglesia (*Redemptoris Missio*, no. 33). La conversión no es completa si falta la conciencia de las exigencias de la vida cristiana y no se pone esfuerzo en llevarlas a cabo (*Ecclesia in América*, no. 27). La Nueva Evangelización nos llama a un proceso continuo de conversión en el cual se pretende cerrar la brecha entre el Evangelio y nuestras actividades diarias dentro de la familia, el trabajo, y la vida social.

Preguntas para la discusión:

- ¿Qué persona en su comunidad sirve de inspiración a los demás para vivir los valores del Evangelio en la vida diaria?
- Da ejemplos de cómo vives tu el Evangelio en la vida diaria.
- ¿Qué te hace difícil vivir el Evangelio en la vida diaria?

Reflexionando sobre Nuestra Tradición de Fe (40 minutos)

Jesucristo no es una idea, sino un individuo concreto e histórico: el Hijo de Dios, que se hizo hijo de María en un tiempo, lugar y cultura determinados, para redimirnos (*La Presencia Hispana en la Nueva Evangelización en los Estados Unidos*, p. 20). Jesús tuvo que enfrentar tradiciones y actitudes de su propia cultura que separaban a las personas de Dios y entre sí. El Evangelio está lleno de ejemplos en los que Jesús transforma estas situaciones esclavizantes al inculturar en ellas los valores del Reino de Dios. Uno de estos ejemplos es la curación el día Sábado, con la que Jesús enseña que el Sábado es para el bien de la persona y no la persona para el Sábado. Al reunirse con pecadores y publicanos, y relacionarse con personas no judías, Jesús enseña que el amor de Dios y su plan de salvación cruza fronteras geográficas y culturales para llegar a todos. Con sus milagros Jesús da testimonio de la voluntad de Dios y esto significa, sobre todo, traer perdón, reconciliación, sanación y liberación para todos. Con su mensaje y acciones Jesus reúne la fe, la vida y la cultura. Jesús afirma lo verdadero y lo bueno que hay en la cultura, y denuncia lo que hay en ella de falso, equivocado o indeseable.

La evangelización consiste precisamente en continuar esta tarea de inculturación: transformar, en nombre de Jesucristo y con el poder del Espíritu Santo, toda creencia, actitud y conducta en nuestra cultura, para que afirmen la vida y la dignidad de cada persona, de acuerdo a los valores y promesas del Reino de Dios. Este proceso de inculturación del Evangelio nos llama a promover al interior de cada una de las culturas a evangelizar una nueva expresión del Evangelio, procurando un lenguaje de la fe que sea patrimonio común de los fieles, y por tanto factor fundamental de comunión (*Directorio General para la Catequesis*, no. 203).

Preguntas para la discusión:

- ¿Qué actividades o acciones realiza su comunidad de fe para dar testimonio del mensaje de fe, esperanza y amor de Jesucristo?
- ¿Qué actitudes, creencias y conductas que se dan en la cultura en que vives, necesitan ser cuestionadas y transformadas por la Buena Nueva de Jesucristo?

Poniendo Nuestra Fe en Acción
(40 minutos)

El Papa Juan Pablo II nos advierte que estamos viviendo una crisis cultural de proporciones insospechadas, en donde los valores evangélicos y humanos fundamentales tienden a desaparecer, y a dar lugar a actitudes y situaciones opresivas que nos separan de Dios y de los demás (CELAM 1992, no. 230). Anteponer las cosas a las personas, enriquecerse a costa del más débil, promover el desprecio racial, educar sin infundir valores morales, son algunos ejemplos de esta crisis cultural. El papa Juan Pablo II llama a una Nueva Evangelización que renueve el compromiso de la Iglesia y de cada creyente para servir de puente entre la fe y la vida, pues una fe que no forma una cultura basada en los valores del Evangelio es una fe estéril (*La Presencia Hispana en la Nueva Evangelización en los Estados Unidos*, p. 16). A fin de responder mejor a este llamado, la Nueva Evangelización exige un "nuevo ardor apostólico" capaz de generar un "nuevo entusiasmo" en la proclamación del Evangelio; y "nuevos métodos" que utilicen en forma efectiva la imaginación, la creatividad, y los recursos técnicos y científicos disponibles para compartir la Buena Nueva.

Pasos para la acción:

- Identificar las acciones que ayudarán a las personas y a las comunidades a cerrar la brecha entre la fe y la cultura. (Una acción que ha sido identificada por los obispos de Estados Unidos es realizar una peregrinación de un día a una catedral o santuario local para orar por una forma nueva de entender y vivir nuestra fe en el mundo).
   — En el estilo de vida de la comunidad de fe (*koinonia*)
   — En la celebración de la Liturgia y la oración (*liturgia*)
   — En la enseñanza de la fe y los valores del Evangelio (*didaché*)
   — En el servicio a los demás y el trabajo por la caridad y la justicia (*diaconía*)
   — En la proclamación que Jesús es el Camino, la Verdad y la Vida, ayer, hoy, y siempre (*kerygma*)
- Desarrollar una estrategia que promueva esta acción con un nuevo ardor apostólico, nuevo entusiasmo, y nuevos métodos.

Recogiendo Nuestras Experiencias
(15 minutos)

- ¿Qué facilitó su participación en la sesión y qué la hizo difícil?
- ¿Hasta qué punto pudieron conocerse mejor y aceptarse mutuamente?
- ¿Se logró alcanzar un conocimiento más profundo de nuestra fe y se logró un compromiso para implementar las acciones identificadas?

Celebrando Nuestra Fe como Comunidad
(25 minutos)

- Himno/canción de apertura
- Invocación o invitación a la oración
- Lectura bíblica
- Oración de acción de gracias o de petición
- La Oración del Señor
- Oración final y el saludo de la paz
- Himno de clausura

REFERENCIAS

La Campaña Católica para el Desarrollo Humano, United States Catholic Conference. Serie Fe y Desarrollo Humano: *Guía Bíblica, Libro de Oración por la Justicia, Rosario Bíblico por la Justicia y la Paz, Vía Cruz y Novena por la Justicia y la Paz* (Washington, D.C.: United States Catholic Conference, 1998).

Catecismo de la Iglesia Católica (Washington, D.C.: United States Catholic Conference, 1994).

CELAM. *Puebla: La Evangelización en el Presente y Futuro de América Latina* (México D.F.: Librería de Clavería, 1979).

CELAM. *Santo Domingo: Nueva Evangelización, Promoción Humana, Cultura Cristiana* (Santafé de Bogotá, Colombia: Ediciones Paulinas, FSP-SAL, 1992).

Comité de Migración, National Conference of Catholic Bishops. *Una Familia en Dios* (Washington, D.C.: United States Catholic Conference, 1995).

Congregación para el Clero. *Directorio General para la Catequesis* (Washington, D.C.: United States Catholic Conference, 1998).

Flannery, Austin, OP, ed. *Concilio Vaticano II* (Northport, N.Y.: Costello Publishing Company, 1992). Solo en inglés.

Juan Pablo II. *Al Aproximarse el Tercer Milenio (Tertio Millennio Adveniente)* (Washington, D.C.: United States Catholic Conference, 1994).

Juan Pablo II. *Christifideles Laici (Sobre la Vocación y la Misión de los Laicos en la Iglesia y en el Mundo)* (Washington, D.C.: United States Catholic Conference, 1988). Solo en inglés.

Juan Pablo II. *La Iglesia en America (Ecclesia in America)* (Washington, D.C.: United States Catholic Conference, 1999).

Juan Pablo II. *On the Permanent Validity of the Church's Missionary Mandate (Redemptoris Missio)* (Washington, D.C.: United States Catholic Conference, 1991). Solo en inglés.

John Paul II. *On Social Concern (Sollicitudo Rei Socialis)* (Washington, D.C.: United States Catholic Conference, 1987). Solo en inglés.

National Conference of Catholic Bishops. *Book of Readings on Reconciliation* (Washington, D.C.: United States Catholic Conference, 1999). Solo en inglés.

National Conference of Catholic Bishops. *Llamados y Dotados para el Tercer Milenio* (Washington, D.C.: United States Catholic Conference, 1997).

National Conference of Catholic Bishops. *Ministerio Hispano: Tres Documentos Importantes* (Washington, D.C.: United States Catholic Conference, 1995). Incluye el Plan Pastoral Nacional para el Ministerio Hispano.

National Conference of Catholic Bishops. *La Presencia Hispana en la Nueva Evangelización en los Estados Unidos* (Washington, D.C.: United States Catholic Conference, 1996).

National Conference of Catholic Bishops. *Reconciliados por Cristo* (Washington, D.C.: United States Catholic Conference, 1997).

National Conference of Catholic Bishops. *Vayan y Hagan Discípulos* (Washington, D.C.: United States Catholic Conference, 1997).

Obispos de la Diócesis de Galveston-Houston. *Muchos Miembros, Un Cuerpo* (Galveston-Houston, Texas: Diócesis de Galveston-Houston, 1994).

Subcomité para el Tercer Milenio, National Conference of Catholic Bishops/United States Catholic Conference. *Abriendo las Puertas a Cristo: Un Marco de Acción para Tertio Millennio Adveniente* (Washington, D.C.: United States Catholic Conference, 1997).

United States Catholic Conference. *Compartiendo la Enseñanza Social Católica: Desafíos y Rumbos* (Washington, D.C.: United States Catholic Conference, 1998).

United States Catholic Conference. *Fundamentos Católicos para la Actividad Económica* (Washington, D.C.: United States Catholic Conference, 1997).

United States Catholic Conference. *Parish Resource Manual: Communities of Salt and Light* (Washington, D.C.: United States Catholic Conference, 1993). Solo en inglés.

La Presencia Hispana en la Nueva Evangelización en los Estados Unidos

En junio de 1995, el Comité de Obispos para Asuntos Hispanos conmemoró el quincuagésimo aniversario del establecimiento de la oficina nacional para el ministerio hispano. Durante su reunión nacional llamada "Convocación '95: La Presencia Hispana en la Nueva Evangelización en los Estados Unidos", realizada en San Antonio, Texas, los obispos recibieron a 500 agentes pastorales quienes participaron en una serie de talleres sobre la fe y la identidad cristiana. Al final de cada taller, surgió un compromiso con la Nueva Evangelización. El sumario de estas declaraciones se convirtió en la "Declaración de Compromiso" que se presentó al cierre de la convocación. Esta declaración hace un llamado a los obispos de los Estados Unidos a compartir sus perspectivas acerca del aporte de los hispanos a la Iglesia. Esta declaración, *La Presencia Hispana en la Nueva Evangelización en los Estados Unidos*, es la respuesta de los obispos de los Estados Unidos a los líderes pastorales acerca de la presencia hispana y la relación entre fe y cultura. En noviembre de 1995, la National Conference of Catholic Bishops aprobó la publicación bilingüe de *La Presencia Hispana en la Nueva Evangelización en los Estados Unidos* y su publicación fue autorizada por el que suscribe.

Monseñor Dennis M. Schnurr
Secretario General
NCCB/USCC

Prefacio

Para conmemorar el quincuagésimo aniversario del establecimiento de una oficina nacional para el ministerio hispano por los obispos católicos de los Estados Unidos, el Comité para Asuntos Hispanos solicitó a la Conferencia Nacional de Obispos Católicos la publicación de una declaración pastoral sobre un aspecto de la Nueva Evangelización; principalmente, sobre la relación entre fe y cultura. La declaración pastoral, *La Presencia Hispana en la Nueva Evangelización en los Estados Unidos*, refleja la experiencia en el ministerio pastoral entre el pueblo católico hispano como un modelo para la Nueva Evangelización. La declaración pastoral reafirma la labor de evangelización entre católicos hispanos en los últimos cincuenta años y da una mirada al futuro y a los desafíos de la Nueva Evangelización, al acercarnos a la celebración del Gran Jubileo del año 2000 y la presencia hispana en la Iglesia Católica al empezar el nuevo milenio.

Líderes católicos de la pastoral hispana de todas partes del país, se reunieron en San Antonio, Texas, del 23 al 25 de junio de 1995, para celebrar cincuenta años del establecimiento de una Oficina Nacional para el ministerio hispano. Este evento, llamado "Convocación '95", tuvo como tema "La Presencia Hispana en la Nueva Evangelización en Estados Unidos." La Convocación incluyó dos sesiones generales dedicadas a los temas de evangelización, misión, cultura y servicio. Se celebraron además veintidós talleres. Hubo ocho talleres en la mañana dedicados a temas doctrinales, teológicos y espirituales tales como: oración y sacramento, vida en el Espíritu, el nuevo *Catecismo de la Iglesia Católica*, Vivir la Iglesia, vocaciones, Evangelizando la Cultura, religiosidad popular y Biblia e Iglesia. Los catorce talleres de la tarde fueron dedicados a temas específicos de preocupación pastoral; en particular, familia, escuela, salud, aborto y eutanasia, jóvenes, justicia social, relaciones inter-raciales y étnicos, asuntos de inmigración, servicios pastorales a los migrantes, misión y servicio, el *Plan Pastoral Nacional para el Ministerio Hispano*, la mujer en la Iglesia y la sociedad, responsabilidad política y estructuras eclesiales para el ministerio hispano. Al concluir la Convocación '95, los participantes emitieron una "Declaración de Compromiso" a la Nueva Evangelización en nuestro país, pidiendo a los obispos que compartieran con toda la Iglesia su visión acerca de la contribución hispana a ésta. Esta Declaración Pastoral es nuestra respuesta al pedido de los líderes pastorales.

La Presencia Hispana en la Nueva Evangelización en Estados Unidos está dirigida a toda la Iglesia en nuestro país. La Declaración de Compromiso dice: "Buscaremos las maneras de compartir con toda la Iglesia en Estados Unidos el progreso realizado en la pastoral hispana." Esto es esencial para la unidad de la Iglesia en nuestro país, ya que todos estamos llamados a su misión de evangelización, culto y servicio.

Dos documentos emitidos por la Conferencia Nacional de Obispos Católicos brindan los fundamentos para la respuesta al llamado a una Nueva Evangelización: *Vayan y Hagan Discípulos* publicado el 12 de febrero de 1993, y el *Plan Pastoral Nacional para el Ministerio Hispano*, publicado el 18 de enero de 1988. Todos los pastoralistas dedicados a la Nueva Evangelización deben familiarizarse con estos documentos, ya que su propósito es guiarnos en esta tarea. En esta respuesta a la Declaración de Compromiso de la Convocación '95, los obispos limitan sus observaciones a sólo un aspecto de la Nueva Evangelización, esto es, a *la relación entre fe y cultura*. Otros aspectos esenciales de la evangelización son tratados en esos dos documentos.

A fin de comprender mejor lo que significa la presencia hispana en Estados Unidos, se ha incluído tres apéndices al documento *La Presencia Hispana en la Nueva Evangelización en los Estados Unidos*. El Apéndice A es el mensaje enviado por el Santo Padre, Juan Pablo II, a los participantes de la Convocación '95. El Apéndice B, incluye una copia de la "Declaración de Compromiso," aprobada por los líderes pastorales que participaron en la Convocación '95, la cual es citada en este documento. El Apéndice C es una breve reseña histórica del ministerio hispano en los Estados Unidos de 1945 a 1995.

+ Roberto O. González, Presidente
Comité de Obispos para Asuntos Hispanos
Conferencia Nacional de Obispos Católicos

LA PRESENCIA HISPANA EN LA NUEVA EVANGELIZACIÓN EN LOS ESTADOS UNIDOS

"En este momento de gracia reconocemos que la comunidad hispana[1] que vive entre nosotros es una bendición de Dios". Con estas palabras empezamos nuestra carta pastoral acerca de la presencia hispana en la Iglesia, hace doce años.[2] Hoy, en los albores del tercer milenio de la historia cristiana, queremos reafirmar y difundir dicha convicción. Declaramos que la presencia hispana en nuestra Iglesia constituye un regalo providencial del Señor en el reto de la nueva evangelización a la que estamos llamados en esta hora de la historia.

Vemos el momento actual como un tiempo de gran oportunidad. Es cierto que este siglo ha sido testigo de algunas de las ofensas más grandes nunca antes cometidas en contra de la dignidad humana. Este ha sido el siglo de guerras mundiales, genocidios y regímenes totalitarios. Todos anhelan un nuevo comienzo, una nueva esperanza, una nueva confianza de que la sed por libertad no es una ilusión vana y que la búsqueda de aquella verdad que nos libera no es un sueño vacío. Este anhelo nos da la oportunidad de proclamar a Jesucristo como la única respuesta a las preguntas que atormentan el corazón humano. Guiados por nuestro Santo Padre, el Papa Juan Pablo II, la Iglesia responde a este reto con la alegre propuesta del *Evangelio de la Vida* como el fundamento de una cultura que verdaderamente responde a todas las necesidades humanas, espirituales y materiales. El *Evangelio de la Vida* proclama que los derechos humanos tienen su origen en la Sabiduría del Creador, que la libertad es inseparable de verdades de las que no somos autores y que la paz es segura, si se funda en una auténtica solidaridad entre hombres y mujeres de diferentes orígenes raciales y étnicos.

Muchos en el mundo entero ven a Estados Unidos como la tierra de la esperanza por la libertad y la justicia. No obstante, nuestro país no ha estado exento de los avances logrados por la "cultura de la muerte" de la que habla el Santo Padre, en la cual los débiles son abandonados a la manipulación de los poderosos. Aún así, cuando miramos hacia el futuro no tenemos miedo. Sabemos que Jesucristo, que ha vencido el pecado y la muerte, es el Señor de la Iglesia, que la guía constantemente, otorgándole la sabiduría para interpretar los signos de los tiempos

> *Este anhelo nos da la oportunidad de proclamar a Jesucristo como la única respuesta a las preguntas que atormentan el corazón humano.*

reconoce la importancia de la contribución de los hispanos en el área de la fe y la cultura. Su Santidad expresa el deseo de que "basados en su rica historia y en su experiencia, la comunidad hispana puede ofrecer una contribución única al diálogo entre fe y cultura en la sociedad norteamericana actual, y de esta forma, abrir nuevos caminos para la propagación del Evangelio en el Tercer Milenio".[5] *Nosotros creemos que ésta es la contribución más importante de los católicos hispanos a la Nueva Evangelización en Estados Unidos.* Por lo tanto, recibimos el compromiso de los participantes en la Convocación '95 de "compartir con nuestros hermanos y hermanas católicos de los Estados Unidos lo que es una fe encarnada en cultura".[6]

FE Y CULTURA

La relación entre la fe y la cultura radica en el corazón de la Nueva Evangelización. La palabra *cultura* viene del verbo latino *colere*, que significa cultivar la tierra. Con el tiempo, la expresión *cultura animi*, la cultura de las almas, vino a designar el proceso de formación personal del individuo. Cuando el proceso de formación personal se llega a entender en términos intelectuales, una "persona culta" es aquella que simplemente tiene muchos conocimientos. Sin embargo, la formación personal es un proceso con elementos intelectuales, afectivos, éticos y prácticos. Toca todo lo que constituye aquello que es característicamente humano. Cultura es lo que configura al ser humano como específicamente humano. El Concilio Vaticano II reconoce a la cultura como el cultivo de los "bienes y valores naturales"[7] a través de los cuales logramos una completa madurez humana[8] por medio del dominio sobre el mundo que fomenta los recursos de la creación. De esta manera, cultura designa la perfección de la persona humana, la construcción de un orden social justo y el servicio de los demás.[9] El documento de Puebla lo resume definiendo cultura como "el modo particular como, en un pueblo, los hombres cultivan su relación con la naturaleza, entre sí mismos y con Dios de modo que puedan llegar a 'un nivel verdadero y plenamente humano'".[10] Como tal, cultura designa el estilo de vida que caracteriza a los diferentes pueblos. Así pues, es apropiado hablar de una pluralidad de culturas.

La Nueva Evangelización se dirige, de modo especial, a aquellos a los que el Evangelio ha sido proclamado pero para los cuales aún no es una experiencia real de vida en todas sus dimensiones. El Evangelio nos da luz en relación a lo que es verdadero o falso, correcto o equivocado, deseable o indeseable. Nos informa y transforma nuestra experiencia con la naturaleza, del paso del tiempo, del trabajo y el descanso, de los demás, del motivo de la vida y del sentido de la muerte. *Estas son las experiencias que caracterizan una cultura.* El Evangelio, por lo tanto, toca los cimientos de todas las culturas. Aunque dirigida a cada persona, la invitación de seguir a Jesucristo tiene necesariamente una dimensión cultural. Sin ella, el Evangelio se convierte en un sistema abstracto de ideas y valores que pueden ser manipulados para excusar pecados personales y sociales. La Nueva Evangelización pretende servir de puente entre la fe y la cultura, mostrando que *una fe que no crea cultura es una fe estéril.*

El punto de partida común y absolutamente esencial de todas las culturas humanas auténticas es el *reconocimiento de la persona humana como valor en sí misma*, como afirma el Concilio Vaticano II.[11] Es decir, que la persona humana nunca debe reducirse a un "instrumento" para alcanzar una meta, por muy buena que sea esa meta. La persona humana, cada persona humana, sin importar las circunstancias, debe ser reconocida y respetada como tal, sin condición alguna. Todas las culturas humanas auténticas dependen de este hecho. *Decir que el Evangelio tiene una dimensión cultural necesaria, es decir que promueve el reconocimiento, la afirmación y el desarrollo de todos los seres humanos como tales.* El Evangelio entonces, nos empuja a la búsqueda de la libertad, la superación personal, el cuidado del débil y del necesitado, y la liberación de estructuras económicas, políticas y religiosas alienantes, tanto de la vida individual como social.

LA OPCIÓN PREFERENCIAL POR LOS POBRES

Cuando el 9 de marzo de 1983, Papa Juan Pablo II manifestó a los obispos de América Latina y del Caribe que el momento actual requiere una evangelización nueva en entusiasmo, expresión y métodos, se refería precisamente al proceso de renovación que la Iglesia en América Latina está llevando a cabo desde el Concilio Vaticano II.[12] Lo esencial de este proceso es reconocer que el éxito en la evangelización ocurre únicamente cuando la fe da forma a la cultura. Es decir, la evangelización es inseparable de la afirmación y la defensa de la dignidad de las personas humanas. Sin embargo, debido a que el Evangelio toca las raíces de las culturas, la verdad acerca de la dignidad humana está destinada a encarnarse en la cultura. Esta afectará las estructuras sociales mediante las cuales la persona humana ejerce dominio sobre los bienes de la naturaleza y sobre la distribución de los frutos de su desarrollo. Estas estructuras deben estar al servicio de la persona humana y son valiosas en la medida en la que reconocen y afirman a la persona misma. Para poder juzgar si éste es o no es el caso, es necesario aceptar la experiencia y *unirse al clamor de justicia de aquellos* que sólo pueden exigir respeto a raíz de su propia identidad como personas. Esta experiencia se convierte en criterio de interpretación de las exigencias del Evangelio en determinadas situaciones sociales.[13] En América Latina, a esta solidaridad se le dió el nombre de "opción preferencial por los pobres".

La Declaración de Compromiso publicada por la Convocación '95 nos recuerda esto cuando reconoce que una señal de una cultura formada por el Evangelio es la existencia de la *opción preferencial por los pobres* en la sociedad. De ahí, el compromiso de "dar testimonio de cómo se incultura en un pueblo la opción preferencial por los pobres, que es parte esencial de la fe católica".[14] *Nosotros recibimos este compromiso y lo reconocemos como una contribución, a la Iglesia en nuestro país, de la reflexión eclesial y de la vida práctica de la Iglesia de Latinoamérica en las últimas décadas.*

La Declaración de Compromiso entiende correctamente este concepto como "la afirmación de la dignidad de la persona humana tal como fue creada por Dios, sin otro propósito que el bien de su existencia".[15] Así pues, los participantes expresan su compromiso de luchar "contra todo intento de instrumentalizar a la persona humana y de valorar sólo su posible contribución al progreso material de la sociedad".[16]

LA CENTRALIDAD DE CRISTO

Para poder entender la profunda razón de la unión entre la opción preferencial por los pobres y el impacto de la fe en la cultura, cabe recordar que la comunión con Jesucristo implica declararse a favor del respeto a la vida en este mundo en todas sus dimensiones. A través de la fe y los sacramentos, entramos en una relación con Jesucristo y con Dios Padre. Adquirimos una visión de la realidad y una experiencia de la naturaleza, de los demás y de Dios, que es consistente con esa relación y que es posible por medio del don del Espíritu de Dios. Esta visión y esta experiencia definen la manera de entender o la *actitud* nacia la realidad que está orientada hacia la consumación del plan de Dios para la Creación al final de los tiempos. Así pues, empezamos a vivir aquí, en esta tierra, la vida del Reino de Dios que se manifestará en toda su magnitud al final de los tiempos. Es esta visión o actitud que se expresa culturalmente a través de estructuras sociales, especialmente aquellas que se refieren al trabajo y al descanso. La Declaración de Compromiso publicada por la Convocación '95 lo expresa de esta manera: "Buscaremos formas para demostrar que nuestros esfuerzos en el área de justicia social son consecuencia de nuestra fe en Jesucristo, el Señor, el centro de la historia y del universo. En la verdad acerca de Jesucristo, verdadero Dios y verdadero Hombre, descubrimos lo que es la persona humana en todas sus dimensiones: individual, social, material y espiritual".[17]

El Evangelio no es un sistema de conceptos para ser enseñados por un maestro a un alumno y adaptarlos a las diferentes circunstancias. El Evangelio es la proclamación de la persona de Jesucristo, de su misión, de sus enseñanzas y de sus promesas. Jesucristo no es una idea, sino un individuo concreto, específico e histórico: el Hijo de Dios, que se hizo hijo de María. Este individuo, y sólo Él, es el Salvador. No hay liberación alguna sin Él. Él se hizo "pobre" y en Él nos solidarizamos con el pobre. Él es el Redentor, la Segunda Persona de la Santísma Trinidad, en quien todos estamos predestinados a alcanzar la perfección como personas humanas por la fe y la incorporación sacramental en su muerte y resurrección salvadoras. Sin esta proclamación de Jesucristo y sin su culto de adoración mediante la fe y los sacramentos no hay una verdadera evangelización.[18]

Por lo tanto, queremos enfatizar la importancia del compromiso de los participantes en la Convocación '95 para la renovación de nuestra "pastoral litúrgica, sacramental y catequética",[19] para la promoción de vocaciones a los ministerios sacramentales del sacerdocio y del diaconado así como a las vocaciones laicas y religiosas. Especialmente, aceptamos el compromiso para un adecuado proceso de formación doctrinal y pastoral basado en la Sagrada Escritura y en el nuevo *Catecismo de la Iglesia Católica*, así como la insistencia en la necesidad de la oración y de las expresiones populares de nuestras creencias religiosas.

TESTIGOS DE ESPERANZA

La vida litúrgica, sacramental y catequética de la Iglesia tienen como fin llevarnos a una relación personal con Jesucristo. Por medio de esta unión con Él, experimentamos el poder del amor de Dios, que es más fuerte que el poder del pecado y de la muerte. Experimentamos la redención de nuestra historia personal y colectiva por medio de un amor más grande que toda la maldad del mundo. Este amor nos muestra lo horrendo que es el pecado, al mismo tiempo que nos despierta a la realidad de la redención y de la verdadera libertad. Así pues, despierta una esperanza "que no espera en vano".[20] La evangelización es la proclamación de esta esperanza enraizada en Jesucristo y que nos compromete a luchar en contra del poder del pecado en nuestras vidas. Es esta esperanza, y no un sueño utópico, la que sostiene nuestra lucha por la liberación y la justicia en el mundo, nuestra opción preferencial por los pobres.

La Iglesia es el pueblo de Dios formado por el Espíritu Santo dentro del cuerpo de Cristo. La Iglesia es el lugar de *communio* o de la comunión interpersonal de fe y de amor con el Señor y entre los creyentes. La vida de la Iglesia es la proclamación, el comienzo y anticipación del Reino de Dios. La Iglesia evangeliza cuando sus miembros proclaman la palabra de Dios, catequizan, dan culto en la liturgia, sirven las necesidades de los demás y dan testimonio de su fe a través de la vida que viven. *El impacto de la fe en las culturas, tal como la opción preferencial por los pobres, debe ser entendido como consequencia de este estilo de vida.*

> *La nueva evangelización requiere la promoción de una cultura de la vida basada en el Evangelio de la vida.*

LA CULTURA DE LA MUERTE

En nuestro país, la mentalidad tecnológica moderna y funcional, crea un mundo de individuos reemplazables e incapaces de una auténtica solidaridad. En su lugar, la sociedad está formada por convenios artificiales creados por intereses poderosos. El terreno común es un creciente conformismo consumista, opaco y estéril, que se ve especialmente entre muchos de nuestros jóvenes, creado por necesidades artificiales promovidas por los medios de comunicación para apoyar los poderosos intereses económicos. El Papa Juan Pablo II ha llamado a esto la "cultura de la muerte". En palabras del Santo Padre esta cultura "está activamente promovida por fuertes corrientes culturales, económicas y políticas portadoras de una concepción de la sociedad basada en la eficiencia La vida que exigiría más acogida, amor y cuidado es tenida por inútil, o considerada como un peso insoportable y, por tanto, despreciada de muchos modos...."[21] En dicha cultura, "la sociedad se convierte en un conjunto de individuos colocados unos junto a otros, pero sin vínculos recíprocos."[22] La nueva evangelización, por lo tanto, requiere que la Iglesia dé refugio y sustento para un crecimiento continuo a aquellos que son rescatados de la soledad de la vida moderna. Requiere la promoción de una cultura de la vida basada en el Evangelio de la vida.

LA CULTURA DE LA VIDA

De aquí la importancia del compromiso a una Nueva Evangelización en nuestro país de los participantes en la Convocación '95 para defender "el valor de cada vida humana desde el primer momento de su concepción hasta la muerte natural".[23] La lucha contra el aborto y la eutanasia es una parte integral de la Nueva Evangelización, así como la lucha contra la pena de muerte, el control de la natalidad, las drogas y el tráfico de armas. Nuestra defensa de la vida requiere "solidaridad con todos aquellos que defienden a las víctimas de la cultura de la muerte en nuestro país, superando toda hostilidad racial o étnica, tratando de ser verdadero fermento de unidad, y luchando contra el racismo y la discriminación que niega acceso a los recursos necesarios para salir de la pobreza en la cual se encuentra inmersa todavía gran parte de la población hispana".[24]

Específicamente, la Declaración de Compromiso llama a reconocer el "derecho a un trabajo digno, a un salario justo, a una vivienda decente, a una educación que respete nuestros orígenes culturales y el acceso a programas de cuidado de la salud dignos del valor de cada ser humano, cualquiera sea su edad".[25] La Convocación '95 también identificó como particularmente urgentes la defensa de la familia, la promoción de la dignidad de la mujer y el cuidado de los ancianos y de los enfermos desahuciados. De importancia particular para nuestros hermanos y hermanas hispanos es la necesidad de rechazar las políticas de inmigración que destruyen a las familias, para buscar en cambio, políticas de inmigración libres de toda motivación racista y de miedos egoístas. Con este mismo espíritu, hemos denunciado frecuentemente el trato injusto a los trabajadores agrícolas migrantes.

Declarar todo lo anteriormente expuesto no es reducir la evangelización y la misión de la Iglesia al mejoramiento de la vida en este mundo.[26] *Evangelii Nuntiandi* insiste en la profunda unión entre la invitación a la fe en Cristo y la promoción de la justicia social. Esta unión es parte del verdadero misterio de fe proclamado a través de la evangelización. Está basada en la relación entre la creación y la redención.[27] En *Redemptoris Missio*, Juan Pablo II confirma esta doctrina y la extiende en término de la *misión profética* de la Iglesia al servicio de los pobres.[28] El Santo Padre habla de la solidaridad de la Iglesia con los pobres como un signo de redención. La Iglesia, dice, es la Iglesia de los pobres.[29] El Santo Padre se refiere específicamente al ejemplo de la Iglesia en Latinoamérica, en donde la opción preferencial por los pobres ha sido reconocida como parte integral de la misión de la Iglesia. En efecto, es esta una de las grandes lecciones centrales a la experiencia de la Iglesia en América Latina, como se expresa en las declaraciones de Medellín y Puebla, y ratificadas en Santo Domingo. Acogemos la importancia dada a este aspecto por nuestros católicos hispanos en la Declaración de Compromiso de la Convocación '95. Vemos esto como un ejemplo de cómo los católicos hispanos son un "puente lógico entre la Iglesia en Estados Unidos y la Iglesia en América Latina",[30] como lo afirma la Declaración de Compromiso.

LA BENDICIÓN DE LA PRESENCIA HISPANA

Junto con el Santo Padre, reconocemos la presencia hispana en nuestra Iglesia como una bendición, como una oportunidad privilegiada para trabajar por una cultura que refleja la verdad acerca de la persona humana revelada en la verdad acerca de Jesucristo. Como escribió el Papa Juan Pablo II a la Convocación '95: "Desde los albores de la evangelización en el Nuevo Mundo, el nombre de Jesucristo y el poder liberador del Evangelio han tomado raíz entre los pueblos de habla castellana en las Américas. La prédica y el testimonio evangélico de los primeros misioneros dieron fruto en vidas de santidad y en el brote de una nueva cultura marcada por una fe profunda y unos valores cristianos auténticos. Hoy, esta herencia viviente continúa siendo una fuente de enriquecimiento para la Iglesia en Estados Unidos, mientras enfrenta el desafío de proclamar la Buena Nueva de nuestra salvación y de edificar el Cuerpo de Cristo en el contexto de una sociedad étnicamente diversa".[31]

En nuestra carta pastoral *La Presencia Hispana: Esperanza y Compromiso*, publicada en 1983 y en el *Plan Pastoral Nacional para el Ministerio Hispano*, de 1987, ya hemos resaltado la contribución hispana a la vida de la Iglesia en Estados Unidos. Es un hecho que *el futuro de la Iglesia en Estados Unidos se verá afectado grandemente por lo que suceda a los católicos hispanos*, quienes constituyen un gran porcentaje de sus miembros. La contribución de los católicos hispanos en Estados Unidos a la Nueva Evangelización y al futuro de la Iglesia, dependerá de la presencia de la Iglesia en la comunidad hispana.

Cuando hablamos de la presencia hispana, es importante entender que estamos hablando de una realidad compleja, variada y dinámica. La Declaración de Compromiso de la Convocación '95 correctamente subraya "la importancia de la presencia hispana en los medios de comunicación social para que se presenten imágenes adecuadas de la realidad de nuestras comunidades, sus verdaderas necesidades y sus contribuciones a la vida de la Iglesia y la sociedad".[32] Los participantes solicitaron a la Iglesia que los programas de educación y formación religiosa en escuelas, universidades, institutos y seminarios, refleje el verdadero significado de la presencia hispana.

En cierto sentido, una nueva identidad hispano-americana está aún en proceso de ser forjada en los Estados Unidos, ya que gente de diferentes culturas latinoamericanas se reúnen, descubren lo que tienen en común y se relacionan con la cultura norteamericana dominante. Esta nueva identidad hispano-americana tomará su lugar junto a todas las otras expresiones de la identidad hispana, teniendo todas un origen común.

La mayoría de los hispanos ha nacido aquí y sus antepasados han estado en nuestro país desde mucho tiempo atrás, algunos incluyendo muchas generaciones. La Convocación '95 proporcionó a los participantes la oportunidad de reflexionar sobre los orígenes de la presencia hispana en nuestra tierra desde mucho antes del establecimiento de las trece colonias inglesas. Hoy, la gran mayoría de los hispanos está comprometida con la misma lucha que todos los grupos anteriores de inmigrantes, principalmente en el cuidado de la familia, del trabajo, de la salud y de la educación. Obviamente, sus necesidades son diferentes a las de aquellos que recién se establecen. Se hace necesario responder de formas diferentes a sus diferentes necesidades. En este sentido, estamos de acuerdo con la necesidad de buscar "las maneras para que los hispanos que han logrado éxito en la sociedad contribuyan con sus talentos para que nuestra experiencia de fe inculturada asista a la Iglesia en la evangelización del mundo profesional".[33]

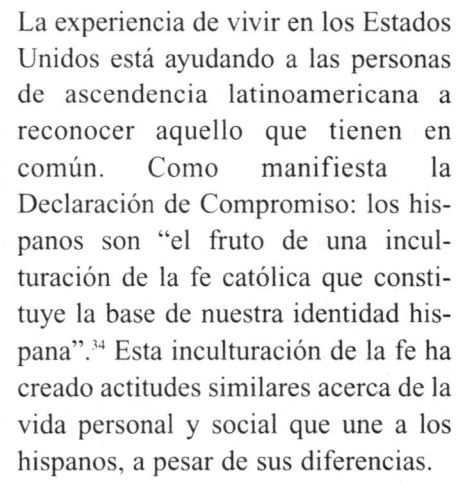

La experiencia de vivir en los Estados Unidos está ayudando a las personas de ascendencia latinoamericana a reconocer aquello que tienen en común. Como manifiesta la Declaración de Compromiso: los hispanos son "el fruto de una inculturación de la fe católica que constituye la base de nuestra identidad hispana".[34] Esta inculturación de la fe ha creado actitudes similares acerca de la vida personal y social que une a los hispanos, a pesar de sus diferencias.

Las culturas hispanas tradicionales conservan muchas experiencias de la persona, de la naturaleza, de los demás y de Dios que caracterizan esta inculturación de la fe. Nos referimos a las actitudes comunes como un espíritu abierto; una disposición abierta a lo inesperado, a lo nuevo o a lo no planeado; a la sencillez; un reconocimiento que la necesidad de compañía y apoyo no es debilidad sino una parte necesaria del crecimiento personal; una fidelidad creativa y una determinación de cumplir las promesas hechas; un sentido de honor y respeto hacia si mismo y hacia los demás; una paciencia y aceptación de seguir el ritmo de la naturaleza; un sentido de caminar juntos hacia un destino común; una verdadera imaginación creativa capaz de elevarse sobre las apariencias inmediatas para alcanzar el meollo íntimo de la realidad; un amor por el hogar y por la tierra y una visión amplia de la familia; una confianza en la Providencia divina; una convicción de que lo que es bueno y correcto es más digno de sacrificio que las satisfacciones inmediatas, que las personas son más importantes que las cosas, que las relaciones personales son más satisfactorias que el éxito material y que la serenidad tiene más valor que la vida en constante actividad. Todo esto se combina con una alegre resignación nacida de la convicción de que la vida es más importante que cualquier frustración temporal. Estas actitudes semejantes, características del "ethos" hispano, son el fruto de la inculturación de la fe católica mediante el extraordinario encuentro con la espiritualidad ibérica, la nativo-americana y la africana ocurrida en los inicios de la historia de los hispanos. *Históricamente, el ethos hispano es inseparable de la fe católica. En realidad, a veces el miedo y la oposición a la presencia hispana están motivados más por un sentimiento anti-católico que por cualquier otro cosa.*

¡Desde luego que los hispanos no son el único pueblo que posee estas cualidades! Estos atributos pertenecen a todos aquellos que son auténticamente humanos. Aún más, como con todo lo que es humano, estas actitudes pueden ser corrompidas por el pecado y pueden ocultar la realidad del prejuicio y del egoísmo. Sin embargo, con el Santo Padre, estamos convencidos de que la presencia en nuestra Iglesia de una gran cantidad de hispanos puede ser entendida espiritualmente como una *oportunidad providencial* para todos nosotros de redescubrir las cualidades necesarias para nuestro servicio a la sociedad en el nombre del Evangelio de liberación de Jesucristo. Estas cualidades no son sólo estereotipos folklóricos. Detrás de ellas, existe una actitud decisiva y valiente, originada en la fe católica y mantenida en medio de las vicisitudes de lo que muchas veces es una vida dura y difícil.

PRESENCIA PROFÉTICA

En nuestra carta pastoral sobre la Presencia Hispana y en el Plan Pastoral Nacional para el Ministerio Hispano, nos referimos a la presencia hispana como *profética*. Esta presencia profética se debe, sobre todo, a aquellos aspectos del ethos hispano que surgen de sus orígenes católicos. Como profética, creemos que la presencia hispana le da a la Iglesia en nuestro país la oportunidad de recordar su misión de preservar y promover una identidad católica en medio de una cultura muchas veces hostil.

Durante casi toda su historia, la Iglesia Católica en los Estados Unidos ha tratado de convencer a la sociedad norteamericana del patriotismo del pueblo católico y de su adherencia a las "verdades fundamentales evidentes" mencionadas en nuestra Declaración de la Independencia. Aunque sigue habiendo anticatolicismo en nuestro país, el esfuerzo realizado ha alcanzado cierto éxito, especialmente después de la Declaración sobre la Libertad Religiosa del Concilio Vaticano II. Sin embargo, en la actualidad, la influencia del secularismo ha suscitado un debate sobre la interpretación correcta de los principios fundacionales americanos.

> *Como profética, creemos que la presencia hispana le da a la Iglesia en nuestro país la oportunidad de recordar su misión de preservar y promover una identidad católica en medio de una cultura muchas veces hostil.*

Algunas de las interpretaciones que se han propuesto, y que se han adoptado aun en decisiones judiciales, son absolutamente incompatibles con nuestra fe. Para poder participar en el debate actual y ayudar a nuestro país a ser fiel a las verdades y valores sobre los cuales se dice que ha sido fundado, es necesario para nosotros, como católicos, apreciar la relación entre la fe y la cultura. La presencia hispana es profética ya que es la portadora de tradiciones que fluyen de una auténtica inculturación de la fe católica.[35] Nuestros esfuerzos por ayudar a los hispanos a que perseveren y crezcan en la fe, nos pondrá en una posición adecuada para entender mejor aquellas corrientes de pensamiento y de experiencia práctica en nuestra sociedad que minan la fe de todos los católicos.

La Iglesia en los Estados Unidos empezó como una iglesia de inmigrantes pobres que lucharon contra la discriminación para poder participar en el sueño americano. No obstante, muchas veces el anticatolicismo los excluyó de su participación en la sociedad. Irónicamente, en nombre de la libertad, la libertad les fue negada; en nombre de la tolerancia, la tolerancia les fue negada y las puertas les fueron cerradas. *Nosotros creemos que nuevamente ésta, más y más, es la situación actual,* extendiéndose aún más allá del catolicismo a todas las expresiones de la fe bíblica que difieren del ethos secularista que busca el dominio cultural en nuestra sociedad.

En el pasado, la Iglesia Católica creó un lugar dentro de la sociedad americana donde el pueblo católico podría ser alimentado y ayudado en la fe al mismo tiempo que se cuidaría de sus necesidades. Esto estuvo acompañado por un esfuerzo implacable para demostrar que los católicos estaban tan totalmente comprometidos a la libertad, al pluralismo y a la democracia como cualquier otra persona en el país. Como resultado de este esfuerzo, la mayoría de nuestros inmigrantes católicos fueron asimilados dentro de la corriente principal en los Estados Unidos. Esto fue posible gracias al compromiso del pueblo norteamericano con los derechos de la persona humana basados en la dignidad intransferible de cada ser humano creado por Dios. Desde luego, hubo diferencias de opinión en relación a esos derechos, su origen y significado final, pero fue posible llegar a un entendimiento común sobre esto basado en las experiencias bíblicas de la vida de los judíos y los cristianos y en la gran tradición sobre la ley natural entendida por todos los seres humanos, sin importar sus diferentes creencias con respecto a religión.

En la presente crisis cultural, este entendimiento común no es siempre posible. Los conceptos cruciales y claves sobre los cuales se basa la discusión son los mismos—conceptos tales como los derechos, las personas, la justicia, la libertad y la felicidad—pero las experiencias que se derivan de estos conceptos no pueden asumirse que son las mismas para todos. Desde luego, debemos continuar el diálogo sobre el cual depende nuestro futuro como nación, buscándolo con serenidad y con respeto para todos, pero siempre debemos tratar de entender las experiencias en la raíz de los conceptos que se discuten. Más importante todavía, debemos *recuperar la dimensión cultural de las experiencias en la raíz de la vida católica.* Es éste un aspecto crucial en la Nueva Evangelización, y la gran presencia hispana en medio de nosotros constituye un recurso providencial en esta tarea. Es por esto que hemos afirmado que *la contribución más importante de los católicos hispanos a la Nueva Evangelización en nuestro país radica en el área de la fe y la cultura.*

ADVERTENCIA PROFÉTICA

La presencia hispana es también una advertencia profética para la Iglesia en los Estados Unidos. Si a los católicos hispanos no se les recibe calurosamente y no se les ofrece un hogar donde puedan sentir nuestra Iglesia como su Iglesia, la pérdida de su identidad católica será un grave golpe a la Iglesia en nuestro país. Habremos perdido una oportunidad de ser verdaderamente católicos mientras esa cultura de la muerte, prevaleciente en nuestra sociedad, busca imponer sus costumbres en todos nosotros.

Así como lo demuestra la llamada a una Nueva Evangelización en Latinoamérica, no podemos dar por hecho la fe católica de los católicos hispanos. Los hispanos no se consideran un pueblo escogido y protegido de un modo especial de infidelidad al Evangelio. Ni tampoco se presentan como ejemplos vivos de fe. Pretender ser así sería un romanticismo intolerable y peligroso. La disposición hacia la fe no es la fe en sí; una fuerte religiosidad no es idéntica a la vida eclesialsacramental en Cristo; la apreciación de los valores personales, de la familia y la comunidad no son suficientes para una vida moral en Cristo. La devastación de familias hispanas debido a las drogas, al alcohol y al libertinaje está bien documentada. También lo está la difícil situación de muchas mujeres hispanas que son víctimas de actitudes machistas, profundamente arraigadas, tal y como nos lo recordaron insistentemente las mujeres presentes en la Convocación '95. Aunque el racismo, la pobreza, los ataques al inmigrante y la discriminación por prejuicios son todavía parte de la experiencia de muchos hispanos, estos vicios también se encuentran presentes en las comunidades hispanas. El compromiso a luchar contra estos males, abrazando una opción preferencial por los pobres es, asimismo, un compromiso de hispanos hacia otros hispanos.

Aún así, con todo, tenemos entre nosotros un precioso regalo traído por nuestros hermanos y hermanas hispanos: un sentido de lo sagrado, una sensibilidad profunda y especial por la belleza de la creación celebrada en forma festiva, un sentido de orgullo en *la hispanidad*, una habilidad de sentir profundas emociones de devoción por los demás, una gran delicadeza en el trato humano, y una sed de lo divino y lo trascendental manifestada en los poderosos símbolos católicos. Nosotros, junto con los participantes de la Convocación '95, creemos que la importancia de este "catolicismo cultural" no debe ser subestimada. Es realmente una bendición, y es bajo estas experiencias de fe hecha cultura que se debe basar la Nueva Evangelización en nuestro país.

LA ESTRELLA DE LA EVANGELIZACIÓN

A esta tarea nos encomendamos, una vez más, a la Reina de las Américas, Nuestra Señora de Guadalupe, mientras buscamos corresponder a la llamada a una Nueva Evangelización. Fue en el seno de María que el Verbo se hizo carne. El misterio de la encarnación es la base de nuestra creencia en el misterio de fe hecho cultura. El *Magnificat* de María es el cántico de nuestra opción preferencial de amor a los pobres. Ella es la mujer, perseguida por el dragón, en cuya compañía el pueblo de Dios, sus hijos, están protegidos de la cultura de la muerte. Es María la que evita que separemos a Nuestro Señor de la carne y lo convirtamos en una figura abstracta y remota. A través de ella, el Señor se hace presencia concreta y tangible redimiendo todos los aspectos de nuestra vida, nuestro compañero y la meta de nuestro peregrinaje hacia la manifestación definitiva del Reino de Dios. Al aceptar el compromiso de nuestros hermanos y hermanas de la Convocación '95, los encomendamos a ellos y a nosotros mismos a Santa María, la Estrella de toda Evangelización.

NOTAS

1. En este documento, el término *hispano* se utiliza como sinónimo de latinoamericano, latino, méxico-americano, hispano-americano, chicano y las demás personas de habla castellana en los Estados Unidos.

2. "La Presencia Hispana: Esperanza y Compromiso", Washington, D.C.: United States Catholic Conference, 1984.

3. Declaración de Compromiso, Convocación '95, 25 de Junio de 1995.

4. Declaración de Compromiso, 9.

5. Carta del Arzobispo G. B. Re, 8 de mayo de 1995 al Obispo Roberto O. González, Presidente del Comité de Asuntos Hispanos de la Conferencia Episcopal, Prot. No. 370.479 (incluída en el Apéndice A).

6. Declaración de Compromiso, 3.

7. *Gaudium et Spes* (GS), 53.

8. Ibid., 57.

9. Cf. GS, nos. 55 y 57.

10. La Evangelización en el Presente y en el Futuro de América Latina. Bogotá: CELAM, 1979, no. 386.

11. Cf. *Gaudium et Spes*, 24.

12. Cf. AAS 75 (1983), pp. 771-779.

13. Congregación para la Doctrina de la Fe (CDF), *Instrucción sobre Ciertos Aspectos de la Teología de la Liberación*, VIII, 1-9.

14. Declaración de Compromiso, 4.

15. Ibid.

16. Ibid.

17. Ibid., 8.

18. Cf. Paulo VI, *Evangelii Nuntiandi*, 22, AAS 68 (1976).

19. Declaración de Compromiso, 8.

20. Cf. Rom. 5,5.

21. Cf. Juan Pablo II, *Evangelium Vitae*, 12.

22. Cf. ibid., 20.

23. Declaración de Compromiso, 5.

24. Ibid.

25. Ibid.

26. CDF, *Instrucción sobre Ciertos Aspectos de la Teología de la Liberación*, VI, 3.

27. CF, *Evangelii Nuntiandi*, no. 31.

28. Juan Pablo II, *Redemptoris Missio*, 43.

29. Ibid., 60.

30. Declaración de Compromiso, 10.

31. Cf. Apéndice A, Carta al Obispo Roberto O. González, op. cit.

32. Declaración de Compromiso, 6.

33. Ibid.

34. Ibid., 3.

35. *Ministerio Hispano: Tres Documentos Importantes.* Washington, D.C.: United States Catholic Conference, 1995.

Apéndices

A. Mensaje del Santo Padre

8 de mayo de 1995

Estimado Monseñor González,

El Santo Padre agradece profundamente que le informaran que el Comité de Asuntos Hispanos de la Conferencia Episcopal auspiciará, del 23 al 25 de junio de 1995, la Convocación '95, un programa de oración y reflexión, dedicado al tema: "La Presencia Hispana en la Nueva Evangelización en los Estados Unidos". Le pide encarecidamente hacer extensivos sus buenos deseos de éxito, a todos los ahí reunidos, por esta iniciativa pastoral tan significativa.

Su Santidad se une a los delegados de la Convocación en su agradecimiento a Dios Todopoderoso por las bendiciones abundantes conferidas a la Iglesia en los Estados Unidos, mediante la profunda fe y testimonio cristiano de generaciones de católicos hispanos. Desde los albores de la evangelización en el Nuevo Mundo, el nombre de Jesucristo y el poder liberador del Evangelio han tomado raíz entre los pueblos de habla castellana en las Américas. La prédica y el testimonio evangélico de los primeros misioneros dieron fruto en vidas de santidad y en el brote de una nueva cultura marcada por una fe profunda y unos valores cristianos auténticos. Hoy, esta herencia viviente continúa siendo una fuente de enriquecimiento para la Iglesia en los Estados Unidos, mientras enfrenta el desafío de proclamar la Buena Nueva de nuestra salvación y de edificar el Cuerpo de Cristo en el contexto de una sociedad étnicamente diversa.

El Santo Padre desea fervientemente que la Convocación de San Antonio, al conmemorar el quincuagésimo aniversario del primer esfuerzo por coordinar el apostolado hispano en los Estados Unidos, fomente un compromiso más profundo y consciente de parte de los católicos hispanos de dar un testimonio efectivo de su fe, de fortalecer el crecimiento de la Iglesia en amor y de servir a Cristo en los más pequeños de sus hermanos y hermanas. Basados en su rica historia y en su experiencia, la comunidad hispana puede ofrecer una contribución única al diálogo entre fe y cultura en la sociedad norteamericana actual, y de esta forma, abrir nuevos caminos para la propagación del Evangelio en el Tercer Milenio. Reconociendo la importancia que tiene la nueva generación para el futuro de la Iglesia en los Estados Unidos, Su Santidad anima a los delegados de la Conferencia a que tomen en consideración la apremiante necesidad de una catequesis efectiva, y que promuevan estructuras que permitan a los jóvenes a responder generosamente a la invitación de servir al Señor en el sacerdocio y en la vida religiosa.

Al final, el éxito de la nueva evangelización se medirá por la respuesta de todos los bautizados al llamado de Cristo a una conversión sincera, a una fe viviente y a una vida de santidad. A los delegados y a todos los reunidos en la Convocación, el Santo Padre les repite las palabras de desafío que dirigió a la comunidad hispana durante su visita pastoral a San Antonio en 1987: "Hoy les toca a ustedes, con fidelidad al Evangelio de Jesucristo, edificar sus vidas sobre la piedra de su fe cristiana. Les toca a ustedes ser evangelizadores de cada uno y de todos aquellos cuya fe es débil o de quienes todavía no se han entregado al Señor. ¡Sean tan entusiastas en la evangelización y en el servicio cristiano como lo fueron sus antepasados! (*Mensaje en la Plaza de Nuestra Señora de Guadalupe, 13 de setiembre de 1987*).

Con estos sentimientos, Su Santidad encomienda a todos los que toman parte en Convocación '95 a la intercesión amorosa de la Inmaculada Virgen María, Patrona de la Iglesia en los Estados Unidos, y les concede cordialmente su Bendición Apostólica como una promesa de gozo y fortaleza en Jesucristo, Nuestro Salvador.

Con mis mejores deseos personales, quedo,

Suyo en Cristo,

+ G. B. Re
Substituto

B. Declaración de Compromiso de la Convocacion '95

1. Alabamos a Dios, quien ha sido bueno con nosotros, por la oportunidad de reunirnos en San Antonio para conmemorar los cincuenta años del establecimiento de lo que ahora es el Comité Nacional de Obispos para Asuntos Hispanos. Celebramos los logros en la pastoral hispana durante este medio siglo, y profundamente conscientes de la Comunión en Cristo Jesús que nos une en una sola Iglesia Católica que peregrina proclamando el Reino de Dios, nos comprometemos a la tarea de una Nueva Evangelización en los Estados Unidos de América. Ofrecemos a nuestros obispos esta "Declaración de Compromiso", ansiosos por escuchar de ellos su visión acerca de la contribución hispana a la Nueva Evangelización.

2. La Convocación '95 ha sido para la comunidad hispano-católica, una experiencia evangelizadora que ya empezó a generar un nuevo ardor, a crear nuevas expresiones y a explorar nuevos métodos para hacer presente el Reino de Dios en nuestra sociedad.

3. Aunque celebramos los cincuenta años de una pastoral hispana organizada a nivel nacional, nuestra reunión en San Antonio nos da la oportunidad de reafirmar los orígenes de nuestra identidad católica. Somos el fruto de una inculturación de la fe católica que constituye la base de nuestra identidad hispana. Celebrando la variedad de manifestaciones de esta identidad en nuestros distintos pueblos de origen, nos comprometemos a compartir con nuestras hermanas y hermanos católicos en los Estados Unidos lo que es una fe encarnada en cultura. De esta manera podremos, todos unidos, luchar contra la cultura de la muerte denunciada por nuestro Santo Padre, Juan Pablo II, dando testimonio de lo que es el Evangelio de la Vida.

4. Nos comprometemos a dar testimonio de cómo se incultura en un pueblo la opción preferencial por los pobres, parte esencial de la fe católica. Por esta opción, comprendemos la afirmación de la dignidad de la persona humana tal como fue creada por Dios, sin otro propósito que el bien de su existencia. Lucharemos contra todo intento de instrumentalizar a la persona humana y de valorar sólo su posible contribución al progreso material de la sociedad.

5. Guiados por esta opción, defenderemos el valor de cada vida humana desde el primer momento de su concepción hasta la muerte natural. Buscaremos formas de afirmar nuestra solidaridad con todos aquellos que defienden a las víctimas de la cultura de la muerte en nuestro país, superando toda hostilidad racial o étnica, tratando de ser verdadero fermento de unidad, y luchando contra el racismo y la discriminación que niegan acceso a los recursos necesarios para salir de la pobreza en la cual se encuentra inmersa todavía gran parte de la población hispana. Insistiremos que se reconozca en toda nuestra sociedad, el derecho a un trabajo digno, a un salario justo, a una vivienda decente, a una educación que respete nuestros orígenes culturales, y el acceso a programas de cuidado de la salud dignos del valor de cada ser humano, cualquiera sea su edad. Discutiendo los problemas de salud, hicimos particular mención a la devastación producida por el SIDA, comprometiéndonos a ser testigos del amor de Dios por todos los enfermos. La contaminación del agua y del medio ambiente también amenazan la salud de muchas de nuestras comunidades, y continuaremos nuestros esfuerzos para que cese esta destrucción de la naturaleza cuyos bienes son para todos los seres humanos.

6. Buscaremos maneras en que los hispanos que han logrado éxito en la sociedad contribuyan con sus talentos para que nuestra experiencia

B. Declaración de Compromiso de la Convocacion '95

1. Alabamos a Dios, quien ha sido bueno con nosotros, por la oportunidad de reunirnos en San Antonio para conmemorar los cincuenta años del establecimiento de lo que ahora es el Comité Nacional de Obispos para Asuntos Hispanos. Celebramos los logros en la pastoral hispana durante este medio siglo, y profundamente conscientes de la Comunión en Cristo Jesús que nos une en una sola Iglesia Católica que peregrina proclamando el Reino de Dios, nos comprometemos a la tarea de una Nueva Evangelización en los Estados Unidos de América. Ofrecemos a nuestros obispos esta "Declaración de Compromiso", ansiosos por escuchar de ellos su visión acerca de la contribución hispana a la Nueva Evangelización.

2. La Convocación '95 ha sido para la comunidad hispano-católica, una experiencia evangelizadora que ya empezó a generar un nuevo ardor, a crear nuevas expresiones y a explorar nuevos métodos para hacer presente el Reino de Dios en nuestra sociedad.

3. Aunque celebramos los cincuenta años de una pastoral hispana organizada a nivel nacional, nuestra reunión en San Antonio nos da la oportunidad de reafirmar los orígenes de nuestra identidad católica. Somos el fruto de una inculturación de la fe católica que constituye la base de nuestra identidad hispana. Celebrando la variedad de manifestaciones de esta identidad en nuestros distintos pueblos de origen, nos comprometemos a compartir con nuestras hermanas y hermanos católicos en los Estados Unidos lo que es una fe encarnada en cultura. De esta manera podremos, todos unidos, luchar contra la cultura de la muerte denunciada por nuestro Santo Padre, Juan Pablo II, dando testimonio de lo que es el Evangelio de la Vida.

4. Nos comprometemos a dar testimonio de cómo se incultura en un pueblo la opción preferencial por los pobres, parte esencial de la fe católica. Por esta opción, comprendemos la afirmación de la dignidad de la persona humana tal como fue creada por Dios, sin otro propósito que el bien de su existencia. Lucharemos contra todo intento de instrumentalizar a la persona humana y de valorar sólo su posible contribución al progreso material de la sociedad.

5. Guiados por esta opción, defenderemos el valor de cada vida humana desde el primer momento de su concepción hasta la muerte natural. Buscaremos formas de afirmar nuestra solidaridad con todos aquellos que defienden a las víctimas de la cultura de la muerte en nuestro país, superando toda hostilidad racial o étnica, tratando de ser verdadero fermento de unidad, y luchando contra el racismo y la discriminación que niegan acceso a los recursos necesarios para salir de la pobreza en la cual se encuentra inmersa todavía gran parte de la población hispana. Insistiremos que se reconozca en toda nuestra sociedad, el derecho a un trabajo digno, a un salario justo, a una vivienda decente, a una educación que respete nuestros orígenes culturales, y el acceso a programas de cuidado de la salud dignos del valor de cada ser humano, cualquiera sea su edad. Discutiendo los problemas de salud, hicimos particular mención a la devastación producida por el SIDA, comprometiéndonos a ser testigos del amor de Dios por todos los enfermos. La contaminación del agua y del medio ambiente también amenazan la salud de muchas de nuestras comunidades, y continuaremos nuestros esfuerzos para que cese esta destrucción de la naturaleza cuyos bienes son para todos los seres humanos.

6. Buscaremos maneras en que los hispanos que han logrado éxito en la sociedad contribuyan con sus talentos para que nuestra experiencia

de fe inculturada asista a la Iglesia en la evangelización del mundo profesional. Subrayamos la importancia de una presencia hispana en los medios de comunicación social para que se presente una imagen apropiada de la realidad de nuestras comunidades, sus verdaderas necesidades y sus contribuciones a la vida de la Iglesia y la sociedad. Reafirmamos nuestro compromiso de solidaridad con los trabajadores agrícolas migratorios, los refugiados, las víctimas de los abusos policiales y los indocumentados. Desarrollaremos metas y estrategias dentro de nuestro ministerio para luchar contra la discriminación que sufre el pueblo inmigrante, trabajando con instituciones políticas y agencias gubernamentales para educar e informar sobre los asuntos que les afectan. Recordamos que los encarcelados por cualquier razón no pierden su dignidad como personas humanas, y trataremos que su cuidado pastoral sea atento a las necesidades particulares de la población hispana en las cárceles.

Queremos que nuestras comunidades hispanas estén a la vanguardia de los esfuerzos por defender la dignidad de la familia como célula fundamental de la sociedad y de la Iglesia. Nos comprometemos a laborar para que se reconozca la dignidad de la vocación a ser madres y padres, y lucharemos por el reconocimiento de los derechos de la mujer y su inestimable contribución a todos los aspectos de la vida social y eclesial. Las mujeres hispanas en la Convocación '95, han llamado nuestra atención a la problemática de la mujer en nuestro país, y nos comprometemos a luchar contra la violencia doméstica, la violación y el maltrato de la mujer, el abandono de las madres solteras, la marginación de la mujer pobre, y la falta de recursos para la educación integral y el desarrollo personal. Hablando de la familia, subrayamos la importancia del respeto de la dignidad de nuestros ancianos de quienes hemos recibido la fe que nos sostiene y anima.

8. Buscaremos formas para demostrar que nuestros esfuerzos en el área de justicia social son consecuencia de nuestra fe en Jesucristo, el Señor, el centro de la historia y del universo. En la verdad acerca de Jesucristo, verdadero Dios y verdadero Hombre, descubrimos lo que es la persona humana en todas sus dimensiones: individual, social, material y espiritual. Nos comprometemos a proclamar y a dar testimonio de lo que es ser el Pueblo de Dios que sigue a Jesús hacia la plena manifestación de su victoria sobre el pecado y la muerte. Por lo tanto, promoviendo una auténtica pastoral de conjunto, haremos todo lo posible para que nuestra pastoral litúrgica, sacramental y catequética, al igual que las estructuras parroquiales, den testimonio de la verdad acerca de la Iglesia fundada por Cristo, para ser fieles a la visión del *Plan Pastoral Nacional para el Ministerio Hispano*, de una Iglesia auténticamente "comunitaria, evangelizadora y misionera, encarnada en la realidad del pueblo hispano y abierta a la diversidad de culturas, promotora y ejemplo de justicia, que desarrolle liderazgo por medio de la educacion integral...que sea fermento del Reino de Dios en la sociedad".

9. Promoveremos el conocimiento del *Plan Pastoral Nacional* y su implementación donde todavía no se haya hecho. Continuaremos buscando expresiones de vida eclesial y cambios estructurales que, en comunión con nuestros obispos y el Santo Padre, nos ayuden a dar un testimonio claro de la verdad acerca de la Iglesia, tales como las pequeñas comunidades eclesiales, movimientos de renovación eclesial, y organizaciones hispanas católicas. En este campo, se hace necesario reforzar las parroquias como centros de vida eclesial en las diferentes regiones. Apoyamos todos los esfu-erzos para fortalecer las escuelas católicas, buscando formas en que la educación católica sea más accesible al pueblo hispano. Subrayamos también la importancia de un ministerio de vocaciones que busque

con esmero particular a hispanos e hispanas llamados al ministerio en la Iglesia como sacerdotes, diáconos y miembros de comunidades religiosas. Reconocemos la necesidad de que las familias hispanas den mayor atención a la vocación al ministerio eclesial, reconociendo la gran bendición que esto representa para ellas. Urgen programas de una formación religiosa adecuada para nuestras comunidades y sus líderes laicos, dando énfasis a un conocimiento profundo de las Sagradas Escrituras como la Palabra de Dios, la doctrina de la Iglesia según el nuevo *Catecismo de la Iglesia Católica*, y el poder incomparable de la oración. Hacemos un llamado a los colegios y a otras instituciones de educación a responder a las necesidades del pueblo hispano, y que los seminarios preparen adecuadamente a todos los futuros sacerdotes a comprender la realidad y la promesa de la presencia hispana en la Iglesia. Afirmamos la importancia de una religiosidad popular que refleje auténticamente el Evangelio como una de las formas más importantes en que la fe se convierte en cultura. En nuestra Convocación '95 se discutió ampliamente la importancia de una pastoral adecuada para nuestros jóvenes, abierta a sus puntos de vista y solicitando sus contribuciones a la vida de la Iglesia. Buscaremos las maneras de compartir con toda la Iglesia en los Estados Unidos el progreso realizado en la pastoral hispana.

10. Concluyendo nuestra Convocación '95, afirmamos nuestro compromiso a buscar formas de continuar y fortalezer el proceso de diálogo, entre nuestras comunidades y nuestros obispos, como en el proceso de los Encuentros y como ha sucedido en esta convocación. No queremos esperar que pasen diez años para otra ocasión igual. Urgimos, por lo tanto, que se formulen planes para lograr una plena contribución de nuestro pueblo hispano en las preparaciones para la celebración del Tercer Milenio de Cristiandad. Como parte de esta preocupación, haremos todo lo posible para ayudar a la preparación y participación de nuestros obispos en el próximo Sínodo para todo el hemisferio americano. Somos el lógico puente entre la Iglesia en Estados Unidos y la Iglesia en América Latina.

11. Regresamos a nuestros hogares y lugares de compromiso eclesial encomendándonos a nuestra Madre, María, la Reina de las Américas, la Morenita, la Virgen de Guadalupe, compañera siempre de nuestros pueblos en la lucha por la libertad, la paz y el respeto de nuestra dignidad.

C. Contexto Histórico del Ministerio Hispano en la Iglesia Católica en los Estados Unidos

El Evangelio fue traído a este continente y a este hemisferio hace más de 500 años. Por tanto, el ministerio hacia las personas de habla hispana y a las personas nativas, ha sido un proceso contínuo y parte integral de la historia de la Iglesia en las Américas. En tiempos más recientes, el ministerio hacia las personas de habla hispana se estableció en las diócesis para responder a las problemáticas pastorales y sociales de cada comunidad hispana en particular.[1] En algunas diócesis, las oficinas de ministerio se establecieron a fines del siglo pasado y a principios del siglo actual. En muchas diócesis del oeste y suroeste del país, se establecieron concilios hispanos durante las décadas de los años 40 y 50.

El primer Comité de Obispos para los de habla hispana fue establecido en 1945 por la *National Catholic Welfare Conference*, bajo el liderazgo del Arzobispo de San Antonio, monseñor Robert E. Lucey. El Comité, con oficinas en la ciudad de San Antonio, tenía como enfoque prioritario, la situación apremiante de los trabajadores migrantes en el suroeste.[2]

Cuando se estableció el Comité de Obispos, la comunidad de habla hispana se encontraba asentada mayormente en los estados fronterizos con México. La presencia hispana se podía ver también en otras partes del país: en el medio oeste, el nordeste y en el estado de la Florida se apreciaba una población hispana significante.

En general, esta población era pequeña y en su mayoría pobre. La mayoría de los trabajadores recibían sueldos bajos, vivían en viviendas deficientes, carecían de cuidados médicos, tenían poca educación u oportunidades educacionales, y recibían una reducida ayuda o asistencia. Desgraciadamente, ni siquiera la iglesia institucional estaba allí para asistirles. Muchos de estos trabajadores habían llegado a los Estados Unidos como "braceros" patrocinados por el *Bracero Program* del gobierno federal que fue establecido durante y después de la Segunda Guerra Mundial para suplir mano de obra a la industria agrícola. Basta decir que la problemática de los trabajadores agrícolas se intensificó durante este período.

Muchas necesidades sociales y pastorales, en diferentes partes del país, impulsaron a los hispanos a formar nuevas asociaciones seculares y eclesiales. Estas asociaciones cobraron importancia ya que la comunidad hispana las utilizó como vehículos para lograr una participación más pro-activa en asuntos de la política pública y para responder a las muchas necesidades de servicios sociales enfrentadas por las familias y comunidades. La respuesta de la Iglesia fue continuar prestando servicios sociales y, más adelante, estableciendo y dando fondos a las diócesis y oficinas regionales e institutos pastorales a fin de coordinar mejor los esfuerzos de la pastoral hispana.[3]

Dentro de este clima de afirmación y apoyo, la Iglesia estableció una oficina para la pastoral de la comunidad hispana extendiendo su énfasis más allá de las problemáticas regionales. En 1968-1970, con la reorganización de la *National Catholic Welfare Conference*, la Oficina Nacional del Comité de Obispos para *el Hispano-Parlante* se convirtió en la Sección de los *Hispano Parlantes*, bajo el Departamento de Desarrollo Social de la recién estructurada *National Conference of Catholic Bishops*.[4]

En 1970, la oficina se trasladó a Washington, D.C. siendo la tarea del director nacional enfocar esfuerzos en lo pastoral yendo más allá de las problemáticas sociales y materiales; incrementar el número del personal para llevar a cabo el desafiante trabajo inmediato; colaborar con organizaciones nacionales e invitarlas a unirse en la tarea que se tenía por delante. El desafío para el Secretariado para Asuntos Hispanos era el de asistir a la Iglesia en su respuesta a las necesidades sociales y pastorales de un número creciente de hispanos católicos. Su misión era la de abogar por las necesidades pastorales y asuntos de naturaleza pública que impactaban la vida de la comunidad hispana. En junio de 1972, estos conceptos se convirtieron en las prioridades y en la base para el Primer Encuentro Nacional Hispano de Pastoral. Según dijo el Papa Pablo VI, el primer Encuentro "despertó tantas esperanzas y tanto entusiasmo".[5]

Las Conclusiones del Primer Encuentro dice que "las personas de habla hispana deben tener mayor participación en el liderato y la toma de decisiones en todos los niveles de la Iglesia estadounidense".[6] Lo que es más, llamaba a la creación de centros regionales y pastorales, coordinados a nivel nacional, con el fin de hacer investigación y reflexión, así como el desarrollo de programas de formación de liderazgo cristiano a todos los niveles de la Iglesia. Finalmente, las conclusiones de los participantes enuncian que "convencidos de la unidad de la iglesia estadounidense" y de los valores de su herencia, ellos sentían "el impulso del espíritu que nos mueve a compartir la responsabilidad en el desarrollo del reino" entre los hispanos y el pueblo de los Estados Unidos.[7]

El período que siguió al Primer Encuentro fue un tiempo en el cual el número de obispos hispanos aumentó, se vio la colaboración con obispos no-hispanos, se vio la renovación de sacerdotes y religiosos hispanos y pro-hispanos, la revitalización de los movimientos apostólicos y un crecimiento prometedor de las pequeñas comunidades de iglesia.

En 1974, la Sección de los Hispano Parlantes fue elevada al rango de Secretariado para Asuntos Hispanos, entrando en vigencia el 1ro de enero de 1975. De inmediato, en el primer año de su creación, el Comité de Obispos llamó a un Segundo Encuentro Nacional para responder a la necesidad de una orientación pastoral más concreta al NCCB. Al año siguiente, el secretariado nacional aprovechó la ocasión del Congreso Eucarístico Internacional que se llevaba a cabo en Philadelphia, para convocar a una reunión de líderes ministeriales a nivel nacional con el propósito de consultar acerca de las prioridades de la comunidad hispana y definirlas, especialmente aquellas que existían a nivel de base. "Surgieron tres grandes prioridades: Unidad y Pluralismo, Educación Integral, Cambio Social (sobre todo más respeto al pueblo hispano). Cada una de estas prioridades prestaba atención especial a los líderes y a los jóvenes".[8]

Los participantes en esta reunión fijaron el verano de 1977 como la fecha para el Segundo Encuentro. Se estableció un comité coordinador nacional, que consistía del personal del Secretariado y de los Directores Regionales. También se incluyó a los líderes de las organizaciones hispanas católicas del país. En enero de 1977, el Comité Ad Hoc de Obispos para el Ministerio Hispano apoyó y ratificó el Encuentro.

En varias de las reuniones que antecedieron al Encuentro, el comité coordinador nacional no tardó en descubrir que "el punto de arranque de este proceso debía ser la Iglesia Diocesana".[9] El número de oficinas diocesanas para personas de habla hispana había crecido de treinta en 1972 a más de cien en 1977. Se incluyó a los directores diocesanos en los procesos de planificación y estos fueron invitados a la reunión Nacional de Directores Diocesanos del Apostolado Hispano. Ochenta y dos directores diocesanos participaron. El tema escogido fue *Pueblo de Dios en Marcha* y el himno oficial, *Un Pueblo Que Camina*. El tema fue la evangelización y otros cinco tópicos relacionados con actividades que describían el concepto de Iglesia que los participantes deseaban encontrar; estos fueron: *ministerios, derechos humanos, educación integral, responsabilidad política y unidad en pluralismo*. Más de cien mil personas de todas partes del país participaron en el proceso.[10] "Las recomendaciones del II Encuentro expresan los deseos de los hispanos de base que quieren tener una iglesia más responsable, multicultural, espiritualmente viva, unida y creativa".[11]

En 1968, la Oficina Regional del Medio Oeste y el Centro Cultural México-Americano (MACC) habían sido establecidos para asistir en la formación, capacitación y desarrollo de oficinas diocesanas y agentes pastorales. En 1974, se fundó el Centro Pastoral del Nordeste en Nueva York. El período que siguió al II Encuentro de 1977, vió la apertura de cinco nuevas oficinas regionales para el ministerio hispano. La oficina del Sureste en 1978, la del Oeste en 1979, la del Noroeste en 1981 y la organización de directores diocesanos en los estados de Norte Central y en la región montañosa en 1984. Estas oficinas y estructuras regionales sirvieron de gran apoyo al apostolado hispano y continúan siendo una parte integral del ministerio hispano hoy en día.

Durante el II Encuentro también se creó un *National Youth Task Force* que más adelante se convertiría en el Comité Nacional Hispano de Pastoral Juvenil. Hoy en día esta organización ha cesado de existir pero hubo varios intentos para reactivarla. En 1987, debido a una reorganización del NCCB, se colocó a la juventud bajo la Oficina para Jóvenes del Secretariado para Laicos y Vida Familiar. En lugar del Comité, las oficinas regionales y diocesanas tomaron la responsabilidad de coordinar el ministerio juvenil hispano.

La fructuosa colaboración que se estableció con organizaciones católicas hispanas durante el II Encuentro, resultó ser una práctica valiosa para el ministerio pastoral. La experiencia y conocimientos de los líderes nacionales fueron elementos valiosos para el Comité Ad Hoc y para el Secretariado para Asuntos Hispanos al momento de formular estrategias pastorales. Todos los participantes se beneficiaron de la coordinación nacional. Ellos vieron la necesidad de mantenerse en contacto y de continuar colaborando con el propósito de implementar las prioridades pastorales nacionales de los hispanos.

Como resultado de la necesidad de continuar con estas reuniones, el Comité Consejero Nacional (NAC) fue creado en 1978 por la Conferencia Nacional de Obispos Católicos a fin de asistir al Secretariado para Asuntos Hispanos. Entre sus miembros estaban los directores y coordinadores de las oficinas y organizaciones regionales, los presidentes de los institutos pastorales, los presidentes de los movimientos apostólicos y los dirigentes de las organizaciones hispanas católicas, tales como PADRES, HERMANAS, Juventud Hispana y el Ministerio Nacional de Trabajadores Migrantes. Luego que el Comité Ad Hoc de Obispos adquirió el rango de Comité Permanente en 1987, el NAC fue desintegrado en 1990 a fin de que el comité se adaptara a la estructura de los comités permanentes de la NCCB/USCC.

Los Obispos Hablan con la Virgen: Una Carta Pastoral de los Obispos Hispanos de los Estados Unidos fue publicada en 1982. Esta carta fué un mensaje del peregrinaje de la comunidad hispana a lo largo de la historia, de su realidad, de cómo la comunidad es artesana de una nueva humanidad, y de su peregrinaje hecho con gozo, valor y esperanza. En 1983, el cuerpo de obispos publicó una carta pastoral sobre el ministerio hispano titulada *La Presencia Hispana: Esperanza y Compromiso*. En este documento, los obispos de los Estados Unidos hicieron un llamado al ministerio hispano, afirmaron los logros dentro del ministerio hispano, enumeraron las implicaciones pastorales urgentes y expresaron su compromiso. Más importante aún, en su carta los obispos llamaban a un tercer encuentro nacional cuyas conclusiones se revisarían y usarían como base para un plan pastoral nacional para el ministerio hispano.

Los obispos pedían al pueblo hispano "que eleve su voz profética una vez más, como hizo en 1972 y 1977, en un Tercer Encuentro Nacional Hispano de Pastoral, de forma que juntos podamos asumir responsablemente nuestras responsabilidades. Pedimos que se inicie el proceso para que tenga lugar un encuentro, desde las comunidades eclesiales de base y las parroquias pasando por las diócesis y regiones, hasta el nivel nacional, para culminar en una reunión de representantes en Washington, D.C., en agosto de 1985".[12] Además, ellos expresaron que reconocían que "la planificación pastoral integral debe evitar adaptaciones meramente superficiales de los ministerios existentes".[13]

El III Encuentro es el fruto de los esfuerzos de muchas mujeres y hombres comprometidos, quienes por muchos años dedicaron su tiempo y energía al proceso de evangelización. El III Encuentro fue un proceso que consistía en 10 pasos que requerían consulta y participación del pueblo a nivel diocesano, regional y nacional. El proceso de 10 pasos incluía: 1) formación de equipos promotores diocesanos (EPDs) y equipos móviles; 2) evaluación del II Encuentro; 3) promoción del III Encuentro mediante la comunicación; 4) consulta local por medio del contacto personal; 5) reflexión local acerca de la consulta y la selección de prioridades para el nivel nacional; 6) reunión nacional de los directores diocesanos y delegados de los EPDs y selección de un tema; 7) estudio y reflexión en el ámbito local sobre el tema nacional; 8) segunda reunión diocesana para sintetizar la reflexión local sobre el tema; 9) encuentro regional sobre las conclusiones diocesanas para uso en el encuentro nacional; y finalmente, 10) el III Encuentro Nacional Hispano de Pastoral.[14]

Cuatro objetivos fueron propuestos por parte del Comité Ad Hoc de Obispos para Asuntos Hispanos para el III Encuentro: a) evangelizador, b) capaz de formar líderes a través del proceso mismo, c) ser desarrollado por las bases y d) debería enfatizar las dimensiones diocesanas y regionales del proceso. Un quinto objetivo vino de la carta pastoral de los obispos, un Plan Pastoral Nacional.[15] Las Oficinas Regionales, los Institutos Pastorales, el Comité Consejero Nacional y los representates de los equipos promotores diocesanos ayudaron a diseñar el proceso, el cual ayudó a conservar el modelo de comunión y participación.

El tema escogido fué *Pueblo Hispano: Voz Profética*, el cual surgió de la Carta Pastoral de los obispos, *La Presencia Hispana: Esperanza y Compromiso*. Unas *Líneas Proféticas Pastorales* prácticas fueron aprobadas y se convirtieron en la "dirección y en las opciones principales de la pastoral hispana".[16]

Voces Proféticas se publicó en 1986 como el documento sobre el contexto histórico, el proceso que se siguió, los compromisos, el seguimiento, la reflexión pastoral y las conclusiones del III Encuentro Nacional Hispano de Pastoral.

Las Líneas Proféticas Pastorales en este documento fueron elaboradas para dar una dirección esencial a la acción pastoral. Entre ellas estaba: la familia como el núcleo del ministerio pastoral, una opción preferencial por los pobre y en solidaridad con ellor, una opción preferencial por la juventud hispana, el propósito de proseguir con una pastoral de conjunto y de continuar el método pastoral de una iglesia evangelizadora y misionera. Las "líneas" también promueven el liderazgo hispano y una "línea de educación integral sensible a nuestra identidad cultural, promotora y ejemplo de justicia, y una línea de valorización y promoción de la mujer reconociendo su igualdad y dignidad, y su papel en la Iglesia, familia y sociedad".[17]

El Plan Pastoral Nacional para el Ministerio Hispano promueve un modelo de Iglesia que es comunitario y participativo. El Objetivo General afirma, profética y poéticamente, la visión de Iglesia que los agentes pastorales y líderes católicos hispanos—y no hispanos— han desarrollado y en la cual han estado participando por muchas décadas. Aunque muchos nuevos líderes y profesionales de la Iglesia no han estado involucrados en el proceso hispano pastoral de los últimos 20 a 25 años, la visión es todavía relevante y es una de las mejores que el ministerio hispano ha desarrollado. En gran parte, el ministerio hispano ha sido afirmado y apoyado por la Iglesia durante este proceso, aunque no siempre al grado esperado. Sin embargo, el propósito de este proceso ha sido siempre desarrollar agentes pastorales responsables de la Buena Nueva y participar en el proceso de construir el reino de Dios, sin importar la edad, cultura, rango económico o género.

"Vivir y promover...mediante una pastoral de conjunto un modelo de Iglesia que sea: comunitaria, evangelizadora y misionera, encarnada en la realidad del pueblo hispano y abierta a la diversidad de culturas, promotora y ejemplo de justicia...que desarrolle liderazgo por medio de la educación integral...que sea fermento del reino de Dios en la sociedad"[18] es el reto que todos los cristianos debemos enfrentar. Por medio de las cuatro Dimensiones Específicas del Plan Pastoral: *Pastoral de Conjunto*, *Evangelización*, *Opción Misionera* y *Formación*, y con los programas y proyectos delineados, la estrategia de implementación del ministerio hispano está ya trazada para la Iglesia. Desde 1987, cuando el Plan Pastoral fue aprobado por la NCCB, el ministerio hispano ha tenido por mandato la implementación del modelo de iglesia vivido por muchos y que ha sido descrito para que todos puedan continuarlo.

En afirmación y apoyo de los esfuerzos pastorales en parroquias, diócesis y regiones dirigidos a y entre hispanos católicos, el Comité de Obispos para Asuntos Hispanos y nueve otros comités de la NCCB/USCC co-patrocinaron Convocación '95, en San Antonio, Texas, del 23 al 25 de junio de 1995. El evento que tuvo lugar en *Incarnate Word College*, enfatizó la intención de los obispos católicos de conmemorar y celebrar, de edificar comunión en el ministerio y de reanudar su compromiso con el ministerio hispano en el quincuagésimo aniversario del establecimiento de una oficina nacional para el ministerio a los hispanos.

Quinientos directores del ministerio hispano y delegados, en representación de 110 diócesis y ocho regiones de la pastoral hispana, se unieron a 35 obispos, 98 sacerdotes, 17 diáconos permanentes, 55 religiosas y más de 300 mujeres y hombres laicos, incluyendo 115 parejas de esposos en esta reunión nacional. Los obispos sirvieron de facilitadores en 23 talleres diferentes tratando con temas relacionados a la identidad cristiana y a la acción cristiana. De las declaraciones de compromiso que se desarrollaron al final de cada uno de los 23 talleres, los participantes a la Convocación '95 dieron su aporte para el desarrollo de una "Declaración de Compromiso" del ministerio hispano que fue utilizado luego por la Conferencia Nacional de Obispos Católicos para desarrollar su declaración pastoral sobre los católicos hispanos en los Estados Unidos titulada *"La Presencia Hispana en la Nueva Evangelización en los Estados Unidos"*.

En la ceremonia de clausura de Convocación '95, el Comité de Obispos presentó la primera Medalla Nacional "Arzobispo Patricio F. Flores" a nueve personas y a una pareja de esposos por su contribución y servicio a la Iglesia y al ministerio hispano. Los beneficiarios y muchos otros semejantes a ellos, continúan haciendo posible la evangelización de los hispanos

NOTAS

1. Conferencia Nacional de Obispos Católicos, *Ministerio Hispano: Tres Documentos Importantes* (TMD); edición bilingüe. Washington, D.C.: United States Catholic Conference, 1995, p. 68.

2. TMD, p. 8.

3. Conferencia Nacional de Obispos Católicos, *Strangers and Aliens No Longer*: Primera Parte. Washington, D.C.: Conferencia Católica de los Estados Unidos, 1993, p. 89-105.

4. Privett, Stephen A. S.J. *The U.S. Catholic Church and Its Hispanic Members: The Pastoral Vision of Archbishop Robert E. Lucey*. San Antonio: Trinity University Press, 1988, p. 65-67.

5. Papa Pablo VI. Mensaje de saludo en las *Conclusiones del II Encuentro Nacional Hispano de Pastoral* (SE). Washington, D.C. Conferencia Nacional de Obispos Católicos/Conferencia Católica de los Estados Unidos, 1978, p. 7.

6. Conferencia Católica de los Estados Unidos, *Conclusiones Primer Encuentro Nacional Hispano de Pastoral (PE)*. Washington, D.C. Division for the Spanish Speaking, 1972, p. 1.

7. PE, p.2.

8. SE, p. 24.

9. Ibid., p. 25.

10. Ibid., p. 26.

11. Galerón, S., R.M. Icaza, R. Urrabazo, eds. *Visión Profética: Reflexiones Pastorales Sobre el Plan Pastoral Nacional para el Ministerio Hispano*. Kansas City, MO: Sheed and Ward and the Mexican American Cultural Center, 1992: p. 192.

12. TMD, p. 19, no. 18.

13. Ibid., p. 18, no. 19.

14. Ibid, p. 30.

15. Ibid., p. 31.

16. Ibid.

17. Ibid., p. 33.

18. Ibid., p. 71.

19. Conferencia Nacional de Obispos Católicos, *Mission Statement: Goals and Objectives 1997-99*. Washington, D.C. Conferencia Católica de los Estados Unidos, 1995, Objetivo 6.6.

Plan Pastoral Nacional para el Ministerio Hispano

PREFACIO

Este plan va dirigido a toda la Iglesia de los Estados Unidos. Enfoca las necesidades pastorales de los hispanos católicos; pero también es un reto a todos los católicos como miembros del mismo Cuerpo de Cristo

Pedimos que este plan se estudie cuidadosamente y se tome en serio porque es el resultado de años de trabajo en que participaron miles de personas que tomaron parte en el III Encuentro. Es una elaboración de estrategias basadas en las Conclusiones de dicho Encuentro.

Nosotros, los Obispos de los Estados Unidos, adoptamos los objetivos de este plan y endosamos los medios específicos para alcanzarlos, como se especifica en el presente documento. Pedimos a las diócesis y parroquias que incorporen este plan, con el debido respeto por las adaptaciones locales. Lo hacemos con un sentido de urgencia y en respuesta al enorme reto que encierra la presencia de un número creciente de hispanos en los Estados Unidos. No sólo aceptamos esta presencia dentro de nosotros como parte de nuestra responsabilidad pastoral, conscientes de la misión que nos encomendó Cristo, sino que lo hacemos con alegría y gratitud. Como dijimos en la Casta Pastoral de 1983, "En este momento de gracia reconocemos que la comunidad hispana que vive entre nosotros es un bendición de Dios."

Presentamos este plan en espíritu de fe: fe en Dios que nos dará la fuerza y los recursos para llevar a cabo su plan divino en la tierra, fe en todo el Pueblo de Dios, y en su colaboración en la grandiosa tarea ante nosotros, fe en los católicos hispanos y en que ellos se unirán con el resto de la Iglesia para edificar todo el Cuerpo de Cristo. Dedicamos este plan para honor y gloria de la Bienaventurada Virgen María bajo el titulo de Nuestra Señora de Guadalupe.

I. INTRODUCCIÓN

✟

Este Plan Pastoral Nacional es el resultado del compromiso expresado en nuestra Carta Pastoral sobre el Ministerio Hispano, *La presencia Hispana: Esperanza y Compromiso*.

Esperamos analizar las conclusiones del III Encuentro de modo que nos sirvan de base para formular un Plan Pastoral Nacional de Ministerio Hispano, que será considerado en nuestra asamblea general en la primera fecha posible después del Encuentro.

El presente plan es una respuesta pastoral a la realidad y a las necesidades de los hispanos en sus esfuerzos por lograr la integración y participación en la vida de nuestra Iglesia, y en la edificación del Reino de Dios.

La integración no debe confundirse con la asimilación. Mediante una política de asimilación, para ser aceptados como miembros de la parroquia, los nuevos inmigrantes son forzados a abandonar su idioma, cultura, valores, tradiciones, y a adoptar una forma de vida y un culto que le son extraños. Esta actitud aleja a los nuevos inmigrantes católicos de la Iglesia y los hace victimas de las sectas y de otras denominaciones.

Integración quiere decir que los hispanos deben ser bienvenidos a nuestras instituciones eclesiásticas en todos los círculos. Deben ser servidos en su idioma siempre que sea posible, y se deben respetar sus valores y tradiciones religiosas. Además debemos trabajar para el enriquecimiento mutuo por medio del intercambio entre las dos culturas. Nuestras establecimientos deben ser accesibles a la comunidad hispana. La participación hispana en las instituciones, programas y actividades de la Iglesia se debe procurar y apreciar.

Este plan busca organizar y dirigir de la mejor manera esta integración. Tiene su origen en nuestra Carta Pastoral y esta basado en el documento de trabajo del III Encuentro y en las conclusiones del mismo. Toma en serio el contenido de estos documentos y busca la manera de implementarlos.

También considera la realidad socio-cultural de los hispanos y sugiere un estilo de ministerio pastoral y modelo de Iglesia en armonía con su fe y cultura. Por esta razón requiere una afirmación explicita del concepto de pluralismo cultural en nuestra Iglesia dentro de la unidad fundamental de la doctrina, como lo ha expresado muchas veces nuestro Magisterio.

Este plan usa la metodología de la *Pastoral de Conjunto*, donde todos los elementos del ministerio pastoral, todas las estructuras y todas las actividades de los agentes pastorales, hispanos y no hispanos, se coordinan en relación a un objetivo común. Integrar este plan dentro del proceso de planificación de las organizaciones, departamentos, y agencias de la Iglesia en todos los ámbitos (nacional, regional, diocesano, parroquial) requerirá de la adaptación local para que todos los elementos del ministerio pastoral operen armónicamente.

El Objetivo General del plan es una síntesis de las Líneas Proféticas Pastorales aprobadas en el III Encuentro, y presenta una visión y orientación para todas las actividades pastorales.

Este documento es también una respuesta al proselitismo de las sectas. Para que sea efectivo es necesario que se renueven las estructuras parroquiales, que haya participación activa de parte de los párrocos y administradores, y una actitud misionera renovada en todos los sectores de la Iglesia.

La Planificación Pastoral es la organización efectiva del proceso total de la vida de la Iglesia para llevar a cabo la misión de ser levadura del Reino de Dios en este mundo. Incluye estos elementos:

- análisis de la realidad en la que la Iglesia debe llevar a cabo su misión;
- reflexión sobre esta realidad a la luz del Evangelio y de las enseñanzas de la Iglesia;
- compromiso a la acción basada en la reflexión;
- reflexión teológica pastoral sobre este proceso;
- elaboración de un plan pastoral;
- implementación;
- evaluación continua de lo que se va haciendo;
- y la celebración de los logros de esta experiencia viva siempre dentro del contexto de la oración y su relación con la vida.

La Pastoral de Conjunto es un ministerio corresponsable y colaborador que incluye la coordinación de los agentes pastorales en todos los elementos de la vida pastoral y las estructuras de la misma, con miras a una meta común: el Reino de Dios.

Este Plan Pastoral es un instrumento técnico que organiza, facilita y coordina las actividades de la Iglesia en la realización de su misión evangelizadora. No es sólo una metodología, sino una expresión de la esencia y la misión de la Iglesia, que es la comunión.

Proceso De Planificación Pastoral

III Encuentro
Realidad
Comunidad Eclesial
Mística
Espiritualidad
Celebración
Realidad:
1. Análisis de la Realidad
2. Discernimeinto
3. Decisión
    Conclusiones del Encuentro
Misión:
4. Reflexión Teológica
5. Plan
6. Implementación
7. Evaluación

II. MARCO DE LA REALIDAD HISPANA

✝

A. Historia

La presencia hispana en las Américas empezó juntamente con el primer viaje del descubrimiento de Cristóbal Colon en 1492, y la primera evangelización cristiana empezó en 1493 en los asentamientos españoles de La Española. El evento fue un encuentro más que un descubrimiento porque los europeos se mezclaron rápidamente con los nativos de las Américas que poseían culturas sofisticadas y desarrolladas, dándose inicio a un nueva era y a un nuevo pueblo, es decir a un verdadero "mestizaje."

En busca de tierras y de trabajadores, los españoles pronto encontraron la región que un día habría de convertirse en los Estados Unidos. En 1513 Ponce de León exploró las costas de La Florida; luego Pánfilo de Narváez trató de establecerse en La Florida en 1527 mientras que al mismo tiempo Nuño de Guzmán avanza en las tierras al norte de México. Los sobrevivientes de la fracasada expedición de Narváez trajeron noticias de muchas tribus y grandes riquezas. Fray Marcos de Niza respondió en 1539 con una expedición a las cercanías de las Rocosas que precedió a la de Francisco Vásquez de Corondo. Un año más tarde, Fray Juan Padilla dio su vida como mártir en las llanuras de Kansas. El Padre Luis Cáncer, un misionero dominico, dio su vida en la Florida en 1549. A pesar de los fracasos, Pedro Menéndez de Avilés siguió adelante y fundo la ciudad de San Agustín en 1565. Misioneros jesuitas llegaron a la Bahía de Chesapeake solo para abandonarla mucho antes que Roanoke. Un mapa de 1529 ilustrado por el cartógrafo de la corte española, Diego Ribero, muestra que los misioneros y exploradores llegaron en el norte hasta Maryland, New York y Nueva Inglaterra y dieron nombres españoles a los ríos y montañas que vieron. Al oeste, aventureros entraban en Nuevo México donde misioneros perdieron la vida en intentos vanos de evangelización. No fue hasta que Juan de Oñate llego en 1598 con decenas de nuevos colonizadores que la estabilidad llegó finalmente. Generaciones antes que los Peregrinos construyeran sus tenues colonias, los misioneros españoles lucharon por traer las Américas al rebaño de Cristo.

En el siglo XVII los misioneros franciscanos levantaron iglesias elegantes en los pueblos de Nuevo México. En las laderas del oeste de Nueva España, los jesuitas integraron rancherías de los indios en eficientes sistemas sociales que elevaron el nivel de vida en la América árida; pero la importancia primaria de la evangelización como piedra angular de la política real española sucumbió ante las ambiciones políticas del siglo XVIII. Las misiones cayeron victimas del secularismo: primero los jesuitas fueron exilados y la orden suprimida; los franciscanos y los dominicos trataron valientemente de detener la ola de absolutismo pero disminuyeron en número rápidamente, y los servicios de la Iglesia para los pobres se desmoronaron.

La independencia arrasó México y las provincias de Nueva España, ahora los estados de una nueva república, cayeron ante los ejércitos de los Estados Unidos. En las provisiones del Tratado de Guadalupe Hidalgo de 1848, los territorios de las viejas misiones fueron anexados a los crecientes Estados Unidos. La Florida española y Luisiana, francesa por un tiempo, eran estrellas en el campo azul de la conquista; y del Mississippi a las costas del Pacifico, las fronteras del mestizaje fueron puestas bajo la ley y las costumbres inglesas.

El siglo XIX se caracterizo por décadas de negligencia y ajustes. Las poblaciones hispanas y nativo-americanas fueron mal servidas e ignoradas. La gente de la meseta continuó moviéndose hacia el norte, como lo venían haciendo por más de un milenio; pero ahora se encontraban con un nuevo imperio que inundaba antiguos sitios familiares y también las familias.

Las condiciones políticas y sociales del siglo XX han seguido incrementando la migración hacia el norte. Nuevas avenidas de inmigración se abrieron desde las islas: portorriqueños, cubanos, dominicanos han invadido la costa este. Los mexicanos continúan su viaje hacia el norte en busca de trabajo y oportunidad. Las condiciones empeoradas de América Central y del sur han añadido miles al flujo de inmigrantes que hablan el mismo idioma que una vez dominara en América del Norte, y ahora es despreciado por muchos que ignoran el profundo poder cultural que ejerce en todo el mundo.

Los Estados Unidos de América no es toda la América. Hablamos de las Américas para describir un hemisferio de muchas culturas y tres idiomas dominantes: dos de la península ibérica y el otro de una isla del Atlántico norte. Ya que la Iglesia es la guardiana de la misión de Jesucristo, tiene siempre que acomodar las poblaciones cambiantes y las culturas en transición del mundo. Si la Iglesia esta impregnada de normas culturales, entonces divide y separa; pero si remplaza normas culturales con la importancia suprema del amor, une a los muchos en el Cuerpo de Cristo sin disolver las diferencias ni destruir la identidad.

B. Cultura

La realidad histórica del Suroeste, la proximidad de los países de origen y la continua inmigración, contribuyeron al mantenimiento de la cultura y el idioma hispano dentro de los Estados Unidos. Esta presencia cultural se expresa de muchas maneras: en el inmigrante que siente el "choque cultural" o en el hispano que tiene raíces en los Estados Unidos que datan de varias generaciones y que lucha con preguntas sobre su identidad, mientras que frecuentemente se le hace sentir como un extraño en su propio país.

A pesar de estas diferencias, hay ciertas similitudes culturales que identifican a los hispanos como pueblo. La cultura expresa principalmente cómo un pueblo vive y percibe el mundo, a los demás y a Dios. La cultura es el conjunto de valores con los cuales un pueblo juzga, acepta y vive lo que considera importante para la comunidad.

Algunos valores que son partes de la cultura hispana incluyen "un profundo respeto por la dignidad de cada persona . . . un profundo y respetuoso amor por la vida familiar . . . un maravilloso sentido de comunidad . . . un afectuoso agradecimiento por la vida, don de Dios . . . y una auténtica y firme devoción a María."

Para los hispanos católicos, la cultura se ha convertido en un modo de vivir la fe y de transmitirla. Muchas prácticas locales de piedad popular se han convertido en expresiones culturales generalmente aceptadas. Pero la cultura hispana, al igual que todas las demás, tiene que ser evangelizada continuamente.

C. Realidad Social

La edad promedio de los hispanos es de 25 años. Este hecho, junto con el flujo continuo de inmigrantes asegura un constante aumento de la población.

La falta de educación y preparación profesional contribuyen a un alto grado de desempleo. Ni la educación pública ni la privada han respondido a las necesidades urgentes de esta población joven. Solo 8% de hispanos se gradúa de universidades.

Las familias se enfrentan a una gran variedad de problemas: 25% de ellas vive en la pobreza y 28% son familias con solo padre o madre.

Gran movilidad, educación deficiente, economía limitada y prejuicio racial, son algunos de los factores que influyen en la poca participación de hispanos en las actividades políticas.

En conjunto, los hispanos son un pueblo religioso. Un 83% considera que la religión es importante. Tienen gran interés en conocer mejor la Biblia y hay un gran apego a las prácticas religiosas populares. A pesar de esto, un 88% no son activos en sus parroquias. Sin embargo, Testigos de Jehová, grupos Pentecostales y otras sectas están aumentando dentro de la comunidad hispana. Según estudios recientes, los pobres, los hombres, y los hispanos de la segunda generación son los que menos participan en la vida de la Iglesia.

Diagnóstico

El patrimonio católico y la identidad cultural de los hispanos están siendo amenazados por los valores seculares de la sociedad americana. Los hispanos participan al margen de la Iglesia y de la sociedad, y sufren las consecuencias de la pobreza y marginación.

Estas mismas personas, debido a su gran sentido religioso, de familia y de comunidad, son una presencia profética frente al materialismo e individualismo de la sociedad. Por el hecho de que la mayoría de los hispanos son católicos, su presencia puede ser una fuente de renovación dentro de la Iglesia Católica en Norteamérica. A causa de su juventud y crecimiento, esta comunidad continuará siendo una presencia importante en el futuro.

El proceso pastoral actual ofrece posibilidades magníficas en el aspecto social y religioso: más participación activa en la Iglesia, una crítica a la sociedad desde la perspectiva de los pobres, y un compromiso con la justicia social.

Al acercarse el año 1992, con la celebración del quinto centenario de la evangelización de las Américas, es más importante que nunca que los hispanos en los Estados Unidos recobren su identidad y su catolicismo, vuelvan a ser evangelizados por la Palabra de Dios, y forjen una unidad muy necesaria entre todos los hispanos que han venido desde todo el mundo de habla hispana.

III. MARCO DOCTRINAL

La misión de la Iglesia es continuar el trabajo de Jesús: anunciar el Reino de Dios y los medios para alcanzarlo. Es la proclamación de lo que habrá de venir y también la anticipación de esa plenitud aquí y ahora en el proceso de la historia. El Reino que Jesús proclama e inicia es tan importante que todo lo demás es relativo ante esa realidad.

La Iglesia, como comunidad, lleva a cabo la misión de Jesús entrando en la realidad cultural, religiosa y social de los pueblos y encarnándose en ellos y con ellos, "en virtud de su misión y naturaleza, no está ligada a ninguna forma particular de civilización humana ni a sistema alguno político, económico o social." Por lo tanto ella puede predicar la necesidad que todos tienen de la conversión, afirmar la dignidad de la persona y buscar la manera de erradicar el pecado personal, las estructuras opresoras, y las injusticias.

La Iglesia, con su voz profética, denuncia el pecado y anuncia la esperanza y de este modo continúa la presencia histórica y palpable de Jesús. Al igual que Jesús proclamó la Buena Nueva a los pobres y la libertad a los cautivos, la Iglesia opta por los pobres y los marginados.

La Iglesia también se identifica con el Cristo Resucitado que se revela como la nueva creación, como la proclamación y realización de nuevos valores de solidaridad con todos; por medio de su simpleza, pacíficamente, por medio de la proclamación de su Reino que implica un orden social nuevo, por medio de un nuevo estilo de Iglesia a modo de levadura, y sobre todo por medio del don que nos dejó de su Espíritu.

Este Espíritu une a los miembros de la comunidad de Jesús íntimamente, y a todos en Cristo, con Dios. Nuestra solidaridad proviene del Espíritu de Cristo vivo en nosotros. El Espíritu impulsa la comunidad a hacer real en esta vida un compromiso profético a la justicia y al amor, y la ayuda a vivir dentro de una experiencia de fe misionera, su unión con Dios.

Esta responsabilidad cae en la Iglesia toda, el Pueblo de Dios: el Papa y los obispos, sacerdotes, religiosos y laicos quienes tienen que llevar a cabo la misión de Jesús con sentido de corresponsabilidad. Todo esto se expresa de manera especial en la Eucaristía. Es allí donde Jesús se ofrece como Victima por la salvación de todos y reta a todo el Pueblo de Dios a vivir según el compromiso de amor y servicio.

IV. ESPIRITUALIDAD

La espiritualidad o mística del pueblo hispano nace de su fe y de su relación con Dios.

La espiritualidad es el modo de vida de un pueblo, el movimiento del Espíritu de Dios, y el enraizamiento de una identidad cristiana en cada circunstancia de la vida. Es la lucha por vivir la totalidad de la vida personal y comunitaria de acuerdo al Evangelio. La espiritualidad da orientación y perspectiva a todas las dimensiones de la vida de una persona, en el seguimiento de Jesús y en el continuo diálogo con Dios Padre.

Este plan pastoral es una reflexión a la luz del Evangelio de la espiritualidad del pueblo hispano. Es una manifestación y respuesta de fe.

Cuando consideramos esta espiritualidad, vemos que uno de sus aspecto mas importantes es el sentido de la presencia de Dios que sirve de estimulo para vivir los compromisos diarios. En este sentido, el Dios trascendente está presente en los eventos y vidas de los humanos. Hasta podemos hablar de Dios como miembro de la familia, con quien conversamos y a quien acudimos no solo en momentos de oración fervorosa sino también en el vivir diario. Así, Dios nunca nos falta. Él es Emanuel, Dios-con-nosotros.

Los hispanos encuentran a Dios en brazos de la Virgen María. Es por eso que María, la Madre de Dios, toda bondad, compasión, protección, inspiración, modelo. . . . está en el corazón de la espiritualidad hispana.

Los santos, nuestros hermanos y hermanas que ya han completado su vida en el seguimiento de Jesús, son ejemplos e instrumentos de la revelación de la bondad de Dios por medio de intercesión y ayuda. Todo esto hace que la espiritualidad de los hispanos sea un hogar de relaciones vivas, una familia, una comunidad que se manifiesta y se concretiza más en la vida diaria que en la teoría.

La espiritualidad de los hispanos tiene como una de sus fuentes las "semillas del Verbo" presentes en las culturas prehispánicas, que consideraban la relación con los dioses y la naturaleza como parte integral de la vida. En algunos casos, los misioneros adoptaron estas costumbres y actitudes; las enriquecieron e iluminaron para que encarnaran la Palabra Divina de la Sagrada Escritura y de la fe cristiana y les dieron vida en el arte y el drama religioso. Todo esto creó devociones populares que preservan y alimentan la espiritualidad del pueblo. Al mismo tiempo, los principios cristianos se expresan diariamente en actitudes y acciones que revelan los valores divinos en la experiencia del pueblo hispano. Esta espiritualidad se ha mantenido viva en el hogar y es una tradición profunda en la familia.

La espiritualidad de los hispanos, una realidad viva a lo largo de su peregrinaje, se manifiesta de muchas maneras: en oración, novenas, canciones y gestos sagrados. Se expresa también en las relaciones personales y la hospitalidad. Otras veces, se muestra como tolerancia, paciencia, fortaleza y esperanza en medio del sufrimiento y las dificultades. Esta espiritualidad también inspira la lucha por la libertad, la justicia y la paz. Con frecuencia se manifiesta en compromiso y perdón como también en celebración, danzas, imágenes y símbolos sagrados. Altarcitos, imágenes y velas en la casa son sacramentales de la presencia de Dios. Las pastorelas, las posadas, los nacimientos, el vía crucis, las peregrinaciones, las procesiones y las bendiciones que ofrecen las madres, los padres y los abuelos son manifestación de esta espiritualidad y fe profunda.

A través de los siglos, estas devociones se han desviado o empobrecido por falta de una catequesis clara y enriquecedora. Este plan pastoral con su énfasis evangelizador, comunitario y formativo puede ser ocasión de evangelización para estas devociones populares y un aliciente para enriquecer las celebraciones litúrgicas con expresiones culturales de fe. Este plan trata de libertar el Espíritu que vive en las reuniones de nuestro pueblo.

El proceso del III Encuentro fue un paso más hacia el desarrollo y crecimiento de esta espiritualidad. Muchos participantes parecen haber expandido su espiritualidad personal y de familia a una espiritualidad comunitaria y eclesial, pasando de reconocer la injusticia individual y hacia la familia a reconocer la injusticia hacia el pueblo. Este crecimiento también se vio en su experiencia de ser Iglesia, en su familiaridad con los documentos eclesiales, en su participación activa en liturgias y oraciones.

La celebración eucarística tiene un lugar especial para este pueblo, que celebra la vida y la muerte con gran intensidad y significado. La liturgia y los sacramentos ofrecen a este pueblo religioso, los elementos de comunidad, la certeza de la gracia, la realidad del Ministerio Pascual en la muerte y resurrección del Señor en su pueblo. Esto es especialmente cierto en la celebración de la Eucaristía, fuente de nuestra unidad, donde se encuentran numerosas posibilidades de enriquecer las celebraciones sacramentales con originalidad y gozo. Estos momentos sacramentales capturan la espiritualidad y mística que brotan de la vocación cristiana y de su identidad hispana.

Reunidos alrededor de una simple y común mesa, Jesús dijo a sus discípulos "hagan esto en conmemoración mía." Fue en esta reunión de amigos que Jesús reveló su misión, su vida, su oración mas intima, y luego les pidió que hicieran lo mismo en su memoria. Les ordeno que hicieran en su vida todo lo que él había hecho, y por lo que él había vivido. Esta costumbre de compartir la mesa ha servido de alimento a los hispanos en su historia. Al igual que los discípulos de Jesús, ellos reservan un sitio para él en su mesa.

La espiritualidad penetra todos los aspectos de la vida y por tanto se manifiesta con gran variedad. En este momento especial de su peregrinaje, los católicos hispanos revelan su espiritualidad por medio de las Líneas Proféticas del III Encuentro que se han resumido en el *Objetivo General* y las *Dimensiones Específicas* de este plan. El Plan Pastoral es por tanto, no solo una serie de metas y objetivos, sino también una contribución al desarrollo, crecimiento, y realización de la vida de fe del pueblo tal como se discierne en el Espíritu de Dios y se encarna en nuestro tiempo.

Durante el proceso del III Encuentro, muchos católicos hispanos han tratado de vivir en dialogo con su Dios que inspira y motiva, con María que acompaña a los discípulos de Jesús. El plan pastoral se basa en las reuniones y el compartir del pueblo hispano. Es una expresión de la presencia de Dios en nosotros. El plan pastoral es una manera de que el Pueblo de Dios exprese su vida con el Espíritu, una vida profundamente enraizada en el Evangelio.

V. OBJETIVO GENERAL

---✝---

VIVIR Y PROMOVER . . .
mediante una pastoral de conjunto
un MODELO DE IGLESIA que sea:
comunitaria, evangelizadora y misionera,
encarnada en la realidad del pueblo hispano y
abierta a la diversidad de culturas,
promotora y ejemplo de justicia . . .
que desarrolle liderazgo por medio de la educación integral . . .
QUE SEA FERMENTO DEL REINO DE DIOS EN LA SOCIEDAD.

MARCO SITUACIONAL DE LA COMUNIDAD HISPANA	MARCO DOCTRINAL
HISTORIA CULTURA REALIDAD SOCIAL	VIDA Y MISIÓN DE JESÚS Y DE LA IGLESIA

DIAGNÓSTICO

OBJETIVO GENERAL

Vivir y promover a través de una pastoral de conjunto un modelo de Iglesia que sea: comunitaria, evangelizadora y misionera, encarnada en la realidad del pueblo hispano y abierta a la diversidad de culturas, promotora y ejemplo de justicia, que desarrolle liderazgo por medio de la educación integral, que sea fermento del Reino de Dios en la sociedad.

DIMENSIONES ESPECÍFICAS
PASTORAL DE CONJUNTO
EVANGELIZACIÓN
OPCIÓN MISIONERA
FORMACIÓN

PASTORAL DE CONJUNTO:
De fragmentación a coordinación

Desarrollar una pastoral de conjunto que en sus estructuras y sus agentes manifieste comunión en integración, coordinación, asesoramiento y comunicación de la acción pastoral de la Iglesia según el objetivo general de este plan.

EVANGELIZACIÓN:
De ser lugar a ser hogar

Reconocer, desarrollar, acompañar y apoyar las pequeñas comunidades eclesiales y otros grupos (Cursillos de Cristiandad, RENEW, Movimiento Carismático, grupos de oración) que unidos al obispo son instrumentos efectivos de evangelización para los hispanos. Estas pequeñas comunidades eclesiales y otros grupos de la parroquia promueven experiencias de fe y conversión, oración, misión y evangelización, relaciones interpersonales y amor fraterno, cuestionamiento profético y acciones para la justicia. Son un reto profético para la renovación de la iglesia y la humanización de la sociedad.

OPCIÓN MISIONERA:
De los asientos a los caminos

Promover la fe y la participación efectiva en las estructuras de la Iglesia y la sociedad de estos grupos prioritarios (los pobres, las mujeres, las familias y la juventud) para que sean agentes de su propio destino (auto-determinación), capaces de progresar y de organizarse.

FORMACIÓN:
De buena intención a preparación

Proporcionar formación de líderes, adaptada a la cultura hispana en los Estados Unidos, que ayude al pueblo a vivir y a promover un estilo de Iglesia que sea fermento del Reino de Dios en la sociedad.

EVALUACIÓN
CELEBRACIÓN—ESPIRITUALIDAD—MÍSTICA

La Presencia Hispana:
Esperanza y Compromiso

I. Llamado al Ministerio Hispano

1. En este momento de gracia reconocemos que la comunidad hispana que vive entre nosotros es una bendición de Dios. Exhortamos a todas las personas de buena voluntad a que compartan nuestra visión de los dones especiales que los hispanos traen al Cuerpo de Cristo, su Iglesia peregrina sobre la tierra (1 Cor 12:12-13).

   Invocando a la Santísima Virgen María para que nos guíe, deseamos especialmente exponer nuestras reflexiones sobre la presencia hispana en los Estados Unidos a los católicos laicos, religiosos y religiosas, diáconos y sacerdotes de nuestro país. Pedimos a los católicos, que como miembros del Cuerpo de Cristo, al desempeñar las funciones que les corresponden, presten verdadera atención a nuestras palabras. La presencia hispana nos estimula a todos a ser más *católicos* y a tener un espíritu más amplio con respecto a la diversidad de la expresión religiosa.

2. Aunque como resultado de esta presencia, la Iglesia ha de afrontar muchas necesidades pastorales, nos agrada que los católicos hispanos expresen el deseo de tener más oportunidad de compartir sus dones históricos, culturales y religiosos con la Iglesia que consideran suya, y a la que ven como parte vital de su tradición. Escuchemos su voz. Hagamos que todos se sientan en la Iglesia como en su propia casa (PHB, I. b & III. c). Seamos una Iglesia verdaderamente universal, una Iglesia acogedora, recibiendo con agrado los dones y expresiones diversas de nuestro credo: "un solo Señor, una sola fe, un solo bautismo, un solo Dios y Padre de todos" (Ef 4:5-6).

3. Los hispanos ejemplifican y fomentan valores esenciales para el servicio a la Iglesia y a la sociedad. Entre estos valores se hallan los siguientes:

   (a) Un profundo respeto por la dignidad de cada *persona* que refleja el ejemplo de Cristo en el Evangelio;

   (b) Un profundo y respetuoso amor por la *vida familiar* en la que toda la "familia extensa" halla sus raíces, su identidad y su fortaleza;

   (c) Un maravilloso sentido de *comunidad* que celebra la vida mediante la "fiesta";

   (d) Un afectuoso agradecimiento por *la vida*, don de Dios y un concepto del tiempo que les permite disfrutar de ese don;

   (e) Una auténtica y firme *devoción a María*, Madre de Dios.

4. Todos tenemos la obligación de apreciar nuestra propia historia y reflexionar sobre el origen étnico, racial y cultural que nos hace ser una nación de inmigrantes. Desde el punto de vista histórico, la Iglesia de los Estados Unidos ha sido una "Iglesia de inmigrantes", cuya historia notable con respecto a la atención prestada a innumerables inmigrantes europeos sigue siendo única. Hoy esa misma tradición debe inspirar a la Iglesia, una autoridad, compasión y determinación similar, al acercarse a los recientes inmigrantes y migrantes hispanos.

   Aunque crece el numero de hispanos en nuestro país seria engañoso insistir solamente en este crecimiento numérico. Fijarse principalmente en el número podría llevarnos con facilidad a ver en los hispanos un gran problema pastoral y pasar por alto, al mismo tiempo, el hecho aún más importante de que constituyen una oportunidad pastoral única.

   Ciertamente las necesidades pastorales de los católicos hispanos son grandes. Aunque su fe es profunda y firme, se halla asediada y mermada por las presiones constantes de la dinámica social de asimilación. Por otra parte, la historia, la cultura y la espiritualidad que animan su fe viva, merecen que todos nosotros las conozcamos, las compartamos y las apoyemos. Su contribución pasada y presente a la vida de fe de la Iglesia merece aprecio y reconocimiento.

   Actuemos juntos para crear una visión pastoral y una estrategia que surgiendo de un pasado memorable, se renueve con el impulso creador del presente.

5. La Iglesia tiene un amplio conjunto de enseñanzas sobre la cultura y la relación íntima de ésta con la fe. "En la propia revelación a su pueblo que culminó con la manifestación plena de su Hijo encarnado, Dios habló de acuerdo a la cultura propia de cada época. En forma similar, en circunstancias diversas, la Iglesia ha existido a través de los siglos y ha utilizado las riquezas de las diferentes culturas en su predicación, para esparcir y explicar el mensaje de Cristo, exa-

minarlo, entenderlo más profundamente y expresarlo más perfectamente en la liturgia y en varios aspectos de la vida de fe" (*GS*, 58).

Del mismo modo que para otros pueblos con una fuerte tradición católica, para los hispanos la religión, la cultura, la fe y la vida, son inseparables. El catolicismo hispano es un ejemplo notable de cómo el Evangelio puede impregnar una cultura hasta sus mismas raíces (*EN*, 20). Pero esto también nos recuerda que ninguna cultura carece de defectos y pecados. La cultura hispana, lo mismo que cualquier otra, necesita ser confrontada por el Evangelio.

El respeto por la cultura se basa en la dignidad de la persona, hecha a imagen de Dios. La Iglesia muestra su estima por esta dignidad, tratando de asegurar que el pluralismo y no la asimilación o la uniformidad, sea el principio que guíe la vida de las comunidades, tanto eclesiales como seculares. Todos nosotros en la Iglesia, debemos hacer que la aceptación de nuestros hermanos hispanos sea más amplia, y que nuestro compromiso hacia ellos, sea más profundo.

Realidad Hispana

6. No hay cultura europea más antigua en nuestro país que la hispana. Los españoles y sus descendientes ya estaban en el sudeste y sudoeste a fines del siglo XVI. En otras regiones de nuestro país la afluencia constante de inmigrantes hispanos ha hecho que estos fueran más visibles en tiempos más recientes. Mirando al futuro se ve claramente que la población hispana en los Esta-dos Unidos cobrará mucha más importancia, tanto en la sociedad en general, como en la Iglesia en particular.

Hace sólo 30 años el censo de los Estados Unidos estimó que había 6 millones de hispanos en el país. El censo de 1980 contó casi 15 millones, cifra en la que no se incluyen los habitantes de la isla de Puerto Rico, los múltiples trabajadores indocumentados, los recién refugiados cubanos, los que han huido de la creciente violencia en América Central y del Sur, ni tampoco otros muchos hispanos omitidos por el censo. Algunos expertos estiman que la población total hispana en los Estados Unidos es por lo menos de 20 millones.[1]

Actualmente los Estados Unidos ocupa el quinto lugar en el mundo, entre los países de habla española. Sólo México, España, Argentina y Colombia tienen mayor número de hispanos.[2]

Los católicos hispanos son muy diversos. Provienen de 19 repúblicas latinoamericanas, Puerto Rico y España. El grupo mayoritario es el de los méxico-americanos que constituyen el 60 por ciento. A éstos les siguen los puertorriqueños, que constituyen el 17 por ciento, y los cubanos que constituyen el 8 por ciento. Los dominicanos, peruanos, ecuatorianos, chilenos, y cada vez más, los centroamericanos; en especial los salvadoreños, lo mismo que otros latino-americanos, están ampliamente representados.

Los hispanos son distintos en su origen racial, su color, su historia, sus logros y manifestaciones de fe y también en el grado de desventaja racial y económica que sufren. Sin embargo, comparten muchos elementos culturales, entre los que se incluyen un catolicismo profundamente enraizado, valores como el del compromiso hacia la familia extensa, el idioma común, español, aunque hablado con diversos acentos.

Los hispanos se hallan en todos los estados de la Unión y en casi todas la diócesis. Aunque muchos, espe-cialmente en el sudoeste, viven en zonas rurales. Más del 85 por ciento se hallan en grandes centros urbanos como Nueva York, Chicago, Miami, Los Angeles, San Antonio y San Francisco. En lugares como Hartford, Washington, D.C. y Atlanta, son prueba de su pre-sencia el numero creciente de anuncios en español e inglés, así como otros grandes barrios hispanos.[3]

Es significativo el hecho de que los hispanos cons-tituyen la población más joven de nuestro país. Su edad promedio, 23.2, es menor que la de los demás grupos. El 54 por ciento de los hispanos tienen aproxi-madamente 25 años o menos.

Condiciones Socioeconómicas

7. En general, la mayoría de los hispanos de nuestro país viven en la pobreza, o casi en la pobreza. Se han producido ciertas mejoras en su situación económica y social en la última generación, en conjunto, pero todavía los hispanos no han empezado a compartir la riqueza de nuestro país; riqueza que ellos han

contribuido a producir. A pesar de las crecientes expectativas, la participación de los hispanos en el proceso político es limitado, a causa de su subdesarrollo económico y social. Por esta razón, están insuficientemente representados en el nivel de los que toman decisiones, tanto en la Iglesia como en la sociedad.

El promedio de ingreso anual de las familias no hispanas es de $5,000 más que el de las familias hispanas. El 22.1 por ciento de los hispanos viven en la pobreza, comparado con el 15 por ciento de la población en general.[4]

Históricamente, el desempleo ha sido siempre mayor entre los hispanos que entre los demás. Los puertorriqueños son los más afectados, con un índice de desempleo que suele ser un tercio más alto que el de los otros hispanos.[5] En tiempos de crisis, como en la depresión económica del comienzo de la década de los ochenta, los hispanos se hallaban entre los últimos para ser contratados y entre los primeros para ser despedidos.

Más de la mitad de los hispanos empleados tienen puestos de trabajo que no son ni profesionales ni administrativos. Trabajan principalmente como braceros en la agricultura, o están empleados en los servicios urbanos. En ninguno de estos dos sectores ha tenido éxito todavía la lucha valerosa de los trabajadores por obtener medios adecuados de negociación y para conseguir una remuneración justa.

La falta de preparación académica y profesional es uno de los factores importantes que mantienen a los hispanos en la pobreza. Aunque ahora los hispanos que terminan los estudios secundarios y universitarios son más que hace diez años, sólo el 40 por ciento de ellos termina la escuela secundaria con éxito, en comparación con el 66 por ciento de la población en general. Los hispanos están insuficientemente representados incluso dentro de la población del sistema escolar católico, en el que representan sólo el 9 por ciento de la población estudiantil.

Las oportunidades educativas en las zonas de gran concentración hispana, con frecuencia, son inferiores a lo normal. Una frustración inicial en la escuela lleva a muchos hispanos a abandonar los estudios sin haber adquirido la preparación necesaria, mientras muchos de los que permanecen en la escuela se encuentran en un sistema educativo que no siempre les apoya. Con frecuencia, los estudiantes hispanos se hallan en una encrucijada cultural. Viven en su hogar según la tradición hispana, al mismo tiempo que en la escuela y en el trabajo sienten que se ejerce presión sobre ellos para que se dejen asimilar y abandonen sus costumbres y tradiciones.

Datos impersonales nos dicen que los hispanos son numerosos, aumentan rápidamente, son de diversas nacionalidades de origen, y se hallan por todos los Estados Unidos. Su situación económica y social es inferior y tienen necesidad de un mayor acceso a la educación y de entrar en el proceso de la toma de decisiones, pero hay una realidad humana detrás de los datos encuestos y a veces desalentadores. Vemos en los rostros de los hispanos una serenidad profunda, una esperanza constante y una alegría llena de vitalidad. En muchos de ellos observamos el sentido evangélico de la gracia y el carácter profético de la pobreza.

II. Logros en el Ministerio Hispano de los Estados Unidos

8. Al intentar responder a las necesidades pastorales de los hispanos, nos basamos en la labor iniciada hace muchos años. Reconocemos con gratitud lo que hicieron hombres y mujeres previsores, hispanos y no hispanos, quienes siendo pioneros en este apostolado, ayudaron a mantener y a enriquecer la fe de cientos de miles de personas. Merece que se les reconozcan sus valerosos esfuerzos.

9. La supervivencia de la fe entre los hispanos en muchos aspectos parece casi un milagro. Incluso en momentos en que la Iglesia oficial no podía estar presente, la fe permaneció debido a la familia (la tradición religiosa familiar proporcionó un ímpetu y dinamismo a los que se debe la conservación de la fe). Pero no dependamos hoy solamente de esta tradición. Todas las generaciones de todas las culturas tienen necesidad de ser evangelizadas (*EN*, 54).

Una de las glorias de las mujeres hispanas, laicas y religiosas, ha sido el papel que han desempeñado alimentando la fe y manteniéndola viva en su familia y comunidad. Ellas han sido, tradicionalmente, las principales formadoras en la oración, las catequistas y con frecuencia, modelos excelentes del discipulado cristiano.

El creciente número de dirigentes laicos y diáconos permanentes (20 por ciento del total de los Estados Unidos) es un signo de que el liderazgo laico de las bases se ha llamado a servir a la Iglesia.

También son dignos de mención los diversos movimientos apostólicos que han ayudado a asegurar la supervivencia de la fe de muchos católicos hispanos. Por ejemplo, los Cursillos de Cristiandad, Encuentros Conyugales, Encuentros de Promoción Juvenil, el Movimiento Familiar Cristiano, Comunidades Eclesiales de Base, y la Renovación Carismática, así como otros más, han sido muy útiles para poner de manifiesto las posibilidades apostólicas de muchas personas, matrimonios y comunidades hispanas. Muchas asociaciones como PADRES y HERMANAS han proporcionado una red de apoyo a sacerdotes y mujeres del movimiento cristiano hispano.

Entre los que han colaborado generosamente en esta tarea figuran las congregaciones religiosas de hombres y mujeres. El hecho de que un porcentaje importante de los sacerdotes hispanos sea religioso es un signo de que dichas congregaciones han dedicado sus recursos, su personal y su energía a esta labor. Las congregaciones religiosas de mujeres han ayudado de forma muy especial a satisfacer las necesidades espirituales y materiales de los braceros agrícolas migrantes, los pobres de las ciudades, los refugiados de América Latina y los indocumentados. Los misioneros norteamericanos que vuelven de América Latina regresan con un gran interés por los hispanos y un deseo de dedicarse a su cuidado.

Ya desde por el año 1940 los obispos mostraron auténtica preocupación por los católicos hispanos al establecer, por iniciativa del arzobispo de San Antonio, Monseñor Robert E. Lucey, una comisión especial con objeto de que se ocupara de los hispanos del sudoeste. En 1912 Philadelphia empezó el apostolado hispano. Nueva York y Boston establecieron oficinas diocesanas para los hispano-parlantes en los años cincuenta. En otras zonas del país también se había dado atención a los hispanos desde temprano.

Más adelante, los constantes esfuerzos de los obispos, quienes reconocieron la necesidad de la presencia hispana en la dirección nacional de la Iglesia, culminaron en el establecimiento en 1970, de la Sección de los Hispano-parlantes de la Conferencia Católica de los Estados Unidos, dentro del Departamento de Desarrollo Social de esta Conferencia. En 1974 la Sección se convirtió en el Secretariado de Asuntos Hispanos de la Conferencia Nacional de Obispos Católicos, y de la Conferencia Católica de los Estados Unidos.

Bajo la dirección de los obispos, y con el apoyo del Secretariado de Asuntos Hispanos de la Conferencia Nacional de Obispos Católicos, los católicos hispanos han sido responsables de dos Encuentros Nacionales de Pastoral. En 1972 y 1977, estas reuniones de personas laicas dedicadas a sus propias comunidades, concluyeron con llamados proféticos a toda la Iglesia. Igualmente, como resultado del Segundo Encuentro Nacional Hispano de Pastoral, celebrado en 1977, se impulsó la pastoral juvenil hispana a nivel regional, diocesano y parroquial, mediante la "*National Youth Task Force*", que se denomina actualmente Comité Nacional Hispano de Pastoral Juvenil.[6]

El nombramiento de obispos y arzobispos hispanos desde 1970 ha acrecentado considerablemente este apostolado. Nos alegramos con todos los católicos hispanos que ven en estos nuevos obispos un signo claro y manifiesto de que la Santa Sede reconoce su presencia y la aportación que son capaces de hacer a la vida de la Iglesia en los Estados Unidos. Los últimos delegados apostólicos han expresado su preocupación por los grupos étnicos y minoritarios de la Iglesia de nuestro país y han pedido a las jerarquías de la Iglesia que atiendan sus necesidades.

En la última década también se han establecido oficinas regionales, institutos pastorales, comisiones y oficinas diocesanas y centros pastorales, todos los cuales se han convertido en instrumentos pastorales eficaces de servicio a los hispanos.

III. Implicaciones Pastorales Urgentes

10. Pedimos a todos los católicos de los Estados Unidos que estudien las posibilidades creativas para responder de forma innovadora, flexible e inmediata a la presencia hispana. Los hispanos y los no hispanos deben actuar unidos, enseñarse mutuamente, aprender unos de otros y juntos evangelizar en el sentido más amplio y completo de la palabra. Hoy, más que nunca, se necesita para atender al pueblo hispano, clero no hispano, especialmente religiosos, sacerdotes y obispos que hayan estado a la vanguardia del apostolado hispano.

La Misión de la Iglesia y la Presencia Hispana

11. Desde una perspectiva eclesial, la evangelización, que constituye la principal misión y finalidad de la Iglesia, no consiste simplemente en llamadas aisladas a la conversión individual, sino en una invitación a unirse al pueblo de Dios (*EN*, 15). Esto se refleja en la experiencia hispana de evangelización, en la que se incluye un importante elemento comunitario, expresado en una visión integral de la fe y en la actividad pastoral que se realiza en comunidad (*II ENHP*, I.4.c).

Esta experiencia se resume en el concepto de pastoral de conjunto, un enfoque y método de acción pastoral surgido de la reflexión común entre los agentes de evangelización (Puebla, 650, 122 y 1307). En la pastoral de conjunto está implícito el reconocimiento de que tanto el sentir de los fieles como las enseñanzas de la jerarquía son elementos esenciales en la concepción de la fe. Este enfoque pastoral reconoce también que la misión pastoral de la Iglesia se ejerce mejor en un espíritu de concordia y apostolado de grupo (*AA*, 18).

Un apostolado hispano eficaz incluye la aplicación de esta experiencia, que puede beneficiar a la Iglesia en todos sus esfuerzos por cumplir su misión. En este sentido, es esencial una visión integral, forjada en común, que acepte como preocupaciones religiosas todas las necesidades humanas y las afronte aprovechando todas las realidades.

Posibilidades Creativas

12. Por consiguiente, invitamos a todos nuestros sacerdotes, diáconos, religiosos y laicos a que consideren las siguientes oportunidades creativas:

a. Liturgia

Nuestra Iglesia, que es universal, "respeta y fomenta las cualidades y dones espirituales de la diversas razas y pueblos" en su vida litúrgica (*SC*, 37). Al aplicar esto a la presencia hispana, se necesitan tomar medidas para celebrar el culto en español o en forma bilingüe, según las tradiciones y costumbres del pueblo al que se sirve. Esto nos debe llevar a estudiar mejor las formas de oración de los hispanos. Es alentador ver que los católicos hispanos, artistas y músicos, ya están haciendo aportaciones a la liturgia en nuestro país.

Es esencial la presencia de liturgistas hispanos en las comisiones parroquiales y diocesanas. Deben hacerse todos los esfuerzos posibles para que esta presencia llegue a ser una realidad.

Como para muchos católicos hispanos el hogar ha sido una verdadera "iglesia doméstica", éste se ha convertido tradicionalmente para ellos en el centro de la fe y del culto. Por consiguiente, se debe valorar y alentar la celebración de las fiestas tradicionales y las ocasiones especiales en el hogar.

La selección del arte litúrgico, gestos y música, junto con un espíritu de hospitalidad, pueden convertir nuestras iglesias y altares en hogares espirituales y crear en nuestras comunidades un ambiente que invite a la fiesta familiar.

b. Renovación de la Predicación

El rescate y proclamación de la Palabra con nuevas imágenes poderosas y liberadoras, es una necesidad ineludible en el ministerio hispano. Así decía el apóstol Pablo: "¿Cómo pueden creer si no han oído hablar de Él? Y ¿cómo pueden oír hablar de Él si no hay nadie que predique?" (Rom 10:14).

Los que predican deben tener siempre presente que la capacidad de escuchar está ligada a la lengua, la cultura y la realidad del que escucha. Al proclamar el mensaje del Evangelio, deben procurar hacer suya esta característica y esta realidad, con el fin de que sus palabras transmitan el verdadero contenido liberador del Evangelio.

Sedientos de la Palabra de Dios, los hispanos desean una

predicación clara y simple del mensaje y de su aplicación a la vida. Reaccionan favorablemente ante una predicación eficaz y con frecuencia expresan un anhelante deseo de una predicación mejor y más eficaz que exprese el mensaje evangélico con palabras que ellos puedan comprender.

Recomendamos encarecidamente que tanto los sacerdotes que se dedican al apostolado hispano, como los sacerdotes de parroquias y los capellanes, se matriculen en cursos de español para que puedan más fácilmente hablar con los hispanos y escucharles. Del mismo modo, pedimos a los diáconos permanentes hispanos, que adquieran una mayor facilidad de predicación y que ejerzan con más frecuencia el ministerio de la Palabra. En este sentido, es necesario la educación continua de los diáconos permanentes, así como la evaluación periódica de su ministerio.

c. *Catequesis*

La catequesis, así como la evangelización inicial, debe partir de la realidad en la que se encuentra el oyente del Evangelio (*EN*, 44). En el caso de los hispanos, esto implica no simplemente el uso del español, sino un auténtico dialogo, con su cultura y necesidades (*NCD*, 229). Puesto que la educación religiosa es un proceso de toda la vida para la persona (*NCD*, 32), las parroquias deben ofrecer en la catequesis un ambiente que impulse en todos los aspectos, la formación progresiva, tanto de los adultos como de los niños. Estos esfuerzos deben ser equivalentes a los de los programas para niños de habla inglesa, en lo que se refiere a su eficacia, al igual que necesitan ser explorados nuevos métodos para adultos.

Igualmente, es esencial que las diócesis patrocinen cursos de formación en español para catequistas hispanos y asegurarse que estos catequistas tengan un material apropiado y eficaz, así como programas en español (*NCD*, 194, 195). Los catequistas deben aprovechar todos los "momentos oportunos" para enseñar la doctrina de la Iglesia a los católicos hispanos. Las celebraciones familiares hispanas[7] como bautismos, quinceaños, bodas, aniversarios, fiestas patrias, novenarios, velorios y funerales, suelen ser excelentes oportunidades para enseñar y también "momentos de gracia", que permiten al catequista basarse en las tradiciones del pueblo y usarlas con ejemplos vivos de las verdades evangélicas (Puebla, 59 y *CT*, 53).

En todo nuestro país existe un profundo anhelo y hambre, "no hambre de pan ni sed de agua, sino de escuchar la palabra del Señor" (Amos 8:11). Pedimos que se hagan esfuerzos continuos para iniciar la formación de grupos de estudio de la Biblia en las comunidades hispanas y preparar a dirigentes hispanos para que guíen y dirijan estos programas bíblicos.

d. *Vocación y Formación de los Ministros Laicos*

En el ministerio hispano debe tenerse como gran prioridad la formación adecuada. En la planificación de esta formación los objetivos de incrementar el pluralismo y la catolicidad determinará los medios a seguir. La formación deberá incluir el conocimiento y la experiencia práctica necesaria para ejercer el ministerio eficazmente, fomentado al mismo tiempo un compromiso serio de servicio.

Aunque los hispanos no tienen suficiente clero preparado para ejercer el ministerio entre ellos, hay entre sus filas muchos laicos dispuestos a responder al llamado de ser apóstoles (*AA*, 3). Desde ese punto de vista, concluimos que el fomento de las vocaciones y la preparación para los ministerios laicos, ayudarán a proporcionar los tan necesitados trabajadores de la viña.

Un modelo en este sentido es la *escuela de ministerios*[8] que ayuda a preparar dirigentes laicos, invita a los jóvenes a una mayor participación en la Iglesia y posiblemente puede convertirse en un lugar de elección de vocaciones sacerdotales y religiosas.

e. *Vocaciones al Sacerdocio y a los Ministerios Religiosos*

La escasez de sacerdotes, religiosos y diáconos permanentes hispanos es uno de los problemas más graves con que se enfrenta la Iglesia en los Estados Unidos. Existen razones históricas para esta lamentable falta de vocaciones hispanas, entre ellas la del descuido. Otra razón importante para que muchos hispanos no perseverasen en continuar su vocación, fue la presencia en seminarios y conventos de expresiones culturales, tradiciones, lengua, relaciones familiares y experiencias religiosas que estaban en conflicto con las suyas. Sin embargo, actualmente nos satisface observar que estos conflictos han disminuido y la situación ha mejorado notablemente. En los últimos años, muchos, y tal vez la mayoría de los seminarios y conventos, han hecho grandes progresos en el sentido de atender las necesidades de los hispanos. Felicitamos a estas instituciones y les exhortamos a continuar mejorando sus programas al servicio del ministerio hispano.

También exhortamos a los seminarios a ofrecer cursos de español, cultura y religiosidad hispana y de ministerio pastoral hispano para seminaristas, sacerdotes, religiosos, diáconos permanentes y todos los que ejercen una actividad pastoral.

En vista de la presente situación, nos comprometemos a fomentar las vocaciones hispanas. Los obispos, sacerdotes, religiosos y laicos deberán animar con más insistencia a los jóvenes hispanos a considerar el sacerdocio y la vocación religiosa. Dirigimos una llamada a los padres hispanos para que presenten la vida y la obra de un sacerdote o religioso como una vocación deseable para sus hijos y se sientan justamente orgullosos de tener un hijo o una hija que sirva a la Iglesia de esta forma. Sin su apoyo firme, la Iglesia no tendrá el número necesario de sacerdotes y religiosos hispanos para atender sus comunidades.

Esto requiere acentuar en las familias hispanas una idea más positiva acerca de los sacerdotes y religiosos, de la que tienen en la actualidad. La presencia de la Iglesia en las comunidades hispanas debe ser de tal modo que los hispanos puedan experimentar la realidad del amor e interés por ellos. Los sacerdotes y religiosos tienen la grave responsabilidad de presentar a los jóvenes hispanos una experiencia positiva y alegre de la Iglesia, e invitarles a considerar el sacerdocio o la vida religiosa al tomar alguna decisión sobre su futuro. Se pide a las oficinas diocesanas de vocaciones que hagan esfuerzos especiales para acercarse a los jóvenes hispanos e invitarles al seguimiento de Jesús en la vocación sacerdotal o religiosa.

Ante todo, la Iglesia de los Estados Unidos debe pedir al Señor de la mies que envíe las vocaciones hispanas que tan urgentemente se necesitan. Pedimos que, con este fin, se hagan oraciones especiales y continuas en las parroquias hispanas y exhortamos a los padres que recen para que uno a más de sus hijos reciba la gracia de una vocación al sacerdocio o a la vida religiosa.

f. Educación Católica

Los educadores católicos de los Estados Unidos tienen en su favor una larga historia de logros y dedicación a la enseñanza y formación de millones de católicos. Ahora deben consagrar su capacidad a satisfacer las necesidades educativas de los hispanos. La educación es un derecho inalienable; y al desarrollar la inteligencia, las escuelas católicas y los institutos de estudio deben también promover los valores y la cultura de sus alumnos (*GE*, 178).

Por consiguiente, pedimos con insistencia a las escuelas y otras instituciones católicas que ofrezcan más oportunidades, incluyendo becas y ayuda financiera a los hispanos que no tienen medios económicos para asistir a ellas.

También recomendamos adaptaciones que respondan de forma adecuada a la presencia hispana en nuestras escuelas. En el plan de estudio debe incluirse la educación bilingüe; los profesores deben estar familiarizados con la lengua hispana, y respetar y comprender la cultura, y la expresión religiosa hispana. Al mismo tiempo, hay que tener cuidado de que la educación bilingüe no impida ni retrase indebidamente el ingreso de los hispanos en la sociedad, tanto política como socioeconómica y religiosa, debido a una incapacidad de poderse comunicar bien en el idioma predominante.

Es importante, no solamente afirmar en los jóvenes hispanos el valor intrínseco de su tradición, sino que también hay que enseñarles la historia y la cultura hispana. La sociedad les dice con frecuencia que la cultura de sus padres, tan profundamente arraigada en el catolicismo, no tiene valor y es extraña. La Iglesia puede enseñarles lo contrario.

La Iglesia también debe convertirse en defensora de los muchos jóvenes hispanos que asisten a las escuelas públicas, haciendo todo lo que esta a su alcance para asegurar que se tomen todas las medidas que satisfagan sus necesidades. Se debe prestar una atención especial a los que han abandonado la escuela, ya sea católica o pública, y que necesitan educación y asistencia especiales para adquirir una preparación técnica.

g. Medios de Comunicación

Vivimos en una era en la que "el medio es el mensaje". La Iglesia ha reconocido este hecho apoyando la modernización de los medios de comunicación que tiene a su disposición. Sin embargo, en su mayor parte, la prensa y los demás medios de comunicación de la Iglesia están muy retrasados en el campo del ministerio hispano. Aunque en la última década se han iniciado algunas publicaciones valiosas en español, la prensa católica ignora, mayormente en su información, las noticias hispanas. Igualmente, aunque se hayan iniciado algunos valiosos esfuerzos bajo los auspicios de la Campaña Católica de la Comunicación y la Red de Telecomunicaciones Católicas de América, a la Iglesia le falta un conjunto sólido de programación en televisión y radio, que responda a las necesidades de la comunidad hispana.

Esto indica la necesidad de mayores esfuerzos que conduzcan a una programación sistemática y planificada y a una información continua sobre los temas relacionados con la comunidad hispana. Se requiere preparar y contratar a hispanos con talento, especializados en el campo de los medios de comunicación y en el periodismo, con el fin de producir material relevante y de actualidad. El material y los programas importados de América Latina puede servir de ayuda a corto plazo, para remediar nuestras deficiencias en este campo.

h. Ecumenismo Efectivo

El Señor Jesús rogó por la unidad de sus discípulos (Jn 17:21) no obstante, la división de las iglesias es un gran obstáculo a la evangelización. Esto se pone de manifiesto en los Estados Unidos en los casos del proselitismo activo que las sectas protestantes llevan a cabo entre los hispanos en una forma antiecuménica. Diversos grupos fundamentalistas dividen a los hispanos y sus familias con una predicación en la que se refleja un espíritu anticatólico que difícilmente puede decirse que proceda del Evangelio de Jesucristo (PHB, II, c).

Nuestra respuesta como católicos no consiste en atacar ni menospreciar a nuestros hermanos de otras tradiciones cristianas, sino en vivir el Evangelio de forma más auténtica con objeto de presentar a la Iglesia Católica como la plenitud de la cristiandad y así mantener la fe de nuestro pueblo hispano. Otras iglesias cristianas han sido parte de la historia de la salvación. La oración, el diálogo y la hermandad en los esfuerzos por atender los asuntos de interés común, siguen siendo importantes para la Iglesia Católica. No obstante, en el contexto hispano, la Iglesia Católica y su tradición han desempeñado el papel histórico más importante con respeto a la incorporación del Evangelio en la cultura. La Iglesia tiene la obligación de continuar esta misión.

i. Juventud Hispana

Deseando ser la luz del mundo y la sal de la tierra, muchos jóvenes hispanos dedican sus energías y su talento a la misión de la Iglesia. Sus principios son profundamente cristianos. Cualesquiera que sean sus circunstancias, se consideran miembros de la familia espiritual dirigida por su madre, la Virgen María. Esto es evidente en su arte, poesía y en otras formas de expresión. No obstante, las presiones del ambiente sobre los jóvenes hispanos para que se adapten y se guíen por principios egoístas, han alejado a muchos de la Iglesia.

Al igual que los jóvenes de otros orígenes, los jóvenes hispanos muestran un espíritu de generosidad con respecto a los que se hallan en una situación económica y social desfavorable. Sin embargo, en el caso de los hispanos, con frecuencia es algo más que sensibilidad con respecto a los pobres; se trata de solidaridad con personas que tienen tan poco como ellos o todavía menos que ellos. Para que no resulten víctimas de sueños de éxito fácil por salir de la pobreza a cualquier precio, necesitan ver que la Iglesia valora su capacidad y sus posibilidades.

Al responder a las necesidades de estos jóvenes, el agente pastoral experto, observará las maravillosas posibilidades implícitas en su energía abundante y en su capacidad para hablar en lenguaje de la juventud. Los jóvenes hispanos comprometidos, saben por su propia experiencia inmediata, como hacer para compartir su visión cristiana con sus semejantes, mediante medios tales como el arte y la música moderna y tradicional hispana.

A los jóvenes hispanos con capacidad de ser dirigentes deben ofrecerse oportunidades de educación religiosa, estudios bíblicos, catequesis y una formación especial, para que se afirme su vocación de servir a la Iglesia. Estos programas deberán tener en cuenta el hecho de que estos jóvenes se educarán mejor en un ambiente familiar y acogedor.

j. La Familia

La tradición del compromiso con la familia es una de las características distintivas de la cultura hispana. Aunque existen variantes entre los méxico-americanos, los puertorriqueños, cubanos y otros hispanos, hay valores familiares y características culturales que son comunes a todos los hispanos.[9]

La familia, ya sea de un solo núcleo o "extensa" ha sido el lugar privilegiado en el que se han enseñado y expresado los principios cristianos y se ha llevado a cabo la evangelización y el desarrollo de la espiritualidad. La familia hispana, a menudo ejemplifica la descripción del Papa Juan Pablo II de oración familiar: "Alegrías y dolores, esperanzas y tristezas, nacimientos y cumpleaños, aniversarios de boda de los padres, partidas, alejamientos y regresos, elecciones importantes y decisivas, muerte de personas queridas, etc., señalan la intervención del amor de Dios en la historia de la familia, como deben también señalar el momento favorable de acción de gracias, de imploración, de abandono confiado de la familia al Padre común que está en los cielos" (FC, 59).

Sin embargo, en nuestra planificación pastoral, no podemos dar por seguro que la familia católica hispana seguirá siendo fuerte y unida. Las familias hispanas de un solo núcleo experimentan las mismas presiones sociales con las que se enfrentan otros grupos étnicos. La unidad de la familia hispana está amenazada, en particular, por el desarraigo causado por los cambios, especialmente de estilo de vida del campo al de la ciudad y del estilo de los países latinoamericanos al nuestro; por la pobreza que sufren una gran proporción de las familias hispanas y por las presiones causadas por el proceso de asimilación que, a menudo, llevan a una separación entre las generaciones dentro de la familia y a una crisis de identidad entre los jóvenes.

Existe una necesidad apremiante de ministerios pastorales que preparen bien a los hispanos para la vida matrimonial, la crianza de los hijos, el asesoramiento de la familia y la educación religiosa. Rogamos especialmente que se tomen medidas para asistir a las familias hispanas en crisis, así como a los divorciados o separados, a los padres o las madres que educan solas a sus hijos y a las víctimas del maltrato de los padres o de uno de los cónyuges.

Invitamos a las familias hispanas, unidas por lazos tan singulares, así como a las de otros grupos culturales, con firmes tradiciones familiares, a cooperar en el proceso del descubrimiento gradual de la plenitud de la verdad de Cristo. "Está en conformidad con la tradición constante de la Iglesia, el aceptar de las culturas de los pueblos, todo aquello que está en condiciones de expresar mejor las inagotables riquezas de Cristo. Sólo con el concurso de todas las culturas, tales riquezas podrán manifestarse cada vez más claramente y la Iglesia podrá caminar hacia una conciencia cada día más completa y profunda de la verdad, que le ha sido dada ya, enteramente por su Señor" (FC, 10).

k. Trabajadores Agrícolas Migrantes

Como se ha observado, los hispanos se mudan de lugar con facilidad y se hallan tanto en lugares rurales como urbanos. Como resultado, tienden a eludir la atención y el cuidado de la Iglesia urbana. Esto pone de manifiesto la necesidad de adaptación en la atención pastoral, especialmente en el caso de los braceros agrícolas migrantes.

Existen tres corrientes principales de migración en los Estados Unidos. En el este, los braceros agrícolas migran de México, América del Sur y Florida hacia el norte, a Nueva York y Nueva Inglaterra, y trabajan en el cultivo de la caña de azúcar, del algodón, el tabaco, la recogida de las manzanas y las uvas. En las llanuras centrales, los braceros van hacia el norte desde Texas a los Grandes Lagos para recoger las cosechas de frutas, verduras y cereales. También hay un número importante de braceros puertorriqueños de temporada, la mayoría de ellos jóvenes y solteros, que trabajan principalmente en el nordeste. En el oeste, los braceros van hacia el norte a través de California, Nevada e Idaho hasta el noroeste; algunos llegan hasta Alaska en búsqueda de empleos de temporada. La migración suele comenzar en la primavera para terminar al final del otoño, cuando los braceros regresan a su lugar de residencia en el sur.[10]

Los abusos que sufren los braceros agrícolas son bien conocidos, sin embargo, nada se hace para ponerles fin. En muchas regiones las condiciones están empeorando. Mujeres y hombres se hallan desmoralizados hasta el punto de que la riqueza de la cultura hispana, los fuertes lazos familiares y la vida de fe profunda, a veces se pierden. Denunciamos el tratamiento de los braceros como mercancía, mano de obra barata, y no como personas. Pedimos a los demás que igualmente denuncien esta situación. Debido a las condiciones económicas, con frecuencia también los niños se ven obligados a tomar parte en la mano de obra. Junto con otros problemas relacionados con las mudanzas, su educación se ve perjudicada. Del mismo modo, nos parece deplorable la violación de los derechos de los trabajadores indocumentados. Todo esto hace que sea apremiante el que la Iglesia apoye el derecho que tienen los braceros agrícolas migrantes a organizarse, con el fin de entablar negociaciones colectivas con los patrones.

La experiencia en el apostolado hispano nos muestra la necesidad de equipos móviles misioneros y otras formas de ministerios ambulantes. Las diócesis y parroquias que están situadas en la ruta de las corrientes de migración, también tienen la responsabilidad de apoyar esta obra y de coordinar los esfuerzos de las diócesis de origen y destino de los braceros.

Sin duda, también, los mismos braceros hispanos, cuya visión rural de la vida se parece tanto a la de Jesús el Galileo,[11] tienen mucho que aportar para ayudar a responder a esta necesidad.

l. *Justicia Social y Acción Social*

La evangelización integral descrita anteriormente como el objetivo principal de la estrategia, pensamos que sería incompleta, sin un complemento activo de doctrina y acción social. Como decimos en nuestra carta pastoral sobre la guerra y la paz, "en la médula de la doctrina social católica está la trascendencia de Dios y la dignidad de la persona. La persona humana es el reflejo más claro de la presencia de Dios en el mundo" (*CP*, 1). Este concepto ha de aplicarse concretamente a la realidad de la presencia hispana y del ministerio que responde a ella.

En los últimos 20 años la doctrina católica ha definido cada vez con más claridad el significado de justicia social. Desde la encíclica *Pacem in Terris* del Papa Juan XXIII hasta la encíclica *Laborem Exercens* del Papa Juan Pablo II, se nos ha venido presentando una doctrina social que define como derechos humanos: un buen gobierno, alimentación, salud, vivienda, empleo y educación. En los Estados Unidos hemos aplicado estas enseñanzas a los problemas de nuestro tiempo y de nuestro país.

Ahora pedimos que se preste atención a las preocupaciones sociales que afectan más directamente a la comunidad hispana, entre ellas el derecho al voto, la discriminación, los derechos de los inmigrantes, la situación de los braceros agrícolas, el bilingüalismo y el pluralismo. Todos son problemas de justicia social de suma importancia para el ministerio hispano y para toda la Iglesia.

La Iglesia, al comprometerse con la doctrina social asume la búsqueda de la justicia como una labor eminentemente religiosa. Las personas dedicadas a esta tarea deben comprometerse, ser informadas y guiadas por aquellas que conocen por experiencia propia, la paradójica bendición de la pobreza, los prejuicios y la injusticia (Mt 6:3). Por lo tanto, pedimos a los hispanos que asuman un papel cada vez mayor en la acción social, y a los no hispanos que traten de buscar, cada vez más, la participación hispana en una auténtica asociación.

m. *Prejuicio y Racismo*

Recordamos que los hispanos han sido víctimas en nuestro país de un prejuicio despiadado. Ha sido tan grande en algunos aspectos que se les han negado los derechos humanos y civiles fundamentales. Aún actualmente los hispanos, negros, los recientes refugiados del sudeste de Asia y los americanos nativos continúan sufriendo de ese tratamiento tan inhumano, tratamiento que nos hace conscientes de que el pecado de racismo persiste en nuestra sociedad. A pesar de los grandes progresos en la eliminación del prejuicio racial, tanto en nuestro país como en la Iglesia, existe aún más necesidad urgente de purificación y reconciliación continua. Es especialmente desalentador saber que algunos católicos mantienen fuertes prejuicios contra los hispanos y otros, y les niegan el respeto y amor debidos a su dignidad humana que es un don de Dios.

Esto es obvio incluso en algunas comunidades parroquiales, en las que algunos no hispanos, se muestran reacios a participar con los hispanos o alternar con ellos en los eventos parroquiales. Exhortamos a quienes manifiestan una actitud tan poco cristiana que analicen su comportamiento a la luz del mandamiento del amor de Jesús y acepten totalmente a sus hermanos hispanos como compañeros en la vida y obra de sus respectivas parroquias. Merecen repetirse las palabras de nuestra carta pastoral sobre el racismo: "el racismo no es simplemente un pecado entre muchos, es un mal radical que divide a la familia humana y no permite la nueva creación de un mundo redimido. Para luchar contra él se requiere una transformación igualmente radical de nuestras ideas y de nuestro corazón, así como de la estructura de nuestra sociedad" (*BSU*, p. 10).

Pedimos a los que dan empleo a hispanos que les proporcionen condiciones de trabajo seguras y adecuadas y les paguen sueldos que les permitan mantener adecuadamente a sus respectivas familias. La condición inhumana de la pobreza extrema impuesta a muchos hispanos, es la raíz de muchos problemas sociales en sus vidas. La justicia más elemental exige que tengan condiciones de trabajo y sueldos adecuados.

n. Lazos con América Latina

Los hispanos que se hallan entre nosotros son un recurso todavía no utilizado, como puente cultural entre el norte y el sur de América. La fuente de la cultura y de la fe hispana se encuentra histórica y geográficamente en América Latina. Por este motivo, una respuesta dinámica a la presencia hispana en los Estados Unidos estará necesariamente ligada a un conocimiento creciente y vinculación con la sociedad y la Iglesia latinoamericana.

América Latina, con más de 350 millones de católicos, continúa experimentado graves injusticias socioeconómicas, y en muchos de sus paises, una carencia grave de los derechos humanos más fundamentales. Estas condiciones son opresivas y deshumanizantes, gestan violencia, pobreza, odio y profundas divisiones en la estructura social y se oponen fundamentalmente a los principios del Evangelio.[12] No obstante, nuestros hermanos católicos de América Latina, especialmente los pobres, suelen ser testigos vibrantes de la liberación que propone el Evangelio, y se comprometen a construir una "civilización de amor" (Puebla, 9).

Debemos continuar apoyando y ayudando a la Iglesia de América Latina. Igualmente esperamos un continuo intercambio de misioneros, puesto que la cooperación que prevemos no es unilateral. Por nuestra parte, debemos continuar enviando a los que estén más preparados para evangelizar en América Latina, incluso a nuestro personal hispano al aumentar este en número. Teniendo en cuenta seriamente las circunstancias de las regiones de las que proceden, damos la bienvenida a los latinoamericanos y a otros sacerdotes, religiosos y religiosas que vienen a atender a los hispanos de los Estados Unidos. Recomendamos que al llegar reciban una preparación especial en el idioma y la cultura para aplicarlas en sus actividades pastorales.

La Iglesia de los Estados Unidos tiene mucho que aprender de la experiencia pastoral latinoamericana; es afortunado tener en la presencia hispana un precioso vínculo humano ligado a esa experiencia.

o. Catolicismo Popular

La espiritualidad hispana es un ejemplo de la profundidad con que el cristianismo puede penetrar las raíces de una cultura. En el transcurso de casi 500 años en América, los hispanos han aprendido a expresar su fe en oraciones y tradiciones que iniciaron, alentaron y desarrollaron los misioneros y que pasaron más tarde de una generación a otra.

Pablo VI reconoció el valor intrínseco del catolicismo popular. Aunque advirtió sobre los posibles excesos de la religiosidad popular, enumeró no obstante algunos valores que, a menudo, tienen estas formas de oración. Señaló que la piedad popular, si está bien orientada manifiesta sed de Dios, estimula la generosidad de las personas y les infunde un espíritu de sacrificio. Puede llevar a una conciencia clara de los atributos de Dios, como son su paternidad, su providencia y su presencia cariñosa y constante (*EN*, 48).

La espiritualidad hispana resalta la importancia de la humanidad de Jesús, especialmente cuando aparece débil y doliente, como en el pesebre y en su pasión y muerte. Esta espiritualidad está relacionada con todo lo que es simbólico en el catolicismo: los ritos, las estatuas e imágenes, los lugares santos y los gestos. Es igualmente una espiritualidad de firmes devociones. La Santísima Virgen María, especialmente bajo títulos patronales como Nuestra Señora de Guadalupe (México), Nuestra Señora de la Divina Providencia (Puerto Rico), Nuestra Señora de la Caridad del Cobre (Cuba), ocupa un lugar privilegiado en la piedad popular hispana.

Se necesita un diálogo más amplio entre la práctica popular y la oficial, de lo contrario la primera podría desprenderse de la orientación del Evangelio y la última podría perder la participación activa de los más sencillos y pobres entre los fieles (Medellín, 3). Una vida eclesial que vibre con un profundo sentido de lo trascendente, como existe en el catolicismo popular hispano, puede ser también un testigo admirable para los miembros más secularizados de nuestra sociedad.

p. Comunidades Eclesiales de Base

De las aportaciones que los hispanos han hecho a la Iglesia en las Américas, una de las más importantes es la formación de las comunidades eclesiales de base. La pequeña comunidad apareció en escena como un rayo de esperanza para afrontar situaciones inhumanas que pueden destruir moralmente a las personas y debilitar su fe. Un sentido revitalizador de hermandad llena de alegría pastoral y esperanza a la Iglesia de América Latina, Africa, Europa y Asia. El sínodo de los Obispos de 1974 fue testigo de una efusión de esperanza por parte de los pastores de

América Latina, que vieron las comunidades eclesiales de base como una fuente de renovación en la Iglesia. Puesto que estas comunidades de base han demostrado ser un beneficio para la Iglesia (*EN*, 58), recomendamos encarecidamente su desarrollo.

La comunidad eclesial de base no es ni un grupo de estudio y discusión, ni una parroquia. Es "el primer núcleo fundamental eclesial que en su propio nivel debe ser responsable de la riqueza y la expansión de la fe, así como del culto del cual es una expresión" (*JPP*, 10). Debe ser una expresión de la Iglesia que libera del pecado personal y estructural; debe ser una pequeña comunidad con relaciones inter-personales; debe formar parte del proceso de evangelización integral y debe estar en comunión con el resto de la Iglesia. El papel de las parroquias en particular es el de facilitar, coordinar y multiplicar las comunidades eclesiales de base en su territorio. La parroquia debe ser una comunidad de comunidades. La comunidad eclesial de base ideal es una comunidad viviente de cristianos cuya participación activa en todos los aspectos de la vida es alentada por un profundo compromiso con el Evangelio.

q. Otras Posibilidades

Exhortamos a los católicos de los Estados Unidos a utilizar sus mejores cualidades creativas para ir mucho más allá de estos primeros pasos, que son simplemente requisitos previos para una acción eficaz.

Una oportunidad para la realización de una acción creativa surge de la presencia de los hispanos en las fuerzas armadas de los Estados Unidos. Exhortamos al Vicario General Castrense a que estudie nuevos medios para llevar a cabo una evangelización integral, con especial atención a esta presencia hispana.

Asimismo, como saben los que ejercen un apostolado en las prisiones, los hispanos encarcelados están en extrema necesidad de atención. Se necesitan agentes pastorales que ayuden en ese campo.

También entre los hispanos hay minusválidos cuyas necesidades especiales se ven agravadas a causa de muchos de los problemas que hemos descrito. Se calcula que casi 2 millones de católicos hispanos tienen una o más enfermedades de incapacitación, entre ellas la ceguera, la sordera, el retraso mental, los problemas de aprendizaje y los impedimentos ortopédicos. Hay una grave necesidad de programas pastorales que estimulen la participación de los católicos minusválidos.

Esto no es más que una lista parcial. Como en todo este documento, nuestro propósito en este caso ha sido no limitar, sino animar a que haya más diálogo, reflexión y acción en esta tarea.

IV. Declaración de Compromiso

13. Somos conscientes de los muchos grupos étnicos y raciales que solicitan legítimamente nuestros servicios y recursos. Asimismo, agradecemos el esfuerzo actual importante, aunque limitado, por llegar a los hispanos de los Estados Unidos, y nos comprometemos junto con los que ejercen con nosotros una labor pastoral, a responder al llamado del ministerio hispano. La conciencia del bien realizado en el pasado y en el presente no debe hacernos lentos en comprender los signos de los tiempos. Nuestros preparativos de hoy facilitarán llevar a cabo la labor del mañana.

Reconocemos la realidad de la presencia de los hispanos de los Estados Unidos, los esfuerzos pasados de los que han tomado parte en el apostolado hispano y la necesidad apremiante de iniciar una nueva labor creadora. Para inaugurar esta nueva era en la Iglesia, tanto los hispanos como los no hispanos, tendrán que someterse a notables adaptaciones. Por otra parte, confiamos en que el compromiso con respecto al apostolado hispano nos conducirá a una reafirmación de la catolicidad y a revitalizar todas las obras para cumplir la misión esencial de la Iglesia.

Compromiso de Catolicidad

14. El carácter universal de la Iglesia comprende a la vez el pluralismo y la unidad. La humanidad con sus culturas y pueblos es tan variada que sólo pudo haber sido forjada por la mano de Dios. La Iglesia reconoce esto cuando dice que "cada una de las partes presenta sus dones a las otras partes y a toda la Iglesia" (*LG*, 13). Sin embargo, la Iglesia sobrepasa todos los límites de tiempo y raza. La humanidad entera está llamada a convertirse en el Pueblo de Dios, en paz y unidad.

El mensaje evangélico que afirma que en la Iglesia nadie es extranjero, es eterno. Como dice el apóstol Pablo, "ya no hay diferencia entre judío y griego, esclavo y libre; no se hace diferencia entre hombre y mujer. Pues todos ustedes son uno solo en Cristo Jesús" (Gal 3:28).

Por consiguiente, el ejercicio de nuestro magisterio respecto al ministerio hispano, nos lleva a invitar a todos los católicos a adoptar una actitud más acogedora con relación a los demás. Los hispanos, cuya presencia en este país está precedida solamente por la de los americanos nativos, están llamados a acoger a sus hermanos, los descendientes de otros inmigrantes europeos y del mismo modo, estos últimos están llamados a acoger a los hispanos recién llegados de América Latina. Libres de una actitud de dominio cultural o étnico, los dones de todos enriquecerán a la Iglesia y darán testimonio del Evangelio de Jesucristo.

Compromiso de Responder a las Necesidades Temporales

15. La evangelización es una labor espiritual que se extiende a todo lo que es humano y busca su realización. El Papa Juan Pablo II nos recordó ésto cuando dijo: "La Iglesia nunca abandonará al hombre, ni sus necesidades temporales, mientras conduce a la humanidad hacia la salvación" (*ABUS*).

Nuestros fieles hispanos afirmaron esta misma realidad en su Segundo Encuentro, en el que aceptaron el compromiso de la evangelización integral, "como el testimonio de la vida al servicio del prójimo para la transformación del mundo" (*II ENHP*, Evangelización, 1).

Por nuestra parte, nosotros como líderes, nos comprometemos una y otra vez a levantar nuestra voz en defensa de la dignidad humana de los hispanos. Recordamos a nuestros agentes pastorales que su trabajo incluye también el esfuerzo de ganar para los hispanos, la participación en los beneficios de nuestra sociedad. Pedimos a todos los católicos de los Estados Unidos que trabajen no solamente *por* los hispanos, sino *con* ellos, para que consigan tomar el lugar que les corresponde en nuestra democracia, así como en plena participación política que constituye para ellos un derecho y un deber. De esta forma, profundizamos nuestra opción preferencial por el pobre que debe ser siempre, según el Evangelio de Jesús y la tradición de la Iglesia, el emblema distintivo de nuestro apostolado (Puebla, 1134).

Llamado a Reconocer la Realidad Hispana

16. Al comprometernos a llevar a cabo una labor junto con los hispanos, y no simplemente en pro de ellos, aceptamos la responsabilidad de reconocer, respetar y

apreciar su presencia como un don. Esta presencia representa más que un simple potencial. Gracias a ella se realiza un valioso servicio a nuestra Iglesia y sociedad, aunque con frecuencia no es reconocido. Es una presencia profética que ha de ser alentada y requerida.

Compromiso de Recursos

17. Igualmente forma parte de nuestro compromiso, como pastores y administradores de los recursos comunes de la Iglesia, la promesa de utilizar estos en el ministerio hispano. Lo hacemos en forma explícita, según el espíritu de las primeras comunidades cristianas (Hechos 2:44).

Esta declaración de compromiso es algo más que una expresión del sentimiento, y en ella está implícito el reconocimiento de que debemos garantizar los recursos económicos y materiales necesarios para conseguir nuestros objetivos.

Vemos la necesidad de continuar apoyando, de forma más permanente, las actuales entidades nacionales, regionales y diocesanas del apostolado hispano. Dadas las limitaciones evidentes de recursos, es igualmente necesario inspeccionar y evaluar más a fondo la labor actual, con el fin de promover un mejor uso del personal, del dinero y de todos los otros medios. Asimismo, es urgente llamar la atención de los administradores respectivos sobre la necesidad de buscar más hispanos capacitados para que sirvan a su comunidad. Se necesitan igualmente más hispanos en las oficinas de la Conferencia Nacional de Obispos Católicos y de la Conferencia Católica de los Estados Unidos, en nuestras oficinas regionales, en las cancillerías, en nuestras escuelas, en nuestros hospitales y en muchas otras entidades de la Iglesia.

Lo que existe actualmente no es suficiente para satisfacer todas las necesidades. Deben realizarse esfuerzos serios, a todos los niveles, para evaluar estas necesidades más cuidadosamente y asignar fondos al ministerio hispano. La Iglesia de los Estados Unidos disfruta de la bendición de disponer de varias instituciones y ministerios cuyas energías pueden y deben aplicarse a esta labor. Debe exhortarse a las escuelas, parroquias, institutos de pastoral, medios de comunicación y diversos ministerios especializados, a que asuman ellos mismos este compromiso.

En vista de auténticas restricciones económicas, nos comprometemos a estudiar nuevas posibilidades de financiamiento. Tenemos conocimiento acerca de fórmulas de administración de presupuestos que estimulan a todos los ministerios y entidades a responder a las prioridades de la Iglesia. Debemos analizar esto al esforzarnos en responder a esta evidente necesidad pastoral.

Convocatoria del Tercer Encuentro

18. Pedimos a nuestro pueblo hispano que eleve su voz profética una vez más, como hizo en 1972 y 1977, en un Tercer Encuentro Nacional Hispano de Pastoral, de forma que juntos podamos asumir responsablemente nuestras responsabilidades. Pedimos que se inicie el proceso para que tenga lugar un encuentro, desde las comunidades eclesiales de base y las parroquias pasando por las diócesis y regiones, hasta el nivel nacional, para culminar en una reunión de representantes en Washington, D.C., en agosto de 1985.

Hacia un Plan Pastoral

19. Aparte del proceso de Encuentro, en el cual tomaremos parte, reconocemos que la planificación pastoral integral debe evitar adaptaciones meramente superficiales de los ministerios existentes. Esperamos analizar las conclusiones del III Encuentro de modo que nos sirvan de base para lograr la formulación de un Plan Pastoral Nacional de Ministerio Hispano, que será considerado en nuestra asamblea general en la primera fecha posible después del Encuentro.

Conclusión

20. Al continuar nuestra peregrinación junto con nuestros hermanos hispanos, manifestamos nuestro compromiso, con el mismo espíritu que nuestros hermanos los obispos de América Latina reunidos en Puebla (*MPLA*, 9).

    (a) Nos dirigimos a toda la Iglesia Católica de los Estados Unidos, laicos, laicas, religiosos, religiosas, diáconos y sacerdotes, para que se unan a nosotros en nuestra promesa de responder a la presencia de nuestros hermanos hispanos.

    (b) Ensalzamos la labor que se ha llevado a cabo en el pasado; nos regocijamos en ella, y prometemos hacer todo cuanto podamos por superarla.

    (c) Vislumbramos una nueva era para el ministerio hispano, enriquecida con los dones de la facultad creativa, puestos providencialmente ante nosotros, y con el Espíritu de Pentecostés que nos llama a la unidad, a la renovación y a la respuesta que pide la llamada profética de la presencia hispana.

    (d) Nos comprometemos a emprender una obra pastoral profunda, consciente y continua para poner de relieve la catolicidad de la Iglesia y la dignidad de todos sus miembros.

    (e) Contamos esperanzados con las grandes bendiciones que los hispanos pueden aportar a nuestras iglesias locales.

Que este compromiso reciba la bendición, el aliento y la inspiración de Nuestro Señor, y que su Santísima Madre, Patrona de América, nos acompañe en nuestra jornada. Amén.

Estudio sobre las Mejores Prácticas de Ministerios Diocesanos entre Hispanos/Latinos

Conferencia de Obispos Católicos de los Estados Unidos
Comité de Asuntos Hispanos
Noviembre, 2006

El documento, *Estudio sobre las Mejores Prácticas de Ministerios Diocesanos entre Hispanos/Latinos* (Study on Best Practices for Diocesan Ministry Among Hispanics/Latinos) es una guía que ha sido preparada por el Comité de Obispos en Asuntos Hispanos de la Conferencia de Obispos Católicos de los Estados Unidos (USCCB), fue revisado por el Director del Comité, el Obispo Plácido Rodríguez, CMF, y ha sido autorizada para su publicación por el que suscribe.

Mons. David J. Malloy, STD
Secretario General, USCCB

Agradecimientos

Expresamos nuestra gratitud a los obispos y al personal de sus archidiócesis/diócesis por participar, y por su apertura y generosidad durante el proceso del estudio. Agradecemos a la Asociación Nacional Católica de Directores Diocesanos del Ministerio Hispano (NCADDHM) y a la Asociación Regional de Directores y Coordinadores para el Ministerio Hispano su liderazgo y colaboración. En particular agradecemos al Sr. Rudy Vargas IV y a la Sra. Elisa Montalvo su valiosa colaboración y guía durante todo el proceso. También queremos dar las gracias al equipo de entrevistadores quienes compartieron la tarea de visitar las archidiócesis/diócesis y luego preparar sus reportes: las hermanas Angela Erevia, Leticia Salazar, la señora Mar Muñoz-Visoso; al Rev. Thomas Florek S.J.; a los señores Miguel León, Ph.D., Alfonso Barros, Ronaldo Cruz y Alejandro Aguilera-Titus.

Antecedentes

Durante su reunión de noviembre del 2004, algunos representantes de la Asociación Nacional de Directores Diocesanos Católicos para el Ministerio Hispano (NCADDHM), y de la Asociación Nacional de Directores Regionales y Coordinadores para el Ministerio Hispano, se dirigieron al Comité de Obispos en Asuntos Hispanos con algunas preocupaciones relacionadas con el cierre de oficinas para el Ministerio Hispano, o que éstas fueran ubicadas bajo la dirección de oficinas de ministerios multiculturales. Las preocupaciones expuestas por esos grupos de ministerios hispanos señalaban que mientras la presencia hispana seguia creciendo y demandando una más fuerte respuesta pastoral, el personal diocesano y/o los recursos del Ministerio Hispano estaban decreciendo en algunas archidiócesis/diócesis. Se pidió al Comité de Obispos que considerara la posibilidad de llevar a cabo una encuesta para ayudar a discernir cuáles eran los mejores modelos de ministerios hispanos diocesanos en ese momento de restructuración. Así fue como el Comité de Obispos dispuso que un equipo desarrollara una estrategia para identificar las mejores prácticas en cuanto a estructuras y funciones diocesanas del Ministerio Hispano. Esta disposición estaba relacionada con la afirmación de la Conferencia de Obispos Católicos de los Estados Unidos (USCCB) en su documento *Encuentro y Misión: una Renovada Estructura Pastoral para el Ministerio Hispano* (Encuentro and Mission: A Renewed Pastoral Framework for Hispanic Ministry), y la necesidad de tener estructuras diocesanas fuertes dentro del Ministerio Hispano.

Propósito

Ofrecer a los obispos modelos que posean las mejores prácticas diocesanas con los ministerios hispanos y que puedan ser utilizadas para ayudar en: (1) la evaluación del nivel de desarrollo del Ministerio Hispano en sus propias diócesis, e identificar los próximos pasos a seguir; (2) aplicar las medidas para asegurar que se lleve a cabo un acercamiento mejor, más sistemático, colaborativo y estructuralmente fuerte del Ministerio Hispano diocesano, (3) desarrollar o actualizar el Plan Pastoral para el Ministerio Hispano en el contexto de una Iglesia culturalmente diversa.

Metodología

Se desarrolló un cuestionario basado en diez guías o indicadores, y fueron seleccionadas veinte archidiócesis/diócesis consideradas como altamente efectivas en su Ministerio Hispano. Todo se hizo en colaboración con la NCADDHM (Asociación Nacional Católica de Directores Diocesanos para el Ministerio Hispano) y de la Asociación Nacional de Directores y Coordinadores Regionales para el Ministerio Hispano. Un equipo de entrevistadores realizó las visitas a las veinte archidiócesis/diócesis seleccionadas. Los indicadores que fueron escogidos se desarrollaron de acuerdo a la experiencia obtenida por el equipo en el terreno pastoral, y en la información ofrecida por los directores diocesanos regionales para el Ministerio Hispano.

Indicadores o Guías

1. Visión
2. Misión
3. Planificación Pastoral
4. Estructura
5. Crecimiento Sostenido
6. Desarrollo y Formación de Liderazgo
7. Proceso en Tomar Decisiones
8. Colaboración
9. Recursos
10. Evaluación

Archidiócesis/Diócesis Identificadas como Ejemplo por tener "Las Mejores Prácticas"

Las archidiócesis/diócesis seleccionadas fueron escogidas por recomendación de las dos organizaciones nacionales mencionadas anteriormente. Las pautas que se consideraron para la selección fueron: la localización geográfica, el tamaño, la población hispana y el porcentaje de ésta en la archidiócesis/diócesis. También el medio ambiente, fuera este rural o urbano, y el grado de desarrollo del Ministerio Hispano.

Por lo menos dos de las archidiócesis/diócesis fueron seleccionadas de entre ocho regiones para poder tener una mayor representación geográfica. Por lo tanto, las archidiócesis/diócesis seleccionadas no necesariamente representan las 20 mejores prácticas de ministerio hispano diocesano de la nación.

Archidiócesis/Diócesis	*Región*
Grand Rapids y Chicago	Norte Centro
Raleigh, Richmond y Charlotte	Sureste
Washington, D.C. y Wilmington	Noreste
Denver y Salt Lake City	Estados de Montaña
Orange, Monterey, San Bernardino y Stockton	Lejano Oeste
Yakima y Portland	Noroeste
Omaha y St. Paul-Minneapolis	Estados de Centro Norte
Galveston-Houston, Fort Worth y El Paso	Suroeste

Resumen de Respuestas

1. Visión

El elemento básico e histórico para lograr un exitoso ministerio entre católicos hispanos debe de estar establecido sobre las bases expuestas en el Plan Pastoral Nacional de 1987 para el Ministerio Hispano (NPPHM por sus siglas en inglés), aprobado por la Conferencia de Obispos Católicos de los Estados Unidos, Todas las archidiócesis/diócesis que participaron en el estudio han reconocido que los hispanos son responsabilidad de toda la Iglesia, y no sólo de algunas parroquias y de sacerdotes dispuestos a atenderlos. Esta clara noción del Ministerio ha hecho que la respuesta del personal parroquial de las archidiócesis/diócesis cambie. Los que antes dudaban si debían responder a la presencia hispana, ahora preguntan cómo deben hacerlo de forma más efectiva. Las veinte archidiócesis/diócesis identificadas por tener las mejores prácticas, tienen un entendimiento sobre el ministerio hispano basado en la NNPHM y en otros documentos formulados por la Conferencia de Obispos Católicos de los Estados Unidos, particularmente *Encuentro y Misión: una Estructura Pastoral Renovada para el Ministerio Hispano* (Encuentro y Misión: A Renewed Pastoral Framework for Hispanic Ministry). En las veinte archidiócesis/diócesis se han llevado a cabo talleres sobre este documento. En dieciséis de ellas los talleres incluían participantes de diferentes oficinas de las archidiócesis/diócesis y de organizaciones e instituciones católicas. Con excepción de las archidiócesis/diócesis que son relativamente nuevas en su desarrollo del ministerio hispano, la visión sobre el ministerio con hispanos ha sido incorporada al trabajo de varias archidiócesis/diócesis y en el de oficinas y organizaciones e instituciones católicas. Esto es evidente por la presencia de un personal profesional responsable de desarrollar a largo plazo en sus oficinas y organizaciones el ministerio entre los hispanos, particularmente en las archidiócesis/diócesis con crecimiento sostenido de hispanos.

2. Misión

Las veinte archidiócesis/diócesis que participaron en el estudio mostraron una fuerte y continuada respuesta a la presencia hispana. El número de católicos hispanos que participan activamente en la vida y misión de la Iglesia ha crecido dramáticamente. Este es el resultado directo del crecimiento continuado de parroquias que tienen ministerios hispanos, particularmente en los últimos diez años. En la mayoría de los casos, el crecimiento ha sido notable ya que en las veinte archidiócesis/diócesis el número de estas parroquias llega a un total de 854. En una de las archidiócesis, el número de parroquias que trabajan con hispanos aumentó de ocho parroquias a cuarenta y una en solo nueve años. El porcentaje de sacerdotes y ministros laicos profesionales que trabajan directamente con católicos hispanos también ha aumentado significativamente de acuerdo a los participantes en la encuesta. Como ejemplo vemos que en una archidiócesis el número de sacerdotes que trabaja directamente con ministerios hispanos aumentó de seis a cuarenta y dos en el término de siete años. Durante este tiempo, el número de líderes laicos hispanos recibiendo sueldo y trabajando en las parroquias aumentó de cuatro a veinte seis. A pesar de este crecimiento, todas las arquidiócesis/diócesis que participaron en la encuesta dijeron que el aumento en la población hispana en las parroquias estaba lejos de lo que debía ser la respuesta pastoral. En los próximos años más parroquias proyectan recibir hispanos. Vale la pena mencionar que todas las arquidiócesis/diócesis participantes esperan que sus seminaristas tomen clases relacionadas con los ministerios hispanos así como clases de idioma y cultura. En algunos casos esta no es solamente una expectativa sino un requisito del obispo ordinario. Además, en dieciséis de las veinte archidiócesis/diócesis encuestadas, el obispo ordinario habla buen español. En las otras cuatro, los obispos pueden comunicarse bastante bien en español y lo hacen en ocasiones especiales.

La participación de los hispanos sigue creciendo en las diferentes parroquias y en los ministerios de las arquidiócesis/diócesis, como son la catequesis, los ministerios litúrgicos, la formación de adultos en la fe, los ministerios para adolescentes y jóvenes adultos, los ministerios con inmigrantes, los ministerios de las cárceles, la evangelización y los servicios sociales. Dentro de la Iglesia hay una proliferación de movimientos apostólicos y programas de evangelización como son los Cursillos de Cristiandad, la Renovación Carismática, las Pequeñas Comunidades Cristianas, RENEW, grupos de estudio de la Biblia, Discípulos en Misión, Jóvenes para Cristo, Movimiento de Jornadas, Neo-catecumenado y otros. El acercamiento a la comunidad hispana en general se lleva a cabo por medio de servicios sociales, eventos culturales, programas de radio y distribución de material impreso. Los hispanos que participan en actividades de acción social, como son los días de cabildeo, los proyectos de apoyo, las campañas de registración electoral, y otras actividades cívicas, también están creciendo en todas las archidiócesis/diócesis que se encuestaron.

3. Planificación Pastoral

La planificación pastoral juega un papel decisivo en el crecimiento sostenido y en la efectividad de los ministerios hispanos. Todas menos tres de las archidiócesis/diócesis encuestadas han desarrollado, o están en el proceso de desarrollar, un Plan Pastoral para el Ministerio Hispano de varios años de duración, que normalmente es de entre tres a cinco años. Las otras tres archidiócesis/diócesis tienen planes de un año de duración. En las archidiócesis/diócesis en las que el ministerio hispano es relativamente nuevo, la Oficina del Ministerio Hispano (OMH por sus siglas en inglés) tiene la responsabilidad de implementar un Plan Pastoral. En contraste, en las archidiócesis/diócesis con una larga historia y experiencia con ministerios hispanos, los planes pastorales son la responsabilidad de diferentes oficinas, instituciones y organizaciones archdiocesanas/diocesanas. En este caso, la Oficina del Ministerio Hispano (OMH) es un agente activo en el proceso de la planificación pastoral de todas la archidiócesis/diócesis. Además, un número de oficinas pastorales y otras organizaciones tienen personal bilingüe directamente responsable del ministerio con hispanos lo cual resulta en una mayor cantidad de hispanos participando en eventos y actividades archdiocesanas/diocesanas (como son la catequesis y los días de ministerios, reuniones juveniles y convenciones, así como celebraciones litúrgicas). Los proyectos en común en las áreas de catequesis, ministerios para adolescentes y jóvenes adultos, y de formación, también son prueba de que existe una planificación pastoral orgánica.

Vale la pena apuntar que entre los encuestados sólo una diócesis tiene una oficina de planificación. También es interesante resaltar que algunas de las archidiócesis/diócesis no tienen establecidos planes pastorales. En el momento de la entrevista, algunos mencionaron que en sus archidiócesis/diócesis estaban llevando a cabo un sínodo, y que ese proceso los llevaría luego a desarrollar un plan.

4. Estructura

Una oficina para el ministerio hispano bien establecida, con un director efectivo con acceso directo al obispo local, es la clave para tener buenas prácticas ministeriales. Diecinueve de las veinte archidiócesis/diócesis tienen un director para el Ministerio Hispano. Trece tienen como director a un laico trabajando a jornada completa; tres tienen religiosas a jornada completa; y tres tienen sacerdotes (dos a jornada completa y uno a jornada parcial).

Las dieciocho archidiócesis/diócesis que tienen directores trabajando a jornada completa, tienen también personal de apoyo, y siete tienen personal asociado. Estas OMH también tienen su propio presupuesto, mientras que en las otras archidiócesis/diócesis el presupuesto para el Ministerio Hispano es solamente un gasto más de las oficinas o departamentos. La mayor parte de los directores tienen acceso directo a un obispo ordinario y cuatro archidiócesis/diócesis están bajo la supervisión del obispo ordinario o del obispo auxiliar. Luego, cuatro están bajo la supervisión del canciller, tres bajo el moderador de la curia, y dos bajo el párroco. En la mayoría de los casos, la OMH se encuentra bajo un departamento, que casi siempre es el de servicios pastorales.

Diecisiete archidiócesis/diócesis tienen personal profesional en sus oficinas diocesanas que han sido empleados, específicamente, para atender a los hispanos. En tres archidiócesis/diócesis la mayor parte del personal es bilingüe–en una de ellas, veintisiete de cincuenta trabajadores profesionales son hispanos y tienen posiciones como directores o como directores asociados.

En tres de las archidiócesis/diócesis, la OMH es la única oficina cuya responsabilidad principal es atender a los hispanos. Una sola diócesis no tiene una OMH pero tiene directores bilingües en la mayoría de sus oficinas diocesanas, y en organizaciones e institutos católicos. La mayor parte de los sacerdotes en esa diócesis son bilingües. Los hispanos constituyen la mayor parte de la población católica de esa diócesis, y la mayoría de sus parroquias ofrecen ministerios en inglés y en español.

5. Crecimiento Sostenido

Se han identificado cuatro etapas diferentes en el desarrollo del ministerio hispano a nivel archidiocesano/diocesano. Cada etapa está definida por una función específica a desarrollar según el ministerio vaya evolucionando:

i. **Etapa Inicial.** En este nivel se encuentra el ministerio hispano en ciertas áreas o parroquias de la diócesis que no tienen coordinación diocesana. Los servicios sociales, centros de apoyo y la instauración de la liturgia dominical en español son las actividades primarias y prioridades principales. Todas las veinte archidiócesis/diócesis han pasado ya esta etapa. Sin embargo, estas prioridades siempre están vigentes en los esfuerzos misionales con la población inmigrante.

ii. **Etapa de Equipo Diocesano.** El Ministerio Hispano es coordinado por la oficina diocesana que ofrece servicios pastorales a los hispanos. Durante esta etapa, la principal meta de la OMH es la de dar apoyo a las parroquias y ayudarlas a recibir a los hispanos. Los católicos hispanos son la responsabilidad de la OMH más que de las parroquias. En esta etapa es fundamental tener sacerdotes y/o religiosos como directores en caso de que haya necesidad de administrar algún sacramento. Cinco de las veinte archidiócesis/diócesis están en esta etapa de desarrollo y avanzan bastante exitosamente hacia la siguiente etapa.

iii. **Etapa de Base Parroquial.** A este nivel el Ministerio Hispano es la responsabilidad de la parroquia y de la OMH. Esta última actúa como un apoyo para las parroquias y otras oficinas pastorales de las archidiócesis/diócesis. En esta etapa, la prioridad mayor debe ser que los hispanos sean la responsabilidad de las parroquias, y es característico que surja un rápido crecimiento en el número de parroquias con ministerios hispanos. También es básico en esta etapa el desarrollo de programas y proyectos para ayudar a las parroquias con sus ministerios hispanos. En esta fase hay también un cambio de quién fungirá como director de la OMH; casi siempre será un director laico o una religiosa, en vez de un sacerdote. También se comienza a emplear personal en la oficina para trabajar con los hispanos en los diferentes ministerios. Doce archidiócesis/diócesis se encuentran en esta etapa de desarrollo. Nueve de ellas tienen directores laicos, dos tienen sacerdotes y una tiene a una religiosa. Todas las archidiócesis/diócesis, excepto una, tienen personal que trabaja en otras oficinas diocesanas y organizaciones católicas (por ejemplo: catequesis, formación de adultos en la fe, formación de adolescentes y jóvenes adultos y Caridades Católicas). Es importante recordar que el funcionamiento de oficinas para el ministerio hispano en las nuevas parroquias resulta un trabajo que no termina nunca y que al comienzo necesita un apoyo fuerte y una planificación pastoral, así como alguna asistencia directa.

iv. **Etapa Integral Diocesano.** A este nivel, la Oficina para el Ministerio Hispano es altamente influyente y comprometida. Las otras oficinas diocesanas están preparadas para ofrecer ayuda a las parroquias en sus esfuerzos pastorales con los hispanos, con sus propias responsabilidades ministeriales. La mayoría de las parroquias que poseen un número significativo de miembros hispanos, ofrecen una amplia variedad de ministerios para hispanos. Dos diócesis han llegado ya a esta etapa, mientras que cuatro van en ese camino. En cinco de seis archidiócesis/diócesis, el director del Ministerio Hispano también trabaja en una oficina archidiocesana/diocesana.

6. Desarrollo de Liderazgo y Formación

Las veinte archidiócesis/diócesis que participaron en la encuesta ven el desarrollo del liderazgo y la formación como sus más altas prioridades, particularmente con dirigentes hispanos laicos. Esto es evidente ya que existen programas diocesanos de formación bien establecidos en dieciocho de las veinte archidiócesis/diócesis. Las otras dos diócesis están aún comenzando esta etapa de desarrollo, y aunque ofrecen oportunidades de formación en los ministerios, no se ha establecido aun un programa más sistemático. Basado en las respuestas generadas por la encuesta, un programa de formación bien establecido posee: 1) un personal específicamente responsable para administrar el programa; 2) un buen equipo; 3) este es valorado y utilizado por un número considerable de parroquias; 4) ofrece formación sistemática, continuada e integral; y 5) es reconocido y está conectado con varias oficinas diocesanas de ministerios.

Siete de las archidiócesis/diócesis tienen una persona trabajando y dirigiendo a jornada completa el programa de formación. En estos casos, el programa tiende a ser más sofisticado pues ofrece una variedad de oportunidades de formación que van desde programas de certificado, programas universitarios con créditos, y/o programas de licenciaturas. Algunas de las archidiócesis/diócesis se están asociando a universidades para promover programas de grado, por lo que no están limitadas solamente a programas de certificación.

En diez archidiócesis/diócesis, el director del Ministerio Hispano es también responsable del programa de formación, siendo esta una posición de jornada completa. En cinco archidiócesis/diócesis, el programa de formación es ofrecido por un instituto regional de pastoral hispana como lo son el Instituto Pastoral del Sureste (Southeast Pastoral Institute (SEPI), el Instituto Pastoral del Noreste o el Centro para Formación de Dirigentes del Medio Oeste.

En once de las archidiócesis/diócesis, el programa de formación fue establecido hace ya más de quince años. Vale mencionar que una vez que un programa es establecido, este crece de forma consistente. Esto se debe en parte al gran nivel de interés mostrado por los dirigentes laicos hispanos en sus formaciones personales. Esto está reflejado en las conclusiones incluidas en la declaración del 1999 de la Conferencia de Obispos Católicos de los Estados Unidos sobre Ministerios Eclesiales Laicos: *La Situación del Asunto* (página 54), y que muestra que los hispanos constituyen el 23 por ciento de los laicos que participan en programas de formación en las archidiócesis/diócesis. Otro factor es la relación que existe entre los programas y las parroquias. Los representantes de las veinte archidiócesis/diócesis hablaron sobre la importancia de tener párrocos que reconozcan la necesidad de ofrecer programas de formación ya que es un medio importante para formar dirigentes dentro de cada parroquia.

Una buena y sólida práctica dentro del ministerio hispano diocesano consiste en tener programas de formación bien establecidos. Este indicador va además acompañado de los esfuerzos que se realicen en los diferentes ministerios, como son la catequesis, los ministerios con adolescentes y con jóvenes adultos, la preparación para el matrimonio y los ministerios con inmigrantes.

Catorce de las veinte archidiócesis/diócesis encuestadas llevan a cabo estos programas de forma regular y continuada, particularmente en el área de la catequesis. Once tienen programas de ministerio hispano para adolescentes y/o jóvenes adultos y algunas han desarrollado sus propios programas, mientras que otras utilizan a los institutos pastorales regionales o nacionales que ya se han mencionado, ó los programas ofrecidos por el Instituto Fe y Vida y el Centro Cultural Mexicano Americano (MACC).

En el área de educación católica, el porcentaje de estudiantes hispanos que asisten a escuelas católicas varía significativamente entre las diferentes archidiócesis/diócesis encuestadas. La disparidad está asociada al tamaño de población hispana y al tiempo de residencia de los inmigrantes en un área específica. Las archidiócesis/diócesis encuestadas que tienen desde hace mucho tiempo una población hispana, muestran que aproximadamente un 20 por ciento de los niños que asisten a colegios católicos son hispanos. Esta cifra se espera vaya en aumento una vez que el número de archidiócesis/diócesis muestren más interés en que la educación católica sea más accesible a los hispanos. En las archidiócesis/diócesis donde la presencia hispana es relativamente nueva, el promedio de hispanos que asisten a escuelas católicas es de aproximadamente el 10 por ciento. Sin embargo, dos de las archidiócesis/diócesis con una presencia hispana relativamente reciente y/o limitada, tienen un promedio elevado de niños hispanos que reciben educación católica.

7. Proceso en Tomar Decisiones

En la encuesta a las archidiócesis/diócesis se incluyó la siguiente pregunta: ¿Cómo calificaría usted a su diócesis en la inclusión de hispanos en los procesos de tomar decisiones? ¿Le daría una puntuación Alta, Buena o Pobre? Las archidiócesis/diócesis encuestadas respondieron de la forma siguiente: seis dijeron que Alta; siete, que Buena, y cinco dijeron que Baja.

Basado en estas respuestas, las archidiócesis/diócesis con una puntuación "Alta" y "Buena" fueron las que tenían OMH muy bien establecidas en sus archidiócesis/diócesis, y su director formaba parte del equipo de trabajo del obispo. De acuerdo a las respuestas, una OMH bien establecida en las archidiócesis/diócesis y que han llegado a la etapa de desarrollo que abarca ya a toda la diócesis (y que incluye hispanos en diferentes departamentos y oficinas de ministerios), reportaron una puntuación "Alta" en cuanto a hispanos que toman parte del proceso de tomar decisiones.

De las cinco archidiócesis/diócesis que indicaron que el nivel de participación de hispanos tomando decisiones era "Bajo," cuatro están en la segunda etapa de desarrollo (enfoque diocesano). Una de ellas está ya bien adelantada en la tercera etapa (establecimiento en la parroquia), pero solamente tiene una persona trabajando a jornada completa con hispanos y que a su vez es director del Ministerio Hispano.

Las siguientes áreas fueron identificadas como básicas en el proceso de tomar decisiones en lo que impacta al Ministerio Hispano: 1) asignaciones de sacerdotes a las parroquias, 2) empleo de personal nuevo; 3) planificación pastoral, 4) eventos y programas diocesanos, 5) adjudicación de recursos y restructuración de estrategias. Además, es también fundamental la participación de hispanos en los consejos parroquiales, en comisiones litúrgicas, en el equipo que trabaja con el sacerdote, y en el comité de vocaciones. En estos equipos, que son los que toman las decisiones, los hispanos van en aumento.

Es bueno el número de hispanos que forman parte de estos consejos parroquiales y/o en comisiones en las archidiócesis/diócesis. Algunas archidiócesis/diócesis no tienen consejos establecidos todavía mientras que otras están en la actualidad en un proceso de sínodo, y tienen una participación significativa de hispanos. La participación de hispanos en la toma de decisiones a nivel parroquial parece ser fuerte. Todas las archidiócesis/diócesis que fueron encuestadas reportaron que la participación de hispanos en sus consejos parroquiales era significativa.

Muchas parroquias tienen un párroco bilingüe, y un número considerable tienen un sacerdote hispano. En las veinte archidiócesis/diócesis encuestadas, el número de parroquias con personal hispano también va en aumento.

8. Colaboración

La colaboración es a la vez fruto y señal de un ministerio hispano muy efectivo. Al igual que en el área de planificación pastoral, la colaboración es mejor intencionada y coordinada en las archidiócesis/diócesis con un largo historial de ministerio hispano. Las seis archidiócesis/diócesis que han llegado, o están próximas a llegar a la etapa de desarrollo en toda la diócesis, reportan un mayor nivel de intercambio de perspectivas y recursos en favor de los católicos hispanos, y también en relación con la Iglesia local. Actividades como los días de catequesis, las convenciones juveniles, las iniciativas de desarrollo de liderazgo, los programas de formación y los días de cabildeo, son comunes en cinco de las veinte archidiócesis/diócesis participantes. En estas cinco, la OMH está asociada a otras oficinas pastorales que tienen una meta o un plan pastoral común con el Ministerio Hispano y que involucra directamente a otros ministerios.

En las archidiócesis/diócesis donde el Ministerio Hispano ha llegado a la etapa de desarrollo parroquial, la OMH se ha convertido en un apoyo para las otras oficinas pastorales y organizaciones católicas. Esto se debe al hecho de que la OMH es la única oficina equipada con el personal, la experiencia y las competencias necesarias para atender a los hispanos. En estas archidiócesis/diócesis la colaboración se lleva a cabo más que nada en la planificación de eventos diocesanos en áreas de ministerios específicos. Cuánto más podría extenderse esta colaboración dependerá, en su mayor parte, de la relación que exista entre sus directores y/o el estilo de colaboración que haya dentro de un departamento, como es, por ejemplo, el de servicios pastorales. La colaboración aumenta significativamente de acuerdo al personal que se emplee en una oficina, departamento o institución católica específica para desarrollar el ministerio entre los hispanos.

En el caso de las archidiócesis/diócesis que se encuentran en las etapas preliminares de crecimiento con el ministerio hispano, la colaboración de la OMH con otras oficinas e instituciones es limitada ya que ésta ofrece servicios directamente a católicos hispanos dejándole poco tiempo libre al personal para otras labores.

Sin embargo, las archidiócesis/diócesis que están en este nivel de desarrollo expresaron que se necesita más colaboración, y que ésta debe aumentar según aumente el ministerio. En general, el concepto de *pastoral de conjunto* (comunión en misión) del Ministerio Hispano incita a sus directores a colaborar. Varias respuestas de la encuesta enfatizan este punto, y ha quedado muy bien ilustrado por un participante que expresó: *"Nosotros le decimos constantemente a nuestros colegas que esto no se refiere a "nosotros," o a "ellos," sino a "todos" porque somos una Iglesia."*

9. Recursos

Todas las archidiócesis/diócesis que participaron dijeron que el personal y los recursos financieros asignados al Ministerio Hispano no alcanzan para lo que se necesita. Diecisiete de las archidiócesis/diócesis encuestadas dijeron que el compromiso de sus archidiócesis/diócesis con los católicos hispanos es generoso pero no suficiente para atender a una población hispana que crece con rapidez. A no ser por dos excepciones, en los últimos años no ha ocurrido reducción de personal en las OMH o entre los hispanos empleados en otras oficinas de ministerios. En tres de ellas ha habido un aumento de personal diocesano que trabaja con hispanos. Cinco reportaron una disminución en su presupuesto debido a las limitaciones económicas que fueron aplicadas a todos los niveles, y tres reportaron un aumento en sus presupuestos en los últimos años.

Mientras que el personal y los recursos en las archidiócesis/diócesis han permanecido casi igual en los últimos años, a nivel parroquial las veinte archidiócesis/diócesis han crecido significativamente. El porcentaje de sacerdotes comprometidos con el Ministerio Hispano ha aumentado del 25 al 65 por ciento en las archidiócesis/diócesis que han llegado a la tercera etapa de desarrollo en la parroquia. Hasta en aquellas archidiócesis/diócesis donde el Ministerio Hispano es aún bastante nuevo, el porcentaje de sacerdotes que trabajan con hispanos es significativo y va en aumento. Es también significativo que doce archidiócesis/diócesis tengan un fondo para ayudar a las parroquias a emplear coordinadores y/o subsidiar parte de los salarios de los sacerdotes que ayudan en el Ministerio Hispano. Dos de ellas dan prioridad a emplear coordinadores para sus parroquias.

En el área de educación católica, nueve de las archidiócesis/diócesis dijeron que estaban haciendo un esfuerzo especial para aumentar el número de estudiantes hispanos en las escuelas católicas. Esto ha resultado en la creación de un fondo monetario para este propósito, o para apoyar a los estudiantes con recursos limitados. Una de las archidiócesis/diócesis se distingue en esta área por tener el porcentaje más alto de estudiantes hispanos en colegios católicos (el 25 por ciento), aunque es una diócesis relativamente pequeña con una población hispana también pequeña.

En el área de mayordomía o servicio a la parroquia, dieciocho archidiócesis/diócesis están involucrando a sus comunidades hispanas en el programa anual de servicio. En la mayoría de las archidiócesis/diócesis, la OMH sirve de apoyo pues ofrece la traducción de materiales e identifica a los dirigentes de habla hispana para ayudar a promover ese tipo de trabajo a nivel parroquial. Algunos OMH ofrecen clases sobre la importancia de desarrollar un sentido de pertenencia a la comunidad de fe y en ser buenos servidores. Una diócesis tiene dos profesionales de habla hispana en la oficina de mayordomía, pero las respuestas de la encuesta reflejan la necesidad de trabajar más en esta área.

10. Evaluación

La evaluación resulta un elemento importante en todas las archidiócesis/diócesis encuestadas. Algunos eventos específicos, como son los días de ministerios, retiros, talleres o estudios, son siempre evaluados. En dieciséis de las veinte archidiócesis/diócesis se llevan a cabo evaluaciones anuales de las OMH. Generalmente, los planes pastorales y los programas de formación son evaluados cuando estos llegan a su fin, pero en algunas archidiócesis/diócesis es necesario implementar un proceso más sistemático.

En cuanto a las pautas empleadas para determinar el crecimiento y la efectividad del Ministerio Hispano en las archidiócesis/diócesis participantes, se utilizaron las siguientes referencias:

- El número de parroquias con Ministerio Hispano
- El número de misas en español y el promedio de asistencia dominical
- El porcentaje de sacerdotes trabajando directamente en ministerios hispanos
- El número de hispanos en el personal diocesano y parroquial, y en consejos parroquiales
- La cantidad y calidad de programas, eventos y actividades para hispanos en las archidiócesis/diócesis, y el número de hispanos participando en ellos
- Número de hispanos que participan en todos los eventos de las archidiócesis/diócesis
- El número de talleres ofrecidos o solicitados por las parroquias y/o por movimientos apostólicos
- El número de personas servidas por agencias de servicios sociales
- El número de sacerdotes, diáconos, seminaristas y religiosos, tanto hombres como mujeres hispanos, que trabajan en las archidiócesis/diócesis, y el número total de sacerdotes bilingües.
- El crecimiento de la población hispana y el porcentaje a la que ha podido llegar la Iglesia

Conclusión

Después de analizar las respuestas en conjunto de las veinte archidiócesis/diócesis que participaron en la encuesta, los siguientes elementos han sido identificados como decisivos para que una archidiócesis/diócesis desarrolle las mejores prácticas del Ministerio Hispano Diocesano.

1. Un elemento histórico y básico para poder desarrollar un exitoso Ministerio Hispano entre católicos es construir dicho ministerio sobre las bases establecidas en el Plan Pastoral Nacional de 1987 para el Ministerio Hispano (NPPHM por sus siglas en inglés) de la Conferencia de Obispos Católicos de los Estados Unidos. La noción de que los hispanos son la responsabilidad de toda la Iglesia y no solo de algunas parroquias y sacerdotes, ha quedado arraigada en todas las archidiócesis/diócesis.

    Lo más relevante: Las veinte archidiócesis/diócesis identificadas por tener las mejores prácticas saben que el Ministerio Hispano está basado en el NPPHM y en otros documentos emitidos por la Conferencia de Obispos Católicos de los Estados Unidos, particularmente el documento *Encuentro y Misión: Una Estructura Renovada para el Ministerio Hispano* (Encuentro and Mission: A Renewed Pastoral Framework for Hispanic Ministry). En las veinte archidiócesis/diócesis se han llevado a cabo talleres sobre este documento.

2. Un ministerio que es cultural y consistentemente específico, atrae a los católicos hispanos a participar de forma más entusiasta en la vida y misión de las parroquias, instituciones católicas, movimientos apostólicos, eventos diocesanos y programas y actividades en general. En las veinte archidiócesis/diócesis el número de parroquias con Ministerios Hispanos llega ya a 854.

    Lo más relevante: Las veinte archidiócesis/diócesis muestran una respuesta fuerte y continuada a la presencia hispana. En una archidiócesis el número de sacerdotes que trabajan directamente con el Ministerio Hispano creció de seis a cuarenta y dos en un plazo de siete años, y el número de dirigentes laicos hispanos trabajando a sueldo en las parroquias creció de cuatro a veintiséis. Durante ese tiempo, las misiones de esas archidiócesis que sirven a hispanos aumentaron de doce a treinta y nueve. En dieciséis de las veinte archidiócesis/diócesis, el obispo local habla buen español. En las otras cuatro, los obispos pueden comunicarse un poco en español y lo hacen en ocasiones especiales.

3. Un proceso de planificación pastoral continuado permite que el Ministerio Hispano esté mejor enfocado, sea más sistemático, mejor organizado y que contribuya a un esfuerzo combinado. El Plan Pastoral para el Ministerio Hispano requiere que se reconozca la presencia hispana en los diferentes departamentos, oficinas e instituciones. Si se planea bien, los recursos serán utilizados al máximo, y se ayudará a evaluar el progreso y el crecimiento de los esfuerzos desarrollados con anterioridad.

    Lo más relevante: Todas, excepto tres de las archidiócesis/diócesis, han desarrollado o están en proceso de desarrollar un Plan Pastoral para el Ministerio Hispano con varios años de duración. Usualmente este es un Plan que se extiende de entre tres a cinco años. Las otras tres archidiócesis/diócesis tienen planes pastorales de un año de duración.

4. Una Oficina para el Ministerio Hispano bien establecida tiene un director competente y/o en su lugar, el personal necesario con acceso directo al obispo local que, hasta cierto punto, es, bilingüe. En las archidiócesis/diócesis donde el Ministerio Hispano está más desarrollado, la OMH se encuentra bajo la supervisión directa del obispo local o un miembro de la curia. En otras archidiócesis/diócesis, el Ministerio Hispano está bajo la supervisión de un departamento, que casi siempre es el de servicios pastorales.

    Lo más relevante: Diecinueve de las veinte archidiócesis/diócesis tienen un director para el Ministerio Hispano. La diócesis que no posee una OMH, tiene directores bilingües en la mayoría de sus oficinas diocesanas y en sus organizaciones e instituciones católicas.

5. La toma de iniciativas en las fases de desarrollo del Ministerio Hispano ofrece un crecimiento sostenido y promueve el progreso. Por medio de las etapas de alcance comunitario, enfoque parroquial, y enfoque diocesano, la OMH pasa de ser una oficina de servicio directo, a una oficina de apoyo, y más tarde será una oficina copartícipe.

Lo más relevante: En las diócesis con un desarrollo avanzado, la Oficina para el Ministerio Hispano es muy influyente y comprometida. Las otras oficinas de ministerios diocesanos tienen los medios necesarios para proveer de recursos a las parroquias en sus esfuerzos pastorales con los hispanos, dentro de su área de responsabilidad pastoral.

6. El desarrollo de un vibrante y bien establecido liderazgo y proceso de formación incluye programas, talleres y actividades en las diferentes áreas de los ministerios. Los programas tienen el personal necesario y crecen constantemente, desarrollando talleres ocasionales, programas de certificación y cursos con licenciatura. Los programas para seminaristas y sacerdotes incluyen cursos de cultura, idioma y ministerio hispano.

Lo más relevante: Dieciocho de las veinte archidiócesis/diócesis tienen establecidos programas diocesanos de formación en español. Esto queda reafirmado en los resultados expuestos en la declaración de la Conferencia de Obispos Católicos de los Estados Unidos de 1999: *Ministerio Laico Eclesial: La Situación del Asunto*, (página 54) (Lay Ecclesial Ministry: The State of the Question). La declaración expone que los hispanos constituyen el 23 por ciento de los laicos que trabajan en programas de formación en las archidiócesis/diócesis.

7. La mejor práctica de ministerio hispano es la que incluye un liderazgo compartido en el cual los hispanos y otro personal bilingüe son miembros del consejo archidiocesano/diocesano y de otras organizaciones que toman decisiones. También, las diferentes oficinas de ministerios tienen personal que es directamente responsable del desarrollo de una pastoral con los hispanos. Un número creciente de sacerdotes, particularmente de párrocos, son bilingües, y los consejos parroquiales con miembros hispanos, aumenta de forma representativa.

Lo más relevante: La archidiócesis/diócesis con los niveles más altos en cuanto a toma de decisiones (seis con puntuación alta, y once con puntuación buena), son las que tienen una OMH establecida y su director forma parte del equipo de trabajo del obispo.

8. La interacción de la OMH con otras oficinas y organizaciones e instituciones católicas hace que el espíritu de colaboración y misión en común pueda ser asimilado y proyectado a otras oficinas y organizaciones e instituciones católicas. Es frecuente que se lleven a cabo proyectos en común en áreas específicamente pastorales, y los programas y eventos en las archidiócesis/diócesis son planificados e implementados con la total o significativa participación de las OMH y por lo tanto, la de los católicos hispanos.

Lo más relevante: La colaboración aumenta significativamente cuando el personal se emplea específicamente para desarrollar un ministerio en un departamento, oficina o institución católica entre los hispanos. En general, el concepto de *pastoral de conjunto* dentro del Ministerio Hispano hace que sus líderes colaboren.

9. Si los líderes del Ministerio Hispano están bien informados, éstos están conscientes de las limitaciones de recursos, y saben que las archidiócesis/diócesis están comprometidas con la presencia de los hispanos. En su mayor parte, el personal y los niveles de presupuesto de los programas de las OMH se administran bien, y se otorgan aumentos cuando los programas están bien estructurados. Los cortes de presupuestos son aplicados por igual, a todos los niveles. A nivel parroquial, los recursos aumentan consistentemente en términos de personal y servicios. La comunidad hispana responde cuando comparte más de su tiempo, talento y tesoro, particularmente cuando los esfuerzos de servicio a la parroquia son consistentes y están siempre en desarrollo.

Lo más relevante: A no ser por dos excepciones, de las veinte archidiócesis/diócesis que realizaron el estudio, no ha ocurrido reducción de personal en los últimos años en ninguna OMH o en otras oficinas de ministerios hispanos. En tres de ellas ha habido un crecimiento en el personal diocesano que trabaja con hispanos, y diecisiete dijeron en la encuesta que su compromiso con los católicos hispanos era generoso.

10. Se establece un proceso de evaluación para medir los logros de las metas reflejadas en el plan pastoral y/o en programas y actividades específicas, y se

obtiene un buen resultado en términos de crecimiento cuantitativo. Es necesario deliberar más con otros ministerios diocesanos y con toda la comunidad respecto al desarrollo y articulación de prioridades, y sobre el camino a tomar en el futuro con los ministerios hispanos.

Lo más relevante: En dieciséis de las veinte archidiócesis/diócesis se llevan a cabo evaluaciones anuales sobre el desempeño de las funciones de las OMH. Los planes pastorales y los programas de formación son generalmente evaluados una vez que estos llegan a su fin.

RESULTADOS MÁS RELEVANTES POR ARCHIDIÓCESIS/DIÓCESIS

Charlotte

- Las oficinas, tanto regional como diocesana del Ministerio Hispano, tienen una estructura bien establecida que provee coordinación efectiva y asistencia a las parroquias que trabajan con hispanos.
- Hay coordinación diocesana con la adolescencia y con la juventud adulta hispana, así como un muy efectivo ministerio con los inmigrantes.
- Está en vigor un Plan Pastoral para el Ministerio Hispano, y la planificación pastoral es un proceso que se realiza de forma continuada.

Chicago

- Hay programas de formación para ministerios laicos y para catequistas bien establecidos que benefician a miles de hispanos, tanto a nivel archidiocesano como parroquial.
- A nivel archidiocesano es fuerte y está bien organizado el ministerio de jóvenes adultos con personal que percibe sueldo y que coordina los esfuerzos.
- La archidiócesis tiene un sólido Ministerio Hispano a nivel parroquial.

Denver

- La Oficina Archidiocesana para el Ministerio Hispano está bien establecida e incluye un coordinador para la pastoral con adolescentes y con jóvenes adultos.
- En el Centro San Juan Diego de esta Archidiócesis se celebran reuniones y que ofrece a la comunidad hispana una gran variedad de servicios pastorales y sociales, así como otras actividades.
- A nivel parroquial, la Archidiócesis tiene un vibrante ministerio con los hispanos. En los últimos diez años el número de parroquias con ministerio hispano aumentó de ocho a cuarenta y dos.

El Paso

- El programa de formación para laicos está muy bien establecido y asiste a más de setecientos hispanos cada año (Instituto Tepeyac).
- El Centro Diocesano de Servicios de Inmigración y Refugiados (DMRS por sus siglas en inglés) es muy efectivo y ofrece consejería sobre inmigración y otros asuntos legales. Todo el personal es bilingüe y muy profesional.
- Prácticamente casi todos los sacerdotes son bilingües, y en la mayoría de las parroquias los hispanos son atendidos tanto en inglés como en español.

Fort Worth

- Un alto porcentaje de directores diocesanos y de directores asociados son hispanos. Todas las oficinas diocesanas poseen los recursos necesarios para trabajar con los hispanos.
- La colaboración entre las oficinas diocesanas es muy grande, y la planificación pastoral se lleva a cabo consistentemente en varias áreas que incluyen: formación de adultos en la fe, catequesis, ministerio con los jóvenes, ministerio con inmigrantes y vida familiar.
- La Oficina del Ministerio Hispano es un canal eficaz para el desenvolvimiento de la Iglesia en actividades cívicas y en proyectos e iniciativas que impacten a los hispanos.

Galveston-Houston

- Tiene una red archidiocesana bien establecida, con representantes para el ministerio con hispanos en cada parroquia.
- Hay programas y proyectos muy efectivos con hispanos que incluyen la catequesis, el ministerio con adolescentes y con jóvenes adultos, la formación en la fe y la formación de dirigentes.

- La colaboración entre las oficinas de la Archidiócesis y otras agencias está bien coordinada por medio de un Plan Pastoral para trabajar con el Ministerio Hispano.

Grand Rapids

- Dentro del ministerio con hispanos, existe una oficina diocesana bien establecida con estructura regional que ofrece coordinación y apoyo a las parroquias que trabajan con hispanos.
- Hay un alto nivel de colaboración con otras oficinas diocesanas, particularmente en lo que se refiere a los adolescentes y al ministerio con jóvenes adultos.
- Durante los últimos años ha estado funcionando el *Plan Pastoral Diocesano Integral para el Ministerio Hispano*, y el crecimiento ha sido muy significativo.

Monterey

- Un vibrante ministerio con inmigrantes llega cada año a miles de hispanos.
- En la diócesis, el Comité Consejero Católico Hispano es una organización efectiva, con una clara visión pastoral.
- Se ha realizado un proceso continuado de planificación pastoral y liderazgo diocesano, que ha resultado en el establecimiento de programas y estructuras que benefician a católicos hispanos en un número creciente de parroquias.

Omaha

- El director de la Oficina para el Ministerio Hispano forma parte del consejo archidiocesano y desarrolla una función clave en todo el proceso de planificación pastoral.
- La arquidiócesis tiene establecido un Instituto para la Formación Pastoral (Instituto Pastoral San Juan Diego).
- La Oficina para el Ministerio Hispano es altamente reconocida por la asistencia que ofrece a la comunidad en asuntos relacionados con la presencia hispana.

Orange

- La pastoral con adolescentes hispanos y con jóvenes adultos ha crecido consistentemente y tiene una presencia muy fuerte en la diócesis y en las parroquias.

- Es considerable la colaboración de la diócesis con instituciones y organizaciones cívicas en lo que afecta a los hispanos.
- Más del 50 por ciento de las parroquias tienen implementado un plan integral con el Ministerio Hispano que incluye: liturgia, educación religiosa, servicio y apoyo, evangelización, así como programas y actividades comunitarias.

Portland, Oregon

- En cincuenta y seis parroquias existe un sólido Ministerio Hispano con sacerdotes bilingües (un número significativo de estas parroquias tiene personal hispano laico).
- La arquidiócesis tiene un buen programa de formación para el Ministerio Hispano (*Comunidades Evangelizadoras*).
- Hay becas especiales para ayudar a las parroquias a emplear laicos que coordinen el Ministerio Hispano.

Raleigh

- Hay un sólido Ministerio Hispano a nivel parroquial (sesenta y seis de setenta y ocho parroquias en la diócesis tienen ministerios con hispanos).
- Un excelente entendimiento de la presencia hispana en la diócesis, y una visión clara del Ministerio Hispano, llevan a una precisa y relevante planificación del proceso pastoral.
- El ministerio con adolescentes y con jóvenes adultos hispanos, y la formación de liderazgo, son programas en constante desarrollo que resultan ser muy exitosos.

Richmond

- La diócesis tiene una Oficina para el Ministerio Hispano bien establecida con una variedad de ministerios.
- Hay un alto nivel de colaboración con otras oficinas y agencias diocesanas, incluyendo la participación de católicos hispanos en actividades de apoyo y eventos relacionados con justicia social (como son, por ejemplo, los días de cabildeo)
- Los programas con el ministerio de adolescentes y jóvenes adultos hispanos, así como la formación de liderazgo laico son actividades en continuo desarrollo y que han resultado ser muy exitosos.

Salt Lake City

- En comparación con la mayoría de las diócesis del país, en esta diócesis un porcentaje considerable de niños de escuelas católicas es hispano (el 24 por ciento).
- Es muy efectiva la Comisión Diocesana para el Ministerio Hispano nombrada por el obispo y que ofrece orientación en el proceso de planificación pastoral.
- En un número creciente de parroquias y movimientos apostólicos que trabajan con hispanos, se están llevando siempre a cabo eventos y actividades diocesanas que ofrecen oportunidades y recursos para la formación en un ambiente proselitista.

San Bernardino

- Un personal altamente capacitado y bilingüe dirige prácticamente todas las oficinas diocesanas y agencias católicas del Ministerio Hispano con una visión clara en una Iglesia culturalmente diversa.
- Los cursos de formación para ministros laicos, la catequesis y los programas de liderazgo a niveles de certificación y de grados universitarios, están bien establecidos y concurridos.
- En muchas parroquias y en programas y actividades diocesanas existe un ministerio muy entusiasta entre adolescentes y jóvenes adultos hispanos.

St. Paul-Minneapolis

- La continuidad de liderazgo del Ministerio Hispano por largos períodos de tiempo, ha resultado en la creación de enlaces sólidos dentro de ese ministerio con una visión en común.
- Siempre se está implementando y evaluando el Plan Pastoral Archidiocesano para el Ministerio Hispano con la participación de dirigentes parroquiales.
- En la Archidiócesis las oficinas de ministerios comparten un sólido conocimiento sobre los hispanos para lograr una mayor colaboración en el futuro.

Stockton

- La Oficina para el Ministerio Hispano es muy efectiva y comprometida, y ha ido evolucionando a través de los años. Los hispanos ocupan puestos en las diferentes comisiones y consejos.
- La diócesis tiene un ministerio muy fuerte con los inmigrantes, ofreciendo una variedad de servicios y recursos, incluyendo un manual para inmigrantes.
- La mayoría de las parroquias tienen un Ministerio Hispano sólido que incluye la catequesis y el ministerio con adolescentes y con jóvenes adultos.

Washington, D.C.

- Hay un Plan Pastoral Archidiocesano para el Ministerio Hispano que es integral y altamente copartícipe.
- La mayoría de las oficinas y agencias archdiocesanas poseen personal bilingüe que es responsable de la Pastoral Hispana.
- La Archidiócesis produce una publicación semanal que es uno de los mejores periódicos católicos del país (El Pregonero).

Wilmington

- Desde la incepción de la Oficina Diocesana para el Ministerio Hispano, existe un liderazgo continuado que ha resultado en una fuerte organización y visión en común del ministerio a nivel diocesano.
- El proceso de planificación pastoral por un largo período de tiempo ha sido consistente, sistemático y orientador.
- La diócesis ha visto un rápido crecimiento en el número de parroquias con ministerios hispanos, así como el desarrollo del ministerio entre los adolescentes y los jóvenes adultos hispanos.

Yakima

- Además de la Oficina para el Ministerio Hispano, cada oficina y agencia diocesana tiene su personal bilingüe.
- Más del 85 por ciento de las parroquias tienen Ministerio Hispano y un párroco y/o vicario parroquial bilingüe.
- La oficina diocesana y la estructura de la pastoral con adolescentes y con jóvenes adultos hispanos, están muy desarrolladas y bien integradas dentro del plan global pastoral diocesano para las juventudes.

Referencias

Conferencia de Obispos Católicos de los Estados Unidos (USCCB). *Encuentro and Mission: A Renewed Pastoral Framework for Hispanic Ministry*. Washington, DC: USCCB, 2002.

USCCB, Committee on the Laity. Lay Ecclesial Ministry: *The State of the Questions*. Washington, DC: USCCB, 1999.

USCCB. *National Pastoral Plan for Hispanic Ministry* (NPPHM; 1987). in *Hispanic Ministry: Three Major Documents*. Bilingual edition. Washington, DC: USCCB, 1995.

Apéndice I
Los Obispos Hablan con la Virgen

Carta Pastoral de los Obispos Hispanos de los Estados Unidos

"Deseo vivamente que se me erija aquí un templo, para en el mostrar y dar todo mi amor, compasión, auxilio y defensa, pues yo soy tu piadosa Madre. A ti, a todos los que están contigo, a todos los moradores de esta tierra y a todos los que me amen, que me invoquen, me busquen y en mi confíen. Escucharé sus lamentos y remediaré todas sus miserias, penas y dolores."

Mensaje de nuestra Señora, diciembre, 1531

SALUDO

Cuatrocientos cincuenta años después de Tu aparición en nuestras tierras, venimos nosotros. Tus hijos, como pastores de nuestro pueblo Hispano de los Estados Unidos del Norte. Venimos llenos de gozo y de esperanza, pero también venimos entristecidos y preocupados por los sufrimientos de nuestro Pueblo.

Somos pastores de un pueblo en marcha. Caminando con nuestro pueblo, hemos venido a Ti, Madre de Dios y Madre nuestra, para recibir nuevo ánimo. Queremos llenarnos de entusiasmo para ir a proclamar las maravillas de Dios que se han realizado en nuestra historia, que se están realizando en este momento vida, y que se realizarán en el futuro.

Aunque muchas veces el mundo no nos ha comprendido. Tú si nos entiendes y aprecias. Pues tú fuiste siempre peregrina. Siempre en marcha. Visitaste en las montañas a Tu prima Isabel (Lc. 1:39-56); Tu Hijo nació al fin de tu larga caminata desde Nazaret hasta Belén (Lc.2:1-7); subiste en peregrinación al Templo para consagrar a Jesús (Lc. 2:21-24); viviste en exilio como extranjera amenazada y perseguida (Mt. 2:13-15); retornaste a Tu tierra después de morir el tirano Rey Herodes (Mt. 2:19-23); y de nuevo te pusiste en marcha hacia Jerusalén para las fiestas de la Pascua (Lc. 2:41-52). Estuviste presente al comienzo y al final del ministerio del Señor: en Caná de Galilea, cuando comenzaron los signos del reino (Jn. 2:1-12) y al pie de la cruz (Jn. 19:25-27). Y aquí, en el nacimiento de las Américas, has aparecido como una señal del cielo (Apoc. 12:1), nueva vida y nueva luz.

Todas tus migraciones, viajes y peregrinaciones las hiciste como mujer pobre, al servicio de Jesús, del Reino de Dios, de los pobres necesitados. Te cubrió el Espíritu. Pusiste en práctica la palabra de Dios y compartiste con el pueblo creyente la vida de Jesús. Después de morir Jesús, esperaste contra toda esperanza y fuiste llamada a los cielos como "predilecta de Dios" (Lc. 1:28).

Tú fuiste la mujer fiel....
Tú formaste el cuerpo de Jesús y lo diste al mundo....
Tú eres la Madre de Dios y nuestra Madre....
Tú eres la Madre de todos los habitantes de estas tierras....
Tú eres la Madre de las Américas

> "Y ahora Dios nos da a conocer este proyecto nacido de su corazón, que formó en Cristo desde antes, para realizar cuando llegara la plenitud de los tiempos. Todas las cosas han de reunirse bajo una sola cabeza, Cristo, tanto los seres celestiales como los terrenales."
>
> *Eph. 1:9-10*

I. NUESTRA PEREGRINACIÓN HISTORICA

Mientras recorres la vida
Tu nunca solo estás
Contigo por el camino
Santa María va

a. Nacimiento de un nuevo Pueblo

En un momento único en la historia de este mundo, se encontraron tres mundos radicalmente distintos y totalmente desconocidos: América indígena, Africa y Europa.

> "América Latina forjó en la confluencia, a veces dolorosa, de las más diversas culturas y razas, un nuevo mestizaje de étnicas y formas de existencia y pensamiento que permitió la gestación de una nueva raza superadas las duras separaciones anteriores."
>
> *Puebla, No.5*

> "Que no se turbe tu corazón....
> ¿No estoy yo aquí, que soy tu Madre?"
>
> *Narración Guadalupana*

> "Mi alma alaba al Señor, y mi corazón se alegra en Dios mi Salvador. Porque Dios ha tomado en cuenta a su pobre esclava, y desde ahora todas las generaciones me proclamarán bienaventurada."
>
> *Lc. 1:46-48*

El enfrentamiento llevo a la muerte y a la esclavitud a muchos pueblos indígenas y los hizo extranjeros en sus propias tierras. Los africanos fueron arrancados violentamente de sus tierras y trasplantados a tierras lejanas como esclavos. Esto inicio un trauma que aun se vive. También inicio un mestizaje que en efecto es el nacimiento de un nuevo pueblo.

En la triple herencia están las raíces de nuestra realidad Latino Americana. Es nuestra identidad, nuestro sufrimiento, nuestra grandeza y nuestro futuro.

Hace 450 años, en el nacimiento de nuestra raza mestiza de América Latina, durante los profundos y agudos dolores de parto de nuestro pueblo, nuestra madre vino a estar con nosotros.

De los cielos vino una gran señal (Apoc. 12:1), una hermosa señora que visito nuestras tierras y nos hablo en nuestro idioma indígena con cariño, amor, ternura y compasión. Esa Señora eres Tú.

Como ella había sido escogida por su pequeñez y humildad, así María escogió a Juan Diego, un humilde Indio. De los muchos de quien podía escoger, escogió a un hombre pobre.

> *Yave dijo:* "He visto la humillación de mi pueblo...He escuchado sus gritos, al maltrato de sus mayordomos. Yo conozco su sufrimiento. He bajado para librar a mi pueblo de la opresión."
>
> *Ex. 3:7-8*

Juan Diego como hijo fiel, escucho a su Madre, confió en ella y acepto Su mandato. El Obispo le pidió la señal, y ella con gusto se la dió – no solamente flores bellas, sino que también le dió la flor de las flores: Su imagen impresa milagrosamente en la propia tilma de Juan Diego.

En un momento doloroso de nuestra historia, Dios nos dió un gran regalo – el retrato de su Madre que también es nuestra Madre. Su imagen es el signo visible de Su presencia amorosa entre nosotros. Una mujer de rostro y corazón compasivo, pero de ojos tristes porque estaba conciente del sufrimiento de su pueblo y oyó sus lamentos.

Desde entonces Tú has compartido nuestros sufrimientos y alegrías, luchas y fiestas y todos nuestros esfuerzos para realizar el Reino de Dios. Tú nos inspiras, nos animas y caminas siempre con nosotros. Eres la fuente de nuestra identidad y de la unidad de nuestro pueblo en las Américas.

Hoy venimos a ti, Madre nuestra, llenos de gratitud y admiración a traerte el retrato de Tu familia, a platicarte nuestra vida y a compartir contigo los anhelos del pueblo Hispano de los Estados Unidos de Norte América.

> "La tierra de las Américas estaba preparada por sus mismas corrientes espirituales para recibir la semilla cristiana."
>
> *Juan Pablo II, Santo Domingo, 25 de enero de 1979*

"Y el Verbo se hizo carne, y habitó entre nosotros."

Jn. 1:14

b. Nuestra Fe

Nuestros antepasados tuvieron un sentido fuerte de religiosidad. Centraban su vida en su Dios. Fueron Pueblo de valores espirituales, de sabiduría y de costumbres humanizantes.

Los misioneros nos trajeron el conocimiento de un Dios personal que a través de Su Hijo nos invita a una nueva vida. El Evangelio purificó y enriqueció las creencias de estas tierras.

Desde entonces, nuestra fe es personal y cultural porque el Verbo se encarnó en nuestra tierra al llegar Su Madre al cerro del Tepeyac. Poco a poco, el Evangelio ha penetrado todo aspecto de nuestra vida y cultura. Es el alfa y omega, el centro de todo nuestro ser. La fe impregna nuestra música, arte, poesía, lenguaje, costumbres, fiestas, y las expresiones de nuestra vida.

Fieles a nuestra tradición, esperamos que el Evangelio siga transformando nuestra vida y nuestra cultura.

c. Nuestro Mestizaje

Nuestro pueblo Hispano de los Estados Unidos de Norte América es un Pueblo mestizado. Es entrelace de sangre y cultura de los pueblos Indígena, Africano y Europeo. En la realidad actual de nuestro pueblo encontramos un nuevo entrelace, el de los pueblos Latino Americano y Estadounidense. De este segundo entrelace comienza a surgir el pueblo Hispano Americano.

Somos un pueblo nuevo y en nuestro ser combinamos las riquezas culturales de nuestros padres. La Santísima Virgen de Guadalupe, nuestra madrecita mestiza, viene a llenar de alegría y bendiciones al doloroso y penoso proceso de nuestro mestizaje.

"El Evangelio encarnado en nuestros pueblos los congrega en una originalidad histórica cultural que llamamos América Latina. Esa identidad se simboliza muy luminosamente en el rostro mestizo de María de Guadalupe que se yergue al inicio de la Evangelización."

Puebla, No. 446

"La religiosidad popular no solamente es objeto de evangelización sino que, en cuanto continente contiene encarnada la Palabra de Dios, es una forma activa con la cual el pueblo se evangeliza continuamente a sí mismo."

Puebla, No. 450

d. Nuestra Cultura

En el desarrollo de este pueblo, se han ido incorporando valores muy hermosos de diferentes culturas que han enriquecido nuestra realidad. Nuestra cultura es rica en imágenes, arte, música, danzas, comidas, poesía y aún con cierto sabor de picardía

Nuestro idioma es rico en expresiones que vienen del Evangelio. Eso facilita la transmisión de la Palabra.

Nuestra fe personal tiene expresiones muy bellas: "Mi Padre Dios", "Nuestra Madrecita María", "Nuestro Señor y Hermano Jesucristo", "Mis Santitos". En nuestros hogares se forma un verdadero ambiente espiritual y muchas casas llegan a ser iglesia doméstica. El altarcito con el crucifijo, con Tu imagen, Madrecita, y nuestros santitos ocupan un lugar especial en el hogar. La veladora y las palmas benditas nos hablan de tu Hijo Santísimo. Nuestra cultura es la expresión del Evangelio encarnado en nuestro pueblo y es una forma rica de transmitir la divina enseñanza a las nuevas generaciones.

"La familia es, por tanto, la primera escuela de las virtudes sociales, que todas las sociedades necesitan. Sobre todo en la familia cristiana, enriquecida con la gracia del sacramento y los deberes del matrimonio, es necesario que los hijos aprendan desde sus primeros años a conocer, a sentir y a adorar a Dios y amar al prójimo según la fe recibida en el bautismo. En ella sienten la primera experiencia de una sana sociedad humana y de la Iglesia."

Gravissimum Educationis, No. 3

e. Nuestras Familias

Es difícil poder explicar este gran don de Dios. Las palabras resultan insuficientes. Para nosotros el sentido de familia se ensancha y abarca en él a padres, hijos, abuelos, tíos y tías solteras, parientes, hijos de crianza, vecinos, padrinos de bautizo y compadres. La familia es la primera escuela de amor, ternura, aceptación, y disciplina y respeto. En nuestros hogares, hemos experimentado vínculos de fraternidad, apoyo mutuo, solicitud unos por los otros y presencia de Dios.

De nuestras familias hemos recibido pensamientos y valores que son el fundamento y la orientación principal de nuestras vidas.

El nuevo Juan Diego que trajo el mensaje del cielo a la Iglesia de Estados Unidos fue también un mensajero humilde: nuestras madres y abuelitas. Ellas enseñaron a los hijos y nietos a orar mientras que los padres luchaban para ganar el pan de cada día. Su voz ha resonado con insistencia: "No dejes tu Misa", "Cásate por la Iglesia", "Que Dios te acompañe". Han marcado en nuestras almas el amor de Dios y han hecho brotar en la nación imagen llena de ternura.

Madrecita, Tú conoces las miserias y las fallas de nuestras familias. No han sido perfectas. Aun con sus defectos, han sido una gran fuente de seguridad, comunidad y felicidad. En los momentos más duros de nuestra marcha histórica, nuestro pueblo jamás ha perdido su alegría de vivir. A través de todos los pesares en la vida, cantamos aun en medio del dolor.

La fe nos ha hecho un pueblo jubiloso. En nuestras fiestas, celebramos el misterio de la vida que en sus éxitos y fracasos, alegrías y tristezas, el nacimiento y aún la muerte es un don de Dios.

"Quienes están familiarizados con la historia de la Iglesia, saben que en todos los tiempos ha habido admirables figuras de Obispos profundamente empeñados en la valiente defensa de la dignidad humana de aquellos que el Señor les había confiado. Lo han hecho siempre bajo el imperativo de su misión episcopal, porque para ellos la dignidad humana es un valor evangélico que no puede ser despreciado sin grande ofensa al Creador."

Juan Pablo II, Puebla, 28 de enero de 1979

---

f. Personas que nos llenan de admiración

Madrecita, nuestra historia está llena de hombres y mujeres que para nosotros han sido una gran inspiración. Han luchado y dado su vida para que nosotros tengamos una vida mejor.

Te damos gracias

- *Por los Indios que sufrieron el dolor de la conquista y lucharon por el bien de su pueblo*
- *Por los Africanos, víctimas de la esclavitud y la humillación*
- *Por los hermosos misioneros que nos trajiste desde España, hombres de visión apostólica, llenos de valor, amor y compasión*
- *Por nuestros héroes ignorados, que han quedado ocultos en la obscuridad*
- *Por los santos que han florecido en nuestra tierra como las rosas del Tepeyac*

Qué alegría Madrecita, al ver tantos que han hermoseado a nuestro pueblo con los dones que les ha dado tu Hijo.

- *Los artistas, escritores, cantantes, y poetas soñadores*
- *Los educadores, los sabios y los técnicos*
- *Los negociantes, agricultores, profesionistas y empresarios*
- *Los trabajadores domésticos y campesinos*
- *Los trabajadores migrantes y los sindicatos organizados para dar fuerza a la voz del obrero*
- *Los políticos que verdaderamente representan al pueblo*
- *Los soldados que han luchado para defender la libertad*

"Como resultado, la Iglesia, a un mismo tiempo 'agrupación visible y comunidad espiritual' avanza como toda la humanidad, y pasa por los mismos avatares terrenos; viene a ser como el fermento y como el alma de la ciudad humana, que en Cristo se ha de renovar y transformar en la familia de Dios."

Gaudium et Spes, No. 40

Madrecita muchas gracias especialmente por los sacerdotes y religiosos, nuestros colaboradores en la viña del Señor, que se han entregado a nuestro pueblo y le han amado de verdad.

Sin la riqueza de sus talentos y la totalidad de su compromiso, el Evangelio de Tu Hijo no se proclamaría en su plenitud.

Le damos gracias a Dios, Madrecita, por habernos llamado a ser apóstoles de Su Hijo en nuestro tiempo. Te pedimos camines con nosotros.

"Pero Cristo nos rescato de la maldición de la Ley haciéndose El mismo maldición por nosotros, pues está escrito: 'maldito todo aquel que está colgado de un palo.' Es así como las naciones paganas habían de recibir en Cristo la bendición de Abraham y es así como recibimos por la fe el Espíritu que fue prometido."

Galatas 3:13-14

II. NUESTRA ACTUALIDAD

Aunque te digan algunos
que nada puede cambiar
lucha por un mundo nuevo
lucha por la verdad

Mucho se ha logrado, pero el sufrimiento sigue. Estamos conscientes de la opresión y explotación de nuestro pueblo. Hemos visto los cuerpos desfigurados por el hambre y entristecidos por el miedo a la ley; hemos oído el llanto de los niños abandonados, maltratados por sus propios padres. Sentimos la soledad de los ancianos ignorados por sus parientes y la depresión de los prisioneros cuyo mayor crimen ha sido el no tener dinero para pagar a quien los defienda. Hemos compartido el dolor y el calor de los campesinos y trabajadores domésticos, los esclavos invisibles de la sociedad moderna. En las Cárceles y campos de detención hay algunos que han venido a nuestro país en busca de trabajo y libertad y se los han tomado como un crimen. Hemos visto a nuestros jóvenes con ojos vacios porque no tienen ilusión en la vida. Hemos estado con múltiples victimas de la violencia que aumenta cada día en nuestros barrios y aún en nuestras familias. No descansaremos hasta que toda injusticia se elimine de nuestra vida.

"Nuestro Sumo Sacerdote no se queda indiferente ante nuestras debilidades, ya que El mismo fue sometido a las mismas pruebas que nosotros, a excepción del pecado."

Hebreos 4:15

Hemos experimentado con nuestro pueblo el miedo que proviene del racismo y la discriminación. Nos paraliza el saber que podremos ser rechazados, ridiculizados o insultados.

Como Juan Diego aceptó su desafío, nosotros aceptamos el nuestro: de ser artesanos de un nuevo pueblo.

a. Nuestra Identidad

Somos un pueblo doblemente mestizado. Estamos en los primeros pasos de nuestra vida como Hispano Americanos.

Todo nacimiento es a la vez gozo y tristeza. Así ha sido el nuestro. El rechazo continuo ha sido parte de nuestra vida cotidiana.

Sin embargo, nuestros padres nos enseñaron a amar a Estados Unidos, aunque la lucha ha sido dura. Nuestro pueblo siempre ha luchado por superarse. Amamos la paz fundada sobre la verdad, justicia, amor y libertad (Pacem in Terris). No hemos tomado armas contra nuestro país y si lo hemos defendido. Hemos luchado para eliminar las injusticias que reinan. El camino ha sido largo, difícil y con muchos obstáculos, pero hemos avanzado y seguiremos adelante con determinación y firmeza.

"Va creciendo de día en día el número de hombres y mujeres que, sea cual fuera el grupo o la nación a que pertenecen toman conciencia de que son ellos los autores y promotores de la cultura de su comunidad...Cree más y más en todo el mundo el sentido de la autonomía y al mismo tiempo de la responsabilidad, lo cual es de capital importancia para la madurez espiritual y moral del género humano....Somos testigos de que está naciendo un nuevo humanismo, en el que el hombre se define por su sentido de responsabilidad hacia sus hermanos y hacia la historia."

Gaudium et Spes, No. 55

b. Nuestros Acontecimientos

Morenita, te damos gracias por las cosas tan hermosas que nos están sucediendo últimamente.

Nuestro pueblo ya empieza a contar en la sociedad. Ya se escucha su voz. Cada día se hace más responsable de las estructuras sociales y religiosas que determinan su vida.

Tus hijos ya han celebrado encuentros de pastoral a nivel nacional.

Los esfuerzos de los campesinos han tenido sus frutos. Mucha de nuestra gente goza hoy día de una vida mejor, gracias a los esfuerzos heroicos de nuestros líderes.

Catorce hijos de nuestro pueblo hemos sido llamados a ser sucesores de los Apóstoles.

Las vocaciones a la vida religiosa y sacerdotal van en aumento.

Han surgido asociaciones y movimientos católicos dedicados al progreso apostólico y social de nuestro pueblo.

Tenemos Centros de Pastoral dedicados a la investigación, reflexión teológica, producción de materiales y formación de agentes de pastoral.

Los obispos han establecido oficinas nacionales y regionales para servir a Tu pueblo.

Le damos gracias a Tu Hijo por todo lo que se está logrando. Pero le pedimos que nos dé la fuerza y valentía para seguir enfrentando los problemas gigantescos de nuestros días. Como dijo Juan Pablo II en México, "Queremos ser la voz de los que no tienen voz". Los pueblos pobres tienen el derecho a nuestro amor y preocupación privilegiada.

c. Desafíos

Hay ciertos desafíos en nuestra sociedad que debemos intentar.

Nuestro mejoramiento en la vida social no quiere decir que nos olvidemos de nuestras raíces–de nuestra tradición mestiza Latino Americana. Entre más apreciemos nuestro pasado, más fuerza tendremos para lanzarnos a la edificación de nuestro futuro.

El desarrollo de una vida más humana no quiere decir que nos dejemos esclavizar y destruir por el materialismo, en consumismo, el anhelo por siempre subir, el afán por el placer constante y la gratificación inmediata.

Todo esto proviene de la idolatría del oro. Estos valores son el cáncer de la sociedad moderna. La modernización de la familia no quiere decir que abandonemos el tesoro más grande de nuestra cultura Hispana. Hoy día la familia está en gran peligro. El divorcio aumenta, los ancianos son olvidados y aún estafados, los niños son abandonados y la juventud hace de la calle, su hogar. El espíritu de individualismo está matando el espíritu comunitario que es la base de la familia.

La unidad de los cristianos no quiere decir indiferencia religiosa. El ecumenismo no nos debe llevar a perder nuestra propia identificación de católicos. Afirmando el ecumenismo, rechazamos todo tipo de proselitismo activo como anti-ecuménico y destructivo de nuestro pueblo. La gran diversidad de grupos fundamentalistas y su espíritu anti-católico dividen a nuestras familias y a nuestros pueblos. Nuestra respuesta no es de luchar contra estos grupos, ni de hablar mal de ellos o de sus intenciones, sino de tomar sus actividades como un desafío para nosotros los católicos a vivir más auténticamente y apostólicamente la vida del Evangelio.

"Yo vine para que tengan vida y la tengan en abundancia."
Juan 10:10

"Yo soy el Camino, la Verdad y la Vida."
Juan 14:6

"Amense uno con otros como Yo los amo a ustedes."
Juan 15:12

"Tuvo compasión y sano a los enfermos."
Mt. 14:13

"Padre, en tus manos encomiendo mi espíritu."
Lc. 23:46

III. ARTESANOS DE UNA NUEVA HUMANIDAD

Ahora que estamos unidos
juntos en la verdad
danos fuerza te pedimos
fuerza para triunfar

a. Un re-descubrimiento del Evangelio

La fuerza más grande de nuestro pueblo viene del re-descubrimiento del Evangelio que es verdad, camino y vida. Es el poder de Dios en nosotros:

- Su luz ilumina el significado de nuestra vida y la meta de nuestra misión
- Su amor transforma nuestros corazones de piedra en corazones humanos
- Su compasión nos mueve a la acción
- Su esperanza nos anima a seguir luchando aún cuando humanamente no hay esperanza
- Su fuerza transforma nuestras debilidades y las convierte en energía para el bien

b. Un re-nacimiento Eclesial

La palabra evangélica toma forma humana en cuanto que penetra, asume y ennoblece nuestra cultura. Se expresa a través de imágenes, símbolos, música, arte y sabiduría, La Iglesia nace de nuestra respuesta a la palabra de Jesús. Hoy día vivimos un verdadero re-nacimiento de la Iglesia mestiza Hispano Americana.

c. Vida Eclesial

La fe nos viene de la Iglesia y nos llama a ser Iglesia. En el tiempo y en el espacio, esta vida eclesial toma diversas formas según las condiciones y necesidades presentes. Vemos con gozo:

- El nacimiento de nueva vida parroquial donde cada miembro pone su talento al servicio de la comunidad. La amplia participación de los feligreses en la misión de la Iglesia es el comienzo de un nuevo día y fuente de gran esperanza para la Iglesia del futuro.
- En las parroquias renovadas, la Iglesia es el centro natural de la vida de la comunidad. La parroquia forma líderes y mueve al pueblo a trabajar unido para el bien de todos.
- Las comunidades eclesiales de base hacen que la persona experimente la fe y se sienta como Iglesia. Pueden y

deben ser una verdadera levadura en las parroquias y en el mundo.

- Los nuevos movimientos familiares y los estudios de la biblia han dado nueva vida a nuestras comunidades.
- La re-actualización de los ministerios ha engendrado una nueva vida eclesial que ha incorporado a muchos en la misión de la Iglesia. Todos somos llamados a participar activamente en el apostolado.
- Los diáconos permanentes, varones preparados y ordenados para el servicio del pueblo de Dios. La dedicación y el celo apostólico de estos hombres hace nuevamente presente a la Iglesia en muchos lugares.

d. Expresiones Populares de la Fe

Los misioneros supieron entender a los indígenas descubriendo sus deseos e inclinaciones para hacer de ellos bases para la evangelización. A las danzas, las hicieron expresiones de fe.

Las peregrinaciones y procesiones daban ocasión a la enseñanza de la doctrina cristiana. Creaban formas como la "Pastorela", las "posadas" y a las "siete palabras" para transmitir el mensaje bíblico por medio de la danza, el teatro, la música y el arte.

Estas expresiones de un pueblo cristiano son verdaderos regalos del Espíritu, y un precioso tesoro de nuestra gente. Invitamos a los dirigentes pastorales y a los catequistas a redescubrir estos valores.

El Señor le dijo a Pablo: "Te basta Mi gracia: Mi fuerza actúa mejor donde hay debilidad. Con todo gusto, pues me alabaré de mis debilidades para que habite en mi la fuerza de Cristo."

2 Cor. 12:9

"La semilla, que es la palabra de Dios, al germinar absorbe el jugo de la tierra buena, regada con el rocío celestial, y lo transforma y se lo asimila para dar al fin fruto abundante. Ciertamente, a semejanza del plan de la Encarnación, las Iglesias jóvenes, radicadas en Cristo y edificadas sobre el fundamento de los apóstoles, toman, en intercambio admirable, todas las riquezas de las naciones que han sido dadas a Cristo en herencia (cf. Sal., 2,8). Ellas reciben de las costumbres y tradiciones, de la sabiduría y doctrina, de las artes e instituciones de los pueblos, todo lo que puede servir para expresar la gloria del Creador para explicar la gracia del Salvador y para ordenar debidamente la vida cristiana."

Ad Gentes, No. 22

"El apostolado de los seglares, que surge de su misma vocación cristiana nunca puede faltar en la Iglesia."

"Es preciso, con todo, que los seglares tomen como obligación suya, la restauración del orden temporal."

Apostolicam Actuositatem, Nos. 1 y 7

"Los cristianos unidos en comunidad eclesial de base, fomentando su adhesión a Cristo, procuran una vida mas evangélica en el seno del pueblo, colaboran para interpelar las raíces egoístas y consumistas de la sociedad y explicitan la vocación de comunión con Dios y con sus hermanos; ofreciendo un valioso punto de partida en la construcción de una nueva sociedad, la civilización de amor."

Puebla, No. 642

"La Iglesia Católica no rechaza nada de lo que es santo y verdadero en esas religiones. Tiene en gran estima la vida y la conducta, los preceptos y doctrinas que, aunque sean muy distintos a sus propias enseñanzas, a menudo reflejan un rayo de la verdad que ilumina a todos los hombres. Pero proclama, y está obligada a anunciar sin cesar, a Cristo que es el Camino, la Verdad y la Vida. (Jn. 1,6)."

Nostra Aetate, No. 2

---

e. Catequesis

La educación religiosa es una tarea de suma importancia en la labor contínua de la Iglesia. A través de la catequesis crecemos y maduramos en nuestro compromiso cristiano.

- La catequesis debe tomar cuenta de la tradición Hispana.
- Métodos apropiados deben ser utilizados, especialmente la radio y la televisión.
- La preparación y motivación del catequista ameritan especial atención

La catequesis hoy, como en tiempos de los misioneros, debe ser basada en las Escrituras y la tradición de la Iglesia, tomándose en cuenta los signos concretos de los tiempos utilizándose los métodos de nuestra tradición: interpretaciones escénicas del Evangelio, expresión artística de los misterios de la fe, y cánticos con contenido catequístico.

f. Liturgia

La celebración comunitaria de la fe es la manifestación de la vida cristiana del pueblo. Para que estas celebraciones sean auténticamente del pueblo, debe utilizarse:

- El idioma local del pueblo en las oraciones, lecturas y predicación
- El arte de nuestro pueblo en las representaciones de imágenes sagradas

Hoy día comienzan a surgir algunas formas de celebrar que incorporan estos principios fundamentales del Concilio Vaticano Segundo. Aplaudimos estos esfuerzos y esperamos que este amanecer litúrgico siga irradiando y pronto llegue a brillar en su plenitud.

"Si la Iglesia no reinterpreta la religión del pueblo latinoamericano, se producirá un vacio que lo ocuparán las sectas, los mesianismos políticos secularizados, el consumismo que produce hastió y la indiferencia o el pansexualismo pagano. Nuevamente la Iglesia se enfrenta con el problema: lo que no asume en Cristo, no es redimido y se constituye en un ídolo viejo con malicia nueva."

Puebla, No. 469

"Los grandes desafíos que nos plantea la piedad popular. Favorecer la mutua fecundación entre liturgia y piedad popular que pueda encauzar con lucidez y prudencia los anhelos de oración y vitalidad carismática que hoy se comprueba en nuestros países. Por otra parte, la religión del pueblo, con su gran riqueza simbólica y expresiva, puede proporcionar a la liturgia un dinamismo creador. Este, debidamente discernido puede servir para encarnar más y mejor la oración universal de la Iglesia en nuestra cultura."

Puebla, No. 465

g. Reflexión Teológica

La teología ayuda a descubrir cómo vivir y proclamar nuestra fe. Toda comunidad eclesial tiene el privilegio y la obligación de descubrir el significado teológico de su vida.

- Agradecemos las contribuciones teológicas de otras comunidades eclesiales locales y, en una manera muy especial, apreciamos la inspiración del pensamiento teológico de América Latina.
- Nuestro pueblo Hispano Americano empieza a identificar el significado teológico de nuestra identidad en Estados Unidos.
- Invitamos a nuestro pueblo a continuar en este proceso.

Cada pueblo y cada generación tiene el privilegio y la obligación de responder a la pregunta de Jesús a Pedro: "¿Y ustedes, quien dicen que soy yo?" (Mt. 16, 15). La respuesta particular de otras iglesias locales nos enriquece, pero al mismo tiempo nos inspira y nos anima a buscar la nuestra. ¿Quién es el Jesús que vive y habla en nuestro pueblo cristiano? Juntos tenemos que buscar, formular, y proclamar nuestra respuesta.

"Es necesario que en cada gran territorio socio-cultural se promueva la reflexión teológica por la cual se sometan a nueva investigación, a la luz de la tradición de la Iglesia universal, los hechos y las palabras reveladas por Dios, consignadas en las Sagradas Escrituras y explicadas por los Padres y el Magisterio de la Iglesia. Así aparecerá más claramente por qué caminos puede llegar la fe a la inteligencia, teniendo en cuenta la filosofía y la sabiduría de los pueblos, y de qué forma pueden compaginarse las costumbres, el sentido de la vida y el orden social con las costumbres manifestadas por la divina Revelación. Con ellos se descubrirán los caminos para una acomodación más profunda en todo el ámbito de la vida cristiana. . . . Serán asumidas en la unidad católica las tradiciones particulares, con las cualidades propias de cada raza, ilustradas con la luz del Evangelio."

Ad Gentes, No. 22

h. Vocaciones

Nos llena de alegría el florecer de nuevas vocaciones de nuestro pueblo. Sin embargo, el número es mínimo en relación a la necesidad. Urge fomentar este apostolado. Muchos hombres y mujeres pueden responder al llamado del Señor.

Nuestra Iglesia mestiza Hispano Americana llegara a su madurez cuando nuestro pueblo tenga suficientes vocaciones no solamente para nuestras necesidades, sino también para la misión universal de la Iglesia.

"Pues la Iglesia profundiza sus más firmes raíces en cada grupo humano, cuando las varias comunidades de fieles tienen entre sus miembros los propios ministros de la salvación en el orden de obispos, de los presbíteros y diáconos, que sirven a sus hermanos de suerte que las nuevas Iglesias consigan, paso a paso, con su clero la estructura diocesana."

Ad Gentes, No. 16

"No me cansare yo mismo de repetir, en cumplimiento de mi deber de evangelizador a la humanidad entera: 'No temáis'. ¡Abrid, más todavía, abrid de par las puertas a Cristo! Abrid a su potestad salvadora, las puertas de los Estados, los sistemas económicos y políticos, los extensos campos de la cultura, de la civilización y el desarrollo."

Juan Pablo II, Discurso de apertura, Puebla, enero 28 de 1979

i. Un seguimiento mas autentico de Jesús

Cristo es nuestro único modelo y como El debemos estar dispuestos a comprometernos y a ser intrépidos en la proclamación de la verdad, siempre llenos de compasión y misericordia.

Nuestro seguimiento de El nos obliga a levantar la voz cuando se quiera destruir la vida y a defender y respetar a todos como personas creadas por Dios. Nos obliga a luchar por la paz y la justicia.

Como El nos abrió nuevos horizontes, así nosotros debemos enaltecer al obrero, al campesino y al trabajador. Debemos ayudar a superar a todo el que busque un mejor lugar en la sociedad.

IV. UN PEREGRINAJE CON ALEGRIA, VALENTIA Y ESPERANZA

La imitación de Cristo nos hace ver a los demás en su dignidad de hijos de Dios

Ahora que estamos unidos
juntos en la verdad
danos fuerza te pedimos
fuerza para triunfar

¡Ven con nosotros a caminar
Santa María, ven!

¡Nos lanzamos hacia el siglo 21!

Conscientes de lo que Dios ha logrado a través de nosotros, llamamos a nuestro pueblo a tomar una actitud de liderazgo para crear una sociedad más humana. La Iglesia somos todos y juntos podemos triunfar.

Invitamos a nuestros hermanos y hermanas seglares a que sean fuertes colaboradores con nosotros en el ministerio. A todos nos dijo Jesús, "Vayan y proclamen la buena nueva". El cristiano por naturaleza es evangelizador. El seglar, si es cristiano, evangeliza.

A los jóvenes y señoritas, en especial, les invitamos a que pongan su entusiasmo, su sentido de compromiso y su sinceridad al servicio del Evangelio. Que sean los jóvenes apostólicos proclamadores del Evangelio a la juventud de hoy.

A nuestros hermanos sacerdotes les invitamos a que sigan viviendo su compromiso. No se desanimen. Caminamos siempre con Jesús. Nunca vamos solos. El nos da la fortaleza para ser fieles conservadores de la fe. Conservemos además nuestras tradiciones y nuestro idioma que son vehículos para transmitir el Evangelio. Formemos a los ministros, seglares y religiosos, que Dios nos da, para que sean efectivos colaboradores nuestros.

Los felicitamos por todo lo bueno que han hecho y les invitamos a que sean el Buen Pastor con nosotros. Sean hombres de oración, devotos hijos de la Guadalupana.

A las hermanas y hermanos religiosos, les invitamos a que sigan dando testimonio del valor de la vida de pobreza, castidad y obediencia en un mundo que valora la riqueza, el placer y el poder. Les felicitamos porque han sido una voz profética por la justicia y la paz, les invitamos a que según el carisma especial de su comunidad se unan a los esfuerzos de la Iglesia local en la cual trabajan para que en colaboración con los obispos y el pueblo de Dios de esa diócesis puedan construir el Reino de Dios.

A las hermanas contemplativas, les invitamos a que sigan brindando a la Iglesia la fuerza de sus oraciones y de su buen ejemplo.

A nuestros hermanos diáconos los invitamos a que se unan a nuestro esfuerzo y al de todo el clero, en el apostolado. Fieles a su vocación de diáconos, sean hombres de servicio para el pueblo. No olviden que el campo principal de su apostolado es su hogar, su comunidad y el lugar de su trabajo.

A los seminaristas les desafiamos a comprometerse seriamente a sus estudios y formación espiritual. El pueblo necesita sacerdotes compasivos, con buen conocimiento de las ciencias sagradas, y sentido profundo de la urgencia de las enseñanzas sociales de la Iglesia.

NUESTRO ADIOS

Oh Madre de las Américas, así como confiaste en Juan Diego, te suplicamos que confíes en nosotros, los obispos hispanos. Que nos mandes a lugares donde nosotros no estamos acostumbrados a visitar; que nos mandes a proclamar Tu mandato: que se edifique un Templo en donde sintamos Tu amor y ternura de Madre. Queremos ser los artesanos y los constructores de este nuevo Templo—una sociedad donde todos podrán vivir como hermanos y hermanas. Queremos edificar el Reino de Dios donde se encuentre la paz porque habrán desaparecido los odios, los celos, la mentira, los pleitos y todo tipo de injusticia.

Madre de Dios
Madre de la Iglesia
Madre de las Américas
Madre de todos nosotros
Ruega por nosotros…

Monseñor Patricio Flores
Arzobispo de San Antonio

Monseñor Roberto Sánchez
Arzobispo de Santa Fe

Monseñor René H. Gracida
Obispo de Pensacola-Tallahassee

Monseñor José J. Madera
Obispo de Fresno

Monseñor Manuel Moreno
Obispo de Tucson

Monseñor Raymundo Peña
Obispo de El Paso

Monseñor Arturo Tafoya
Obispo de Pueblo

Monseñor Juan Arzube
Obispo Auxiliar de Los Angeles

Monseñor Gilberto Chávez
Obispo Auxiliar de San Diego

Monseñor Alphonse Gallegos
Obispo Auxiliar de Sacramento

Monseñor Francisco Garmendia
Obispo Auxiliar de New York

Monseñor Ricardo Ramírez
Obispo Auxiliar de San Antonio

Monseñor Agustín Román
Obispo Auxiliar de Miami

Monseñor René Valero
Obispo Auxiliar de Brooklyn

Apéndice II
Carta de los Obispos Hispanos/Latinos a los Inmigrantes

Los obispos hispanos/latinos de Estados Unidos nos saludaron temprano hoy, día de la Virgen de Guadalupe, con su propia versión muy especial de las mañanitas: una carta abierta a los inmigrantes. La carta está firmada por 33 obispos y fue publicada simultáneamente desde Los Angeles y San Antonio, sede de los dos arzobispos hispanos de más alto rango.

El texto completo de la carta con la lista de obispos que la firman se reproduce a continuación. 12/20/11

ESTAS SON LAS MAÑANITAS . . . DE LOS OBISPOS HISPANOS

Muy estimados hermanas y hermanos inmigrantes,

¡Que la paz y la gracia de Nuestro Señor Jesucristo estén con todos ustedes!

Nosotros los obispos hispanos/latinos de Estados Unidos abajo firmantes les hacemos saber a quienes se encuentran en nuestro país sin papeles que no están solos ni olvidados. Reconocemos que todo ser humano, documentado o no, es imagen de Dios y por lo tanto tiene un valor y dignidad infinitos. Les abrimos nuestros brazos y nuestro corazón y los recibimos como miembros de nuestra familia católica. Como pastores, les dirigimos estas palabras desde lo más profundo de nuestro corazón.

De una manera muy especial queremos agradecerles los valores cristianos que nos demuestran con su vida—el sacrificio por el bien de sus familias, la determinación y perseverancia, el gozo de vivir, su profunda fe y su fidelidad a pesar de la inseguridad y tantas dificultades. Ustedes contribuyen mucho al bienestar de nuestra nación en el ámbito económico, cultural y espiritual.

La crisis económica ha impactado a toda la comunidad estadounidense. Lamentablemente, algunos aprovechan este ambiente de incertidumbre para despreciar al migrante y aun culparlo por esta crisis. Sembrar el odio no nos lleva a remediar la crisis. Encontraremos el remedio en la solidaridad entre todos los trabajadores y colaboradores—inmigrantes y ciudadanos—que conviven en los Estados Unidos.

En sus rostros sufrientes vemos el rostro verdadero de Jesucristo. Sabemos muy bien el gran sacrificio que hacen por el bien de sus familias. Muchos de ustedes hacen los trabajos más difíciles, con sueldos miserables y sin seguro de salud o prestaciones salariales o sociales. A pesar de sus contribuciones al bienestar de nuestro país, en lugar de ofrecerles gratitud, se les trata como criminales porque han violado la ley de inmigración actual.

Estamos también muy conscientes del dolor de las familias que han sufrido la deportación de alguno de sus miembros; de la frustración de los jóvenes que han crecido en este país y cuyos sueños son truncados por su estatus migratorio; de la ansiedad de aquellos que están en espera de la aprobación de su petición de residencia permanente; y de la angustia de quienes viven cada día bajo la amenaza de ser deportados. Todas estas situaciones claman a Dios por una solución digna y humana.

Reconocemos que en ocasión las acciones tomadas con respecto a los inmigrantes les ha llevado a sentirse ignorados y abandonados, incluyendo cuando no se han escuchado voces que se levanten ante las falsedades que se promueven dentro de nuestra sociedad. Por medio de la Conferencia de Obispos Católicos de Estados Unidos (USCCB) hemos abogado ante el Congreso estadounidense por un cambio a la ley de inmigración que respete la unidad de la familia, e incluya pasos ordenados y razonables para que personas sin documentos puedan obtener la ciudadanía. La nueva ley deberá incluir un programa de visas para trabajadores que respete los derechos humanos de los inmigrantes, les provea las necesidades básicas para vivir y facilite su ingreso a nuestro país para trabajar en un ambiente seguro y ordenado. Así mismo, continuamos abogando por la justicia económica global que facilite el empleo de nuestros hermanos y hermanas en su tierra de origen y les provea lo suficiente para vivir con dignidad.

El pueblo inmigrante es una fuerza revitalizadora para el país. La falta de una reforma migratoria justa, humana y eficaz debilita el bien común de toda la unión americana.

Nos duele y nos apena que muchos de nuestros hermanos y hermanas católicos no hayan apoyado nuestras peticiones por un cambio a la ley de inmigración que proteja sus derechos, mientras ustedes contribuyen con su trabajo a nuestro país. Les prometemos que seguiremos trabajando para obtener este cambio. Conocemos lo difícil que es el camino para llegar y para entrar a Estados Unidos. Por eso estamos comprometidos a hacer lo que podamos para lograr un cambio de ley que les permita entrar y vivir en este país legalmente, y no se vean ustedes obligados a emprender un camino peligroso para proveer a sus familias. Como pastores que se preocupan por el bienestar de todos ustedes, les debemos decir que consideren seriamente si es aconsejable emprender su camino hacia acá antes de que se logre un cambio justo y humano en las leyes de inmigración.

Sin embargo, no vamos a esperar hasta que cambie la ley para darles la bienvenida en nuestras iglesias a los que ya están aquí, ya que San Pablo nos dice, "Ustedes ya no son extranjeros ni huéspedes, sino conciudadanos de los que forman el pueblo de Dios; son familia de Dios" (Ef. 2:19). Como miembros del Cuerpo de Cristo que es la Iglesia, les ofrecemos alimento espiritual. Siéntanse bienvenidos a la Santa Misa, la Eucaristía que nos alimenta con la palabra y con el cuerpo y la sangre de Jesús. Les ofrecemos programas de catequesis para sus hijos, y los programas de formación que nuestros esfuerzos diocesanos nos permiten poner a su alcance.

Los ciudadanos y residentes permanentes de este país no podemos olvidar que casi todos, nosotros o nuestros antepasados, hemos venido de otras tierras, y juntos con inmigrantes de varias naciones y culturas hemos formado una nueva nación. Ahora debemos abrirles el corazón y los brazos a los recién llegados, como nos lo pide Jesús cuando nos dice, "Tuve hambre y ustedes me alimentaron; tuve sed y ustedes me dieron de beber; pasé como forastero y ustedes me recibieron en su casa" (Mt 25:35). Estas palabras del Señor Jesús se pueden aplicar a los inmigrantes entre nosotros. Tuvieron hambre en su tierra de origen, tuvieron sed al pasar por el desierto, y se encuentran entre nosotros como forasteros (ver Daniel G. Groody, CSC, "Crossing the Line," *The Way*, Vol. 43, No.2, abril 2004, p. 58-69). Su presencia nos invita a ser más valientes en la denuncia de las injusticias que sufren. A imitación de Jesús y de los grandes profetas, debemos denunciar las fuerzas que los oprimen, y anunciar la buena nueva del Reino con nuestras obras de caridad. Oremos y luchemos para que estos hermanos y hermanas nuestras tengan las mismas oportunidades de las cuales nosotros nos hemos beneficiado.

Vemos en ustedes migrantes a Jesús peregrino. La Palabra de Dios migró del cielo a la tierra para hacerse hombre y salvar a la humanidad. Jesús emigró con María y José a Egipto, como refugiado. Migró de Galilea a Jerusalén para el sacrificio de la Cruz, y finalmente emigró de la muerte a la resurrección y ascendió al cielo. Hoy día, sigue caminando y acompañando a todos los migrantes que peregrinan por el mundo en búsqueda de alimento, trabajo, dignidad, seguridad y oportunidades para el bien de sus familias.

Ustedes nos revelan la realidad suprema de la vida: todos somos migrantes. Su migración es un fuerte y claro mensaje de que todos somos migrantes hacia la vida eterna. Jesús nos acompaña a todos los cristianos en nuestro peregrinar hacia la casa del Padre, el reino de Dios en el cielo (Ver *Tertio Millennio Adveniente* No. 50).

Les rogamos que no se desesperen. Mantengan su fe en Jesús migrante que sigue caminando con ustedes, y en la

Santísima Virgen de Guadalupe que constantemente nos repite las palabras dichas a san Juan Diego, "¿No estoy yo aquí que soy tu Madre?" Ella nunca nos abandona, ni nos abandona san José quien nos protege como lo hizo con la Sagrada Familia durante su emigración a Egipto.

Como pastores queremos seguir abogando por todos los inmigrantes. Con san Pablo les repetimos: "No se dejen vencer por el mal; antes bien, venzan el mal con la fuerza del bien" (Rom. 12:21).

Que Dios todopoderoso, Padre, Hijo y Espíritu Santo los acompañe y los bendiga siempre.

Sinceramente en Cristo Salvador,

Los Obispos Hispanos/Latinos de Estados Unidos

Most Rev. José H. Gómez
Archbishop of Los Angeles

Most Rev. Gustavo García-Siller, MSpS
Archbishop of San Antonio

Most Rev. Gerald R. Barnes
Bishop of San Bernardino

Most Rev. Alvaro Corrada del Rio, SJ
Apostolic Administrator of Tyler
Bishop of Mayaguez, PR

Most Rev. Felipe de Jesús Estevez
Bishop of St. Augustine

Most Rev. Richard J. García
Bishop of Monterey

Most Rev. Armando X. Ochoa
Apostolic Administrator of El Paso
Bishop-designate of Fresno

Most Rev. Plácido Rodríguez, CMF
Bishop of Lubbock

Most Rev. James A. Tamayo
Bishop of Laredo

Most Rev. Raymundo J. Peña
Bishop Emeritus of Brownsville

Most Rev. Arthur Tafoya
Bishop Emeritus of Pueblo

Most Rev. Daniel E. Flores
Bishop of Brownsville

Most Rev. Fernando Isern, DD
Bishop of Pueblo

Most Rev. Ricardo Ramírez
Bishop of Las Cruces

Most Rev. Jaime Soto
Bishop of Sacramento

Most Rev. Joe S. Vásquez
Bishop of Austin

Most Rev. Carlos A. Sevilla, SJ
Bishop Emeritus of Yakima

Most Rev. Oscar Cantú, STD
Auxiliary Bishop of San Antonio

Most Rev. Arturo Cepeda
Auxiliary Bishop of Detroit

Most Rev. Manuel A. Cruz
Auxiliary Bishop of Newark

Most Rev. Rutilio del Riego
Auxiliary Bishop of San Bernardino

Most Rev. Eusebio Elizondo, MSpS
Auxiliary Bishop of Seattle

Most Rev. Francisco González, SF
Auxiliary Bishop of Washington, DC

Most Rev. Eduardo A. Nevares
Auxiliary Bishop of Phoenix

Most Rev. Alexander Salazar
Auxiliary Bishop of Los Angeles

Most Rev. David Arias, OAR
Auxiliary Bishop Emeritus of Newark

Most Rev. Octavio Cisneros, DD
Auxiliary Bishop of Brooklyn

Most. Rev. Edgar M. da Cunha, SDV
Auxiliary Bishop of Newark

Most Rev. Cirilo B. Flores
Auxiliary Bishop of Orange

Most Rev. Josu Iriondo
Auxiliary Bishop of New York

Most Rev. Alberto Rojas
Auxiliary Bishop of Chicago

Most Rev. Luis Rafael Zarama
Auxiliary Bishop of Atlanta

Most Rev. Gabino Zavala
Auxiliary Bishop of Los Angeles

Fiesta de Nuestra Señora de Guadalupe, Diciembre 12, 2011